SEMPER FI—VIETNAM

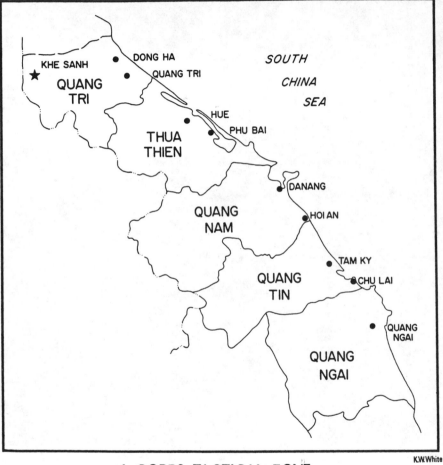

KHE SANH

DONG HA

QUANG TRI

QUANG
TRI

SOUTH

CHINA

SEA

HUE

PHU BAI

THUA
THIEN

DANANG

QUANG
NAM

HOI AN

TAM KY

QUANG
TIN

CHU LAI

QUANG
NGAI

QUANG
NGAI

K.W.White

I CORPS TACTICAL ZONE

SEMPER FI VIETNAM

From Da Nang to the DMZ
Marine Corps Campaigns, 1965–1975

Edward F. Murphy

PRESIDIO

BALLANTINE BOOKS • NEW YORK

A Presidio Press Book
Published by The Ballantine Publishing Group

Copyright © 1997 by Edward F. Murphy

www.ballantinebooks.com

Library of Congress Cataloging-in-Publication Data

Murphy, Edward F., 1947–
    Semper fi—Vietnam : from Da Nang to the DMZ : Marine
Corps campaigns, 1965–1975 / by Edward F. Murphy.
        p.   cm.
    Includes bibliographical references
    ISBN 0-89141-562-9 (hardcover)
    ISBN 0-89141-705-2 (paperback)
    1. Vietnam   Conflict,   1961–1975—United   States.
2. Vietnamese Conflict, 1961–1975—Campaigns 3. United
States. Marine Corps—History—Vietnamese Conflict,
1961–1975. I. Title.
DS558.M87   1997
959.704'3373—dc21   97-7246
                                                          CIP

Printed in the United States of America

This edition printed in 2000

Contents

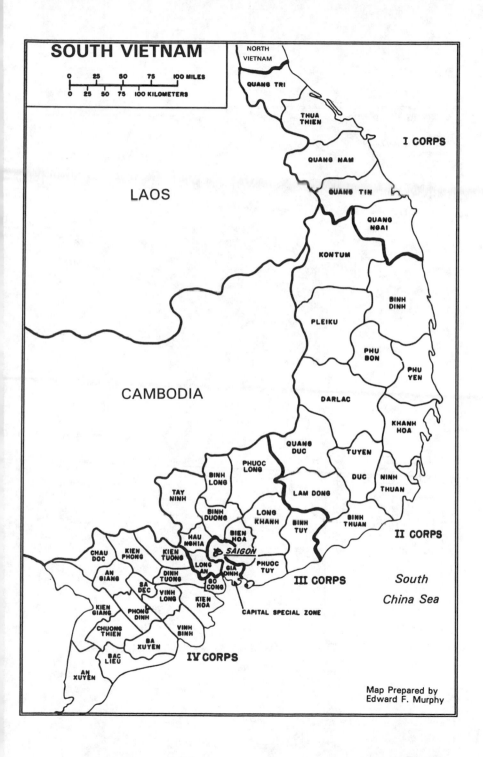

SOUTH VIETNAM

0   25   50   75   100 MILES
0 25 50 75 100 KILOMETERS

NORTH VIETNAM

LAOS

CAMBODIA

QUANG TRI

THUA THIEN

QUANG NAM

QUANG TIN

QUANG NGAI

KONTUM

BINH DINH

PLEIKU

PHU BON

PHU YEN

DARLAC

KHANH HOA

QUANG DUC

TUYEN DUC

NINH THUAN

PHUOC LONG

LAM DONG

BINH LONG

TAY NINH

BINH DUONG

LONG KHANH

BINH TUY

BINH THUAN

HAU NGHIA

BIEN HOA

SAIGON

CHAU DOC

KIEN PHONG

KIEN TUONG

DINH TUONG

LONG AN

GIA DINH

GO CONG

PHUOC TUY

AN GIANG

SA DEC

VINH LONG

KIEN HOA

KIEN GIANG

PHONG DINH

CHUONG THIEN

VINH BINH

BA XUYEN

BAC LIEU

AN XUYEN

CAPITAL SPECIAL ZONE

I CORPS

II CORPS

III CORPS

IV CORPS

South China Sea

Map Prepared by
Edward F. Murphy

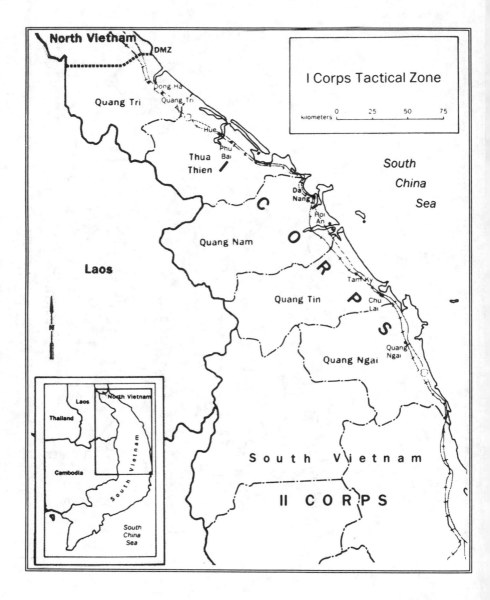

I Corps Tactical Zone

kilometers 0 25 50 75

North Vietnam

DMZ

Dong Ha

Quang Tri

Quang Tri

Hue

Thua
Thien

Phu
Bai

Da
Nang

Hoi
An

South

China

Sea

Laos

Quang Nam

C

O

R

P

S

Tam Ky

Quang Tin

Chu
Lai

Quang Ngai

Quang
Ngai

N

Laos

North Vietnam

Thailand

South Vietnam

Cambodia

South
China
Sea

South   Vietnam

II CORPS

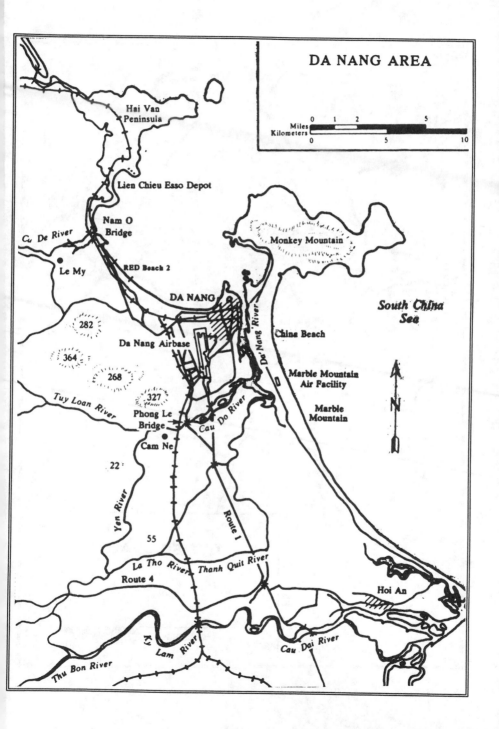

DA NANG AREA

Miles
Kilometers

Hai Van
Peninsula

Lien Chieu Esso Depot

Nam O
Bridge

Cu De River

Le My

RED Beach 2

Monkey Mountain

DA NANG

South China
Sea

282

Da Nang Airbase

China Beach

364

268

Marble Mountain
Air Facility

327

Tuy Loan River

Phong Le
Bridge

Cau Do River

Marble
Mountain

N

Cam Ne

22

Yan River

55

Route 1

La Tho River

Thanh Quit River

Route 4

Hoi An

Ky Lam River

Cau Dai River

Thu Bon River

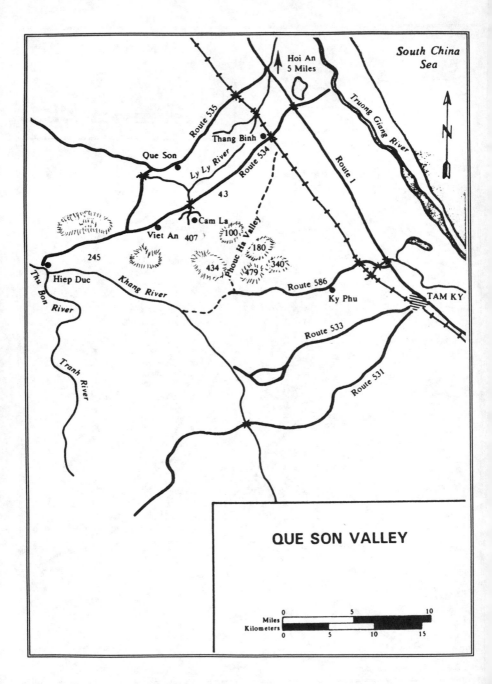

South China Sea

Hoi An
5 Miles

N

Route 535

Truong Giang River

Que Son

Thang Binh

Ly Ly River

Route 534

Route 1

43

Cam La

Viet An

407

100

180

Phouc Ha Valley

245

434

479

340

Route 586

Thu Bon River

Hiep Duc

Khang River

Ky Phu

TAM KY

Route 533

Tranh River

Route 531

QUE SON VALLEY

Miles
Kilometers

0   5   10

0   5   10   15

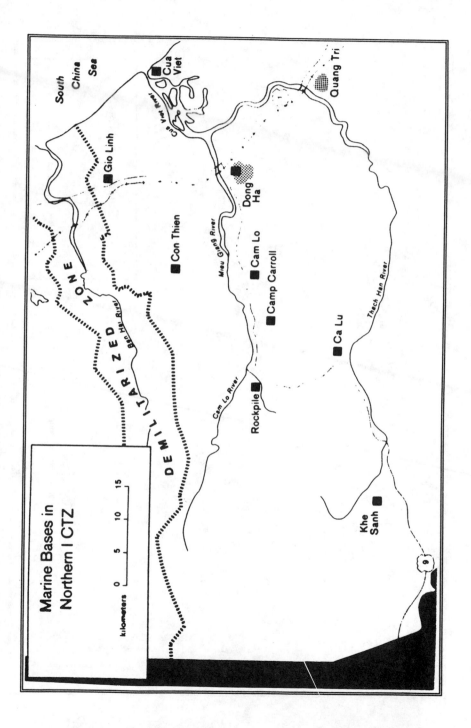

Marine Bases in
Northern I CTZ

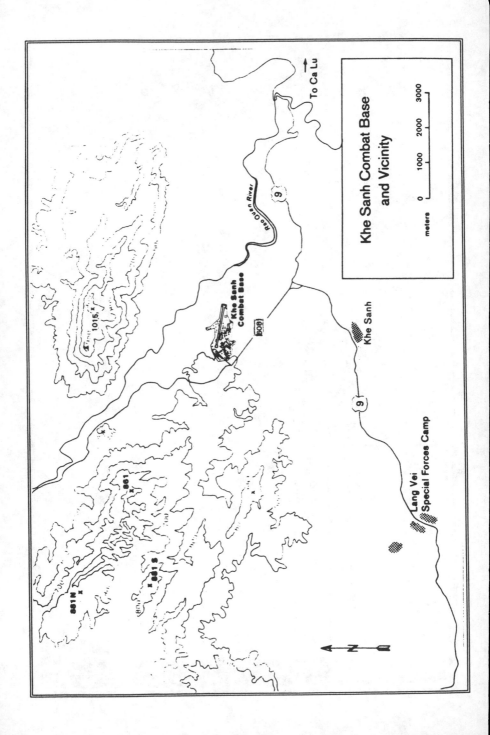

Khe Sanh Combat Base
and Vicinity

meters   0   1000   2000   3000

To Ca Lu

Rao Quan River

Khe Sanh
Combat Base

9

Khe Sanh

9

Lang Vei
Special Forces Camp

1015

881N

881S

N

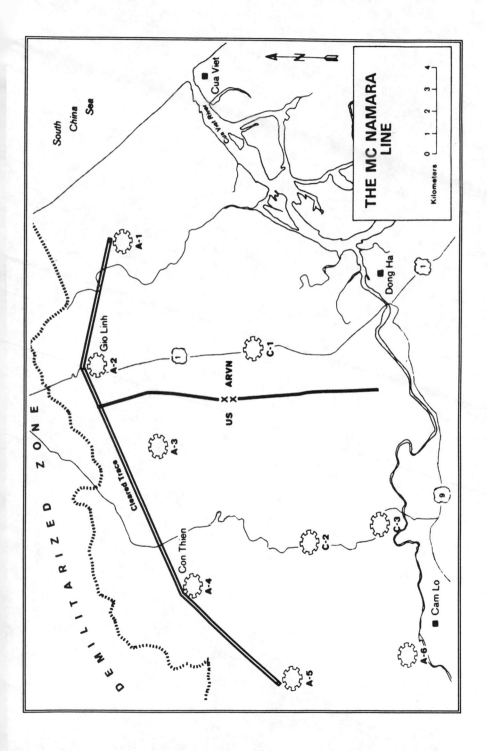

Foreword

My third war began in May 1968 when I took command of the 3d Marine Division. For more than three years this illustrious unit had been fighting the North Vietnamese Army regulars and the Viet Cong insurgents on scores of battlefields all across northern South Vietnam. In more than thirty years as a Marine, few of my assignments were as challenging.

In my previous wars, at the battles of Guadalcanal, Peleliu, Inchon, and the Chosin Reservoir, my men and I fought for clearly defined objectives. We had to secure that beachhead, take that island, capture that hill. We met the enemy on the battlefield, defeated him, and claimed victory.

Unfortunately, it wasn't that way in Vietnam.

There were no clear-cut objectives. Our target was simply the enemy's forces. Once we destroyed the enemy on a hill we departed to seek him elsewhere, leaving the terrain to be reclaimed by our foe. Sites of hard fought battles and numerous casualties were abandoned because we did not have enough manpower to occupy our entire area of operations. As a result, we surrendered to the enemy the initiative to select the time and place to fight. It was a very frustrating way to fight a war.

Yet, despite this handicap, the fighting prowess of the individual Marines never wavered. Whether it was a brief skirmish at a soon forgotten night ambush site or a pitched battle at a well-protected fire support base, the Marines in South Vietnam fought with all the valor and tenacity of their brethren of earlier wars.

Many of the Marines' major battles in the Vietnam War are well-documented: Khe Sahn, Hue, Dong Ha and Operation Dewey Canyon in the Da Krong Valley, to name but a few. Semper Fi—

Vietnam is the first book to present the full story of the Marine
Corps infantry from their arrival in 1965 to their departure in 1972.
This history is skillfully written to provide a rich blend of command
strategy and heroic individual exploits. Mr. Murphy has not only
been able to present an interesting and highly readable account of
Marine Corps infantry operations in South Vietnam but also perfectly captures the spirit of the gallant men who fought the battles
and took the casualties.

Semper Fi—Vietnam will be enjoyed by veteran and non-veteran
alike and will become a popular staple of any Vietnam War library.

General Raymond G. Davis, USMC, (Ret.)
Medal of Honor recipient, Korean War

Chapter One
1965

At 0545 on 8 March 1965, the four ships of the U.S. Navy's Amphibious Task Force 76, the *Mount McKinley, Henrico, Union,* and *Vancou-
ver,* steamed into the harbor of Da Nang, South Vietnam. Slicing
through four-foot-high waves, the vessels moved into position three
thousand meters offshore. A raspy, clanging sound challenged the
morning air as four heavy anchors pulled thick chain links to the
bay's bottom. The eyes of hundreds of anxious U.S. Marines crowd-
ing the ships' railings peered through the haze of a light drizzle,
furtively searching for a glimpse of the distant shoreline.

Rear Admiral Don W. Wulzen, the task force commander aboard
the *Mount McKinley,* ordered at 0600, "Land the landing force!" H
hour was 0800.

The well-armed Marines moved into position to begin the ship-
to-shore movement. As they clambered down rope nets slung over
the ship's steel sides, the weather suddenly worsened. The waiting
landing craft bounced dangerously on the building waves. Mooring
lines snapped under the strain. Soon the harbor's surface teemed
with white-capped swells stretching to ten feet in height.

At 0730 Admiral Wulzen ordered the landing postponed one hour
so that larger, heavier, more stable landing craft could be brought
into position. Once they were lashed securely alongside the trans-
ports, the troops resumed climbing down the treacherous nets. The
loaded vessels moved into position for the run to the beaches.

Many of the young men crouching nervously in the bobbing craft
had fathers and uncles who had made landings on Pacific Ocean islands during World War II, just two decades earlier. These assaults
had been deadly affairs. Enemy artillery shells had crashed among
the assault waves, spreading brutal death. Casualties during these

1

landings had been horrendous. Fortunately, the only casualties the Marines of this generation were apt to experience this day would be from seasickness. The rolling surf heaved the boats up and down as they neared the beach.

Corporal Garry Powers jumped from his amphibious tractor into knee-deep water at 0903 and splashed his way ashore. This first Marine would soon be followed by tens of thousands more as the United States commenced a controversial ten-year effort to keep South Vietnam from falling to the Communists. The journey to the beaches of Da Nang had begun ten years earlier.

The Geneva Accords of 1954 ended France's colonial role in what was then known as French Indochina. The accords divided the new country into a Communist-supported government north of the seventeenth parallel and an anti-Communist regime to the south. Despite the accords Ho Chi Minh, North Vietnam's leader, launched a subversive effort to overthrow the government of South Vietnam and reunite the country.

The United States enthusiastically supported South Vietnam's desire to remain free of Communist domination. To help the fledgling country, in 1954 it established a Military Assistance Advisory Group (MAAG) in the capital of Saigon to train the newly created South Vietnamese Armed Forces. As the insurgents' terrorism escalated in the early 1960s the United States took significant steps to strengthen its ally. By the end of 1962 more than twelve thousand American military personnel were in South Vietnam. Among them were eighteen U.S. Marines serving as advisers to the infant South Vietnamese Marine Corps and a Marine Corps helicopter squadron.

With this major expansion in commitment, the United States abolished the MAAG in February 1962. It was replaced by the Military Assistance Command, Vietnam, a more comprehensive structure, headed by U.S. Army General Paul D. Harkins.

Despite this massive infusion of American aid, the fragile South Vietnamese government was continually torn by internal dissidence. A series of violent clashes between Buddhist monks and President Ngo Dinh Diem's national police resulted in the arrest of the insurgent Buddhist leaders in August 1963. The crisis continued, culminating in the assassination of Diem in November. The turbulent period of political instability that followed witnessed numerous coups and countercoups. South Vietnam's leaders changed so rapidly during this time that it was often difficult for the Americans to know who was in charge of the country on any given day.

This continued instability was not lost on Saigon's enemies, the North Vietnamese–supported Viet Cong (VC). Taking full advantage of the situation, the VC struck again and again. After repeatedly thrashing the much vaunted Army of the Republic of Vietnam (ARVN), the VC next turned to terrorist tactics designed to demoralize the civilian population. Among the targets were U.S. military personnel and installations.

In retaliation, in late July and early August 1964, U.S.-trained South Vietnamese naval commandos aboard fast-moving torpedo boats attacked two islands north of the demilitarized zone dividing the two countries. Though they did little physical damage, the attacks infuriated the North Vietnamese. They struck back, attacking the U.S. Navy destroyer *Maddox* in the Gulf of Tonkin with their own torpedo boats on 2 August. A second attack against the *Maddox* and the recently arrived *Turner Joy* came two days later. President Lyndon B. Johnson responded by sending naval aircraft on bombing missions against targets in North Vietnam.

The next major event came on 31 October when Viet Cong sappers hit the U.S. Air Force base at Bien Hoa, northeast of Saigon. Four Americans died and five U.S. planes were destroyed in the attack. On Christmas Eve, a VC terrorist bomb exploded in the downtown Saigon Brink Hotel, which served as an American bachelor officers' billet. One American naval officer died and fifty-eight more suffered injuries in the massive blast.

Relative quiet reigned over the country for the next few weeks. Then, in the early morning hours of 7 February 1965, Viet Cong infantry attacked two U.S. Army installations near Pleiku, in South Vietnam's mountainous Central Highlands. The fifteen-minute ground assault left 8 Americans dead and more than 125 wounded.

Elevated to the presidency after the assassination of John F. Kennedy in November 1963, Lyndon B. Johnson fought a bitter campaign during the summer and fall of 1964 to be elected in his own right. Regarding the building crisis in South Vietnam, he frequently stated his objections to sending "American boys to do what Asian boys should be doing . . ." Once elected and safely in office, Johnson wasted no time in committing U.S. forces to the war. Less than twelve hours after the Pleiku attack, U.S. naval fighter-bomber aircraft from the carriers *Ranger, Hancock,* and *Coral Sea* hit military targets near Dong Hoi, North Vietnam. The next day, in the second stage of Operation Flaming Dart, land-based U.S. Air Force F-100 Supersaber jet fighters launched from the Da Nang air base. They struck guerrilla staging and communications centers near Vinh Linh and Chap Le, just across the demilitarized zone.

In a televised speech that same evening, President Johnson announced the air raids to the American public, saying: "We have no choice but to clear the decks and make absolutely clear our continued determination to back South Vietnam." The president further stated that he had ordered dependents of American servicemen stationed in South Vietnam to return home. He then declared, "I have ordered the deployment to South Vietnam of a HAWK air defense battalion. Other reinforcements, in units and individuals, may follow."

Though the logic of sending a surface-to-air guided missile weapons system to South Vietnam, which had never been threatened with air attacks, and never would, escaped many, nevertheless the orders went out. On Okinawa the Marines' 1st Light Antiaircraft Missile (LAAM) Battalion got the nod.

Battery A, 1st LAAM flew into Da Nang on the night of 8–9 February. The rest of the battalion, traveling by ship, arrived over the next week. By 16 February the five-hundred-plus Marines of the 1st LAAM occupied positions surrounding the Da Nang air base. America's leaders were convinced that this show of force would persuade North Vietnam's leaders to curtail terrorist attacks.

They were wrong.

On 10 February, the Viet Cong attacked a U.S. Army enlisted men's barracks at coastal Qui Nhon in Binh Dinh Province. Twenty-three American soldiers died; another twenty-two were wounded. President Johnson immediately ordered another round of air strikes. Naval warplanes from the carriers and ground-based aircraft from Da Nang headed north on 12 February under Operation Flaming Dart II.

Significantly, President Johnson referred to these raids not as reprisals but as "air operations" provoked by "continued aggression." The next day, heeding the recommendations of his key military advisers—Secretary of Defense Robert S. McNamara and the Joint Chiefs of Staff—Johnson opted to begin a program of "measured and limited air action jointly with South Vietnam against selected military targets in North Vietnam . . ." The air attacks would be regularly scheduled several times per week with two or three major targets on each operation. The new campaign was called Rolling Thunder.

Though the first strikes had been scheduled for 20 February, renewed South Vietnamese political instability put Operation Rolling Thunder on hold. The day before, a military coup aimed at the current premier, Gen. Nguyen Khanh, failed. However, after a subsequent vote of no confidence from the Armed Forces Council, Khanh departed the country. The leadership of South Vietnam was again in doubt.

Confronted with an unstable political situation just as a massive air campaign was commencing, Gen. William C. Westmoreland, the new commander, U.S. Military Assistance Command, Vietnam (MACV), had grave reservations about the ability of the ARVN forces to protect the U.S. air base at Da Nang and the HAWK battalion. He ordered his deputy, Lt. Gen. John L. Throckmorton, to determine what level of U.S. ground forces would be needed for adequate security. Throckmorton responded within twenty-four hours. He recommended two battalions of Marines be deployed to guard the Da Nang complex.

General Westmoreland concurred. He sent the request to his immediate superior, Adm. Ulysses S. Grant Sharp, Jr., commander in chief, Pacific, on 22 February. Admiral Sharp forwarded his positive endorsement of Westmoreland's request to the Joint Chiefs of Staff.

However, in a separate, private, back-channel cable to President Johnson, the U.S. Ambassador to South Vietnam, retired U.S. Army general Maxwell Taylor, expressed strong reservations about committing U.S. ground troops to South Vietnam. After the first contin-

gent of American forces arrived, Taylor said, "It will be very difficult
to hold the line" on further force commitments. Without a doubt, Taylor predicted, ARVN commanders would soon relinquish other
"ground force tasks" to the Americans. These tasks were sure to es-
calate, the ambassador asserted, leading to his chief worry: "The
white-faced soldier, armed, equipped, and trained as he is, is not a
suitable guerrilla fighter for Asian forests and jungles. The French
tried to adapt their forces to this mission and failed. I doubt that U.S.
forces could do much better."

Despite Taylor's prescient view, Washington cabled him on 27 February that the Marines would land. Taylor was to so inform the South
Vietnamese government. On 1 March, the minister of the South Vietnamese Armed Forces, Gen. Nguyen Van Thieu, and the Vietnamese
chairman of the Joint General Staff, Gen. Tran Van Minh, approved
the landing. Fearing opposition by some segments of the South Vietnamese population, Thieu and Minh requested that the landing of
the Marines be accomplished as "inconspicuously as possible."

Two battalions from the 3d Marine Division's 9th Marine Expeditionary Brigade (MEB) had been aboard ships of the U.S. Seventh
Fleet sailing off South Vietnam's coast since January. Several times
the shipboard Marines had been within hours of hitting the beaches.
Each time a cooling off of the crisis alleviated the landing. Now, however, word for the Marines to go ashore had come directly from
Washington. There would be no last minute reversal of these orders.

Brigadier General Frederick J. Karch, a dapper-looking, mustache-
sporting veteran of two bloody World War II island campaigns, had
taken command of the 9th MEB on 22 January 1965. As the assistant
division commander, Karch had made several visits to the country
over the previous year. He did not like what he saw. In his opinion
the ARVN were so weak that if Marines were to land in Vietnam he
felt they should "make it North Vietnam, not South. If we go into
Da Nang, we'll disappear into the countryside and never be heard
from again."

Nonetheless, when Karch got his orders he went to work. Spread
aboard the four ships of naval amphibious Task Force 76 were the
2d and 3d Battalions, 9th Marines. (The Marine Corps does not

use the traditional identifier "Infantry Regiment" or "Artillery Regiment" in referring to its units. Instead, it simply refers to a regiment with its numerical designator followed by "Marines." Thus, the 1st Marines is actually the 1st Marine Infantry Regiment.) The 2d and 3d Battalions served as the battalion landing teams (BLT). (The BLT is the basic Marine unit in an assault landing. The team's core is an infantry battalion reinforced by other mission-necessary combat and service units.) Karch selected BLT 3/9 to make an amphibious landing at Da Nang. The Marines would go ashore at Red Beach 2, north and west of the city. Once ashore, they would be carried by trucks to defensive positions at the air base. As a reserve, BLT 2/9 would remain aboard ship.

The second of the two battalions would come directly from 3d Marine Division units on Okinawa. The 1st Battalion, 3d Marines would be airlifted directly to Da Nang soon after the arrival of BLT 3/9.

After completing a flurry of activities ashore related to getting his units ready for the actual landing, General Karch returned to his command ship, the *Mount McKinley*, on the evening of 6 March. Late the next day Admiral Wulzen handed Karch a dispatch. "Close Da Nang. Land the landing force," the message read.

Karch turned to Wulzen. "Don, do you think in Washington they know what time it is in Da Nang? This means a night landing if we close Da Nang at this point."

Besides that, the task force was experiencing the worst weather it had yet encountered while traveling around the South China Sea. Waves were cresting at four feet in a strong wind. Visibility was limited to two hundred meters. Karch contacted his headquarters. The orders were modified; the landing would commence the next day.

No enemy action awaited Corporal Powers. Instead, when he reached the top of the beach a South Vietnamese beauty queen placed a fragrant lei over his helmeted head. A short distance away a stone-faced, lei-draped General Karch watched as the four rifle companies of BLT 3/9 crossed the wet sand. Within thirty minutes Company L had boarded trucks and started for the airfield. It was soon followed by Companies I and K; Company M remained behind to provide security for the unloading of the battalion's equipment.

As the Marines of BLT 3/9 began digging in at Da Nang air base, air force C-130s carrying members of 1/3 from Okinawa entered South Vietnamese airspace. The first planeload touched down at 1300. Enemy snipers on nearby hills fired numerous rounds at the planes during the landings, but there were no injuries. By late afternoon two companies, B and C, plus the battalion headquarters had arrived. Company A arrived a few days later. Company D was already in-country providing security for a Marine helicopter squadron.

Though they did not know it at the time, the Marines of the 9th MEB had turned a corner in U.S. involvement in South Vietnam's internal conflict. Their arrival presaged a seven-year war that eventually called into question America's role in world affairs, divided America's citizenry like no issue since the Civil War, and cost the lives of nearly 55,000 members of the U.S. armed forces.

Acclimating to their strange new surroundings occupied the Marines' first few weeks in South Vietnam. Few members of the expeditionary forces had ever experienced the enervating heat and humidity of this tropical country. The fetid odor of the human waste used as fertilizer in the surrounding rice paddies assaulted the senses. Throughout the day, peasants dressed in pajama-like clothing and sporting conical straw hats worked the paddies behind heaving water buffalo. Inside the air base's perimeter, ARVN soldiers lounged lazily as Marines worked under the debilitating sun to prepare their defensive bunkers. About the only time the South Vietnamese soldiers stirred was to beg for American cigarettes.

If daytime scenes appeared bucolic, the arrival of sunset quickly changed that perception. Gunfire and explosions erupted at dusk. Marines nervously watched bright tracers cut colorful swaths across the night sky. From distant bamboo thickets, mortar shells flew skyward to crash in the paddies. The Marines were learning that the war in South Vietnam was unlike anything for which they'd been trained.

Indeed, U.S. Marines were not trained for defensive roles. They were hard-charging warriors tasked with carrying the war to the enemy rather than waiting for the enemy to come to them. But their hands were tied. In their landing order of 7 March, the Joint Chiefs of Staff had been clear: "The U.S. Marine force will not, repeat will not, engage in day-to-day actions against the Viet Cong." As General

Westmoreland told General Karch, the Marines would protect the Da Nang airfield, but "overall responsibility for the defense of the Da Nang area remains an ARVN responsibility."

As a result of this restriction, the Marines' tactical area of responsibility (TAOR) covered about eight square kilometers of relatively unpopulated terrain. It encompassed the airfield and the high ground to the west where the HAWK missile batteries were ensconced. Security of the area to the south and east of the air base remained the province of the ARVN.

With the Marines straining at their shackles, General Westmoreland took up their cause with Washington. He strongly recommended that U.S. forces in South Vietnam be increased and their role enhanced. Only by adopting his suggestions, Westmoreland argued, could the Viet Cong be blunted and the resolve of the ARVN stiffened.

President Johnson concurred. On 1 April, he approved a twenty-thousand-man increase in U.S. forces in South Vietnam, including additional Marines. More significantly, Johnson also authorized a change in the mission of the 9th MEB to allow them to participate in "active combat," under guidelines to be established by the secretary of defense.

The Marines wasted no time in sending more troops to South Vietnam. On 10 April, BLT 2/3 landed across the beaches of Da Nang. Four days later BLT 3/4 began arriving. Two companies of 3/4 were immediately flown north to garrison the small airstrip at Phu Bai, about ten kilometers south of the old imperial capital of Hue. By the end of April the 9th Marine Expeditionary Brigade consisted of four infantry battalions and a four-squadron aircraft group, as well as artillery and support units. Total troop strength neared nine thousand.

General Westmoreland clarified the president's order on 14 April by providing the 9th MEB with a concept of operations divided into four areas. First, the Marines would establish defensive bases. Then they would conduct deep reconnaissance patrols of the enemy's avenues of approach. Third, they would undertake offensive action as a reaction force in coordination with the ARVN. Finally, the Marines would undertake an "intensifying program of offensive operations to fix and destroy the VC in the Da Nang area."

General Karch immediately tried to implement his new orders. Unfortunately, the local ARVN commander agreed to only a six-square-kilometer increase in the Marines' TAOR. There was also a small increase in the defensive area for the 3/4 companies at Phu Bai. On 20 April Marines at both locations began their patrol activities, extending out as far as ten kilometers.

Two days later the Marines and the VC tangled for the first time. A patrol of men from Company D, 3d Reconnaissance Battalion and three dozen ARVN bumped into a VC force of more than one hundred men about thirteen kilometers southwest of Da Nang. After a flurry of small arms fire the patrol leader radioed for help. A company from 1/3 boarded helicopters and choppered into the area. The combined force chased the VC for several kilometers, but the enemy disappeared into the heavily foliaged countryside. In this precursor of tens of thousands of firefights, the Marines killed one VC while having one of their own wounded. The Phu Bai Marines had their first contact on 24 April. A small force of Viet Cong surprised a recon squad's night defensive position on a hilltop two kilometers south of Phu Bai. The fight ended in minutes, but each side lost two men.

While the Marines patrolled their new TAORs, a high-level conference in Honolulu reached a major conclusion regarding U.S. efforts in South Vietnam. The conferees, led by Defense Secretary McNamara, agreed that the war was going to get worse before it got better. They thus authorized an increase of forty-two thousand troops for service to South Vietnam. Among them were five thousand additional Marines in three infantry battalions and three jet aircraft squadrons. These reinforcements would establish a new enclave at Chu Lai, seventy kilometers south of Da Nang in Quang Tin Province.

The previous year Lt. Gen. Victor H. Krulak, commander of the Fleet Marine Force, Pacific, had surveyed the coastal plain dividing the two southern provinces of I Corps, Quang Ngai and Quang Tin. (For command control purposes, the ARVN high command had divided South Vietnam into four corps tactical zones: I Corps, the northernmost, consisted of the country's five northern provinces.) Krulak selected the area as the future site of an airfield. Because the site was not marked on his map, Krulak dubbed it Chu Lai, the Mandarin Chinese characters for his name. The Marines planned to construct an air base there with an eight-thousand-foot by one-hundred-foot runway, as well as taxiways, parking, and maintenance facilities.

Although the Marines initially expected the landing to be opposed, MACV assured them that the ARVN would secure the landing site. They were right.

At 0730 on 7 May, transport ships offshore disgorged their combat troop–laden amphibious vehicles. Thirty minutes later the first vehicle nudged onto the beach. As at Da Nang two months earlier, a group of South Vietnamese maidens passed out leis to the sweat-soaked Marines. As BLTs 1/4 and 2/4 came ashore, a cluster of dignitaries and members of the press watched from nearby. The riflemen ignored them.

What they couldn't ignore was a large banner strung from trees behind the beach courtesy of the U.S. Army advisers assigned to the local ARVN forces. In huge letters no one could miss, the banner's greeting declared: "AHOY MARINES! WELCOME ABOARD! AREA SECURED." Pushing past the humiliating sign, the Marines moved inland to begin digging in. It was an uneventful landing. The only casualties were four men suffering from the effects of the high heat and humidity.

By late afternoon the men of BLT 1/4 had set up several kilometers inland. Elements of the 3d Recon Battalion had also arrived from Da Nang. They secured the beachhead's southern flank. The next day the advance party of the navy's Mobile Construction Battalion 10, which would build the air base, arrived. The hard-working Seabees immediately went to work.

A few days later BLT 3/3 arrived from Okinawa. The 3d Recon Battalion then returned to Da Nang.

With the arrival of 3/3, seven of the 3d Marine Division's nine infantry battalions, most of its artillery, and many support units were in South Vietnam. As a result, on 6 May, the 9th MEB became the III Marine Expeditionary Force. However, because the term *Expeditionary* had negative connotations for the Vietnamese dating back to the French Expeditionary Force of the early 1950s, General Westmoreland requested a name change. The Marines complied. On 7

May, they redesignated their troops the III Marine Amphibious Force (MAF). At the same time, the headquarters of the 3d Marine Division, under Maj. Gen. William R. Collins, opened in South Vietnam. General Karch returned to Okinawa.

General Collins's stay in South Vietnam did not last long. On 5 June, Maj. Gen. Lewis W. Walt assumed command of both III MAF and the 3d Marine Division. A stocky, rugged former college lineman, Walt was one of the Marine Corps' most decorated officers, holding two Navy Crosses and the Silver Star for combat service in World War II and Korea. He would bring a high level of aggressiveness and experience to the Marines during their early years in South Vietnam.

Almost immediately, General Walt pushed MACV for an expansion of his TAOR and a more aggressive role for his men. General Westmoreland agreed. On 15 June, he authorized the III MAF to commence independent search and destroy missions in their TAORs. The Marines wasted no time in complying. Daily combat patrols set out from the enclaves at Phu Bai, Da Nang, and Chu Lai (where the airfield was completed on 1 June, testifying to the outstanding capabilities of the Seabees). Contact with the VC escalated.

Soon after he took over, General Walt had a survey made of the area around Da Nang. It didn't surprise him that more than 150,000 civilians lived within a few kilometers of the air base. As far as he was concerned, this information proved, "We were in the pacification business." Walt concurred with the opinion of Marine Corps commandant Gen. Wallace M. Greene, Jr., who told the Joint Chiefs of Staff, "The real targets in Vietnam were not the VC and the North Vietnamese, but the Vietnamese people."

Walt encouraged a variety of civilian pacification programs. Among them was the establishment of medical clinics in the villages and hamlets around Da Nang. Marines and their navy medical corpsmen volunteered their free time to provide medical assistance to needy villagers. Navy doctors also freely gave of their time to treat the civilians, many of whom had never before received medical care. Other members of III MAF also gave of their off-duty time to help build schools, churches, and clinics for villages.

A unit of the 3d Marines initiated a more ambitious project. Operating by itself at Phu Bai, 3/4 decided to develop the platoons of the South Vietnamese Popular Forces (PFs), essentially a loosely organized local militia, stationed in the nearby villages. First Lieutenant Paul R. Ek asked for Marine volunteers to work with the PFs. In a week's training he taught them as much as he could about Vietnamese customs and the country's political situation. Each of the four squads was then assigned to a PF platoon.

Each PF platoon took up residence in a hamlet. The Marines lived, ate, slept, and worked with the villagers. At night they sent patrols into the nearby countryside to interdict any marauding VC. Over time it was hoped that the presence and help of these combined action platoons (CAPs) would persuade the peasants to disavow the Viet Cong.

As the CAP program developed through the summer and fall of 1965, its effectiveness became apparent. Nocturnal visits by VC recruiters to hamlets dropped dramatically. The villagers grew more confident and began supplying the Marines with information on the local VC.

General Walt believed in the CAPs. In September, in an obvious break with official MACV policy, he said, "The Marines have never felt that the war stands to be won by the grand maneuvers of large forces, by brilliant marshalship in the Tannenberg or Chancellorsville image, but rather in the villages." Though the CAPs would expand and make major contributions to the war effort in future years, General Walt's support of the program would bring him into conflict with General Westmoreland.

With all this increased activity, General Walt needed more troops. He requested the remaining battalions of the 3d Marine Division be sent from Okinawa to South Vietnam. His timing could not have been better. Expansion of U.S. forces in South Vietnam was once again under consideration by General Westmoreland.

Westmoreland, limited to a force of just nine infantry battalions (seven Marine and the two army battalions of the 173d Airborne Brigade, which had arrived in-country in May), did not feel that this was adequate to help the ARVN hold back the VC. On 7 June, he asked the Joint Chiefs of Staff (JCS) for the remaining two battalions of the 3d Marine Division, two more army brigades, and an airmobile division.

Negotiations between MACV and the JCS continued for several more weeks. It was finally decided on 22 June that allied aid to South Vietnam would consist of forty-four maneuver battalions, the majority to be American, with South Korea and Australia contributing several units (although the American taxpayer would bear the full cost of allied deployment). Though he'd just increased his forces fivefold, Westmoreland still wanted more. He told the JCS that the forty-four battalions were nothing more than "a stopgap measure to save the ARVN from defeat."

Unwilling to undermine the on-site commander's decisions, the JCS acquiesced to Westmoreland's request for even more troops. At the same time, Washington gave Westmoreland permission to commit U.S. forces to battle "in any situation" where their use was judged necessary to strengthen ARVN positions. America's long slide into the morass of the Vietnam conflict was gathering speed.

One area where Westmoreland saw fit to use his newly authorized manpower was at Qui Nhon, in Binh Dinh Province in the II Corps Tactical Zone. The massive U.S. Army logistical base being built there in anticipation of the imminent arrival of several full army divisions was too lucrative a target for the VC to ignore. As a result, Westmoreland requested that a Marine battalion be deployed immediately from Okinawa to protect the base. Admiral Sharp agreed but suggested that it would be easier to send in the Special Landing Force (SLF) of the Seventh Fleet. (The SLF was a shipboard battalion landing team that formed the Fleet Marine Force's floating reserve. Through an administrative technicality, command of the SLF rested with the U.S. Navy's Seventh Fleet commander, not MACV. Thus, personnel assigned to the SLF were not counted against the in-country manpower allocation. Plus, MACV had to request their deployment for specific operations. Throughout the war individual Marine battalions rotated between SLF service and assignment to the III MAF. (This gave the battalions an opportunity to refit and retrain their personnel after a tour as an in-country unit.) Westmoreland accepted the modification, because it would be relatively easy to reembark the Marines once the army units arrived.

On 1 July, BLT 3/7, the SLF, came across the beaches at Qui Nhon. They remained on station for a week before being relieved by BLT 2/7 and returning to Special Landing Force duty. Significantly, the arrival of these 7th Marine units in the war zone signaled a major expansion of the Marine Corps' presence in South Vietnam, for they were a part of the California-based 1st Marine Division.

Although General Westmoreland proved to be correct in his prediction that the VC would find the new American bases too tempting to ignore, when their attack finally did come, it still caught everyone by surprise. In the early morning hours of 1 July, a Viet Cong sapper team crept onto the air base at Da Nang. Before the sentries could react, the infiltrators destroyed three aircraft and damaged three more. Enemy small arms fire wounded three Marines as they chased the sappers off the base. Several blood trails were discovered at daybreak, but no enemy casualties were found.

Despite the relatively light damage, the spectacular nature of the attack caught the attention of America's senior officers. Within hours of the attack General Walt received inquiring phone calls from all his superiors, ranging from General Westmoreland to Defense Secretary McNamara.

General Walt used the political interest in the attack to expedite to South Vietnam the deployment of the balance of the 3d Marine Division from Okinawa. All remaining division units arrived in-country by 6 July. Walt also pressured the local ARVN commander for a major expansion of the Marines' TAOR, particularly south and east of the air base. Permission was granted almost immediately.

Marine patrols entered the expanded TAOR for the first time on 12 July. The entire region was densely populated with innumerable clusters of villages and hamlets. South of Da Nang, the area below the east-west–running Cau Do River was of particular concern. Intelligence information indicated that the Viet Cong were thickly embedded in nearly every hamlet and had been for a generation. They strongly resisted the Marines' incursion into their territory.

Company B, 1/9, lost three men killed and four wounded that first day when the VC opened fire on them in the hamlet of Duong Son (1)*, about two kilometers south of the Cau Do River. Only the timely arrival of Marine close air support broke the enemy's ranks.

That same day, an eighteen-man patrol from Company A, 3d Reconnaissance Battalion, came under heavy fire from an estimated one hundred VC about twenty kilometers southwest of the air base. When his radioman was hit by enemy fire, the patrol leader, 1st Lt. Frank S. Reasoner, ignored the heavy volume of fire and moved to his side to render aid. Reasoner, providing covering fire as the radioman crawled to safety, killed two VC and silenced an automatic weapon. Despite this, the VC wounded the radioman again before he reached cover. Again ignoring the intense enemy fire, Reasoner bounded to the man's aid but was mortally wounded before he reached him. Reasoner's self-sacrifice brought him a posthumous Medal of Honor, the first earned by a Marine in South Vietnam.

Determined to keep the VC off balance and under pressure, the Marines intensified their activity south of Da Nang. Almost daily, patrols of company strength or greater moved through the thatched huts of the villages looking for the enemy, their weapons, and their supply caches. More often than not, the Marines came up empty-handed as their crafty foe eluded these searches. But they frequently found irrefutable evidence of the VC's presence.

One such patrol brought the Marines some unneeded publicity. On 3 August, Company D, 1/9, commanded by Capt. Herman B. West, Jr., swept the hamlet of Cam Ne, just south of the Cau Do River. Though they found no VC, they did uncover nearly three hundred *punji* stick traps (sharpened bamboo sticks covered with human feces and embedded in camouflaged shallow holes designed to impale a foot), three grenade booby traps, six antipersonnel mines, and one multiple booby-trapped hedgerow. Sporadic sniper fire harassed the Marines as they moved through Cam Ne, causing several friendly casualties.

* Because several hamlets comprising a village often carried the same name, military maps identified them with a numerical suffix.

Frustrated, the Marines burned a number of thatched huts. A television crew, accompanying CBS news correspondent Morley Safer, captured Marines igniting the straw huts with their cigarette lighters. Though these "Zippo Squads" were responding to the small arms fire they had taken, when the film clip played on American television Safer noted, "If there were Viet Cong in the hamlet they were long gone." These comments made the Marines seem undisciplined, vindictive, and brutal. This story seemed to set the tone for press coverage for the balance of the Vietnam War.

During the summer, General Westmoreland made several command decisions that greatly escalated the Marines' role in the war. The most significant one came on 30 July. He advised General Walt to undertake larger offensive operations against the VC at greater distances from his base. Reminded by Walt that MACV's April instructions restricted III MAF to reaction missions in support of South Vietnamese units actually engaged with the enemy, Westmoreland rescinded those restrictions on 6 August. Walt could now use his Marines in whatever manner he desired. It didn't take General Walt long to launch his first offensive operation of this new war.

Operation Starlite

Throughout July the 3d Marine Division's S-2 (Intelligence) office had repeatedly turned up information regarding a large Viet Cong buildup south of Chu Lai. Even MACV's intelligence staff reported that the VC might attack the Marines' garrison at Chu Lai with as many as three regiments.

The enemy's intent became clear on 15 August when a member of the 1st VC Regiment surrendered to the ARVN. During his interrogation the enemy soldier revealed that his regiment, numbering almost fifteen hundred men with supporting units, had established its base in the Van Tuong village complex, fifteen kilometers south of Chu Lai and about two kilometers inland. The attack on Chu Lai would be launched from there.

Once General Walt learned of this, he sprang into action. Meeting with his senior commanders, Walt made it clear that he wasn't going to wait for the enemy to strike. He now had the authority and enough troops at his disposal to go on the offensive. In a whirlwind of activity over the next forty-eight hours, Walt's staff put together the attack plan. Two battalions would be involved. Three companies of 3/3 would make an amphibious landing at Green Beach to the south and east of Van Tuong, blocking the VC's southern escape routes. The battalion's fourth company, Company M, would move overland from Chu Lai to setup a blocking position four kilometers northwest of the landing beaches.

Just after the amphibious landings, Marines of 2/4 would be air-assaulted into three landing zones (LZs) forming an arc southwest of Van Tuong. LZ Blue, the southernmost of the LZs, sat two thousand meters west of Green Beach. Company H, 2/4, would touch down there. Two thousand meters northwest, Company E, 2/4, would land at LZ White. LZ Red, two thousand meters farther north, would accept the helicopters carrying the Marines of Company G. Once on the ground the three companies would attack northeast toward Phase Line Banana, just short of Van Tuong (1).

General Walt selected Col. Oscar F. Peatross, the commander of the 7th Marines, as overall commander of the assault. Peatross's 3/7, then the Special Landing Force, would act as reserve. Because 3/7 was then at Subic Bay in the Philippine Islands, 18 August was selected for D day, allowing them ample time to arrive offshore. (Historically, Marine regiments had operated with their own organic battalions. Beginning with Operation Starlite, III MAF began the practice of shuffling battalions, and even individual line companies, among regiments without regard to their historical lineage. Although this habit allowed quick response to developing tactical situations, it created many morale problems. Subordinate commanders had little chance to develop a working relationship with their superiors, or the regimental staff. Combat commanders frequently operated without knowing who commanded the adjacent units. As companies and platoons were switched around, confusion over the proper chain of command often resulted.)

In the planning sessions the operation was designated "Satellite." However, a harried operations clerk, working by flickering candlelight due to a generator failure, typed the name as "Starlite." Rather than redo all the stenciled forms, the name Starlite was accepted.

Operation Starlite began when Company M, 3/3, left Chu Lai on the morning of 17 August aboard amphibious vehicles. They landed near their blocking position, then began their inland trek. Before dawn on 18 August they were in position and ready.

The first 155mm artillery shells slammed into the LZs at 0615 on 18 August, throwing earth and vegetation skyward. Within minutes, hundreds of shells had ripped into the ground. Then twenty Marine A-4 Skyhawks and F-4 Phantoms screamed in at low level. Tons of bombs and gallons of napalm blanketed the target area. Thick rolls of black smoke filled the air.

At Green Beach another flight of Skyhawks sprayed the target area with deadly 20mm cannon shells. Just off shore heavy machine guns, mounted on the amphibious craft, added their fire to the din. Under this covering fire Companies I and K, 3/3, hit the beaches at 0630. Facing only intermittent sniper fire, the anxious Marines quickly moved through An Cuong (1), the hamlet closest to the sea. By 0730 battalion commander Lt. Col. Joseph E. Muir had set up his command post a kilometer west of the village. He was soon joined by Colonel Peatross and his staff. The battle was going well.

Inland, the staccato beat of helicopter rotors signaled the arrival of Company G, 2/4, at LZ Red at 0645. Forty-five minutes later the men of Company E and the command group of 2/4, including Lt. Col. Joseph R. Fisher, jumped from their helicopters at LZ White. At about the same time, Company H alighted at LZ Blue. The cordon around Van Tuong (1) was in place.

Company G easily moved off their LZ. They encountered only minor resistance as they searched two hamlets near their touchdown site. Continuing to the northeast, they linked up with Company M, 3/3, by early afternoon.

To the south Company E ran into trouble as soon as it moved off LZ White. From a ridgeline north and east of the LZ, the VC used mortars and automatic weapons fire to stifle the company's advance. Diving for cover, the Marines aimed their M14 rifles and M60 machine guns uphill. Maneuvering by squads, the company crept up the hill. Together, grizzled noncommissioned officers and baby-faced, inexperienced enlisted men destroyed one enemy bunker after another. Finally, after several hours of dogged fighting, the Marines threw the VC off the hills. After evacuating their casualties the company resumed its northeast advance.

In the meantime, along the coast, Company K, 3/3, had advanced nearly two thousand meters north, halting at Phase Line Banana. There, VC forces entrenched on the high ground between them and Van Tuong (1) drove them to the ground. Responding rapidly, Colonel Muir ordered Company L forward from its reserve position at Green Beach. Following a blistering mortar barrage, the two companies stormed the hill. Sharp, close-quarters fighting raged across the hill as the Marines used rifle fire and grenades to dig out the VC. Not until midafternoon was the fight over. The Marines then dug in for the night.

So far, Colonel Peatross was pleased. The battle was developing as planned, his forces were in position and advancing, casualties were light, and the enemy was cornered. His troops would be in Van Tuong (1) the next morning. Then word of the plight of Company H, 2/4, reached the colonel. His optimism faded.

Landing Zone Blue straddled the boundary between the two assault battalions. This one-square-kilometer area was bounded by three hamlets: An Thoi (2) on the north, Nam Yen (3) on the south, and An Cuong (2) to the east. The ground was a patchwork of rice paddies, meandering streams, hedgerows, woods, and built-up areas, all interspersed by a maze of twisting trails. Two small knolls dominated the area: Hill 43, about three hundred meters southwest of Nam Yen (3), and Hill 30, four hundred meters north of An Cuong (2). Landing Zone Blue sat between Hill 43 and Nam Yen (3). To the planners it seemed an ideal site for Company H, 2/4, to land and start its movement to the northeast. What the operations staff didn't know was that the 60th VC Battalion already occupied the area.

The first incoming UH-34 helicopters carrying Company H caught the VC by surprise. The aircraft dropped their loads and departed safely. It was a different story for the following flights. Vicious enemy machine-gun fire from Hill 43 sliced through the formations. The choppers' thin aluminum skin offered little resistance to the heavy slugs. The firing was so intense that one helicopter pilot later remarked, "You just had to close your eyes and drop down to the deck."

The riflemen pouring out of the helicopters formed a rough defensive perimeter. Not yet fully aware of what he faced, company commander 1st Lt. Homer K. Jenkins sent one platoon to handle the enemy on the hill. The other two platoons started toward Nam Yen (3). Violent blasts of enemy small arms fire drove both groups of men to the ground. Realizing now that he didn't have the strength to take both positions at once, Jenkins pulled his platoons back to the LZ. As they regrouped Jenkins called for help. Soon jets were strafing and bombing both the hill and the village. When they finished Jenkins sent all three platoons up the hill. The fighting was fierce. Well-entrenched Viet Cong sent a hail of small arms fire down on the Marines. Finding little cover on the hillside, the attackers pressed forward, moving by leaps and bounds. The novice but well-disciplined Marines went after their foe aggressively. Unused to a bold enemy, the VC soon broke under the pressure. Fleeing into the nearby underbrush, the enemy left behind more than a dozen dead, a heavy machine gun, forty rifles, and one wounded man.

To avoid casualties from the air strikes called in by Lieutenant Jenkins on Nam Yen (3), Company I, 3/3, moving inland from Green Beach, halted along a streambed about one kilometer east of Nam Yen (3). Despite this caution, two Company I members were lightly wounded by friendly bomb fragments. At the end of the bombing run, Capt. Bruce D. Webb advanced his Marines northward along the streambed until they reached a point opposite An Cuong (2). Enemy fire immediately slashed through the company's ranks. Webb requested permission to attack An Cuong (2) even though it lay in 2/4's territory. Colonel Peatross agreed.

Consisting of twenty-five to thirty huts, An Cuong (2) was surrounded by heavily wooded areas and bamboo thickets. A camouflaged trench line connected a series of interlocking tunnels. An Cuong (2) was a perfect VC stronghold.

Webb led his Marines in clearing the first few huts. Halfway through the village a Viet Cong guerrilla rolled a grenade at Webb's feet. The intrepid captain died in the blast. Three other Marines fell wounded. Seconds later two enemy mortar rounds exploded nearby.

Three more Marines went down. Lieutenant Richard M. Purnell, the executive officer, quickly assumed command. After reorganizing his rattled men, Purnell led them through the village. A short time later the company had punched through the enemy's defenses. Company I held An Cuong (2). The Marines killed more than fifty VC in the process. After the friendly casualties were evacuated, Colonel Muir ordered Purnell to head northeast to help Company K with its fight near Phase Line Banana.

In the meantime, Lieutenant Jenkins brought his company forward from Hill 43 toward An Cuong (2) to link up with Company I. He bypassed Nam Yen (3) to the east, mistakenly believing that Company I had cleared it, too. Jenkins learned the unfortunate truth when VC in Nam Yen (3) and on Hill 30 pounded his company with small arms and mortar fire. The savage fire badly wounded five men in the lead platoon. Frantic calls of "Corpsman up!" echoed across the field. Accurate Viet Cong automatic weapons fire prevented any corpsmen from reaching the wounded. Fully mindful of the danger, LCpl. Joe C. Paul picked up his M60 machine gun and splashed across a paddy. Taking up an exposed position between the casualties and the enemy, Paul unleashed burst after burst of fire into the enemy's positions. His selfless action diverted the VC's fire long enough for corpsmen to pull the wounded men to safety. Struck by enemy fire and knocked from his gun, Paul ignored his painful wounds and crawled back to his weapon. Firing again and again, he was mortally wounded before he could return to cover.

Jenkins, realizing he again faced more enemy than he could handle, now ordered his company back to LZ Blue. They started back about 1400. Then, unexpectedly, medical evacuation helicopters began landing amidst the company, scattering the men. The lead platoon was isolated in the resulting confusion. As the men maneuvered, concealed VC took them under fire. They were pinned down. Surprise relief for the trapped platoon came in the form of two squads from Company I that had been left behind to protect a downed helicopter.

During the ensuing firefight one of the Company I squad leaders, Cpl. Robert E. O'Malley, who had already distinguished himself in the fight at An Cuong (2), bravely charged the enemy emplacement. His deadly M14 fire drove the VC from their position. O'Malley was hit twice in this encounter but still helped pull several other casualties to safety. Fighting together, the two small Marine units made it to An Cuong (2). Meanwhile, Jenkins and his remaining platoons fought their way back to LZ Blue, arriving there at 1630. They were ordered to dig in and await reinforcements. The reinforcements never made it to Jenkins. Instead, they were diverted to rescue a supply column that had been ambushed just west of An Cuong (2).

Just after noon the column, consisting of five LVTs (landing vehicle, tracked) and three tanks, left the 3/3 regimental command post (CP) to resupply Company I, which had just cleared An Cuong (2). Somehow, the little force got lost in the thick woods. They ended up on a trail that took them between An Cuong (2) and Nam Yen (3). There VC recoilless rifle fire and a mortar barrage suddenly blasted the unsuspecting supply train. Viet Cong infantry swept out of the foliage. The column's radioman called for help, but in his panic he kept the microphone's transmit button depressed the whole time. As a result, the supply column's exact position was unknown. For more than an hour the radioman cried that the men were surrounded and needed help.

A relief force consisting of the nearly spent Company I, some headquarters personnel, and the one remaining tank was hurriedly organized at the regimental CP. Led by Maj. Andrew G. Comer, 3/3's executive officer, the Marines headed for the column's last known position about an hour after it was attacked. Just after they crested Hill 30, the VC opened fire. A recoilless rifle round slammed into the tank, disabling it. Seconds later VC rifle fire and mortar shells saturated the area. Within minutes, five Marines were dead and seventeen were wounded. Comer called in supporting artillery and air strikes. The high explosives scattered the enemy.

Comer then ordered Lieutenant Purnell to take Company I through An Cuong (2) to find the supply column. Initially, Purnell experienced only light resistance. As he neared the trapped men, however, the enemy fire increased. Soon he was pinned down. Meanwhile, Comer and his command group were hit by intense enemy small arms fire from a wooded area to their right front. They took cover in the nearby rice paddies.

At this juncture, the two errant squads from Company I and the platoon from Company H, 2/4, joined Comer. He sent the two Company I squads to Hill 30 for evacuation and kept the Company H platoon with him.

While Lieutenant Purnell struggled to fight his way to the trapped supply column, Colonel Peatross obtained the release of Company L, 3/7, from the SLF reserve force aboard the *Iwo Jima,* anchored off Green Beach. After checking in at 3/3's CP, Company L headed out, following Comer's route. Enemy fire hit them as they neared An Cuong (2) from the east. Four Marines were killed and fourteen were wounded. Recovering quickly, Company L drove forward, finally forcing the VC to break contact as night fell.

Deciding that it was too risky to continue searching for the supply column, Colonel Muir now ordered Company L, 3/7, to reverse direction and link up with Companies K and L, 3/3, near Phase Line Banana. Company I, 3/3, pulled back to the regimental CP. Purnell's company had suffered particularly heavy casualties that day, losing 14 dead and 53 wounded of its 177 members. The supply column, no longer in danger, was ordered to remain in place for the night. That evening Colonel Peatross brought the two remaining reserve companies, I and M, 3/7, ashore.

The next day, Peatross issued his orders to continue the battle. He planned to keep on tightening the cordon around Van Tuong (1) and the adjacent Phuoc Thuan Peninsula. Companies K and L, 3/3, and Company L, 3/7, were to attack north toward Van Tuong (1), the original objective. Companies E and G, 2/4, would advance eastward, eventually linking up with the Marines moving northward. Companies I and M, 3/7, would rescue the supply column, then set up blocking positions at An Thoi (2) to prevent any VC from slipping southward. Company H, 2/4, and Comer's group were ordered back to the regimental CP; Jenkins's company suffered fifteen killed and thirty wounded in the fighting. Company M, 3/3, would maintain its blocking position on the north.

The renewed attack commenced at 0730 on 19 August. The various companies found pockets of stiff resistance as they advanced across the rugged terrain. The region was thick with rice paddies ringed by dikes and hedgerows, which hampered control, observation, and maneuverability. The VC fought back from well-concealed bunkers, trenches, and caves. Frequently, Marines would complete sweeping an area only to be fired on by VC from the rear as they moved on. The Marines would then reverse direction and dig the enemy out or blow up their tunnels. Nonetheless, by 1030 Companies E and G, 2/4, had linked up with the 3/3 units near Van Tuong (1). The combined force then swept the rest of the peninsula. Organized enemy resistance on Phuoc Thuan Peninsula had ceased.

Meanwhile, at 0900 Companies I and M entered An Cuong (2). The enemy had fled. A short time later remnants of the supply column were found. Of twenty-three men originally with the column, five were dead and nine were wounded. The Marines counted sixty dead VC in the area. After evacuating the survivors, the two companies continued to An Thoi (2).

Operation Starlite continued for five more days because General Walt felt that some enemy soldiers remained behind in underground hiding places. Before beginning this mop-up phase, Colonel Peatross released 2/4 and 3/3 on 20 August, replacing them with 1/7. The fresh Marines, together with 3/7 and units from the 2d ARVN Division, killed another 54 VC before Operation Starlite officially ended on 24 August. In all, 614 VC were killed, 9 prisoners were taken, and 109 assorted weapons were captured. The Marines suffered 45 dead and 203 wounded.

Despite some confusion, the Marines won the battle of Chu Lai. Credit belonged not only to the infantry but to the supporting arms as well. Masterful employment of both artillery and close air support, brought to within two hundred meters of pinned-down infantry, frequently proved decisive in breaking the VC's defenses.

At the same time, the Marines learned that the VC were far more than a ragtag collection of rebellious peasants. Indeed, the Viet Cong were well-armed, well-led, brave, and resourceful. They employed excellent battlefield techniques, quickly isolating small units and punishing them with massed firepower. They exploited every opportunity given them, including using as bait a pinned down unit, then ambushing the relief force. The VC were not afraid of the Marines and would not be easily beaten.

The young, mostly inexperienced Marines learned that they were the equal of their fathers and older brothers who had fought a crafty foe in World War II and Korea. They could take what the VC dished out and give it back to him with a vengeance. Though they made skillful use of their supporting firepower, it was individual heroism that often made the difference. Six Navy Crosses, including a posthumous one to Captain Webb, would be awarded to Marines for their bravery in Operation Starlite. Corporal O'Malley and Lance Corporal Paul earned Medals of Honor, the latter posthumously.

Other lessons were learned as well. The allotted two gallons of water per man per day proved woefully inadequate in South Vietnam's oppressive heat. The quota was immediately doubled. The M14 semiautomatic rifle proved too heavy and bulky. A search for a lighter weapon began immediately.

Operation Starlite was a major morale booster for the Marines. They had met the VC in a pitched battle and defeated him. They had passed the first big test. What they didn't know was that there would be many more tests in the future.

Based on the success of Operation Starlite, General Walt planned to continue the battering of the 1st VC Regiment. Intelligence sources indicated that the enemy unit had retreated to the Batangan Peninsula, about twelve kilometers south of Van Tuong. The III MAF planned a three battalion assault there beginning 7 September.

Operation Piranha began at 0555 that day when eight A-4s strafed White Beach on the Batangan Peninsula's north shore for twenty minutes. Then a single A-4 laid a smoke screen along the beach while the other jets turned their attention inland. There they blasted LZs out of the thick vegetation with five-hundred-pound "Daisy Cutter" bombs.

At 0635 the first wave of amphibious tractors carrying members of Companies A and C, 1/7, nosed onto the sand. Within twenty minutes the entire battalion was ashore. The enemy's response was a few poorly aimed sniper rounds. The Marines quickly moved inland and established defensive positions.

At 0730, UH-34Ds carrying assault elements of 3/7 swooped in from the north to LZ Oak, about three kilometers southwest of White Beach. The aircraft deposited their human cargo without incident. Over the next three hours the helicopters ferried in the rest of the battalion. The aircraft then went to pick up ARVN troops.

Following the extensive press coverage that the Marines had received for their successes in Operation Starlite, the local ARVN began openly criticizing them. The South Vietnamese felt slighted because not only had they not had a role in the operation, they had not even been told about it until the landings had occurred. This secrecy stemmed from the I Corps commander, Maj. Gen. Nguyen Chanh Thi. All too aware of the security leaks from his staff, Thi had kept information about Operation Starlite to himself. That fact, however, did not prevent the South Vietnamese from feeling excluded from their own war.

Consequently, two ARVN battalions were given roles in Operation Piranha. After dropping the Marines at LZ Oak, sixteen of the UH-34Ds headed south to load elements of the ARVN 2/4 and the South Vietnamese Marine Corps' 3d Battalion. These units were landed at LZs Birch and Pine, respectively, to the southwest of the Batangan Peninsula. They would conduct a sweep to the northeast toward the An Ky Peninsula, south of Batangan.

During the three days of Operation Piranha, only 1/7 had any significant contact with the VC. On the second day, its Company B discovered a VC field hospital in a large cave near the center of the peninsula. Enemy soldiers within the cave fired on the Marines, killing two and wounding five. When the VC refused to surrender, Marine engineers detonated a large charge of dynamite in the cave. Sixty-six VC died in the blast.

The allied force claimed 178 VC killed during Operation Piranha, with a total of 5 Marines and ARVN killed and 47 wounded. Considering the size of the allied force, Operation Piranha could hardly be deemed a success. In fact, by questioning villagers, the Marines learned that the 1st VC Regiment had fled the area starting several days before the operation began. It was almost as if they'd received advance notice of the plans. And, as soon as the allied troops withdrew, the VC returned. The Batangan Peninsula would remain an enemy stronghold for years. In 1968 it was the site of the infamous My Lai Massacre of civilians by soldiers of the U.S. Army's Americal Division.

For the three months following Operation Starlite, the Viet Cong refused to meet the Marines in battle. Though the units of the 3d Marine Division mounted more than half a dozen operations outside their enclaves, they uncovered few VC. More often than not, enemy resistance was limited to sporadic, ineffective sniper fire.

It was during the lull in the early fall that General Westmoreland finalized his plan for fighting the Vietnam War. Because the plan contained no specific objectives, Westmoreland's directive was more a guideline for conducting the war than a strategy in the conventional sense. Westmoreland divided the war into three phases. The first, ending in 1965, was simply to commit those American and allied forces necessary to halt the losing trend. The second phase, beginning in 1966, foresaw those forces taking the offensive in select high-priority areas. At some distant, to-be-determined date, phase three—the complete destruction of the enemy's forces—would commence.

Based on MACV's guidelines, III MAF developed its own concept of operations within I Corps. Primarily it emphasized the "ink blot" approach, whereby the III MAF was to secure and maintain its coastal enclaves, then gradually expand them as manpower and resources became available. Eventually the three enclaves would meet, and the involved populous coastal areas would be secure.

Within this framework, III MAF produced a "balanced strategy" for the war. Its three main components consisted of a counterguerrilla campaign within the TAORs, offensive operations against enemy main force units outside the TAORs, and an expanded pacification campaign within the villages in order to destroy the Viet Cong's infrastructure and return the people's loyalty to the government of South Vietnam.

It soon became clear that there existed a significant difference between MACV and III MAF as to where the enemy posed the greatest threat. General Walt was convinced that his first priority was to rid the populous and rice-rich Da Nang region of the Viet Cong. General Westmoreland, on the other hand, desired to destroy enemy main force units in the country's interior.

The MACV commander appreciated General Walt's concerns with pacification efforts. However, Westmoreland preferred that III MAF maintain a three- or four-battalion reaction force that could respond to large enemy unit sightings. This conflict of emphasis remained a sore point between MACV and III MAF for more than a year before it was resolved.

Tasked with fighting both a big-unit war and an antiguerrilla campaign, General Walt requested more troops. He advised MACV that he needed a second full Marine division to execute his mission. As a result, the 1st Marine Division shifted its headquarters from Camp Pendleton, California, to Okinawa. Several of the division's individual battalions were already in South Vietnam or in the Special Landing Force. By early 1966 the entire division would be in-country.

As III MAF increased in size, General Westmoreland toyed with the idea of placing it under I Field Force command. (Because the South Vietnamese already used the corps designator, MACV developed the field force concept to avoid confusion. Thus, a field force was essentially an American corps but with the additional responsibilities of supply and pacification, as well as an advisory role to the local ARVN commander.) Headquartered in Nha Trang, I Field Force operated in the ARVN II Corps geographical area. General Westmoreland considered placing III MAF under I Field Force, thus creating another link in the chain of command below him, but he did not do so. Concerned about interservice rivalries, Westmoreland opted to allow III MAF to report directly to him.

The Viet Cong did not remain idle for long. On the night of 27–28 October, they hit both the newly completed Marble Mountain helicopter facility east of Da Nang and the Chu Lai airfield.

At Chu Lai about twenty VC sappers sneaked onto the base. The first notice the Marines had of trouble was when an aircraft blew up. In the fire's light, sentries caught ghostly glimpses of the loincloth-clad sappers running among the planes, spraying them with machine-gun fire and throwing satchel charges. The sentries tracked down and killed fifteen of the sappers, but not before two jets were destroyed and six more were severely damaged.

The Viet Cong attack at Marble Mountain was larger, better organized, and more destructive. Some ninety main-force VC attacked the base under a barrage of mortar fire. As at Chu Lai, the attack caught the airfield defenders by surprise. The sappers raced across the tarmac, tossing explosive charges at the neatly parked helicopters. Firing automatic weapons at the sentries, the sappers finally withdrew after a thirty-minute rampage. They left behind seventeen of their own dead and four wounded plus nineteen destroyed helicopters, eleven severely damaged craft, and another twenty that were badly damaged. Three Marines died and ninety-one were wounded in the attack.

The attacks vividly demonstrated that the Viet Cong were the ones who chose when and where the war intensified.

Operation Harvest Moon

On 17 November, a revitalized 1st VC Regiment overran the small ARVN garrison holding Hiep Duc, in Quang Tin Province. This district capital sat at the western end of a fertile valley that constituted one of the most strategic areas between Da Nang and Chu Lai. Bordered on both north and south by rugged mountain ranges, this region, known to the Marines as the Que Son Valley, would remain bitterly contested throughout the Vietnam War.

The next day, Marine helicopters airlifted reinforcing ARVN troops into an LZ east of Hiep Duc. Unknown to the pilots, a North Vietnamese Army (NVA) antiaircraft battalion held well-entrenched positions on the nearby hills. The first wave of troop-carrying helicopters landed unopposed. Then, just as the second wave touched down, the NVA let loose. The heavy 12.7mm slugs slammed into the UH-34Ds. As soon as the ARVN cleared their helicopters, the pilots pulled pitch and flew away. The other waves were halted while air strikes were ordered. Twenty minutes after the enemy opened fire, the first A-4s and F-4s were dropping bombs on the NVA positions. In another twenty minutes the troop lift resumed. Once the ARVN battalion was on the ground and formed up, it headed west for Hiep Duc. Bitter fighting raged for the rest of the day, but, with the help of Marine close air support, the South Vietnamese troops recaptured the important town by nightfall.

However, before the ARVN could exploit their victory, the VC over-ran the isolated outpost at Thach Tru in southern I Corps. Strapped for manpower, General Thi withdrew his two battalions from Hiep Duc and sent them south. While the ARVN fought to hold on to Thach Tru, General Walt recognized that the 1st VC Regiment was in an excellent position to reenter the Que Son Valley, threatening other ARVN outposts at Que Son and Viet An, in the center of the valley. Over the next two weeks he met several times with General Thi. Both commanders agreed that they needed to launch a sizable attack against the VC before they could establish a firm base of operations.

As a result, on 5 December, General Walt established Task Force (TF) Delta under his assistant division commander, Brig. Gen. Melvin D. Henderson, to control the Marine operations in the com-bined Operation Harvest Moon/Lien Kiet 18. Two battalions, 2/7 and 3/3, were assigned to TF Delta.

Three days later the 5th ARVN Regiment left Thang Binh headed southwest toward Hiep Duc, twenty-five kilometers away, along Highway 534. About halfway to their first day's objective, a point south of Que Son, the 70th VC Battalion hit the ARVN with a fero-cious close-quarters attack. In the first fifteen minutes, one third of the ARVN force was destroyed. A surviving U.S. Army adviser later said, "They attacked in a mass and hit us from all sides. People were dropping left and right." The survivors retreated to the northwest. Reinforcements arrived late that afternoon, but they didn't deter the VC. At 0645 the next morning they struck again. In the heavy fighting that followed, the VC overran the regimental command post, killing the ARVN commander. The surviving ARVN troops fled into the nearby hills.

As soon as he learned of the ARVN's situation, General Hen-derson ordered his Marines into action. The 2d Battalion, 7th Marines jumped aboard UH-34D helicopters at Tam Ky, at the east-ern edge of the valley, and headed for an LZ eight kilometers west of the decimated ARVN unit. Once on the ground the Marines moved easily eastward and set up a night perimeter two kilometers from the LZ.

Meanwhile, the 3d Battalion, 3d Marines were at a staging area five kilometers north of Thang Binh. Helicopters, normally assigned to the SLF, picked the Marines up there and rushed them to an LZ southeast of the shattered ARVN unit. One and a half hours later, at 1530, 3/3's lead unit, Company L, made contact with the ARVN. Together, the allies set out for Hill 43, just a kilometer to the northwest.

Halfway there, a VC force estimated at two hundred opened fire. A brutal firefight raged into the evening. Burdened by the skittish ARVN, the Marines were unable to overcome the foe. Supporting artillery and air strikes finally drove away the VC. The battalion established a night defensive perimeter and then called in medical evacuation helicopters to take out the eleven dead and seventeen wounded Marines.

The next day General Henderson ordered the two Marine battalions to advance toward each other, squeezing the VC between them. Any escape route to the south would be blocked by 2/1, the SLF, which was being helilifted into position that morning.

Company F, 2/1, was the first unit into the LZ near Cam La, five kilometers southeast of Que Son. Before the first helicopters had finished disgorging their Marine infantry cargo, the VC blasted them with machine-gun fire from the high ground to the south. Several helicopters were hit. While they limped off, the rest of the battalion headed to an alternate LZ farther west.

Company F, meanwhile, was having a hard time. Besides the machine-gun fire pinning them down in the open rice paddies, VC mortar rounds crashed down on the Marines.

With the rest of 2/1 unable to move toward Company F, General Henderson ordered 2/7 to the rescue. Company E, 2/7, set out. As the company neared the trapped Marines, its right flank was raked by a vicious blast of enemy fire. Struggling forward, dragging their casualties with them, members of Company E reached a position where they could provide supporting fire to Company F. Under this cover the pinned-down Marines inched their way backward, finally linking up with Company E. The trapped Marines' ordeal had lasted ten hours. Together, the two companies suffered more than one hundred casualties, including twenty dead.

That night General Walt replaced General Henderson as task force commander. Brigader General Jonas M. Platt, assistant division commander at Chu Lai, took command of Task Force Delta. His first action was to order another company to reinforce 2/1. Company G, 2/7, arrived at the perimeter at 0300 on 11 December.

During an aerial reconnaissance of the battlefield later that day, General Platt was surprised that his aircraft wasn't fired on. He surmised that the enemy had slipped into Phuoc Ha Valley, smaller than the Que Son Valley and paralleling it seven kilometers to the southeast. Platt ordered B-52 strikes in Phuoc Ha Valley for the morning of 12 December. When the heavy bombers finished their runs, the infantry-laden helicopters darted in. The 3d Battalion, 3d Marines landed on Hills 100 and 180, overlooking the northern approaches to the valley. The 2d Battalion, 1st Marines deployed farther to the south.

The next morning, the two battalions entered the valley from both directions. Though they uncovered several large supply caches, they found no sign of the 1st VC Regiment. The Marines spent several more days patrolling the valley but encountered little organized resistance.

While those two battalions swept Phuoc Ha Valley, 2/7 searched for the VC along the northern bank of the Khang River, about ten kilometers south of Que Son. For the next week the battalion advanced eastward toward Tam Ky. Though the enemy fired a few sniper rounds at the column, the weather was a bigger problem.

Constant monsoon rains dogged the Marines' every pace. The ground was so saturated that fifty-four men suffered from immersion foot. They were evacuated during a temporary break in the weather on the morning of 18 December. After the medevac, Company G took the point, or lead position. They were followed by Company F, then the Headquarters and Service (H&S) Company. Company H, 2/9, which had replaced the badly mauled Company E, 2/7, brought up the rear. The column moved along a narrow road that snaked its way through hedgerow-lined rice paddies. Company G had just passed through the village of Ky Phu, about ten kilometers west of Tam Ky, when well-concealed VC from the 80th Battalion opened fire. From his position with the H&S Company, Lt. Col. Leon N. Utter, the battalion commander, quickly ordered Company G to deploy to the south of the road. He then radioed Company F to hurry forward into supporting positions.

As soon as Company F exited the east edge of Ky Phu, enemy mortar rounds dropped on the H&S Company, caught west of the village in open paddies. Two VC companies charged out of the nearby woods intent on isolating the H&S Company and the battalion command group. Utter now radioed Company F to reverse direction and assault the attacking VC.

With this help the H&S Company fought its way into the relative safety of Ky Phu. Company H, 2/9, at the rear of the column, now found itself completely isolated and under attack from the rear and both flanks. The heavy blasts of enemy fire killed the company commander and his radioman in the first few minutes of the battle. Responding valiantly, the artillery forward observer, 1st Lt. Harvey C. Barnum, on temporary duty from his post in Hawaii, immediately assumed command of the company. Rallying the decimated company, Barnum organized a tight defensive perimeter. With the help of several UH-1E Huey gunships, he destroyed a key enemy position. With the letup in enemy fire, Barnum then called for a medevac. Standing fully exposed to the enemy's fire, Barnum directed the helicopters into an LZ, then oversaw the loading of the wounded. With that task completed he turned his attention back to the VC. Under his fearless guidance the company cleared out the remaining enemy. Four hours after his fight began, Barnum, who would receive a Medal of Honor for his exceptional courage, led Company H into Ky Phu.

By nightfall the fighting around Ky Phu was over. The 80th VC Battalion left 104 of its members dead on the battlefield. The Marines suffered 11 killed and 71 wounded.

Operation Harvest Moon officially ended on 20 December when all its maneuver battalions returned to their enclaves. The allies claimed 407 enemy killed and 33 captured. The ARVN lost 90 killed, 141 wounded, and 91 missing, mostly in the first two days of the operation. Marine casualties were 45 killed and 218 wounded.

Operation Harvest Moon was the last major Marine operation of 1965. In the final six months of the year, the Marines conducted fifteen battalion-sized or larger operations. Through them they were learning about their enemy and how he fought. The Marines were becoming experienced combat veterans, adept at fighting the determined foe. Unfortunately, the Marine Corps' policy of rotating its troops out of the war zone after a thirteen-month tour, assuming they had survived death or serious injury, meant that many of the lessons learned in the early days were doomed to be relearned over and over again as the years passed.

Something that did survive the changing personnel was the slang the Marines used to describe their life in the war zone. Riflemen in South Vietnam referred to themselves as "grunts" in a sardonic reference to the sound they made when they hoisted their eighty-to ninety-pound packs onto their backs. Patrols were called "humps." The countryside became the "boonies." Viet Cong were known as "Charlie," and North Vietnamese regulars were "Mister Charles." Everyone's ultimate destination, the United States, was known as "the world," as in "When I get back to the real world." But before that could happen, there was a lot of war to fight.

Overall, the senior Marine commanders, as well as MACV, were pleased with the performance of the troops during the first six months of the war. In their evaluations they felt that their troops had responded aggressively against the main-force Viet Cong and North Vietnamese regular army units they'd met in battle. And, though not wholly supported by MACV, the III MAF pacification efforts seemed to be taking hold. More South Vietnamese civilians were living without fear of the Viet Cong. With the increase in troops scheduled for 1966, General Walt felt positive that his forces would soon have the upper hand.

If he had had any idea of what the future would hold, though, he might not have been so optimistic.

Chapter Two
1966

As the second year of the war in South Vietnam began, the III MAF faced a multifaceted and confusing situation. The Marines' primary responsibilities were the three coastal enclaves and their respective surrounding TAORs. The largest of these was Da Nang, centrally located in the heart of I Corps' Quang Nam Province. More than 250,000 South Vietnamese lived in the 700-plus square kilometers of this TAOR. The headquarters of the III MAF, the 3d Marine Division headquarters, and the 1st Marine Aircraft Wing all were located in Da Nang. Two regiments, the 3d and the 9th Marines, consisting of six maneuver battalions, operated there, along with the supporting artillery of the 12th Marines.

Seventy kilometers to the south was the Marines' second-largest enclave, centered in Chu Lai. Its TAOR covered more than 300 square kilometers, in which lived more than 100,000 people. The two regiments operating out of Chu Lai, the 4th and 7th Marines, with five maneuver battalions and supporting artillery, were responsible for the two southernmost provinces of the I Corps Tactical Zone, Quang Tin and Quang Ngai.

The smallest enclave was at Phu Bai, in Thua Thien Province, just ten kilometers south of Hue. Only one hundred square kilometers in size, this TAOR existed primarily to protect the small airstrip located there.

Though the Marines had conducted several large-scale operations against Viet Cong main force units in 1965, the Marine commander's major concern was still the well-organized VC political and guerrilla substructure. In General Walt's mind the Marines' main objective was to win the loyalty of the population for the government: eliminate the VC from the hamlets and villages and you would win. As far as

Walt was concerned, it made little sense for his troops to sweep through a village, clear it of VC, then move on, leaving the gate wide open for the VC to return. Combined-action platoons (CAPs) were a means to address this problem. A typical CAP consisted of a squad of Marines, usually fifteen men, assigned to a village—ultimately providing security and improved relations with the villagers.

Although General Westmoreland acknowledged the benefits of the CAP, he did virtually nothing to encourage their use. He argued that he simply did not have the manpower to put fifteen American Marines or soldiers in every village in South Vietnam.

Consistent with his 1965 guidelines for conducting the war, General Westmoreland's tactical plan for victory was also divided into three phases. First was "search and destroy." This involved large allied units operating in the field where they would "find, fix, and destroy" enemy forces and their base areas. Next would come "clearing operations" to find any guerrilla forces remaining after a large-scale search and destroy operation. Finally, "securing operations" would provide a permanent defense, as well as a stable social and political environment in which village pacification efforts would be conducted.

Because of manpower limitations, Westmoreland divided the responsibility for these three phases among the available forces. American troops, with their superior handling of supporting firepower, would conduct most of the search and destroy operations. The ARVN troops would follow up with the clearing operations. Finally, South Vietnamese Regional Forces (RFs) and Popular Forces (PFs) would carry the burden of securing the villages and nearby countryside.

One major flaw existed with Westmoreland's plan. Just months earlier he had pleaded for the deployment of U.S. troops, arguing that the ARVN were incapable of protecting only a few air bases. How he now expected them to handle the much more difficult task of providing security for more than twelve thousand hamlets remained unexplained.

The search and destroy phase of Westmoreland's strategy was nothing more than a war of attrition: simply kill more of them than they killed of us. Westmoreland himself stated it bluntly: "We'll just go on bleeding them until Hanoi wakes up to the fact that they have bled their country to the point of national disaster for generations." Though his pronouncement was prophetic, Westmoreland had no idea when he made it that it would eventually apply more to the United States than to North Vietnam.

Because territorial gains were not a goal of his war, Westmoreland had to have some other way of measuring success. For progress reports he turned to the management techniques he'd learned while earning his master's degree at Harvard Business School in the early 1950s. Headway would be measured by a variety of quantifiable indices. The most notorious of these was the body count. After a battle, enemy dead would be counted and compared with allied casualties. The higher the friendly ratio, the greater the allied victory. This measurement was abused as the war dragged on. Commanders at every level exaggerated the enemy body count in order to enhance their own status and earn promotions or medals.

Another measure was "battalion days in the field." This was an effective way to gauge the ARVN, who were notoriously reluctant to venture from their secure bases, but not a good way to evaluate Americans who did not exhibit this inhibition. The fact that less than one percent of all patrols actually resulted in enemy contact was ignored in the statistical contest. Accumulation of figures acceptable to higher headquarters became an end in itself for most American infantry units.

As might be expected, the Marines challenged Westmoreland's strategy. Feeling that their primary responsibility lay with the enclaves they had established, III MAF had developed tactics designed to provide security for the local population. They likened their strategy to a "spreading ink blot," and planned to work their way outward from their enclaves, enlarging the secure areas up and down the coast where the vast majority of South Vietnam's population lived.

General Krulak enthusiastically supported III MAF's plan. A special adviser to the Joint Chiefs of Staff on counterinsurgency in the early 1960s, Krulak felt that "there was no virtue at all in seeking out the enemy in the mountains and jungles, that so long as they stayed there they were a threat to nobody, that our efforts should be addressed to the rich, populous lowlands."

Krulak further argued: "It is our conviction that if we can destroy the guerrilla fabric among the people, we will automatically deny the larger units the food and the intelligence and the taxes and the other support they need. At the same time, if the big units want to sortie out of the mountains and come down where they can be cut up by our supporting arms, the Marines are glad to take them on, but the real war is among the people and not among the mountains."

Activities during the Marines' early months in South Vietnam were for the most part consistent with General Krulak's policy, with the notable exceptions of Operations Starlite and Harvest Moon. To help eradicate the VC in the hamlets and villages, the Marines undertook a demanding pattern of near-constant patrolling. Coupled with the CAP squads, these patrols maintained a strong, highly visible Marine presence among the population.

So convinced was III MAF of the benefits of its strategy that it even petitioned MACV to accept pacification efforts as "days in the field." MACV turned them down flat.

In an effort to force his view on III MAF, in November 1965, Westmoreland sent his MACV operations officer, Brig. Gen. William E. DePuy, to I Corps to review the Marines' counterguerrilla campaign. It came as no surprise when DePuy reported to Westmoreland that he was "disturbed . . . that all but a tiny part of the I Corps area is under the control of the VC." He further noted that the Marines were "stalled a short distance south of Da Nang." He recommended that III MAF be "directed" to conduct large-scale multibattalion offensive operations against the VC "at least two weeks out of every month."

General Westmoreland agreed with DePuy's analysis. However, to avoid an interservice argument he opted not to have a direct confrontation with General Walt. In his memoirs he said he would rather "issue orders for specific projects that as time passed would gradually get the Marines out of their beachheads."

Though General Walt graciously said that the differences between Westmoreland and him were primarily of emphasis, others saw it differently. Colonel Edwin H. Simmons, III MAF operations officer, acknowledged that "there were some fairly fundamental differences in the two approaches."

General Krulak later said, "Our efforts belonged where the people were, not where they weren't. I shared these thoughts with General Westmoreland frequently, but made no progress in persuading him."

Marine commandant General Greene felt that Westmoreland was overly concerned about the big unit war. "From the very beginning," General Greene said, "the prime error had been the failure to make the population secure."

The strategic philosophies proved different enough that General Greene carried his concerns to the Joint Chiefs of Staff. Though the chiefs expressed interest, they opted to settle the dispute according to the main standard of military tradition: support the on-site commander.

In a letter to General Walt dated 21 November 1965, General Westmoreland succinctly stated the mission of the III MAF as "[conducting] military operations in I Corps in support of and in coordination with CG, I ARVN Corps and in other areas of the Republic of Vietnam to defeat the VC. . . ."

Working within these general guidelines, and recognizing the futility of continued conflict with his superior officer, General Walt established III MAF's campaign plan for 1966. The Marines would make a three-pronged effort, with the major emphasis on search and destroy operations. Counterguerrilla operations and pacification efforts would still be conducted, but not to the extent that General Walt felt appropriate.

Because of the proportionately stronger forces available in the sparsely populated Chu Lai enclave it was selected to be the main TAOR in which to start major search and destroy operations against the VC's main-force units. Following this, III MAF planned to expand both the Chu Lai and Da Nang TAORs until a linkup was accomplished. Then, III MAF planned to turn its attention to the north of Da Nang all the way to the DMZ and to the south of Chu Lai to the II Corps border. The Marine commanders felt that they could secure the entire coastal plain by the end of 1966.

Operation Double Eagle
Consistent with his policy of forcing III MAF to go on the offensive, on 7 December 1965, General Westmoreland issued orders for

it to conduct an operation in late January 1966 against enemy forces concentrating along the border between the I and II Corps tactical zones. Because intelligence reports indicated that enemy forces operating in southern Quang Ngai Province had their base areas in northern Binh Dinh Province, Operation Double Eagle would be the first major operation of the war coordinated across corps boundaries. The III MAF units, supported by units of the 2d ARVN Division, would strike any enemy forces found in Quang Ngai Province. At the same time, units of the U.S. Army's 1st Cavalry Division (Airmobile), in conjunction with elements of the 22d ARVN Division, would launch Operation Masher (later White Wing) in northern Binh Dinh Province to find and destroy the enemy's base areas.

To command III MAF's share of the operation, General Walt reactivated Task Force Delta. The task force commander would again be General Platt. Using staff personnel from his own assistant division commander's group, the 4th and 7th Marines, as well as divisional personnel, General Platt went to work. The area of operations (AO) for Double Eagle encompassed more than seven hundred square kilometers. Inland from the white sand beaches, the terrain quickly became crossed by a network of rivers, streams, and marshes. At the AO's western edge sat a range of jungle-clad mountains, with steep rises and deep valleys. After surveying the land, Platt reached two conclusions: his planners would have to make heavy use of helicopters, and the terrain significantly favored the enemy.

Task Force Delta's intelligence section estimated that more than 6,500 enemy troops occupied the AO. Their main forces were identified as the 18th and 95th North Vietnamese Army Regiments and the 2d VC Main Force Regiment. All three units were reported to be operating within 15 kilometers of the coast. Additionally, more than a dozen independent Viet Cong companies called the area home.

Based on all this information, General Platt divided Operation Double Eagle into three phases. In the initial phase, Marine reconnaissance units would be inserted inland well before D day in order to establish the whereabouts of the enemy. Next, two infantry battalions would make an amphibious assault on D day. General Platt hoped to fool the enemy into thinking that the Marines were ashore only to conduct limited sweeps in the coastal area. Thus, he kept two battalions in reserve for the exploitation phase—the main effort—signaled by B-52 bomber strikes, called "Arc Light missions," on suspected enemy locations. Helicopters would carry these Marines inland to cut off any enemy troops fleeing the massive bombardments.

As planned, the reconnaissance forces established their base at the Special Forces camp at Ba To on 12 January. The first patrols went out the next day. Almost immediately they began seeing small groups of VC.

On 24 January the 1st Cavalry Division launched Operation Masher/White Wing. Four battalions of cavalrymen air-assaulted into the Bong Son plain, just south of the provincial border. Joining the soldiers were six ARVN airborne battalions and six infantry battalions from the 22d ARVN Division. Farther north, elements of the 2d ARVN Division moved into blocking positions north of the Marines' AO.

Dawn of 28 January, D day for the amphibious landing phase of Operation Double Eagle, broke overcast, and rainy. Despite heavy seas, Lt. Col. James R. Young's BLT 3/1 came ashore at 0700 as planned at Red Beach, just north of Duc Pho. The Marines quickly moved inland with no opposition. By noon BLT 2/4, now commanded by Lt. Col. Rodolfo L. Trevino, was also ashore and in position.

Adverse weather continued to plague the operation, restricting Marine operations to within eight thousand meters of the beach for the next few days. But the bad weather couldn't stop the exploitation phase of the operation. The Arc Light raids were scheduled for 30 January. General Platt asked for a postponement of the air raids, but MACV said "take 'em or leave 'em." He took them.

Low clouds and poor visibility prevented any helicopter operations until the afternoon of 31 January. Then UH-34 helicopters carried Lieutenant Colonel Trevino's 2/4 twenty kilometers inland to the Ba To River valley, north of the Special Forces camp. They quickly moved two kilometers northeast to Hill 508 to exploit one of the Arc Light raids.

On 1 February, General Platt committed his reserve forces. Two companies of Lt. Col. William F. Donahue's 2/9 were lifted from

Quang Ngai City to an LZ on the high ground seven kilometers northwest of where 2/4 had landed the previous day. At the same time, 2/3 swept the flatlands to the east.

Over the next few weeks the Marines encountered only small bands of VC. As one company commander said, "The VC would hit us, then pull out. They wouldn't stick around." Despite the concentration of Marine units in the AO, there was no heavy fighting.

In contrast, the cavalrymen to the south fought several pitched battles with the 18th NVA Regiment from 28 January to 3 February. To prevent these enemy forces from fleeing to the north, General Platt started moving his units south on 3 February.

In fast-moving teams consisting of two rifle companies supported by an 81mm mortar platoon, the Marines crisscrossed the southern portion of Double Eagle's operational area. Supported by nearly two thirds of III MAF's available helicopters, the Marines would swoop into an area, search it, then reboard the aircraft for further movement.

Eventually, it became apparent that the enemy had somehow managed to slip through the cordon. The Marine ground units were gradually pulled out until, by 17 February, General Platt had closed Operation Double Eagle. The Marines had killed 312 enemy soldiers and captured 19 at a cost of 24 dead and 156 wounded.

Task Force Delta itself had nearly closed down when III MAF advised General Platt that the 1st VC Regiment had been spotted in the Que Son Valley. Platt was ordered to reactivate TF Delta and deploy seventy kilometers north for Operation Double Eagle II.

Elements of four battalions began moving into the old Operation Harvest Moon area by truck and helicopter on the morning of 19 February. The 3d Battalion, 1st Marines moved by truck from Chu Lai to the north of Tam Ky, where it set up blocking positions. Helicopters carried 2/7, BLT 2/3 of the SLF, and 2/9 into LZs farther southwest in the Que Son sector. From there they attacked northeast toward 3/1.

The 1st VC Regiment was not there. For the next ten days the attacking Marines swept the area. They uncovered numerous supply dumps but found no major enemy units.

By 1 March, Operation Double Eagle II was over.

* * *

Pacification remained the main objective of both the 3d and 9th Marines operating in the Da Nang TAOR. The 3d Marines, commanded by Col. Thell H. Fisher, had responsibility for the sparsely populated sectors north and west of Da Nang. Colonel John E. Gorman's 9th Marines operated south and east of the city.

In the early months of 1966, the 3d Marines focused their efforts in the previously untouched An Hoa region, thirty kilometers southwest of Da Nang. Once identified as a potential major industrial area, An Hoa had long been under the protection of ARVN forces. However, repeated attacks by the VC in 1964 and 1965 proved the South Vietnamese army's inability to effectively control the area. To keep the Viet Cong off balance, two battalions of the 3d Marines conducted sweeps in the area in January 1966. Military results were minimal—the VC simply fled into the mountains to the west.

From a pacification standpoint, however, success was achieved. Several hundred peasant residents, tired of the Viet Cong influence, asked to be evacuated to more secure hamlets. In coordination with local South Vietnamese officials, the relocation was accomplished.

In their sector of the Da Nang TAOR, the 9th Marines conducted a number of search and destroy operations during the first months of 1966. Most resulted in only minimal contact with the enemy. In fact, the worst casualties resulted from booby traps. During the month of February, for example, 12 of the regiment's 17 killed in action died as the result of hidden explosive devices, as did 120 of the 150 wounded. The infantrymen were experiencing one of the most frustrating, and deadly, aspects of the war in South Vietnam.

In contrast to the large forces at Chu Lai and Da Nang, the northernmost enclave at Phu Bai consisted of only 2/1 under Lt. Col. Robert T. Hanifin, Jr., and supporting artillery, engineer, and logistical units. In order to protect the airstrip at Phu Bai, Hanifin was forced to have his small force of Marines constantly patrolling their one-hundred-square-kilometer TAOR.

The biggest operation for Hanifin's Marines during early 1966 was New York, conducted from 26 February to 3 March. The operation began as a joint Marine-ARVN task force deployed against a VC unit reported to be occupying the Pho Lai village complex about seven kilometers northwest of Hue. Reinforced by two companies from Da Nang, Hanifin's Marines moved by truck and helicopter to the jump-off line near the village complex on 26 February. Attacking that night, the assault companies quickly advanced through the villages—without finding the VC.

After returning to Phu Bai the next day, the Marines responded to a new threat. While they had been moving north to Pho Lai, ARVN forces had engaged the VC on supposedly pacified Phu Thu Peninsula, immediately to the east of Phu Bai. Though his men were tired, Hanifin immediately sent three companies to reinforce the ARVN. Launching a frontal assault on the well-prepared enemy positions, the Marines quickly broke through the VC's lines, sending the foe scattering in small groups. The Marines chased them for several days, killing more than 120 VC while losing 17 of their own.

Operation Utah

On 3 March, Col. Bruce Jones, the U.S. Army senior adviser to the 2d ARVN Division, visited General Platt at his headquarters at Chu Lai. Jones said that he had good intelligence information that the 21st NVA Regiment had taken up residence in an area about ten kilometers northwest of Quang Ngai City. Based on Jones's information, General Platt ordered the 7th Marines, together with the 2d ARVN Division, to mount an attack.

Eager to tangle with the North Vietnamese regulars, Colonel Peatross flew that evening to meet with General Lan at his headquarters at Quang Ngai City. Within hours the allies had agreed to a combined operation using one battalion of ARVN airborne infantry and one battalion of Marines. The paratroopers would land first and secure the LZ. Once the Marines were on the ground the two battalions planned to move southeastward on opposite sides of Highway 527, a one-lane dirt track. They would continue on that road until the highway joined up with Route 1, about ten kilometers north of Quang Ngai City.

The selected landing zone sat just southwest of Chau Nhai (5), about fifteen kilometers northwest of Quang Ngai City. Surrounded by rice paddies, Chau Nhai (5) was overlooked by Hills 97 and 85, just to the southwest, and Hill 50, about one kilometer to the northwest. After clearing Chau Nhai (5), the South Vietnamese troops were to clear Hill 50.

The newly designated Operation Utah moved rapidly from the planning stage to execution. When Colonel Peatross returned to Chu Lai late on 3 March, he notified Lieutenant Colonel Utter that his 2/7 would be going on the operation. Responding as a true Marine, Utter had his three companies ready for pickup at dawn the next day.

Early on 4 March, Marine A-4s and F-4s dropped from the sky to bomb and strafe the target area. Despite this heavy preparatory fire, the Marine helicopters carrying the first wave of the 1st ARVN Airborne Battalion were peppered by intense 12.7mm antiaircraft fire as they neared the LZ. All four of the protective UH-1E Huey gunships were hit, with one crashing in a cloud of dust and smoke. Marine jets were called in to napalm the suspected enemy gun sites. Within minutes one of the F-4s was severely damaged by the enemy guns. Its pilot headed east to the South China Sea, where the two crew members ejected safely.

Despite the brutal NVA response, the airlift continued. Half of the twenty UH-34s in the first wave took hits from the enemy weapons. The brave Marine pilots ignored the fire. By 1030 the entire ARVN battalion was on the ground. The helicopters immediately began ferrying in Lieutenant Colonel Utter's Marines. By 1040 the 1st Platoon of Company F was on the ground. Over the next hour the pilots brought in the rest of Company F, Company G, and the battalion command group. Then, to the surprise of even the most combat experienced, the enemy fire increased. The arrival of Company H was postponed for ninety minutes while jets again bombed the enemy positions.

Once the troop lift ended, Lieutenant Colonel Utter detailed a platoon from Company H to secure the LZ. He also sent a platoon from Company G fifteen hundred meters across the paddies to the southwest to protect the Huey downed earlier until it could be extracted. He then ordered the rest of his battalion to secure Hills 97 and 85 as planned. Only light resistance from distant snipers harassed the column of Marines as they walked precariously along the paddy dikes.

It was a far different story to the north. Though they experienced only scattered resistance as they swept through Chau Nhai (5), the paratroopers ran into a firestorm as they neared Hill 50. Concentrated small arms and automatic weapons fire drove the ARVN to the ground. Unwilling to attack alone, the ARVN commander radioed Utter for help.

Utter instantly reversed his column and headed north to aid the ARVN. Via radio messages he learned that the paratroopers' commander planned to move his battalion around to the northwest side of Hill 50. With this information, Utter placed his Company F on the left to tie in with the ARVN's right. Company G would attack up the center while Company H held the exposed right flank.

As Utter later said, "We got off to a good start. It was fairly even ground, we had a nice even line with good contact, there was enough excitement to keep everyone on his toes, air was on station, and artillery was within range and in position."

All went well as the high-spirited Marines crossed the first few hundred meters. Then the NVA let loose with a fury. From well-concealed positions the enemy soldiers unleased a barrage of heavy fire on the advancing line of troops. Two full battalions of the 21st NVA Regiment pounded Utter's battalion with all they had. Wisely, the enemy commander had waited to open fire until the Marines were too close to make use of their supporting arms. Utter had no choice but to continue his frontal attack.

Company G pushed ahead in the center. Taking cover behind the dikes as needed, the Marines pressed forward. The rifle squads leaped forward a few meters at a time, ignoring the brutal machine-gun fire that actually chewed up the earthen berms. Finally, the Marines broke through the enemy's line. Unfortunately, Lieutenant Colonel Utter could not exploit this gain, because his flanks were being ripped up by an enemy meat grinder.

On the right, Company H battled its way forward through thick vegetation. It was on the verge of cutting into the enemy's first line of defense when an NVA company suddenly slammed into its right rear flank. The company commander was forced to give up his advance as he turned to meet this unexpected challenge.

Over on the left flank, vicious enemy fire slashed into Company

F. More than a dozen men went down. With his two lead platoons pinned down, company commander Capt. Jerry D. Lindauer rushed forward. Enemy rounds suddenly ripped into his arm, shattering it and spinning him to the ground. Ignoring the pain, Lindauer arose and continued on. He reached his 2d Platoon but learned that the 1st Platoon was cut off. He called for supporting fire. Soon artillery shells from Battery M, 4/11, were pounding the hill in front of him.

About this time Lieutenant Colonel Utter radioed for the ARVN airborne to close the growing gap on Lindauer's left flank. To his surprise the ARVN commander refused. Try as he might, Utter could not get the South Vietnamese to join the battle. Captain Lindauer bitterly recalled: "During the entire day I was not aware that the ARVN airborne battalion did anything except view our critical situation as detached observers."

The NVA didn't miss the opportunity. They poured people into the breach. Utter wrote in his after-action report: "We were taking it from three sides, the front and both flanks, and from an enemy who was literally hugging us so we couldn't use our supporting arms."

As the fierce fighting raged into the late afternoon, Utter faced a desperate situation. All three of his companies were running low on ammunition, supporting artillery and air were limited, casualties were increasing, the NVA were well dug in, and darkness was rapidly approaching. He had no choice: he ordered his troops to pull back.

While under heavy fire the Marines began inching backward, the able bodied pulling the wounded with them; the dead were left behind. The enemy moved right along with Company H, chasing them until the company's 60mm mortars succeeded in holding them off.

Once the battalion had put one hundred meters between itself and the enemy, the jets roared in. Soon the enemy positions were engulfed in napalm and bomb explosions. The line companies pulled back to Chau Nhai (4), about one kilometer east of the morning's LZ. Soon dirt was flying as the grunts dug fighting holes.

At his Chu Lai headquarters, General Platt immediately reacted to the ongoing battle. Concerned that the enemy might flee, as they had during Operation Double Eagle, he had Colonel Peatross send 3/1 to an LZ north of Hill 50. They'd then attack southward from there. Platt then ordered Lt. Col. P. X. Kelley (a future commandant of the Marine Corps) to take his battle-tested 2/4 the next morning into an LZ two kilometers south of Utter's night defensive position. From there they would link up with Utter's command.

Utter's men fought the NVA all night on 4–5 March. Using artillery, air support, and flare ships, the men repulsed several major ground attacks. Ammunition became so low that several helicopters dared the heavy enemy fire to drop ammo loads directly to the front-line platoons and squads. The helicopters took an incredible pounding but delivered the badly needed rounds.

Lieutenant Colonel Kelley's men started into their LZ at 0830 on 5 March. Even though F-4s had bombed the new landing zone, heavy enemy machine-gun fire blistered the lead helicopters. Several were badly damaged. Three UH-34s crashed into the LZ. Ignoring the heavy fire, the eight remaining aircraft ferried in the entire battalion by 1000.

The fresh Marines immediately spread out. As they proceeded toward Chau Nhai (4), VC emplaced in nearby hamlets opened fire. Within minutes two of Kelley's three companies were heavily engaged. They remained so until 1100 when General Platt ordered Kelley to continue his mission. Leaving the attached Company B, 1/7, at the LZ to guard the downed UH-34s, Kelley disengaged his remaining rifle companies. Sweeping to the east to bypass the VC, Kelley's column reached Utter at midafternoon. Once there they dug in with 2/7.

In the meantime, events to the north clearly illustrated that the North Vietnamese were controlling this battle. Lieutenant Colonel Young's 3d Battalion, 1st Marines had moved rapidly south across the wide expanse of rice paddies in order to link up with the ARVN airborne on Hill 50. At 1030 the battalion's easternmost company, Company M, bumped into a force of well-dug-in NVA just outside of Chau Nhai (3), which sat to the east of Hill 50. The Marines hit the ground. With his Company M heavily engaged, Young sent Company L wide to the west. Anxious to join the ARVN, he had the company dispatch a platoon to move straight to Hill 50. When the 3d Platoon arrived there, they received a deadly surprise: there were no ARVN on Hill 50, only NVA.

The enemy soldiers were sited in elaborate fortifications. Dense hedgerows and bamboo fences concealed their fighting holes. An extensive network of deep tunnels kept them safe from all but direct hits. It was going to be tough to dig them out.

Young's Marines were up to the task. Despite the odds they pressed forward, using their training and raw courage to take on the enemy. For more than three hours the fighting raged. Finally, the last enemy defender was killed. Hill 50 was at last in allied hands.

If this fight wasn't enough for the battalion, Company M still had its hands full outside of Chau Nhai (3). No matter what they tried, the Marines could not budge the enemy force, now estimated at a full battalion. Young even sent Company I on a wide flanking movement to hit the enemy from the east. It did no good. The NVA were dug in too well.

Finally, as darkness neared, Young was forced to pull out. He moved Company L off of Hill 50. It joined Company M well to the north of Chau Nhai (3), where the two battered companies set up a tight night defensive perimeter (NDP). Company I, unable to disengage, held up for the night just east of the village.

It had been a costly day for 3/1. Thirty-two of its members were dead and ninety were wounded. And the Marines had nothing to show for it.

After reviewing the situation that evening, Generals Lam and Platt decided that they had the enemy surrounded. The Hill 50–Chau Nhai village complex was encircled by four Marine battalions and three ARVN battalions. At dawn they'd tighten the noose, trapping and destroying the enemy. It was a good plan. Unfortunately, the NVA had a better one.

To the south, Company B, 1/7, had spent 5 March patrolling the LZ near An Tuyet (1), where they and the two organic companies of 2/4 had landed that morning. The lone company guarded three helicopters downed during the bitterly opposed landing. Once the damaged aircraft were extracted, Capt. Robert C. Prewitt had his men dig in for the night. In the morning they would march out and rejoin 2/4.

At 2300 a violent rain of enemy mortar shells fell on the isolated company. The hot shards of steel kept the grunts deep in their fighting holes. Under this cover fire, two full companies of NVA infantry laid siege to the LZ. Desperate for help, Captain Prewitt brought artillery fire to within mere meters of his own position. Only this wall of deadly steel kept the enemy at bay. Not until 0130 the following morning did the NVA troops pull back. Still, they filled the air above the Marines' shaky perimeter with a near constant stream of machine-gun bullets and mortar shells.

At first light, Lieutenant Colonel Kelley led his 2d Battalion, 4th Marines from their night bivouac to Captain Prewitt's help. By the time they closed in on their old LZ, the fight was over, the enemy gone.

To the north following a two-and-a-half-hour air and artillery bombardment on the position, the allied battalions closed on Hill 50. As they neared the site of the previous day's fight, the Marines realized that the enemy had fled. By noon Young's battalion occupied the hill. The troops soon uncovered the tunnel and bunker complex. Documents found in the bunkers indicated that the hill had served as an NVA regimental headquarters.

While the other allied units pulled out of the area, 3/1 spent the rest of 6 March and most of the next day exploring, then destroying, the tunnels on Hill 50. Besides large quantities of supplies and extensive documents, the Marines found more than 140 enemy dead.

In all, the Marines claimed to have killed nearly 600 NVA. Besides the casualties that Young's battalion suffered on 5 March, another 66 Marines were killed and 188 were wounded.

Lieutenant Colonel Utter summed up this first fight with the North Vietnamese regulars by noting, "They're not superman. But they can fight."

On 9 March 1966, North Vietnamese Army troops launched a well-coordinated ground assault on the U.S. Army Special Forces camp at A Shau, about fifty kilometers southwest of Phu Bai in western Thua Thien Province. Despite ferocious resistance from the camp's defenders, the NVA overran A Shau four days later. The fall of the camp increased the possibility of enemy infiltration into the central I Corps area.

To counter this threat, Walt, recently promoted to lieutenant general, made plans to strengthen the garrison at Phu Bai. He ordered BLT 3/4 to move directly to Phu Bai from Okinawa rather than to its originally scheduled debarkation point of Da Nang. At the same time, he ordered Col. Donald W. Sherman to move the headquarters of his 4th Marines from Chu Lai to Phu Bai and assume operational control of the TAOR. In addition, two battalions of Republic of Korea Marines would be sent to Phu Bai when they arrived in-country in a few weeks.

Walt's rapid response to this serious threat apparently stymied the NVA's plans. They made no attempt to move to the coast. However, MACV intelligence reported that NVA troops were along the demilitarized zone separating the two warring countries and near the Khe Sanh Special Forces camp in northwestern Quang Tri Province. The Marines continued their close watch over these ominous developments to the north.

As III MAF completed its first full year in South Vietnam, several major command changes took place. Between August 1965 and January 1966, two regiments of the 1st Marine Division, the 1st and the 7th Marines, had joined their brethren from the 3d Marine Division in South Vietnam. By March 1966, only the division's 5th Marines, the 2/11 artillery battalion, and a few support units still remained on Okinawa.

On 29 March 1966, Maj. Gen. Lewis J. Fields arrived at Chu Lai. In a formal ceremony that afternoon he officially opened the headquarters of the 1st Marine Division. At the same time, he took control of all Marine ground forces at Chu Lai and became deputy commander of III MAF.

During April and May, two battalions of the 5th Marines, the 1st and 2d, arrived at Chu Lai, releasing 2/4 and 3/1 to move north to Da Nang. On 27 May, Col. Charles F. Widdecke brought the headquarters of the 5th Marines to South Vietnam; his remaining battalion, 3/5, would deploy to the war zone later in the summer.

Earlier, on 18 March, General Walt had relinquished command of the 3d Marine Division to devote more time and energy as commanding general (CG) of III MAF. Major General Wood B. Kyle, a double recipient of the Silver Star for heroism in World War II, took command of the division.

1st Marine Division

The 1st Marine Division wasted no time in getting involved in the war. Between April and June it conducted ten battalion-sized operations outside the Chu Lai TAOR. Most, however, resulted in only minimal contact with the enemy. In one, though, Operation Hot Springs, in April, the 7th Marines tangled with the 1st VC Regiment in the area northwest of Quang Ngai City. The Marines killed more than 150 of the enemy and captured 23 weapons.

Despite these search and destroy operations, the major effort of the 1st Marine Division continued to focus on pacification. Besides the combined-action platoons that the division fielded, the two other main pacification programs were County Fair and Golden Fleece.

Begun in February 1966, County Fair operations emphasized coordination with South Vietnamese forces to reestablish government control over a village without alienating the residents. At the beginning of a County Fair, Marine forces would cordon off the target village while South Vietnamese troops gathered the villagers at a central collection point. The ARVN troops then searched the village for any VC or contraband. At the same time, South Vietnamese government officials processed the villagers (taking a census and issuing ID cards) and provided medical care and entertainment (pro-government plays and music). The Marines remained in the background, providing logistical support and security as needed. The County Fair technique proved so successful in ferreting out the VC that General Westmoreland ordered them conducted in other corps areas, although he changed the name to Hamlet Festival.

Begun during the 1965 fall harvest season, Golden Fleece operations provided Marine security to farmers while they harvested their crops. These operations allowed the peasants to retain their produce while denying the Viet Cong the sustenance they needed to operate.

At the beginning of June 1966, the 1st Marine Division consisted of more than seventeen thousand men organized into two regiments of infantry, the 5th and 7th Marines, four battalions of artillery in the 11th Marines, plus supporting units. These forces allowed the division to expand its TAOR to more than five hundred square kilometers from the three hundred square kilometers it covered at the start of the year. Long-range plans called for the TAOR to expand northward until it joined up with the Da Nang TAOR at Tam Ky, the capital of Quang Tin Province.

The immediate future, however, called for an excursion into the Do Xa region, southwest of Chu Lai near the western border of I Corps. Intelligence sources placed an enemy headquarters in the area. Under pressure from MACV to run an operation there, Brig. Gen. William A. Stiles, assistant division commander since late April, began the planning. Just as Stiles and his staff completed their work, III MAF intelligence officers learned that the 2d NVA Division had entered the Que Son Valley. Generals Walt and Fields instantly recognized the threat to this strategic area and postponed the Do Xa operation. Instead, on 13 June they ordered an extensive reconnaissance effort to be made between Tam Ky and Hiep Duc.

Operation Kansas

The new operation began on the afternoon of 13 June when the command group of the 1st Reconnaissance Battalion and thirteen-man recon team helicoptered onto Nui Loc Son, a small mountain ten kilometers northeast of Hiep Duc and smack in the middle of the Que Son Valley. Over the next twenty-four hours, six more recon teams flew in by helicopter to take up their positions at strategic sites ringing the valley.

The recon patrols were to report on enemy activity and, when possible, call in artillery or air strikes on their formations. Once the NVA's positions were verified, up to eight battalions on alert—four Marine and four ARVN—could be air-assaulted into the valley to attack the enemy.

The team working south of Hiep Duc found the enemy first. Within hours after taking up their position on heavily wooded Hill 555, the Marines spotted several various-sized enemy groups that appeared to be training in the area. On the afternoon of 14 June, a scout dog accompanying an enemy patrol picked up the Marines' unfamiliar scent. As the patrol moved toward them, the team's lieutenant called for an emergency extraction. Within minutes a helicopter swooped into a nearby clearing. The Marines hastily scrambled aboard. Soon they were safely back at Chu Lai.

Five of the remaining six teams reported only occasional sightings of the enemy over the next two days. However, almost from the moment they took up positions on the five-hundred-meter Nui Vu hill mass anchoring the east end of the valley, Team 2 had spotted numerous enemy formations transiting the region. Using an ARVN artillery battery sited at a Special Forces camp seven kilometers to the south, the team leader, SSgt. Jimmie L. Howard, a crewcutted blunt-mannered, decorated Korean War veteran, called for numerous fire missions on the enemy.

Though Howard prudently called for artillery only when a spotter plane or helicopter was in the vicinity, the enemy soon realized that it was more than a coincidence that their formations were getting blasted by the high explosives. On the night of 15 June, a U.S. Army patrol from the Special Forces camp spotted a battalion-sized enemy force moving toward Nui Vu. The patrol quickly radioed the information to its headquarters. But it was too late. At 2130 Howard heard NVA troops massing at the bottom of the hill. He called for artillery.

The next few hours passed quietly. Then, just after midnight, one of Howard's men spotted a shadowy figure sneaking furtively up the hill. Before he could shout a warning, a barrage of enemy grenades fell among the Marines. The fight was on.

Almost immediately, dozens of NVA soldiers swarmed out of the darkness. Firing their weapons on full automatic, they rushed toward Howard's little band. As tracer rounds cut brilliant swaths of light across the ink-black sky, the recon Marines fought back. The repetitive blasts of small arms fire were frequently punctuated by the sharp crack of hand grenades exploding among the rocks. Occasional screams of pain signaled a fallen warrior. Though badly outnumbered, Howard's band fought bravely. Facing the enemy with resolute determination, the recon Marines drove off the attackers.

Howard used the resulting lull to call his commander, Lt. Col. Arthur J. Sullivan, at Nui Loc Son. "You gotta get us outta here," he pleaded. "There are too many of them for my people!"

Sullivan called for extraction helicopters. A short time later the UH-34s arrived. Before they could reach Howard's position, however, long fingers of light surrounded the helicopters as enemy machine gunners opened fire on them. The aircraft turned back.

Sullivan radioed the bad news to Howard. There were no more helicopters to send. The team was on its own until daylight.

Artillery fire, close air support, and helicopter gunships ripped into the enemy throughout the long night, but the NVA still launched three more strong ground attacks against Team 2. By the thinnest of margins the intrepid little band held on. By 0400 six of Team 2's eighteen members were dead. Howard was temporarily paralyzed below the waist from shrapnel wounds, and every other man had been hit at least once. Ammo supplies were so low that some Marines resorted to throwing rocks at the enemy; others fired captured AK-47 rifles. But still they fought.

The violent ordeal of Team 2 finally ended when helicopters landed Company C, 1/5, at the base of Nui Vu at dawn. The relieving force fought its way to Howard against scattered but strong resistance. After Howard and his surviving men were evacuated, Company C continued the battle for control of the hill. Not until midafternoon did the NVA finally disengage and withdraw. They left behind forty-two dead.

Howard's patrol became the most decorated unit of the Vietnam War. Fifteen members of Team 2 received the Silver Star, two the Navy Cross, and Sergeant Howard the Medal of Honor for his gallant leadership.

The second phase of Operation Kansas was to have consisted of a massive exploitation of the recon teams' findings by the eight battalions of infantry: four from III MAF and four from the 2d ARVN Division, including two South Vietnamese Marine Corps battalions. Unfortunately, on 17 June, the day before the first assault was scheduled, General Walt advised General Stiles that the ARVN units were not going to be available. Due to an internal political crisis that had been brewing all spring, the ARVN I Corps commander needed his forces to quell an uprising in Hue.

Generals Walt and Stiles agreed to continue the recon efforts, supporting them with the artillery batteries already in place. For the next five days the small recon teams moved throughout the Que Son Valley. In all, they reported 141 sightings of enemy forces. In most cases, artillery or air strikes were called in, dispersing the enemy. Operation Kansas ended on 22 June without further significant contact with the enemy. Although the large ground operation originally envisioned by its planners did not materialize, Operation Kansas did prevent the NVA from massing in the Que Son Valley.

* * *

When Operation Kansas ended, General Fields informed III MAF that he was ready to commence his delayed excursion into the Do Xa region. General Walt agreed to the plan submitted and obtained the necessary clearances from MACV and the ARVN I Corps.

To explore the Do Xa region, General Fields planned to duplicate the tactics used in Operation Kansas. First, recon teams would be inserted throughout the AO. Based on their findings, infantry units would then be helicoptered in to pounce on any enemy that were sighted.

Operation Washington began on 6 July when Lieutenant Colonel Sullivan set up his 1st Reconnaissance Battalion headquarters at Hau Doc, about twenty-five kilometers west of Chu Lai. For the next eight days his recon teams ranged over the rugged, jungle-covered four hundred square kilometers of the AO. In all, only forty-six sightings of enemy forces totaling two hundred personnel were made. Ground combat and supporting fire resulted in just thirteen enemy dead and four prisoners taken.

Because of these dismal results, General Fields ended the operation on 14 July. He later told attendees of a commanders' conference that he didn't think there were any appreciable enemy forces in the Do Xa region.

Soon afterward sources reported that the NVA were once again on the move in the Que Son Valley. All three regiments of the 2d NVA Division had reportedly left their mountain sanctuaries to return to the valley. On 30 July, General Fields ordered Colonel Widdecke to conduct multibattalion search and destroy operations around Hiep Duc. Elements of the 2d ARVN Division would participate in the operation, too.

According to the plan, a task force from the 2d ARVN Division would move southwest from the hamlet of Thang Binh toward Que Son. At the same time, three South Vietnamese Marine Corps battalions would take up blocking positions to the west of Que Son. This classic hammer-and-anvil maneuver would destroy the 2d NVA Division.

To prevent any NVA forces from escaping, the 5th Marines would helicopter into LZs south of Que Son. The infantry would search the area and engage any enemy found there. If no contact developed, the Marines would then move either by foot or helicopter to a new area. Any heavy contact would result in other Marine units "piling on" to help the original unit.

Operation Colorado began early on 6 August when UH-34 helicopters carried the grunts of 2/5 into LZs near Hiep Duc. They touched down, and riflemen spread out around the landing zones without incident. Because of the absence of enemy contact, the arrival of the regiment's 1st Battalion was delayed twenty-four hours while new LZs for it were found south of Hiep Duc.

The only significant action that first day occurred in the AO of the South Vietnamese Marines. They took enemy fire as soon as they landed. In the resulting three-hour fight, the South Vietnamese Marines killed fifty NVA and took twenty prisoners.

The U.S. Marines encountered only limited enemy resistance during the first three days of Operation Colorado. Then, on the morning of 10 August, Lt. Col. Harold L. Coffman's 1/5 came under long-range sniper fire as it moved east in a heavy rainstorm toward Ky Phu, the scene of intense fighting in December 1965. By 1500 the column had passed through Ky Phu and was approaching the tiny hamlet of Cam Khe. Company A, in the lead, spotted thirty NVA running across a nearby rice paddy. In a blaze of rifle fire the Marines cut down the enemy. The column resumed its march, but after advancing a short distance other NVA ambushed it. Within minutes all three companies were heavily engaged at close quarters.

The heavy, driving rain and low ceilings prevented supporting aircraft from helping the pinned-down Marines. So close was the fighting that neither artillery nor naval gunfire could provide assistance. The firefight continued unabated until 1730, when the rain finally stopped and the sky cleared. In minutes Huey gunships and A-4s roared earthward to strike the enemy's positions. Company C then rolled over a line of well-entrenched NVA, breaking the back of the enemy force. As night fell the remaining enemy pulled out. Regardless, Lieutenant Colonel Coffman surrounded his battalion's night laager with artillery and naval gunfire.

The next day Coffman's Marines surveyed the battlefield. They found more than one hundred NVA bodies. Fourteen Marines died and sixty-five were wounded in the firefight.

The Marines had only minor contact with the NVA during the rest of the operation. The ARVN units to the north, however, experienced several more sharp clashes before the operation ended on 22 August.

Although Operation Colorado was planned to be but the first of a series of operations in the valuable and strategic Que Son Valley, increased fighting elsewhere prevented the Marines from returning there until April 1967.

In early October, Maj. Gen. Herman Nickerson took command of the 1st Marine Division. A Marine since 1935, Nickerson had served in both World War II and Korea and had commanded the 1st Marine Division prior to its movement to South Vietnam. Because the 3d Marine Division had recently been fighting the NVA along the demilitarized zone (DMZ), one of Nickerson's first acts was to move his division's headquarters north to Da Nang. General Stiles assumed command of the Chu Lai TAOR, operating there as Task Force X-ray. The 7th Marines retained operational control of the Chu Lai TAOR, and the 5th Marines operated farther north between Tam Ky and Da Nang. Both regiments patrolled vast geographical areas, which greatly reduced their effectiveness.

During the remaining months of 1966, the 1st Marine Division focused its main effort on pacification programs. A number of Golden Fleece and County Fair operations were conducted throughout the fall months, helping the peasants to feel more secure in their villages.

3d Marine Division

The 3d Marine Division had a hard time pacifying the Da Nang TAOR in the spring of 1966 because of a major South Vietnamese political crisis. On 11 March, the popular commander of the ARVN I Corps, Lt. Gen. Nguyen Chanh Thi, was removed from command by the South Vietnamese National Leadership Council because he was viewed as a political threat to Premier Nguyen Cao Ky. Almost immediately, supporters of General Thi organized general strikes in Da Nang and Hue, paralyzing the cities and seriously impeding the flow of supplies to III MAF units.

Over the next few weeks, protests by the dissidents became de-

cidedly anti-American; their leaders accused the Americans of in-
terfering in South Vietnam's internal affairs by supporting Premier
Ky. The situation grew so serious that American civilians, nonessen-
tial military personnel, and foreign nationals were evacuated from
Da Nang in early April. Marine units had to be pulled out of the field
to guard allied installations in Da Nang and Hue.

Tensions heightened throughout the spring. A number of con-
frontations between Marines and the dissidents contributed to the
taut atmosphere. A major confrontation on 18 May involved General Walt himself. On that day South Vietnamese Marines had been
clearing dissident forces from a section of Da Nang. When the Vietnamese Marines attempted to cross a vital bridge over the Da Nang
River, the rebels' leader announced that he would blow up the bridge
if the Marines crossed it.

Because of the critical importance of the bridge to the U.S.
Marines' supply line, General Walt went to meet the dissidents'
leader. As Walt crossed the contested span on foot, he was confronted
by a rebellious South Vietnamese warrant officer. The diminutive soldier threatened to blow up the bridge with Walt on it unless the
Americans withdrew. Neither man would budge. Finally, the South
Vietnamese gave the signal to blow the bridge. To Walt's everlasting
surprise, the charges failed to ignite. Nearby U.S. Army engineers
quickly rushed onto the structure and defused the explosives. General Walt calmly returned to his jeep.

Not until the end of May did resistance by the armed dissidents
in Da Nang collapse. In Hue, however, the demonstrations continued. Protesters stormed the U.S. consulate on 1 June, burning it and
several other buildings. Premier Ky ordered riot-control police into
the city. Acting with restraint, the police cleared the city streets of
the protesters. By 18 June, the rebel leaders were under arrest. Government forces regained firm control of Hue by the next day.

General Walt walked a very fine line throughout this difficult period. His primary interest, of course, was fighting the war. Each time
he had to redeploy his troops during the crisis or react to the dissidents, his attention was diverted from the war effort. And the major
effort of III MAF in the spring of 1966 focused on expanding the Da

Nang TAOR and solidifying the government's control over myriad hamlets and villages in the surrounding countryside.

The 9th Marines were responsible for the southern approaches to Da Nang. The regiment's commander, Col. Edwin H. Simmons, planned a series of operations designed to eradicate the Viet Cong infrastructure from within his TAOR. The first was Operation Kings, launched on 18 March. The operation's AO lay south of Route 4 and north of the Ky Lam River, about ten kilometers south of Da Nang. Although reported to MACV as a search and destroy mission, Operation Kings was actually designed to be a long-term occupation of the area.

Originally controlled by 2/9's commander, Lt. Col. William F. Donahue, Kings initially concentrated on the AO's eastern reaches. When enemy contact there proved sparse, the troops moved westward. As they did, command of the operation passed to 3/3's Lt. Col. Joshua W. Dorsey III.

Although enemy contact was rare, the VC weren't about to let the incursion go unnoticed. On the night of 24–25 March, Company E, 2/9, under the operational control of 3/3, was set up in a night defensive position about one kilometer north of Route 4 and three kilometers north of the hamlet of Phong Thu. At 0030 sentries detected a small force of VC trying to enter the company's perimeter. Rifle fire and grenades drove them off. Thirty minutes later a seventy-five-round enemy mortar barrage pounded the Marines' perimeter. Then two companies of VC attacked out of the night. The intense firefight raged for more than an hour. Eventually, under a blistering barrage of supporting artillery fire, the VC pulled back. Although five Marines died in the fight, at least forty VC were also killed.

The next day two companies from 3/3 were helicoptered in to pursue the remnants of the attackers. Companies L and K landed at dawn about four kilometers southwest of Company E's position. Moving northeast, the fresh companies met heavy resistance from VC occupying well-prepared positions. Stopped cold, the Marines needed close air support before the resistance ended.

On 27 March, the two companies continued their attack. Once again heavy enemy fire stopped them. Superb close air support again broke the back of the VC defenses. The following day the two units from 3/3 reached Route 4, their final objective. With that goal attained, Operation Kings ended.

Because of the continuing political crisis in Da Nang during the spring months, government troops were frequently pulled from the field and sent to the city. In several instances, in displays of solidarity with the dissidents, ARVN units simply walked away from their outposts. As a result, the VC quickly reentered many of the areas cleared during Operation Kings. Some even armed themselves with weapons left behind by the ARVN.

Originally, the 9th Marines had planned to follow Operation Kings with a one-battalion operation near An Hoa, south of the Ky Lam River. Not until late April, though, was 3/9 assigned to Operation Georgia. On 21 April the Marines, supported by ARVN and PFs, arrived at An Hoa. Battalion commander Lt. Col. William W. Taylor divided the region into company-sized TAORs. Working with the ARVN, the Marines conducted numerous County Fair and Golden Fleece operations throughout the area.

Only moderate enemy resistance was encountered during most of Operation Georgia. However, heavy fighting did break out on the afternoon of 3 May when Company M stumbled on two enemy companies holding a hamlet north of An Hoa. Four hours of intense ground fighting, supported by air and artillery, raged before the Marines drove off the VC. The Marines lost five dead and fifty-four wounded.

Operation Georgia officially ended on 10 May. However, in reality it, like Operation Kings, was part of a continuing effort to expand the Marines' TAOR around Da Nang. Colonel Simmons's next step in this effort began on 4 May, when he ordered a renewal of search and destroy missions in the area north of the Ky Lam River. Still demonstrating the type of tactical thinking that worked in World War II and Korea but failed miserably in South Vietnam, Simmons planned three distinct phases for his Ky Lam campaign. First, his forces would spend the month of May clearing the area south of Da Nang to the La Tho River. Then, in June, the Marines would push south five kilometers to the Ky Lam River. The final phase would come in July, when the Marines would work their way eastward to reach the city of Hoi An.

Colonel Simmons had four battalions under his control for this campaign—all three from his 9th Marines plus 2/4. These units would use the same tactics employed during Operations Kings and Georgia: the maneuver companies would sweep their sectors, employing supporting artillery and air support "imaginatively and vigorously."

The first major action of the Ky Lam campaign came on the morning of 12 May, two days after the campaign started. A fourteen-man patrol from Company B, 1/9, was ambushed by a VC force in an area south of the La Tho River at the western edge of the AO. When the rest of the company rushed to the patrol's aid, the VC took them under fire, too. Soon they were pinned down, unable to advance or retreat. Despite air and artillery support, the fight raged most of the day.

In the middle of all this, two badly wounded Marines from the missing patrol staggered into Company B's perimeter. Suffering from shock, they managed to convey that they were the only survivors.

Although reinforced by Company D and a platoon from Company A that afternoon, Company B still could not conquer the enemy. Not until night fell did the VC disengage, slipping away across the Thu Bon. The next day Company B went looking for its missing members. They found all twelve of them dead, some executed at close range.

Desperate to avenge these deaths, the Marines spent the next two days searching for the enemy in the numerous, well-fortified villages and hamlets in the AO. Although the villagers frequently provided valuable information on the VC's movements, the Marines were unable to follow up these tips. A flare-up of the political crisis in Da Nang resulted in many of the ARVN troops again abandoning their posts. Consequently, the Marines had to take up these defensive positions. The Ky Lam campaign effectively ended on 25 May.

Once the dissident forces in Da Nang surrendered, General Kyle planned for Colonel Simmons to renew his campaign. Because of the relocation of several battalions from the Chu Lai TAOR to Da

Nang, General Kyle ordered Simmons to conduct a "conventional linear type of attack of all forward units to push the front lines forward." At the same time, Kyle would realign his available forces, greatly reducing the overtaxed 9th Marines' TAOR.

On 7 June, the new Operation Liberty began with the heavy crash of preparatory artillery fire. The shells blasted thirty-five target areas in front of the infantry. With all available rifle companies at the front, the renewed sweeps started. The enemy responded with nothing more than light small arms fire. In fact, most friendly casualties resulted from enemy-sewn mines and booby traps.

By 15 June, the regimental realignment was complete. The 9th Marines had their TAOR reduced by nearly half, to just two hundred square kilometers, as the 3d Marines moved to their west and the 1st Marines took over their eastern flank.

With all the infantry regiments in their new positions, Operation Liberty continued through the end of June. Enemy resistance was light and scattered; the aggressive movement of the rifle companies prevented the VC from offering any major, organized resistance. At the end of Operation Liberty, the Marine commanders were confident that they could at last pacify the Da Nang enclave.

The action heated up on 4 July when Company K, 3/9, was violently attacked three kilometers northeast of An Hoa. Assigned to protect the engineers working on the Liberty Road, which connected Da Nang and An Hoa, the company had patrolled the area for several days without finding any sign of the foe. Then, just before noon on that Independence Day, a flurry of Viet Cong rifle grenades suddenly dropped out of the blazing hot sky. The missiles exploded with violent effectiveness among the grunts. One of the amphibious tractors accompanying the weary column was knocked out immediately. As the frantic Marines scrambled to find cover, mortar shells erupted among them. Seconds later, repeated bursts of enemy small arms and automatic weapons fire tore into the men. The company was pinned down.

Two companies were rushed to Company K's aid. For more than two hours the three units battled the well-armed VC. Finally, as night neared, the enemy commander pulled out his troops. In all, eight Marines died and sixteen were wounded in the ambush.

Based on evidence found at the site, Marine intelligence identified the enemy unit as part of the Viet Cong R-20 Battalion. When this information reached General Walt, he immediately authorized the 3d Marine Division to initiate Operation Macon, with five battalions. As planned, Operation Macon would begin with the rifle companies of 3/9 continuing to sweep around An Hoa. Two battalions of the 3d Marines would then be helilifted into LZs to the northeast. The 3d Battalion, 9th Marines would then turn in that direction and push the VC into the waiting Marines.

Early on the morning of 6 July, the artillery tubes of the 12th Marines pumped more than five hundred rounds of high explosives into the LZs. Then CH-46s appeared on the horizon. Within minutes they had settled in a cloud of dust and disgorged their cargo of infantrymen.

The next day 3/9 headed northeast. Reinforced by fourteen tanks, the battalion reached the lines of 1/3 on 10 July. Only scattered handfuls of VC had been found along the way. The results of this phase of Operation Macon were disappointing.

The following day the new commander of the 9th Marines, Col. Drew J. Barrett, opened phase three. The companies of 1/3 wheeled and swept east while 3/9 retraced its steps to the west.

Neither battalion had any significant contact during this phase. The Marine riflemen continued crisscrossing the scrub-covered ground, splashing through rice paddies, and slowly working their way through thick tangles of undergrowth, but they found no VC. With the R-20 Battalion apparently out of the area, Colonel Barrett ordered Operation Macon closed out on 14 July.

Later that same afternoon, a Marine recon patrol spotted four hundred VC assembling about ten kilometers east of An Hoa. The patrol immediately called for both artillery and air strikes. Within minutes the lethal shells and bombs slammed into the enemy formation. The barrage killed at least thirty-five but, more importantly, scattered the rest.

Because of this reappearance of the R-20 Battalion, Colonel Barrett revived Operation Macon. All activity in the An Hoa AO would fall under its umbrella. Barrett, and General Kyle, wanted to maintain a strong presence in the region to not only keep the enemy off balance but also to guard the engineers while they finished the Liberty Road.

As July turned into August, enemy contact decreased. Colonel Barrett reduced his operational force to just 3/9. The rest of the summer saw these Marines constantly patrolling the AO. Only occasionally did any significant contact develop. By the last week of October, enemy sightings were so rare that it was decided to end Operation Macon on the twenty-eighth. In the 117-day operation, 380 enemy were killed at a cost of 24 Marines dead and 172 wounded. Even when the operation ended, though, nothing really changed for the 9th Marines. The rest of the division had moved north while they stayed behind, attached to the 1st Marine Division to protect An Hoa. Under this cordon, Marine engineers and Navy Seabees came to An Hoa to finish work on the promising industrial site.

While the Marines were battling to expand their TAORs in central and southern I Corps, General Westmoreland turned his attention to northern I Corps. He became convinced that the NVA would soon attempt to capture the former imperial capital of Hue. Its loss, he knew, would provide the NVA and VC a far greater political than military victory.

In early April, MACV intelligence sources confirmed Westmoreland's suspicions with information that the 324B NVA Division had taken up positions just north of the DMZ. Other sources said that at least three, and possibly four, NVA regiments had moved into Quang Tri and Thua Thien Provinces. Finally, MACV learned that the enemy had created the Tri-Thien-Hue Military Region, with a headquarters location about twenty-five kilometers west of Hue.

General Walt and his III MAF intelligence staff, however, interpreted the same information differently. None of them believed that the enemy had any more than three regiments in the whole northern area. Further, General Walt felt that the new presence of the 4th Marines at Phu Bai had drastically reduced the enemy's influence in the Hue area. The regiment's extensive patrolling had resulted only in limited contact with enemy forces. In addition, the 1st ARVN Division, based in Hue, had not seen any increase in enemy activity.

Despite General Walt's misgivings, MACV insisted that III MAF conduct a one-battalion operation near the isolated U.S. Army Special Forces camp at Khe Sanh, in the far northwestern corner of

Quang Tri Province. Sitting on a broad plateau six kilometers east of the Laotian border and twenty kilometers south of the DMZ, Khe Sanh was overlooked by high hills and mountains. The camp existed because it controlled the east-west–running Route 9, a logical corridor for any NVA infiltrating from the west. General Westmoreland eventually wanted to use the camp as a jumping-off point for his long-hoped-for invasion of Laos. His idea was to cut the infamous Ho Chi Minh Trail infiltration route running from North Vietnam to various points in the south.

Under heavy pressure from MACV, General Kyle finally ordered Colonel Sherman's 4th Marines to send one battalion to Khe Sanh for the operation. Sherman selected 1/1, then opconned to the 4th Marines, under the command of Lt. Col. Van D. Bell, Jr., for the excursion. Though Operation Virginia was originally scheduled to begin on 5 April, adverse weather postponed its commencement until 18 April.

Lieutenant Colonel Bell's three rifle companies (Company D was opconned to the 3d Marines at Da Nang) would first search for the NVA northeast of Khe Sanh, then to the northwest, and finally to the southwest. An ARVN infantry battalion would search the southeast quadrant.

On 19 April, helicopters ferried the Marines into position. From their LZs northeast of the camp, Companies A and B moved westward toward Company C, already in place six kilometers north of Khe Sanh. Over the next three days the wary Marines scoured the countryside. They found absolutely no sign of the enemy. On 23 April, the battalion pulled back to Khe Sanh.

Because of the battalion's lack of success, Lieutenant Colonel Bell canceled the rest of Operation Virginia. Instead, acting on a suggestion from the division G-2 (operations officer), Bell decided to march his battalion east along Route 9. Little more than a rutted cart path meandering through the northern jungle, Route 9 had not been traveled during the war. Traversing the route would not only spot any NVA infiltrators but would be a significant political and military accomplishment.

To provide security for his exposed infantry, Bell established an artillery fire support base at Ca Lu, twenty kilometers east of Khe Sanh. The III MAF also moved 3/4 to Dong Ha, the eastern terminus of Route 9, as a quick reaction force in the event that Bell's Marines ran into trouble.

Outside of the oppressive heat, 1/1 experienced no difficulty during its five-day trek to Ca Lu. On May 1, after a day's rest, the Marines were carried by truck the final ten kilometers to Dong Ha. There, Generals Westmoreland and Walt greeted the weary foot troops. Though Bell's battalion was the first allied unit to traverse Route 9 in more than eight years, the results of Operation Virginia proved inconclusive.

The division conducted several other operations during May and June in the northern reaches of I Corps, including rushing the venerable 2/4 to Dong Ha at the end of May to guard against a perceived NVA invasion. None of these operations resulted in any serious tangling with the enemy.

Not until late June did the Marines find the NVA. On 23 June, an ARVN patrol in the Quang Dien District, about twenty-five kilometers northwest of Hue, had a sharp clash with two battalions of the 6th NVA Regiment. Colonel Sherman quickly worked out plans for a combined operation with the Hue-based 1st ARVN Division. Operation Jay called for 2/4 to land at the northern edge of the AO, which was bounded by the meandering O Lau River on the north and west, Route 1 on the south, and the Gulf of Tonkin on the east. The battalion would then proceed to the southeast, sweeping toward blocking positions held by 2/1 about six kilometers away. The ARVN units involved in the operation would establish blocking positions to the north to prevent any enemy reinforcements from reaching the area. Colonel Sherman established his forward CP just north of the village of Phong Dien at the southern end of the AO.

At 0800 on 25 June, nineteen CH-46s carrying the first wave of Lieutenant Colonel Kelley's Marines started their descent into LZ Raven. By 1015 the battalion was on the ground and moving southeast. The terrain it crossed was flat but heavily covered with paddy dikes, scrub growth, hedgerows, bamboo, and tree lines defining numerous hamlets. These natural obstacles provided excellent cover and concealment opportunity for any waiting enemy force.

Kelley's battalion, consisting of Companies E, F, and H, crossed the first two thousand meters southeast of the LZ without incident. As they approached the hamlet of Ap Chin An, however, heavy enemy small-arms fire suddenly ripped into the advancing Marines. Kelley immediately sent his Company H around to the north to flank the hamlet. He then called for air, artillery, and naval gunfire to blast Ap Chin An. Despite this bombardment, the two lead companies of 2/4 still could not continue forward.

At the southeastern end of the AO, Lieutenant Colonel Hanifin's 2/1 had landed at LZ Shrike at 1100, then set up its blocking positions. At 1420 Colonel Sherman ordered Hanifin to move forward fifteen hundred meters to take some of the pressure off Kelley's hard-pressed Marines. As 2/1 complied with the new orders, it came under heavy fire from strong NVA forces in the hamlet of My Phu, adjacent to Ap Chin An. Hanifin also called for supporting fire but still was not able to advance.

In coordination with Hanifin, Kelley then sent his Company E on a wide flanking move to the southeast in an attempt to link up with Company H, 2/1, maneuvering to its northwest. The NVA, emplaced in well-dug-in positions in the two villages, spotted the movement and poured heavy mortar and automatic weapons fire on the two companies, forcing them to the ground. Though the members of each company could actually see one another, the intense enemy fire prevented the physical linkup.

Unable to continue, the two battalions settled in for the night. They would resume the attack in the morning. But, at 2100, NVA troops stormed out of Ap Chin An and headed straight for Kelley's Company H. Though the embattled Marines repulsed the attackers, it was a close call. Only the timely arrival of accurate supporting fire kept the enemy at bay.

The next morning, following a heavy preparatory barrage of artillery and air bombardment, the two battalions renewed their attack. Although there was some resistance, it soon became apparent that the bulk of the NVA had fled, leaving behind rear guards to slow down the Marines.

Still it wasn't until 1600 on 26 June that the two battalions finally linked up. Together, they finished clearing the two hamlets just before nightfall. Over the next two days, the Marines policed the battlefield. They found large quantities of abandoned equipment and a total of eighty-two enemy bodies. The Marines lost twenty-three of their own with fifty-eight wounded.

On 28 June, Colonel Sherman removed 2/1 from the battlefield. Kelley's 2/4 remained in the area to continue patrolling and mopping up, but the fighting was over. Operation Jay came to an end on 3 July.

During this activity in northern Thua Thien Province, evidence continued to mount that the enemy was building his forces in northern Quang Tri Province. The 1st ARVN Division reported that several new large NVA units had crossed the DMZ. General Westmoreland still believed that the enemy was planning a major offensive action south of the DMZ. To more accurately gauge the enemy's presence, General Westmoreland ordered General Walt to conduct extensive recon patrols in the area. Operating from bases at Dong Ha and Cam Lo, the patrols began on 20 June. Any doubts that General Walt and his staff might have had about the accuracy of the MACV intelligence reports were quickly dispelled. Major Dwain A. Colby, commander of the reconnaissance troops, reported that every patrol "encountered armed, uniformed groups and no patrol was able to stay in the field for more than a few hours, many for only a few minutes."

To support the recon efforts, at the end of June, Colonel Sherman ordered 2/1 north to Dong Ha. For the next several weeks the recon patrols continued to scour the countryside. Everywhere they looked they either found the enemy or signs of him. So thick were the NVA that between 4 and 14 July, fourteen of eighteen recon patrols had to be pulled out early because of enemy contact.

About this time two NVA deserters confirmed the presence of the 324B NVA Division south of the DMZ. The stated objective of the enemy force was to drive the ARVN out of Quang Tri Province.

Based on this, General Kyle recommended to General Walt that his division go north and drive out the enemy. Walt agreed. He then went to General Westmoreland. The MACV commander needed little persuasion to concur with the proposal.

Operation Hastings

Brigadier General Lowell E. English, the 3d Marine Division's assistant division commander, met with Maj. Gen. Ngo Quang Truong, the 1st ARVN Division commander, and Colonel Sherman in Hue on 11 July. The three commanders agreed that a Marine task force would conduct operations in northern Quang Tri Province just south of the DMZ. The insertion would be an extension of Operation Hastings, the code name of the ongoing reconnaissance effort. The ARVN forces would operate to the south of the Marines.

General Walt met with General Westmoreland in Hue the next day. After the command briefing that outlined the plan for Operation Hastings, Westmoreland not only approved it but authorized Walt to transfer up to an entire division to Quang Tri Province.

Initially, though, Walt told General Kyle to just establish a forward headquarters for the 4th Marines at Dong Ha. Kyle then reactivated TF Delta, with General English as its commander. Four infantry battalions—2/1, 1/3, 2/4, and 3/4—plus an artillery battalion, 3/12, made up the task force. On 14 July, General English established his headquarters at Cam Lo.

The terrain of TF Delta's new operational area varied from coastal plain to steep, rugged, jungle-clad mountains. Around Cam Lo and Dong Ha, the ground is relatively flat. To the north, rolling hills begin. All are covered with dense scrub and elephant grass. Thick stands of trees fill many of the valleys. Villages and hamlets, many with masonry buildings, dot the countryside. Farther north and west, sharp ridges and steep hills climb to more than five hundred meters in height. The heavy jungle foliage covering the rough terrain made ground travel extremely difficult, if not impossible. And helicopter landing zones were few and far between.

Based on intelligence reports, General English decided to seek the enemy in the Song Ngan Valley. This heavily forested area lay just two kilometers south of the DMZ. Hills 200 and 208 dominated the valley's southwestern end; Hill 100 guarded the northeast approaches. It was on Hill 208 that the 324B NVA Division was believed to have set up its command post.

The plans called for 3/4, under Lt. Col. Sumner A. Vale, to land at LZ Crow, situated between Hills 200 and 208. Five kilometers to the northeast, 2/4, now commanded by Lt. Col. Arnold E. Bench, would come into LZ Dove, about one kilometer east of Hill 100. Bench's battalion would then push southwest toward Hill 208 and 3/4.

The 2d Battalion, 1st Marines (later replaced by 1/1) guarded Dong Ha; 1/3 protected General English's headquarters at Cam Lo. As a diversion, the SLF, 3/5, would make an amphibious assault along the coast northeast of Dong Ha. Once the SLF battalion was established ashore, its control would pass to General English. In the meantime, the 1st ARVN Division would conduct operations north of Dong Ha and west of Route 1.

At first light on 15 July, a flight of A-4s dropped out of the sky over the Song Ngan Valley. Hurtling earthward, the screaming Skyhawks unleashed tons of bombs on the two LZs. As thick, dark clouds rose skyward, F-4 Phantoms raced in at treetop level. With pinpoint accuracy they dropped napalm-filled canisters on the target. Huge sheets of black-accented flames burst among the foliage, sucking up the oxygen and killing all living creatures.

Once the jets had finished, the artillery tubes of 3/12 at Cam Lo opened fire. Beginning at 0725 and lasting twenty minutes, the howitzers poured hundreds of rounds of high-explosive shells on the LZs. As they finished, the staccato beat of helicopter rotors echoed over the valley. At 0745 the first wave of CH-46s carrying the Marines of 3/4 hovered over LZ Crow. Within minutes the troops were on the ground and fanning out around the LZ.

The initial landings passed uneventfully. By the time the second wave dropped into the tight LZ, the NVA were ready to respond. Suddenly, enemy small arms fire filled the air. In taking evasive action, two CH-46s collided and fell earthward. A third helicopter, maneuvering to avoid the crashed pair, slammed into a tree. Two Marines died and seven were injured in the crashes. Later that day enemy fire hit another helicopter. Belching flame and smoke, it hit the ground near Lieutenant Colonel Vale's CP. Thirteen men died and another three were injured in this mishap. The sardonic Marines quickly dubbed the area "Helicopter Valley."

Lieutenant Colonel Bench's Marines began arriving at LZ Dove about 0935. Once on the ground the three companies (one company from each battalion had remained behind at Phu Bai) started advancing southwest toward 3/4. Though there was no enemy contact, the oppressive heat, high humidity, and difficult terrain greatly hampered the battalion's progress. Conditions were so bad that by midafternoon it had moved only three kilometers.

It was another story at Vale's end of the valley. While Company I secured the LZ, Company L moved west to occupy Hill 200. No sooner had Company L left the perimeter than it was peppered with small arms fire. The company hit the ground.

Vale sent Company K to the south to cross the Song Ngan, which ran between LZ Crow and Hill 208. It, too, started taking enemy fire almost as soon as it left the LZ. Just a few hundred meters to the south, members of Company K stumbled on a two-hundred-bed hospital hidden deep in the dense foliage. After killing the four stay-behind guards, the Marines pressed on. The closer they came to the river, the heavier the enemy fire became. Each time they neared the bank, a wall of lead greeted them. Four times the company tried to ford the river. Four times deadly enemy fire lashing out of the nearly impenetrable jungle drove the men back. Company K's commander, Capt. Robert J. Modrzejewski, finally decided to pull back his company and form a tight, night defensive perimeter. They'd try again in the morning.

While Modrzejewski's company dug in, enemy machine-gun and mortar rounds suddenly raked Company I and the battalion CP. At 1930 Lieutenant Colonel Vale reported to General English that he was completely surrounded. But then, thirty minutes later, the enemy's fire slackened. Vale told English that he thought the enemy had retreated. Then, at 2015, the NVA hit Modrzejewski's company. For the next three hours, Modrzejewski's company battled the determined foe. The pitch-black darkness hid the NVA from the Marines, who resorted to flinging hand grenades blindly into the jungle. Modrzejewski later said, "It was so dark we couldn't see our hands in front of our faces, so we threw our trip flares [into the jungle] and called for a flare plane. We could hear and smell and occasionally see the NVA after that. In the morning we found twenty-five bodies, some of them only five meters away, stacked on top of each other." Eventually the NVA slithered back into the jungle, but they still harassed a nervous Company K throughout the night.

Realizing that he was badly outnumbered, Lieutenant Colonel Vale asked for help. General English immediately ordered 2/4 to abandon its mission and go directly to Vale's aid by moving along the easier terrain bordering the river.

Early the next morning a heavy shower of enemy mortar rounds again fell on Vale's CP. While Marine jets and artillery blasted the suspected gun sites, Company K again tried to ford the Song Ngan. As before, heavy enemy small arms fire blasted the Marines. With his troops pinned down in the jungle, Modrzejewski called for air strikes.

To the northeast, Bench's battalion headed out shortly after dawn. Though the men fought the NVA on and off throughout the day, suffering nine casualties including two dead, they arrived at Vale's location by 1500.

Though there were now six Marine rifle companies facing them, the NVA did not back off. During the night of 16–17 July, they struck again. As before, the heaviest attacks tore into Company K. Modrzejewski's company, positioned about eight hundred meters south of the two battalion CPs, was hit about 1930. Screaming, yelling, and firing a variety of automatic weapons, and nearly invisible from more than two meters away, the NVA tore into all sides of Company K's thin perimeter. Over the next four hours the embattled Marines threw back three intense ground attacks, one of which was stopped just five meters from them. Modrzejewski displayed gallant leadership that night, but he credited accurate artillery fire, and a flare ship that stayed on station all night, with helping him hold back the NVA. In the morning his men found seventy-nine NVA bodies around their laager site. Combined with the twenty-five they had killed the night before, Company K had acquitted itself very well. Suprisingly, only one Company K Marine was killed; five were seriously wounded and forty were slightly wounded in the fight.

On the morning of 17 July, Lieutenant Colonel Vale abandoned any plans he still had to take Hills 200 and 208. Instead, he sent Company L to help Modrzejewski. That evening General English changed the plans of the two battalions. On 18 July, 2/4 would move out of the valley, heading northeast to a position about fifteen hundred meters south of the DMZ. Vale's 3/4, meanwhile, would stay behind to destroy the three downed helicopters and a cache of NVA ammo uncovered by Company L. When that was done they would follow 2/4 to the northeast.

In the meantime, 3/5, the SLF, which had successfully completed its amphibious landing on 16 July, would be airlifted into a parallel valley about three kilometers to the south of Helicopter Valley. There the Marines would not only exploit a B-52 strike made on 17 July but act as a blocking force for any NVA escaping from the Song Ngan area.

At midmorning on 18 July, 2/4 started its trek back to the northeast. The battalion moved without interference. By 1500 Bench's men had established a defensive perimeter at their new position. At 1400 Vale's battalion began its movement to trace 2/4's steps out of the valley. Vale ordered Company K to remain behind to provide security for the engineers blowing the ammo and helicopters. At 1430, the NVA hit.

Enemy mortar shells fell first, crashing down all across the LZ and the battalion area with thundering booms. Lieutenant Colonel Vale and some of his headquarters staff were still at their CP. Because their fighting holes had already been filled in, all Vale and his staff could do was double-time to the east. They did.

Company K wasn't so lucky. Pinned down by the mortars, the men were further immobilized by bursts of heavy automatic weapons fire blasting them from three sides. The 1st Platoon, led by SSgt. John J. McGinty, was some distance from the rest of the company. Before Modrzejewski could get to the platoon, the attacking NVA had successfully isolated it.

Wearing pith helmets and new green uniforms, and firing AK-47 semiautomatic rifles, scores of NVA infantry swarmed toward McGinty and his thirty men. Firing as fast as they could reload magazines, the trapped Marines killed dozens of the enemy, but still they kept coming. McGinty later said, "We just couldn't kill them fast enough."

Unable to reach McGinty, Modrzejewski called for air and artillery support. Within minutes both were hitting as close as fifty meters from his lines. At one point in the fight some NVA swarmed over one of the nearby downed helicopters. Modrzejewski called in a jet. "Napalm got about twenty of them, and then another forty in the middle of the landing zone," he recalled.

Lieutenant Colonel Vale rushed Company L back to the aid of Company K, which was battling for its life. Not until just before 1700 were the relieving Marines able to break through. Laying down a heavy base of fire, they finally freed McGinty and his trapped men. Everyone then pulled back, bringing their wounded but leaving the dead in the tall elephant grass. A short time later two platoons from Company I arrived to help, too. With the enemy at last repulsed, the exhausted Marines formed a ragged column of walking wounded, wounded to be carried, and able-bodied men. They proceeded upstream.

By 1900 the two battalions had again joined up. Casualties had been heavy. Company K alone suffered 14 dead and 49 wounded, out of a prebattle strength of 130. McGinty's platoon alone had suffered 8 dead and 14 wounded. The NVA casualties were estimated at 138 dead. Both Modrzejewski and McGinty would later be decorated with the Medal of Honor for their valor.

The next day Company K was pulled from the field for rebuilding, but the rest of the two battalions remained in place. They spent the next two weeks crisscrossing the valley looking for the NVA. However, the elusive foe avoided contact. For all practical purposes the battle for Helicopter Valley was over.

Heavy fighting did erupt to the south where 3/5 was operating. On 24 July, Lt. Col. Edward J. Bronars ordered his Company I to establish a radio relay station atop Hill 362, about seven kilometers southwest of Hill 200. Captain Samuel S. Glaize's company had no problems getting to the top of the hill. However, when Glaize sent his 2d Platoon down the far side, the NVA suddenly opened fire. Blazing away with AK-47 and machine-gun fire from well-established fighting positions hidden deep within the heavy jungle, the NVA easily mowed down the Marines.

Under covering fire from their buddies at the top of the hill, a few 2d Platoon members at the rear of the column scrambled to safety. The NVA then crept out of the jungle and mercilessly murdered any living Marines. Only by playing dead did a few of them survive this brutal massacre.

Next, four NVA mortars started dropping rounds across the top of Hill 362. Because they had not been able to dig any holes, the members of Company I were ripped apart by the shells. The pounding lasted for two hours before a Marine helicopter gunship finally arrived and silenced the enemy weapons.

As soon as he learned of Company I's ordeal, Lieutenant Colonel Bronars ordered Company K to their relief. These fresh troops made it to within three hundred meters of Company I's position before renewed heavy enemy fire stopped them cold. Company K was forced to dig in for the night where it was. To add to the already bad situation, heavy rainsqualls that evening hampered the evacuation of casualties. Only eleven wounded from Company K were pulled out before the medevac operation was called off.

The sister companies spent a terror-filled night on Hill 362 as NVA mortar shells pounded them continually. Enemy soldiers probed the Marines' lines all night, appearing as shadowy ghosts in the misty jungle. One young Marine later said, "The Commies were so close we could hear them breathing." By dawn, however, the enemy was gone. Company K pushed forward and finally linked up with Glaize's company. It had been a tough fight. Company I alone suffered one hundred casualties—eighteen dead and eighty-two wounded. Marines policing the battlefield found only twenty-one enemy bodies in the nearby jungle.

The fight on Hill 362 marked the end of large-scale action during Operation Hastings. General Kyle met with General English on 26 July. After reviewing the situation, Kyle ordered the battalions withdrawn. Over the next few days the Marines departed their AOs. On 30 July, 3/5 returned to the control of the Seventh Fleet as the SLF. General English deactivated his task force headquarters on 1 August. Control of Operation Hastings passed to the 4th Marines, now commanded by Col. Alexander D. Cereghino. The operation officially ended on 3 August.

Marine intelligence believed that the 324B NVA Division had either moved north of the DMZ or slipped into the impenetrable jungle to the west. Westmoreland disagreed. Not only did he think that the 324B Division was still south of the DMZ, but his intelligence specialists reported that two more NVA divisions, the 304th and 341st, were preparing to cross the DMZ.

Operation Prairie

To monitor NVA activities in Quang Tri Province, III MAF authorized Operation Prairie to commence on 3 August 1966. The

original units participating in the operation included 2/4 at Dong
Ha, a howitzer battery from 3/12, and a variety of supporting units,
including a platoon of tanks, an antitank platoon, engineers, and logistical troops. The primary element of Operation Prairie, however,
was the 1st Force Recon Company.

The plan for Operation Prairie called for five-man recon teams
to be inserted by helicopter along suspected enemy routes. If the
teams found the NVA, they could call for artillery, helicopter gunships, or close air support to bombard them. If these weapons
proved insufficient, rifle companies would be airlifted into the
scene.

Once again it didn't take long for the recon Marines to find the
enemy. Operating four kilometers north of the Rockpile, a promi-
nent terrain feature west of Cam Lo, a recon team spotted a good-
sized NVA force on 6 August. After calling artillery fire down on the
enemy, the team suddenly found itself threatened by other NVA. A
reaction platoon from Company E, 2/4, was rushed into the area to
help the recon Marines. By the time it arrived on the scene, though,
the enemy had slipped away.

The combined force searched for two days but could not reestablish contact. On 8 August, the troops were being lifted out of a quiet
LZ when the NVA suddenly opened fire on the helicopters from a
nearby ridge. Then, without warning, enemy soldiers poured out of
the jungle, surrounding the twenty-five Marines still on the ground.
The stranded men quickly set up a defensive perimeter. Within minutes the NVA killed the Company E lieutenant and his platoon
sergeant. Command of the beleaguered unit passed to the recon
team leader. He called for air strikes and artillery. Within minutes
both were pounding the NVA back into the jungle.

At Dong Ha the Company E commander, Capt. Howard V. Lee,
rounded up seven volunteers as a relief force. Two UH-34 gunships
flew alongside the troop-carrying helicopter. Deadly accurate enemy
fire forced all three ships to land some distance from the trapped
men. That didn't stop Lee, though. Disregarding the marauding enemy, and accompanied by just two other men, Lee broke through
the jungle to join his isolated troops. For the rest of the night the
stoic Marines, aided by artillery fire and helicopter gunships, fought

off the NVA. At dawn on 9 August, Company F, soon followed by the rest of Company E, reached Lee and his men. As usual, the NVA had pulled out. Captain Lee received a well-deserved Medal of Honor for his brave actions.

This fight convinced Colonel Cereghino that the enemy was indeed operating in strength in Quang Tri Province. On 13 August, he established a regimental forward CP at Dong Ha and ordered 1/4 north from Phu Bai. Once the fresh battalion arrived, 2/4 headed west along Route 9 toward the Rockpile, about twenty kilometers away, on 17 August. The men made it about halfway before strong, enemy machine-gun fire from Hill 252, south of the road, forced them to a halt. Air and artillery support were called in, but neither could budge the well-dug-in enemy soldiers. Lieutenant Colonel Bench then brought up tanks from Cam Lo. When they arrived, the two M48 behemoths fired point-blank at the enemy positions. This support finally allowed the infantry to capture the hill the next day. The Marines then continued on and established a night defensive perimeter north of the Rockpile.

During the next six days, 2/4's infantry companies fanned out and looked for the NVA in the dense jungle. They found them nearly everywhere. Hardly a day went by without some element of 2/4 making contact with the NVA. The clashes were always deadly but brief. Before artillery or air support could be brought to bear on the slippery enemy, they had pulled out, leaving the Marines to evacuate their wounded and dead before renewing the search.

On 21 August, from the eastern slopes of a sharply contoured northwest-southeast–running hill mass just northwest of the Rockpile, the enemy began firing a 12.7mm machine gun at resupply helicopters servicing the Marine recon team atop the Rockpile. Despite repeated air strikes and artillery missions, the automatic weapon kept firing away. Lieutenant Colonel Bench ordered Company E to find and destroy the NVA weapon.

The sixty men of Company E, still understrength from its fight on 9–10 August, jumped from helicopters east of the suspected enemy location on the newly named Razorback Ridge on the afternoon of 23 August. Fanning out across the steep hillside, the Marines immediately noticed numerous caves, some quite large. All appeared to be empty. About 1630, while preparing to end their search, the Marines heard voices coming from one of the caves. The new company commander, Capt. Edwin W. Besch, deployed his men around the cave's entrance in hopes of taking a prisoner. Suddenly, NVA hidden in nearby caves opened fire. The enemy's fire was so intense that the Marines were pinned down, unable to move, within minutes.

Lieutenant Colonel Bench, advised of Company E's perilous situation, immediately formed a composite relief force, consisting of a platoon each from Companies F and G and his headquarters company. Led by the S-3, Capt. John J. W. Hilgers, the makeshift relief force landed at the base of the Razorback late that evening. Fighting uphill, the relieving Marines reached the trapped men just after midnight. At daybreak the combined force repulsed a vicious ground attack from NVA streaming from the caves. By midmorning on 24 August, the fight for the Razorback was over. The Marines suffered twenty-one dead and ninety-nine wounded, but the NVA had lost a key position from which they could have captured the Rockpile.

The rest of August and early September were relatively quiet in Quang Tri Province. Colonel Cereghino decided to expand his AO to include the Con Thien region, which lay due north of Cam Lo and just three kilometers south of the DMZ. He ordered Lieutenant Colonel Bench to take his battalion on a reconnaissance-in-force sweep of the area. Company H, 2/4, and a platoon of tanks from Company C, 3d Tank Battalion headed north from Cam Lo early on 7 September. That afternoon helicopters carried the rest of the battalion northward to LZs spaced around Con Thien. The very next day Company G found a force of NVA about one kilometer northeast of Con Thien. The resulting firefight lasted three hours and cost five Marines their lives. On 9 September, Bench's Companies E and F, supported by tanks, found a dug-in NVA company just south of the DMZ. From trenches extending deep into the DMZ, the enemy raked the Marines with heavy machine-gun fire. Only the direct fire of the tanks finally broke the enemy resistance. The Marines swept the area for several more days but found no more NVA. Bench's battalion returned to Cam Lo on the thirteenth.

A few days later combat action intensified to the west. Acting on intelligence reports that the NVA were establishing a stronghold on the Nui Cay Tre ridgeline in the rugged, jungle-covered mountains three kilometers north of the Rockpile, Colonel Cereghino ordered 1/4, under Lt. Col. Jack Westerman, to probe north. On 15 September, Companies B and D started through the dense, triple-canopied jungle.

At noon the next day the NVA struck. The two companies were immediately surrounded by a full battalion of NVA. For the next two and a half days the battle flared. Marine air and artillery constantly pounded the NVA, but the enemy wouldn't give up. Not until elements of the reinforcing 2/7 reached the two encircled companies on the evening of 18 September did the NVA sneak away. In spite of the intensity and duration of the fight, friendly casualties were surprisingly light: only nine Marines were killed.

Colonel Cereghino sent 1/4 back to the Rockpile on 19 September, and 2/7 continued on to the Nui Cay Tre area. The closer they moved to the ridgeline, the heavier the enemy fire became. After two days of this, Cereghino pulled 2/7 back to the Rockpile, too. He not only felt that Nui Cay Tre was too well defended for the forces he had, but the NVA had reoccupied the Razorback. From there they again threatened the Rockpile. Cereghino decided he had to clean out the Razorback before he could tackle Nui Cay Tre.

On 22 September, two companies of Lt. Col. John J. Roothoff's 2/7 attacked up the western slope of the Razorback. That day and the next passed uneventfully. Then on the twenty-fourth, well-concealed NVA in mutually supporting bunkers unleashed a vicious sheet of automatic weapons fire on Company G. Burdened with heavy casualties, the company could not withdraw. Lieutenant Colonel Roothoff ordered Company F to aid its embattled sister company. Company F made only a few hundred meters before it, too, was ambushed and pinned down. By the end of the day the two companies had suffered thirteen killed and forty-five wounded. Once again, Marine close air support prevented a larger disaster. Under this protective umbrella of high explosives, the two rifle companies recovered their casualties from the dense undergrowth and retreated to safety. The next day Colonel Cereghino sent Roothoff's mauled battalion back to its parent regiment at Chu Lai for rebuilding. It was replaced on the battlefield by 2/9.

Stymied at the Razorback, Cereghino now decided to have another crack at Nui Cay Tre. He sent Lt. Col. William J. Masterpool's 3/4 against Nui Cay Tre from the east. Following a heavy artillery barrage on the morning of 22 September, CH-46s brought the battalion into its LZ, about four kilometers east of the hill mass, or just south of Hill 362. Starting forward, the Marines soon encountered the most difficult terrain they'd yet faced. A six-foot layer of tangled brush covered the ground. Trees up to eight feet thick had such a dense canopy of leaves that whatever sunlight penetrated cast an eerie, netherworld pall over the jungle. Forward movement was limited to mere meters per hour as the enervated Marines hacked through the thick jungle with machetes. Sometimes they had to wait for bombs or napalm to blast or burn the jungle ahead of them before they could move.

Not until 26 September did Company L, 3/4, secure Hill 400, the battalion's first objective. Along the way it became obvious that the Marines were deep in enemy territory. Company commander Capt. Roger K. Ryman said, "As we got closer to [Hill] 400 . . . we saw more and more enemy positions, including enough huts in the ravines to harbor a regiment, and piles and piles of ammunition. NVA bodies lying around and hastily dug graves were signs we were moving right behind them."

At 0730 the next day Company K pushed southwest from Hill 400 preparatory to the battalion's movement toward Hill 484, three kilometers to the west. The enemy soon hit them with such fury that by noon the company was surrounded, with eight dead and twenty-five wounded. Not until late that afternoon did the NVA break contact. Lieutenant Colonel Masterpool dispatched the rest of the battalion to link up with Company K and set up a multicompany night defensive position (NDP).

At the crack of dawn the next morning, Company K started out of the NDP. Almost immediately the Marines ran into NVA in heavily reinforced bunkers. Captain James J. Carroll pulled back his men and called for artillery. As soon as the barrage ended, the NVA attacked. Heavily camouflaged, the enemy soldiers were barely visible as they poured out of the jungle. The fighting was so intense that one of Carroll's sergeants later said, "You couldn't tell who was firing, Charlie or us. They had everything—mortars, heavy weapons, and mines—and they even had ladders in trees for spotters to climb and direct fire." Elements of Companies I and M arrived just in time to help Captain Carroll's Marines throw back the enemy.

The fighting raged until late on 28 September. The three companies then withdrew and consolidated back atop Hill 400. After being resupplied, Lieutenant Colonel Masterpool continued his methodical movement toward Hill 484. By the evening of 3 October, the battalion was in position. The next morning, Company M sent a platoon against the bunkers guarding the hill. It was soon thrown back. Another platoon moved around the right flank. It, too, fell back under a barrage of NVA grenades. Unable to make any progress, Company M retreated. Then, Marine jets unleashed high explosives on the hill all the rest of the day and into the next morning. At 1000 on 5 October, Company M again charged forward. Resistance was tough, but by 1330 the Marines controlled Hill 484.

The hard-won victory was tarnished by the friendly fire deaths of three Marines on Hill 400, including Capt. James Carroll. He was later posthumously awarded the Navy Cross for his valor during the fight for Hill 484. The artillery base on the plateau west of Cam Lo was renamed Camp Carroll in his honor.

The 3d Battalion, 4th Marines suffered twenty dead in taking Nui Cay Tre. More than fifty more were wounded. The enemy suffered at least one hundred dead. From then on Nui Cay Tre would be known as "Mutter's Ridge" after Lieutenant Colonel Masterpool's radio call sign.

This intense fighting raised General Westmoreland's concerns about the enemy's intentions for Quang Tri Province. He believed that the NVA would move more troops across the DMZ, increasing the pressure on III MAF. Even worse, he feared that the enemy might try to outflank the Marine strongholds at the Rockpile and Dong Ha by slipping troops into the province via the mountainous terrain of northwestern Quang Tri Province. To blunt these movements Westmoreland suggested General Walt put Marines at Khe Sanh.

General Walt resisted. His staff supported him, feeling that Khe Sanh had no military value. In fact, General English thought that the loss of Khe Sanh would have absolutely no effect on any operations in Quang Tri Province. "It's far away from anything," he said. "You could lose it and you really haven't lost a damn thing."

The Marines' position was negated on 26 September when MACV intelligence pinpointed an NVA base camp just fourteen kilometers northeast of Khe Sanh. Rather than lose face by being ordered by MACV to reinforce Khe Sanh, General Walt issued the necessary orders himself. On 29 September, 1/3 was lifted by C-130 transport planes from Da Nang directly to Khe Sanh. The troops immediately began extensive patrolling of the rugged, inhospitable terrain surrounding the base. They occasionally saw the enemy but made no significant contact.

At about this time, MACV intelligence received reports of a major buildup of enemy forces all along the DMZ. As a result, General Westmoreland became convinced that the North Vietnamese were preparing for a massive attack into Quang Tri Province. One intelligence analysis even predicted a three-division invasion in less than three days. Though that did not happen, III MAF reactivated Task Force Delta on 1 October. General English set up his command post at Dong Ha and assumed responsibility for Operation Prairie from Colonel Cereghino. General English had six infantry battalions (1/4, 3/4, 2/5, 1/3, 2/9, and 3/7) supported by artillery and other units in TF Delta when he took command.

With all this increased activity in Quang Tri Province, General Walt ordered the 3d Marine Division to move its headquarters north from Da Nang to Phu Bai. When General Kyle opened his new headquarters there on 6 October, he also deactivated TF Delta. In its place he established at Dong Ha a division forward headquarters under General English. At the same time, Operation Prairie transitioned from a specific operation to an area of operations. Also, responsibility for the important Da Nang TAOR transferred to the 1st Marine Division.

The Marines were ready, but the expected NVA offensive never materialized. In fact, enemy contact dropped off sharply right after the fight for Mutter's Ridge. The III MAF continued to hear of large enemy formations around the DMZ, but if they were actually there they stayed hidden.

By the end of 1966, III MAF reduced the force in Quang Tri Province to just one regiment, the 3d Marines, operating with four infantry battalions. The 4th Marines moved south to participate in Operation Chinook near Hue.

Operation Prairie, which would extend into 1967, had prevented the NVA from establishing a major base in Quang Tri Province. But the cost had been high: two hundred Marines were killed and more than one thousand were wounded. Reported enemy deaths were a little more than one thousand. And the shuffling and reshuffling of Marine units had adversely affected the ongoing pacification efforts favored by III MAF.

As the Marines' second year in South Vietnam ended, General Walt felt that the North Vietnamese leaders were succeeding in their efforts to draw his combat troops away from the populous coastal plain into the rugged interior mountains, where the NVA could win a war of attrition. With III MAF strength at nearly seventy thousand men in two infantry divisions, a full air wing, and a logistical command, General Walt now commanded the largest force of U.S. Marines deployed overseas since World War II. And the Marines were fighting two distinctly separate wars: the 3d Marine Division conducted a more or less conventional ground campaign in northern I Corps, and the 1st Marine Division continued the combination of large unit operations with major pacification efforts in the south. This separation of effort would continue into 1967.

Chapter Three
1967

The long line of combat-loaded Marines snaked through the thick vegetation surrounding the thatched huts of Thuy Bo. The hamlet was fifteen kilometers southwest of Da Nang and just west of the north-south railroad berm that bisected the region. The riflemen approached Thuy Bo cautiously. The grunts had been patrolling this northern edge of the area they called Go Noi Island for several days without seeing any sign of the enemy. They didn't really want to find any now. The next morning the company would leave the field for several days of well-deserved rest. Once they swept through Thuy Bo, they'd set up a night defensive perimeter. At first light, helicopters would take them back to their base camp.

Suddenly, any thoughts the riflemen had of rest and recreation were shattered by the heavy bark of a .50-caliber machine gun. Seconds later, the sharp crack of AK-47s rose to a crescendo. The Marines dove for cover. For some it was too late. Frantic cries of "Corpsman up!" filled the air. Immediately, the valiant navy medics hastened forward under the grazing fire, intent only on reaching the wounded.

While they tended to the casualties, the company commander deployed his platoons in flanking maneuvers. Heavy fire forced the advancing troops to seek shelter behind nearby rice paddy dikes. The captain then radioed for both artillery fire and air strikes on the hamlet. A short time later the explosives slammed into Thuy Bo, tossing the fragile thatched huts skyward. Despite this pounding the enemy soldiers refused to give ground. For all the rest of the day and into the night, the fight continued. The enemy was so well entrenched that the bombs and artillery shells did them little damage. The

Marines could neither advance nor retreat. They spent a miserable night in their exposed positions.

At dawn, the mud-soaked Marines arose from the rice paddies. They assaulted the village, firing their rifles from the hip as they pressed forward. Only sporadic fire greeted them. Within fifteen minutes the company was through Thuy Bo. The enemy was gone. The company lost 6 dead and 26 wounded. Though they claimed to have killed 101 enemy soldiers, there weren't that many bodies in the village. The body count was simply an estimate based on what damage the artillery and air had probably done.

This action of Company H, 2/1, on 31 January 1967, was typical of the combat experienced by the 1st Marine Division as the third year of the war in South Vietnam began.

More often than not, when the enemy was found, it was he who initiated the contact. Just as it had to Company H, the foe would ambush a Marine unit, cause casualties, then flee to its hiding places. Neither side gained any military advantage as a result of these violent meetings.

According to General Westmoreland's grand scheme for the war, 1967 was to be the year in which large-scale battles between American and North Vietnamese forces resulted in resounding victories for the former and bitter defeats for the latter. To this end MACV and the Vietnamese Joint General Staff issued their 1967 Combined Campaign Plan. A major strategic change for 1967 involved assigning to the ARVN primary responsibility for pacification efforts. American forces would now not only have to carry out the bulk of the offensive operations against the NVA and VC but also most of the tactical tasks previously performed by the ARVN.

The North Vietnamese, of course, had their own plans for fighting the war in South Vietnam in 1967. As allied forces extended their control over more of the populated regions of the country, North Vietnam's leaders continued to plan to draw American forces away from their bases and into the countryside. As North Vietnamese General Vo Nguyen Giap observed, "We will entice the Americans close to the border and bleed them without mercy." There, the inhospitable terrain blunted the American's advantage of superior firepower. And, while the allies were engaged in the wilds of South Vietnam, their pacification programs would be stymied.

1st Marine Division

Operating in I Corps' three southernmost provinces—Quang Nam, Quang Tin, and Quang Ngai—the 1st Marine Division was very active. In the first three months of 1967 the division sent out more than thirty-six thousand company-sized operations, patrols, and ambushes. The bulk of these, to be sure, resulted in little or no contact with the enemy. They did, however, deny the enemy the freedom of movement he had once enjoyed across the area.

In the joint U.S.-Vietnamese Combined Campaign Plan for 1967, the Duc Pho District of Quang Ngai Province was specifically identified as an area where III MAF units were to replace ARVN units so that the latter could be used elsewhere in pacification programs. Duc Pho, the southernmost district of the province, had long been dominated by the Viet Cong. Though the ARVN did maintain a presence there, they generally confined themselves to a few outposts and the district capital of Duc Pho. Only on rare occasions did they leave the security of their bases. As a result, the VC had constructed numerous extensive fortifications throughout the area. To eliminate those, the 1st Marine Division would replace the ARVN units in Operation Desoto.

The operation began on 27 January when Company L, 3/7, and four 105mm howitzers of Battery I, 12th Marines relieved the ARVN troops atop Nui Dang, a 140-meter hill northeast of Duc Pho. At 0800 the next day, Marine helicopters ferried Companies I and M, 3/7, into LZs north of Nui Dang. Under intermittent sniper fire the Marines moved out to occupy hamlets sitting northwest and northeast of the LZs. Company M then turned north, crossed the Song Quan River, and continued toward Tan Tu.

Heavy enemy fire suddenly erupted from the small hamlet, stopping the advance before it had gone very far. Following an artillery barrage and air strikes, the riflemen tried again. Once more strong enemy resistance forced the Marines to the ground. They dug in for the night. The next day the battalion commander, Lt. Col. Raymond J. O'Leary, sent both Companies I and M into the fray. Most of the enemy had fled, and by early afternoon the two rifle companies had not only secured Tan Tu but pushed on to the next village north, Sa Binh.

On 30 January, Company I headed east toward Hai Mon. The sporadic enemy small arms fire that greeted the infantrymen quickly escalated to include heavy machine guns. By late afternoon Company I, burdened with casualties and low on ammo, broke contact and pulled back to the west. Company M fought its way to Company I, providing the latter with much needed ammo. Throughout the night, while the two companies evacuated their casualties, artillery and naval gunfire pounded Hai Mon, all but leveling the village.

Over the next few days the two companies continued searching the area. On 3 February, Companies L and M, 3/5, joined the operation. Two days later the new commander of 3/7, Lt. Col. Edward J. Bronars, again directed his forces against Hai Mon. Attacking from the east, Bronars used his two fresh companies in the assault. Beginning early on the morning of 5 February, an intense artillery, air, and naval gun bombardment blasted the target area. Despite this, as the grunts neared what remained of Hai Mon, they took machinegun and recoilless rifle fire. After again calling in supporting arms, the rifle companies spotted about fifty VC fleeing across the adjacent Song Tra Cau River. While helicopter gunships attacked the fleeing enemy, the Marines finally occupied Hai Mon. They discovered a vast, sophisticated bunker and tunnel complex. Engineers called in to destroy the network used thirty-six hundred pounds of explosives to do so.

Operation Desoto continued throughout February. Little was accomplished on the daily company and platoon sweeps of the AO. Enemy contact was generally limited to snipers and the occasional squad of VC. The rifle companies set up numerous ambushes every night but rarely had anything in the morning to justify their efforts.

While 3/7 continued operating in the Nui Dang–Nui Dai area, Operation Deckhouse VI commenced near Sa Huynh, at the tip of Quang Ngai Province. According to the plan, the SLF, BLT 1/4, would destroy any enemy in the area to pave the way for the construction of a U.S. Army Special Forces camp at the site. Then the Marines would turn north to link up with the Operation Desoto forces. At 0800 on 16 February, the rocket ships USS *Clarion River* and *White River* unleashed a barrage of missiles on the LZs inland from the beaches. At 0855 the first wave of troop-laden helicopters lifted from the deck of the USS *Iwo Jima*. A short time later Company A, 1/4, had been deposited on the ground. The hardworking helicopters soon ferried in the rest of the BLT. Only a few scattered sniper rounds greeted the Marines during this maneuver.

After four days it became apparent that the VC were no longer in the area. Brigadier General William A. Stiles, the assistant division commander controlling Operation Desoto through TF X-ray, assumed operational control of BLT 1/4. He ordered the BLT to proceed northeast on a search and destroy mission. In the meantime, Lieutenant Colonel Bronars's Marines assumed blocking positions south of Nui Dai. Five days later the two forces met up. Though BLT 1/4 had had no major contact with the enemy, they had uncovered a number of supply caches and fortified positions.

Phase two of Operation Desoto/Deckhouse began on 26 February when 1/5 and two ARVN battalions landed at LZs northwest of Duc Pho, then headed northeast. With 3/7 holding blocking positions to the south, BLT 1/4 then made an amphibious assault northeast of Duc Pho. Once ashore it headed to the southwest. None of the forces made any contact with the enemy.

In preparation for yet another amphibious assault, BLT 1/4 was then ferried back to its ships. On 27 February, less than fifteen hours later, the SLF Marines came ashore ten kilometers north of Duc Pho. Though the Marines who were lifted into an LZ fifteen hundred meters inland received strong, enemy small arms fire upon landing, the amphibious landing proceeded without a hitch.

For the next two days the SLF swept to the southwest. The Marines stayed in near constant contact with a fleeing band of enemy soldiers but were never able to catch them. On 3 March, UH-34s and CH-46s carried the BLT back to its ships. Inland, 1/5 and the ARVN infantry found evidence of an enemy presence but made little contact. They, too, left the operational area on 3 March.

General Stiles continued Operation Desoto with just 3/7. While improving their base on Nui Dang, the Marines kept expanding their AO. The constant pressure of patrolling Marines forced the VC to abandon their fortified hamlets. By the end of March nearly all the assigned AO had been swept and cleared. Intelligence reports indicated that the VC had fled westward. When Operation Desoto ended on 7 April, more than fifty-five square kilometers of Duc Pho District were under allied control. As a result, Revolutionary Development pacification teams, a U.S. Central Intelligence Agency–sponsored civic action effort, were soon making progress toward restoring government control in southern Quang Ngai Province.

The continued requirement to relieve ARVN units so that they could form the new Revolutionary Development teams, plus the redeployment of several 1st Marine Division units north to bolster the 3d Marine Division's efforts along the DMZ, severely strained troop availability in southern I Corps. General Walt recognized that these manpower shortages meant that his forces were barely capable of holding their own. If they were to regain the initiative, III MAF needed additional troops.

The MACV saw the problem, too. With enemy pressure continuing against the 3d Marine Division along the DMZ, and the 2d NVA Division again on the prowl in the southern area of I Corps, General Westmoreland made plans to reinforce the Marines. On 7 April, elements of the 1st Cavalry Division relieved 3/7 at Duc Pho. (The deployment of the cavalrymen was only temporary; the 3d Brigade, 25th Infantry Division would replace them by the end of April.) Two days later the four battalions of the 196th Infantry Brigade arrived at Chu Lai. On 20 April, Task Force Oregon, under Westmoreland's former chief of staff, Maj. Gen. William B. Rosson, became operational and assumed control of all U.S. Army units in southern I Corps. During the first week of May, a brigade of the 101st Airborne Division joined Task Force Oregon. The airmobile soldiers immediately opened an offensive operation south of Quang Ngai City. Eventually, Task Force Oregon developed into the U.S. Army's Americal Division and assumed operational responsibility for Quang Tin and Quang Ngai Provinces.

The arrival of these U.S. Army units allowed III MAF to concentrate its efforts on the three northern provinces of I Corps. As a result, the 7th Marines moved north from Chu Lai to Da Nang on 13

April. The 5th Marines took over responsibility for the Que Son Valley on 25 April.

With the arrival of the U.S. Army units and the repositioning of the Marine regiments, III MAF once again returned to the Que Son Valley. As per the 1967 Joint Combined Campaign Plan, the ARVN outpost on the hill complex of Nui Loc Son, about midway between Hiep Duc and Que Son, was taken over by Marines. Company F, 2/1, relieved the ARVNs. The rifle company immediately began intensive patrol and civic action programs throughout the central Que Son Valley area.

As Col. Emil J. Radic, commander of the 1st Marines, acknowledged, the activities of Company F, which operated under his direct control, were planned "to create a situation." The Marines' nemesis, the 2d NVA Division, took the bait.

Operation Union and Union II

As envisioned by the operations staff of the 1st Marines, Operation Union would begin as soon as Company F made a significant contact with the enemy. Then, elements of the regiment's 3d Battalion would be lifted in to reinforce the company. If a major battle broke out, other rifle companies from the 1st Battalion, as well as the opconned 3/5, could be flown in.

Early on the hot, humid morning of 21 April, Company F, commanded by Capt. Gene A. Deegan, left the Nui Loc Son outpost. As the Marines headed east across the wide valley floor, they occasionally fired on several small bands of NVA. Around 0700 the company's scouts spotted a large enemy force entering Binh Son (1), a hamlet four kilometers to their northeast. Deegan took his company after the NVA but was stopped by a vicious blast of enemy fire. The riflemen inched their way back to the safety of a tree line. At 0930 Deegan called for artillery and air strikes. Ninety minutes later Company F again headed for Binh Son (1). The two lead platoons had barely crept past the hamlet's first few thatched huts when heavy enemy small arms and automatic weapons fire stopped them in their tracks. Artillery and air strikes again hit the enemy, but Deegan's platoons remained pinned down.

By this time, Companies I and M, 3/1, as planned, had landed at an LZ fifteen hundred meters north of Binh Son (1). Unfortunately, the LZ was hotly contested. The fresh companies battled their way to Deegan, who by this time had been seriously wounded. Late in the afternoon the lead elements of 3/5 landed east of the fight, then headed west to link up with the embattled forces. After dark, 1/1 arrived at Nui Loc Son. Despite the darkness they immediately moved to the battle.

The fighting raged on into the next day. The Marines finally cleared Binh Son (1), then chased the fleeing NVA to the north. While in retreat the enemy was repeatedly pounded by accurate artillery fire and air strikes. The chase continued for several more days, but the enemy got away.

On 25 April, the 5th Marines took over the operation, permitting the 1st Marines to return to the Da Nang TAOR; Company F, 2/1, however, stayed at Nui Loc Son. The 5th Marines' units continued patrolling the area but found no major enemy formations. Despite this, Marine intelligence sources continued to report large numbers of the enemy in the area.

To force the enemy's hand, Col. Kenneth J. Houghton, commander of the 5th Marines, decided to send Lt. Col. Peter L. Hilgartner's 1/5 into the mountains north of Hiep Duc. For the first few days after the 1 May landing, enemy contact was light. Then, as the battalion continued west along the ridgeline, the contacts became more numerous and more intense.

In the meantime, while 1/5 struggled through the mountainous terrain, SLF Alpha, BLT 1/3, under Lt. Col. Peter A. Wickwire, entered the Que Son Valley and began a sweep northwest of Que Son village. They, too, found the enemy resistance increasing as they neared the mountains.

On 10 May, Hilgartner's Company C came under heavy fire from a well-entrenched enemy force as it moved up the southwestern slope of Hill 110, four kilometers north of Que Son. Though they took the hill, Company C then found itself pinned down by heavy machine-gun and rifle fire from a higher hill mass to the southeast. The company commander called for help.

Companies B and C, 1/3, were the closest available reinforcements. They immediately moved toward the fighting, but they hadn't proceeded very far through the thick vegetation before determined enemy fire stopped them. Artillery fire and air support couldn't help them, because the foes were too close. These two companies now called for help, but only a single platoon of Company A made it into a nearby LZ before heavy fire drove off the succeeding helicopters. Then a UH-34 went down, closing the LZ.

Lieutenant Colonel Hilgartner now ordered his Company A, operating about two kilometers to the east, to help the two 1/3 companies. As Company A, 1/5, neared the fight, it, too, came under heavy enemy fire. As the company commander was aggressively urging his men forward, four Marine F-4s dropped out of the sky. Mistaking Company A for the NVA, the jets fired. Eight rockets burst on the hillside, filling the air with jagged chunks of red-hot metal. Five Marines died and twenty-four were wounded. Company A wasn't going anywhere for the rest of the day.

As the only remaining unengaged unit, Hilgartner's command group and his Company D fought their way to a nearby hill overlooking the battle site from the southeast. The battalion mortar men immediately went to work dropping rounds onto the enemy's positions below them. At 1530, Company M, 3/5, landed at Hilgartner's position. Company D then pushed forward and finally linked up with Company C. Together, they drove the enemy to the northwest. The two companies from BLT 1/3 also pursued the NVA into the rugged hills but soon lost them.

After the fight 116 enemy dead were found; 33 Marines were killed and another 135 were wounded.

Though BLT 1/3 returned to SLF control on 12 May, the other three battalions—1/1, 1/5, and 3/5—remained in the AO. For the next five days the Marines stayed in nearly constant contact with the enemy. The generous use of artillery and air support killed dozens of enemy soldiers. The last significant contact occurred on 15 May when members of 1/5 stumbled on a sizable enemy bunker complex. After a heavy preparatory barrage of artillery fire, the Marines attacked. Resistance was light—most of the NVA had already fled.

On 16 May, 1/1 left the Que Son Valley to return to Da Nang. The next day Colonel Houghton officially closed down Operation Union. In all, the twenty-seven-day campaign had cost the Marines 110 dead and 473 wounded. A body count revealed 865 enemy dead.

Despite these massive losses, enemy activity in the Que Son Valley continued nearly unabated. Colonel Houghton decided to launch another operation with the local ARVN. The 1st Battalion, 5th Marines would establish blocking positions at the west end of the valley, while three ARVN ranger battalions advanced southwest from Thang Binh. Two battalions from the 6th ARVN Regiment would, in the meantime, sweep northwest from Tam Ky. In coordination with the others, 3/5 would helicopter into LZs in the southern portion of the AO and push northeast.

Operation Union II opened on the morning of 26 May when helicopters carried the Marines of 3/5 into LZ Eagle, about five kilometers east of Nui Loc Son. Intense enemy fire erupted almost as soon as the first helicopters appeared. In the opening minutes a CH-46 was shot down; it crashed alongside the LZ. L and M Companies, which landed safely, attacked north to relieve the pressure on the LZ. They quickly found themselves up against a well-entrenched enemy force. Using air strikes and artillery, the Marines finally overran the enemy positions, but the fighting lasted nearly all day. A total of 118 NVA bodies were found on the battlefield. The Marines lost 38 killed and 82 wounded, including a badly injured battalion commander.

After this, activity fell to occasional sporadic exchanges of rifle fire with distant enemy units. The four friendly forces maneuvered through their AOs as planned, finding few fresh signs of the enemy. With such poor results, the ARVN pulled out of the operation on 29 May.

Colonel Houghton, however, didn't give up so easily. He sent his two battalions to the southern edge of the valley. From there they would sweep to the northeast. On 30 May, 1/5 and 3/5 landed at LZs about eight kilometers southeast of Nui Loc Son. Light sniper fire harassed the two battalions as they pushed northeast. On 2 June, with 1/5 on the right, they swung left, proceeding northwest toward the site of the 26 May fight. The objective was Vinh Huy village, about a kilometer east of LZ Eagle.

Just before 0930 a force of two hundred NVA dug in to the east of Vinh Huy took the two lead companies of 3/5 under fire and halted their progress. Heavy fighting raged for the next four hours, but the resolute Marines persevered and finally overran the enemy.

While 3/5 fought, Lieutenant Colonel Hilgartner's 1/5 tried to flank the enemy to the right. Two of his companies, D and the attached Company F, 2/5, soon found themselves in serious trouble. While crossing an open rice paddy, automatic weapons fire from a bordering hedgerow raked the column. Pinned down by a deadly crossfire from the well-situated enemy machine guns, the Marines called for supporting fire. When the artillery barrage ended, Company F again started forward. Halfway to the hedgerow, bursts of deadly fire from two previously unseen NVA machine guns tore into the lead platoon. More than half a dozen men fell wounded or dying. The rest dropped behind the low paddy dikes, trapped. Taking the initiative, company commander Capt. James A. Graham quickly organized his small headquarters group into an assault team and, ignoring the bitter crossfire, boldly led his men in an attack on the enemy positions. He and his gallant squad wiped out one of the machine-gun nests, reducing the fire on the trapped men.

While the wounded were pulled to safety, the intrepid commander went after the second automatic weapon. Unsuccessful, and wounded twice, Graham ordered the rest of his group to pull back. He would stay behind to protect a young Marine too badly wounded to be moved. Graham's dying words on his radio were that twenty-five NVA were attacking him. Graham earned a posthumous Medal of Honor for his deliberate sacrifice.

With both his battalions heavily engaged, Colonel Houghton asked that the division reserve be released to him. The new commander, Maj. Gen. Donn J. Robertson, a World War II Navy Cross recipient who had just taken command of the division the previous day, sent 2/5 to Houghton. By 1900 two companies of fresh Marines were on the ground northeast of the enemy strongpoint. In darkness they moved toward the fight. They hadn't gone very far when they bumped into an NVA force fleeing north. The meeting engagement didn't last very long; both sides were eager to move on. Nonetheless, the Marines suffered twenty casualties fighting their way through the enemy.

This sudden appearance of reinforcements caused the remaining NVA to disengage and withdraw to the southeast. While artillery chased the fleeing NVA, the Marine battalions spent the rest of the night consolidating their positions and treating their wounded. Medevac helicopters took the most seriously wounded to hospitals that same night.

The next morning all three battalions policed the battle area. They counted 476 dead NVA. The Marines lost 71 killed and 139 wounded.

While the Marines gathered their dead, NVA working parties entered the area to collect their own dead. Advised of the unusual situation, Colonel Houghton declined to engage the enemy. For the rest of 3 June, in one of the more bizarre incidents of the war, the two foes worked side by side as they searched the tall grass for the bodies of their fallen comrades.

The day following the undeclared truce, the Marines went after the fleeing NVA but were unable to catch them. Two days later Houghton ended Operation Union II. His Marines had thwarted the enemy's efforts to strengthen their hold on the important valley, but everyone knew that the NVA wouldn't give up easily.

During the rest of the summer the allied units intensified their efforts against NVA infiltration into the Que Son Valley. With two battalions of the 5th Marines operating on a more-or-less permanent basis in the valley, and with the pressure applied by Task Force Oregon to the south, the enemy pulled back into the surrounding mountains.

Thirty kilometers to the north, guerrilla activities kept the 1st and 7th Marines occupied around Da Nang. In mid-July the enemy moved 122mm rockets into firing positions around the city. On the night of 14 July, 50 of these high-trajectory, 12,000-meter-range, high-explosive rockets slammed into the Da Nang airfield. Though the response was swift, the damage was done. Eight Americans died and 176 were wounded. The rocket attack also destroyed 13 barracks and 10 aircraft and damaged 40 other aircraft.

The 1st Marine Division immediately extended its protective cordon, the "Rocket Belt," around Da Nang from eight kilometers to twelve. Daily patrols fanned out in all directions. More often than not the Marines found only booby traps and mines. The rocket attacks continued. It was a very frustrating way to fight a war.

In late July word reached III MAF that the 3d NVA Regiment and the 1st VC Regiment had entered the Que Son Valley east of Hiep Duc. On 9 August, General Robertson authorized TF X-ray to begin Operation Cochise to throw them out. The new assistant division commander, Brig. Gen. Foster C. LaHue, would control the 1st and 3d Battalions of the 5th Marines, and BLT 1/3 from the SLF, as the maneuver elements of TF X-ray.

On the morning of 11 August, 1/5 and 3/5 helicoptered into LZs south of Nui Loc Son, while BLT 1/3 took up blocking positions several kilometers to the east. Over the next three days there were frequent encounters with small bands of VC as the two maneuver battalions swept east. Twice on the night of 16 August the enemy attacked 1/3's defensive perimeter. With the help of accurate artillery fire, the grunts easily repulsed the enemy.

As planned, phase one of the operation ended on 18 August, and 3/5 was pulled out of the AO. The two remaining battalions were helicoptered to Hiep Duc; from there they moved northeast toward Que Son. Though intelligence had reported a sizable enemy force operating in that area, the Marines never found them. Operation Cochise officially ended on 28 August.

Though this operation forced a major portion of the 2d NVA Division to abandon the Que Son Valley, III MAF had no illusions that this was only temporary. The NVA would not easily relinquish the densely populated, rice-rich region.

In fact, with South Vietnam's national elections scheduled for early September, the NVA planned to return to the Que Son Valley and disrupt the voting. The Marines reacted by stepping up their patrol activity. One of these patrols ended in an action that led to some of the heaviest fighting of the year for the 1st Marine Division.

Operation Swift

On 4 September, the day after election day, Company D, 1/5, was attacked at its night defensive position near Dong Son (1), about twelve kilometers southwest of Thang Binh. Just before dawn, small arms fire and mortars raked the Marines from positions less than one hundred meters away. A UH-1E gunship soon arrived to help, but the enemy still succeeded in breaching the western end of the

perimeter. Company commander Capt. Robert F. Morgan led a reaction force that drove the intruders out of his NDP, but he died in
the effort. The executive officer then took command and called for
air strikes as soon as light permitted. He also asked for reinforcements. Lieutenant Colonel Hilgartner ordered his Company B to assist Company D.

As Company B neared the battle site at about 0830, they were
struck by strong fire from NVA in Dong Son (1), nestled in a bend
of the Ly Ly River just west of Company D's NDP. Captain Thomas
D. Reese asked for a load of tear gas to be dropped on the village.
A short time later, a Huey dropped four hundred pounds of the irritant on the enemy. The NVA broke and fled north across the river.
Reese's men killed more than two dozen of the fleeing North Vietnamese. Company B then secured the eastern end of Dong Son (1).

At about this time, 3/5 received orders to release two of its companies to 1/5. By 1300 Companies K and M, 3/5, had joined up with
Hilgartner's command group four kilometers east of Dong Son (1)
at Chau Lam (1). While this relief force assembled, Companies B and
D cleared the west end of Dong Son (1) of the few remaining NVA,
then dug in.

Lieutenant Colonel Hilgartner then started moving his troops toward Dong Son (1). Company K took the lead, followed by Hilgartner and his command group, while Company M protected the rear.
As the column headed west they found numerous signs indicating
the presence of a large body of enemy. Anticipating a fight, Hilgartner immediately ordered Company M to move up on the right,
abreast of Company K. As they crossed a wide, open rice paddy, the
enemy cut loose.

Heavy small arms and automatic weapons fire erupted from a
large NVA force deployed in an L-shaped ambush. Company M's 1st
Platoon was hit hard. Within minutes it was pinned down in the rice
paddy. The company commander, 1st Lt. John D. Murray, sent his
2d Platoon to their aid. As the Marines crossed over a small knoll, a
full company of well-entrenched NVA attacked them. While the 2d
Platoon fought for its life, the 1st Platoon managed to pull back and
take up positions with the rest of the company at the top of the knoll.
The bold NVA quickly surrounded the beleaguered company. Within

minutes the first of more than two hundred deadly mortar rounds started pounding the grunts. Murray ordered tear gas dropped on the enemy, hoping it would allow his 2d Platoon to break loose. Unfortunately, the gas drifted back over the Marines. Few of them carried gas masks, so they suffered as much as the NVA.

When the gas cleared, the NVA again attacked the isolated platoon. Ignored the charging enemy, Sgt. Lawrence D. Peters stood in the open and pointed out targets to his squad. Even after being badly wounded in the leg, Peters continued to lead his men in repulsing the attackers until he was mortally wounded later that evening.

During the earlier march from the LZ, the 3d Battalion's chaplain, navy Lieutenant Vincent R. Capadonno, had moved with Company M. When the fighting started, Capadonno rushed across the bullet-swept knoll to the 2d Platoon. During the course of the afternoon, the chaplain repeatedly braved the enemy fire to give aid to wounded Marines. Several times he left the 2d Platoon's perimeter to carry seriously wounded men uphill to Company M's main position. Even after being wounded himself, Capadonno refused to give up. He continued to treat casualties, pray with the dying, and pull men to cover until he was cut down by a burst of enemy machine-gun fire.

Company K had a rough time of it, too. All afternoon and into the evening, they battled the dug-in NVA. Captain Joseph R. Tenny repeatedly led his company in brave attacks against the enemy but was unable to gain the upper hand. As night neared, Tenny was forced to pull back and set up positions around Hilgartner's command group.

As darkness fell, air strikes and supporting artillery pounded the enemy positions. A key enemy antiaircraft gun emplacement on nearby Hill 63 was finally silenced by a well-aimed bomb from a Marine A-6 Intruder. The loss of that weapon seemed to signal the end of the heavy fighting.

That night, UH-34 medevac helicopters carried out the wounded; other helicopters brought in much needed ammo supplies and the men of Company I, 3/5, as reinforcements. To the west, Company D, 1/1, and the 3/5 command group joined up with Companies B and D, 1/5. Unwilling to face the strengthened night defensive positions, the NVA pulled back.

After policing the battlefield on the morning of 5 September, the Marines counted 130 dead NVA soldiers. The Marines lost 54 killed and 104 wounded.

Operation Swift officially began that day as Col. Stanley Davis, now commanding the 5th Marines, ordered his 1st and 3d Battalions to pursue the NVA to the south. At midafternoon on 6 September, Company B, 1/5, came under heavy fire near Vinh Huy (3), which bordered the southern mountains. Within minutes the 3d Platoon was pinned down in a rice paddy, unable to move due to the extremely heavy automatic weapons fire coming from the NVA. Captain Reese sent his 2d Platoon on a flanking movement to the right, but enemy fire stopped it also. Reese next tried to maneuver his 1st Platoon farther to the right, but it, too, was soon stopped by the vicious enemy fire.

While the NVA concentrated on the 1st Platoon, the 3d Platoon withdrew from the open rice paddy. The enemy now turned their attention to the 2d Platoon. Boldly charging headlong across the open paddies, the NVA came at the trapped men from straight on and the right flank. One platoon member later said, "We looked up and saw many NVA in full uniforms, packs, and cartridge belts running across the rice paddy at us. We started shooting and we could see them falling, but they didn't stop and more and more of them kept coming. Nothing could stop them; it was like they were doped up."

With the enemy nearly on top of them, 2d Lt. John E. Bracken, the platoon leader, ordered a fifty-meter withdrawal to a shallow trench. The NVA pressed their attack. Soon they were within grenade range. One thudded down near Bracken and his command group. The platoon guide, Sgt. Rodney M. Davis, sacrificed his own life to save the others by covering the missile with his body as it exploded.

With more than a dozen dead and as many wounded, Bracken knew that he couldn't hold out much longer. He called for tear gas to cover his withdrawal back to the battalion's perimeter. The maneuver worked. Those men still on their feet carried the more seriously injured several hundred meters to safety. The platoon's dead remained on the battlefield. When the rest of Company B scurried into the perimeter, the battalion consolidated its position for the night and called for supporting fire. Even though artillery rounds were hitting within fifty meters of the battalion's lines and air strikes were dropping bombs just one hundred meters out, the NVA still managed to creep into the perimeter. The Marines hunted them down in the dark and killed them before they did any damage. Throughout the night the NVA punished the battalion with mortar and rocket fire. Not until early the next morning did they pull back into the mountains. The fight cost the battalion another thirty-five dead and ninety-two wounded.

While 1/5 was heavily engaged on the afternoon of 6 September, 3/5 fought its own battle about three kilometers to the east at Hill 43. After taking Hill 48 earlier that afternoon without any significant resistance, Lt. Col. Charles B. Webster ordered his Company I to occupy nearby Hill 43, about one kilometer to the southwest. As the lead platoon neared the base of the hill, the NVA unleashed AK-47s, which erupted with their distinctive popping. Displaying great gallantry, the grunts overran the enemy line. As they pressed onward, more enemy fire hit the line. Soon the entire company was under fire. By maneuvering his platoons, Capt. Francis M. Burke tried to flank the enemy, but no matter which way they turned, heavy automatic weapons fire ripped into them, forcing them to seek cover.

Lieutenant Colonel Webster rushed his Company K to assist Burke. The two companies joined up just before dark. After recovering a number of casualties that had been left forward of the company's front, the two units crawled back to a more defensible position. And a good thing they did: twice that night the determined NVA launched full-scale ground attacks, supported by heavy machine-gun fire. The second human wave assault broke through a weak spot in the perimeter. Only after furious hand-to-hand fighting were the North Vietnamese ejected. In a lull in the fighting just before midnight, Company M entered the perimeter. Even with these reinforcements, it took a dose of tear gas to finally halt the enemy. After that only a few enemy mortar rounds fell on the grunts. The Marines were so well dug in, however, that the explosives did no damage. A welcome dawn revealed 88 enemy bodies sprawled across the landscape. The battalion lost 34 killed and 109 wounded in the day's action.

The three days of heavy fighting had not only badly depleted the battalions but also demonstrated the incredible courage of individual Marines. Medals of Honor were posthumously awarded to Lieutenant Capadonno and Sergeants Peters and Davis. Five Navy Crosses, including one to Lieutenant Murray, were awarded for exceptional gallantry during the fighting.

More fighting erupted on 10 September when a platoon from Company H, 2/5 (opconned to 3/5), was decimated by an NVA company hidden in a small village two kilometers northeast of Vinh Huy (3). When the rest of the company moved to the platoon's aid, they, too, were hit hard by a devastating barrage of automatic weapons fire. Though reinforced by Company M, 3/5, the Marines didn't overcome the NVA defenders until air strikes dropped 250 pound bombs and tear gas canisters on the village. When the Marines searched the village ruins they found 40 dead NVA. Nine Marines were killed and another two dozen were wounded in the four-hour fight.

Operation Swift ended on 15 September, and once again the Marines had thrown the 2d NVA Division out of the Que Son Valley. Intelligence reports indicated that both the 1st VC and 3d NVA Regiments were chewed up and required extensive rebuilding. But, as before, the Marines knew that the NVA would return.

While the 1st Marine Division was engaged in the Que Son Valley, a major senior command change occurred. General Walt, commander of III MAF since its inception in 1965, turned over command to his deputy, Lt. Gen. Robert E. Cushman, Jr., on 1 June 1967. A Marine since his graduation from the Naval Academy in 1935, Cushman had survived the Japanese sneak attack on Pearl Harbor. Later, his personal gallantry during the ferocious battle for Guam earned him a Navy Cross.

Because of the heavy fighting in the Que Son Valley in September, and the continued pressure along the DMZ affecting the 3d Marine Division, General Cushman asked MACV for additional forces to help hold the line in southern I Corps. General Westmoreland agreed. Thus, on 4 October, the 3d Brigade, 1st Cavalry Division joined the Americal Division at Chu Lai, at which point the Americal Division assumed responsibility for all operations in the Que Son Valley. This freed the 5th Marines to move north to Hoi An, replacing the 1st Marines. This regiment then headed north to fight along the DMZ under the operational control of the 3d Marine Division.

The division's combat operations for the rest of 1967 were conducted primarily around Da Nang in a continuing effort to reduce rocket attacks on the important city. One of the major operations launched to accomplish this was Foster, beginning on 13 November. It was conceived after the VC viciously attacked a refugee settlement village just twenty kilometers south of Da Nang, killing and wounding more than one hundred civilians. Supported by BLT 2/3 from the Special Landing Force, the 3d Battalion, 7th Marines landed by helicopter west of An Hoa at 0900 that day. On the subsequent area sweep the riflemen had numerous contacts with small bands of fleeing VC. The ground forces also found many supply caches and bunkers. By the time Operation Foster ended on 30 November, the Marines had destroyed thousands of bunkers, tunnels, and shelters and captured nearly ninety tons of rice.

In retaliation for these efforts, the local VC intensified their terrorist activities against the local populace, particularly against refugee camps. The attacks, instead of rallying the people to the Viet Cong's side, had the opposite effect of strengthening the government's hand. To maintain the peasants' loyalties, all the allies had to do was successfully implement the government's pacification programs. That, however, would prove to be a tough, unappreciated, unrewarding, and deadly task.

3d Marine Division

As 1967 began, Operation Prairie was still in effect in Quang Tri Province. To protect the province against any invading NVA, Brig. Gen. Michael P. Ryan, commander, 3d Marine Division (Forward) and assistant division commander, had six infantry battalions, two recon companies, and a variety of supporting units. The major bases from which these units operated began on the east at Gio Linh, ten kilometers inland from the South China Sea and just below the DMZ. Fifteen kilometers southwest sat Con Thien. Twenty kilometers south of Gio Linh was Dong Ha, the province's largest combat base and the command post for the 3d Marine Division (Forward). Cam Lo was located ten kilometers west of Dong Ha on Route 9. The 12th

Marines' artillery pieces, along with a battery of U.S. Army 175mm guns, occupied Camp Carroll, seven kilometers farther west on Route 9. An intermediate base was at the Rockpile, another ten kilometers west. The last, and most westerly, of the Marines' combat bases in Quang Tri Province was Khe Sanh, just a few kilometers east of the Laotian border.

The NVA avoided major ground combat during January. However, they did harass allied positions with frequent mortar and rocket attacks.

Operations Prairie II and III

For administrative reasons General Ryan closed down Operation Prairie on 31 January. Operation Prairie II, with an identical mission, began the next day. The same low level of enemy contact persisted during the first few weeks of the new operation. Then, reconnaissance activity and intelligence sources revealed that the NVA had used the lull, and the Tet Truce of 8–12 February, to significantly increase their presence along both sides of the Ben Hai River, which bisected the DMZ. (Tet, the Buddhist festival welcoming the lunar new year, is the most highly regarded of all Vietnamese holidays and is celebrated enthusiastically by all factions of Vietnamese society.)

To counter this new threat, General Ryan requested permission to fire artillery into and north of the DMZ. This was no simple tactical decision. The political realities of the war had prevented any previous allied violation of the DMZ. As a result, enemy troops used the zone as a sanctuary. Keenly aware of the ramifications of an approval, General Cushman passed the request to MACV. From there it traveled up the chain of command all the way to the White House. Permission was granted on 25 February. Over the next two days Marine artillery units dropped thousands of rounds into the previous inviolate DMZ. The NVA were on notice that they could no longer consider the area a safe haven.

The enemy didn't take this change lying down. On 27 February, heavy NVA mortar, artillery, and rocket fire started blasting both Con Thien and Gio Linh. The latter was particularly hard hit. More than four hundred high-explosive shells slammed into the base in just one seventeen-minute period on the twenty-eighth.

While these bases were being hit, on the morning of 27 February a recon team from the 3d Marines, operating about five kilometers northwest of Cam Lo, tangled with the lead elements of what turned out to be an NVA regiment. Colonel John P. Lanigan, the 3d Marines' commander, dispatched Company L, 3/4, and a platoon of tanks to help. Within a short time the company commander reported that he was bogged down in rugged terrain. Thick brush as high as twelve feet blocked his route.

Lanigan was hard pressed for additional troops. His 3d Battalion was heavily involved in an operation west of the Rockpile. His 2d Battalion, commanded by Lt. Col. Victor Ohanesian, was in the process of rotating back to Okinawa. Only Company G, a part of Company F, and a portion of the battalion command group were left at Camp Carroll; the rest of the 2d Battalion was already aboard ship. The replacement battalion, 3/9, was not in any position to mount a relief of the recon team. Lanigan had no choice: he ordered Capt. Carl E. Bockewitz to take his Company G to help the recon team.

Despite the fact that Bockewitz had had a premonition that very morning that he would not survive another operation, he obediently led his Marines out of Camp Carroll. Because rough terrain and falling darkness greatly hampered its movement, Company G did not reach the beleaguered recon team until just before midnight. Bockewitz set up an NDP, treated the wounded, and called for a protective curtain of artillery fire around his position.

In the meantime, Company L, 3/4, had been attacked by a strong enemy force. Close-quarters fighting raged most of the afternoon. Finally, the massive firepower of the accompanying tanks broke the enemy's resolve and allowed the company to proceed. A short distance farther, one of the tanks threw a track. It couldn't be repaired. Unwilling to abandon the vehicle, Colonel Lanigan ordered Company L to dig in around it for the night.

The next morning Lanigan decided to commit the rest of the available elements of 2/3 to the relief effort. Lieutenant Colonel Ohanesian planned to first link up with his Company G, then attack to the east, driving any NVA into the waiting Company L. However, after Company L was hit by a 150-round mortar attack followed by three determined ground attacks beginning at 0630 that morning, Colonel Lanigan ordered Ohanesian to head for them first.

Ohanesian reached Company L at 1030. He immediately led an attack on the nearby high ground. The fighting raged for more than an hour, but the Marines persevered and finally threw the NVA off the hill. The battalion operations officer, Maj. Robert F. Sheridan, who fought in the battle, was shocked at the large number of well-equipped NVA soldiers encountered by the Marines during this maneuver. "In my year in Vietnam I had never seen this number of NVA troops in the open," he said later.

At the same time that he sent Ohanesian on his way, Colonel Lanigan ordered Company G, and the recon Marines, to occupy Hill 124, about two kilometers to their east and about the same distance west of Ohanesian. The hill, which was the commanding terrain feature in the area, overlooked the enemy's likely route of withdrawal back to the DMZ. But the NVA were already waiting. As Company G ascended the hill at about 1030, well-concealed NVA on both flanks unleashed a deadly blast of small arms and automatic weapons fire. In the brutal six-hour firefight that followed, seven Marines, including Captain Bockewitz, were killed and eighteen more were wounded. Not until late that afternoon, and then only with the help of the supporting artillery fire, could Company G pull back to safety.

Anxious to extricate his embattled rifle companies, Colonel Lanigan ordered Company M, 3/4, to rescue Company G. By midafternoon on 28 February, the fresh Marines had landed by helicopter on Hill 162, to the north of Hill 124. They immediately headed south. To their surprise they met only light resistance on the way.

At 1430, Ohanesian's command group, with the two platoons of Company F, headed toward Company G, too. Company L, 3/4, and the tanks remained behind. It wasn't easy to leave the security of the perimeter. The threat of enemy contact hung heavily in the air. Major Sheridan recalled that the men knew "full well we were walking into a hornets' nest. We knew we were outmanned and outgunned. One could almost smell the enemy."

The Company F platoons led the way for Ohanesian's group. The terrain that the Marines traversed was covered with thick brush, confining them to a narrow trail. The last man in the column hadn't even left the perimeter when the enemy opened up. One moment it was dead silent; the next moment, automatic weapons fire cut into the column from the front and both flanks. Then, enemy mortar shells walked up and down the trail. Hand grenades thrown by enemy soldiers concealed in the brush fell on the Marines. Unable to disperse his troops or gain fire superiority, Ohanesian ordered a withdrawal.

As the troops inched their way backward, firing into the brush at the unseen enemy, an enemy grenade plopped down in the middle of a group of tightly packed men. Private First Class James Anderson reached out, scooped up the device, and curled around it. The explosion killed him, but the other Marines survived. Anderson would receive the Medal of Honor posthumously.

Burdened with more than one hundred casualties, moving back to Company L's position was a major task for the column. According to Major Sheridan, "All radios had been hit and casualties continued to mount. Moving the dead and wounded out of the killing zone required feats of bravery beyond comprehension. Lieutenant Colonel Ohanesian was carrying the last of the wounded toward the perimeter when an explosion mortally wounded him, three other Marines, and myself. None of us could walk, and others had to leave the relative safety of their holes to come get us."

Major Sheridan, despite his painful wounds, took command of the shattered remnants of the battalion command group and the Company F platoons. Directing a fighting withdrawal, he got the column back to the perimeter still held by Company L and the tanks. Marauding NVA instantly closed to within twenty meters of the perimeter, attacking with small arms and grenades. Sheridan called for medevac helicopters for the more than one hundred wounded. They arrived a short time later, only to be driven off by strong enemy fire. The casualties would have to spend an agonizing night in the field. Despite artillery fire and air strikes, the close-quarters fighting persisted throughout the night.

When he was told that Ohanesian was down, Colonel Lanigan dispatched his executive officer, Lt. Col. Earl R. DeLong, to take over command of 2/3. Unable to reach his new command by helicopter due to the intense enemy fire, DeLong instead joined Company F, 2/9, heading out from Cam Lo on foot to reinforce the embattled battalion. Not until 0340 on 1 March, did DeLong reach his new command's perimeter. With the reinforcements' arrival, the NVA began pulling out.

About noon that day Company G, 2/3, and Company M, 3/4, arrived on the scene, too. These companies swept the nearby area, but the NVA were long gone. That afternoon the survivors of 2/3 headed to Cam Lo to continue their journey to Okinawa.

That same day, Colonel Lanigan dispatched two additional battalions, 1/9 and 3/3, to pursue the NVA. The retreating enemy eluded the Marines until 3 March, when an aerial observer sighted three large groups of NVA moving toward the DMZ carrying bodies. Massive air strikes and artillery were ordered. A follow-up sweep by 1/9 the next day found more than two hundred dead NVA scattered across the ground.

On 18 March, following a series of battalion sweeps between Cam Lo and Con Thien, Operation Prairie II ended. The sweeps uncovered a number of mass graves and several supply caches, but it was obvious that the enemy had abandoned the area. Enemy casualties were placed at 694 killed. The operation cost the Marines 93 dead and 483 wounded.

Colonel Lanigan started Operation Prairie III immediately after Prairie II ended. Though the NVA's offensive efforts had been blunted, III MAF knew it was only temporary. In anticipation of their return, III MAF authorized retention of five infantry battalions and four artillery battalions in the Prairie III area. Despite vigorous patrols by the rifle companies, enemy contact was light during the first few weeks of the new operation. Enemy offensive action consisted of mortars, artillery, and rocket attacks on both Gio Linh and Con Thien.

Though not specifically a part of the Prairie series of operations, a significant achievement occurred on 19 March: Route 9 was opened all the way to Khe Sanh. The 11th Engineer Battalion had labored for months against mines, bad weather, and enemy ambushes to complete the formidable task. This new ability to resupply the distant combat base by truck rather than by air greatly reduced the logistical burden on the supply depot at Dong Ha.

Ground action in Quang Tri Province picked up on 24 March. That day, 1/9 stumbled on an NVA battalion in well-prepared defensive positions southeast of Con Thien. Several hours of heavy fighting, including air and artillery strikes, ensued before the enemy pulled out. The Marines pursued the enemy force, encountering frequent sniper fire and harassing mortar fire, but the NVA slipped away. Two days later, 1/9 was relieved by 3/9. The new battalion was to conduct night ambushes in the area just north of Cam Lo.

During their first two days in the field, the fresh Marines saw no enemy soldiers. Then, on the night of 30 March, Company I, 3/9, was busy establishing night ambush positions around Hill 70, about ten kilometers northwest of Cam Lo. Without warning, deadly NVA mortar shells dropped out of the night sky, pounding the 2d Platoon and the company command group atop Hill 70. As the Marines dove for cover to escape the flesh-ripping chunks of jagged metal, at least a full company of heavily armed NVA swarmed out of the surrounding jungle. As the enemy soldiers neared his position, Capt. Michael P. Getlin frantically called for supporting fire. From their bases kilometers away, the artillerymen responded with precision. The exploding howitzer shells drove off the attackers. Both the 1st and 3d Platoons then tried to reach their buddies, but the enemy stopped them with perfectly placed automatic weapons fire.

Suddenly, the NVA poured out of the jungle a second time. Within minutes they had swarmed over the company. Desperate hand-to-hand battles raged across the dark hillside. Second Lieutenant John P. Bobo, the Weapons Platoon commander, lost his right leg when an enemy mortar round erupted at his feet. First Sergeant Raymond G. Rogers fought his way to Bobo through the swarming enemy, patched him up, and, at the lieutenant's request, propped him up in a firing position. The gallant Bobo kept blazing away at the NVA until they killed him as they ran through his position.

When Rogers learned that Captain Getlin and the executive officer were dead, he took command of the remnants of the company. He managed to make contact with a Huey helicopter flying in the area. Rogers directed the helicopter's gunfire on the enemy, but still they kept coming. Although seriously wounded, Rogers established a last-ditch defensive position with six other wounded men. From there they held off the swarming NVA until artillery fire and the Huey's gunfire finally broke the attack.

When reinforcements reached Company I the next day, sixty-seven NVA bodies were found in the area. Sixteen Marines were killed and forty-seven were wounded in this bitter fight. Lieutenant

Bobo received a posthumous Medal of Honor for his heroic action, and Captain Getlin was awarded a posthumous Navy Cross for his bravery. First Sergeant Rogers survived his wounds to wear his Navy Cross.

Operation Prairie III ended on 19 April. The very next day, Operation Prairie IV began in the same place with the same units. During this period, the 9th Marines were able to deploy north to Dong Ha from Da Nang because Task Force Oregon had assumed control of I Corps' southern two provinces. This realignment of forces was designed to give III MAF more maneuverability and flexibility in dealing with the NVA's threats across the DMZ. Unfortunately, it didn't turn out that way.

The McNamara Line

Defense Secretary Robert S. McNamara was as much the architect of the Vietnam War as any other single man. One of the Pentagon's original "Whiz Kids" from the World War II era, McNamara had built a successful business career after the war, culminating with his selection as president of the Ford Motor Company in 1960. A few months later, President-elect John F. Kennedy tapped him to be his secretary of defense.

McNamara's rise to power was based primarily on his unwavering adherence to the philosophy of quantitative analysis. This discipline reduced any problem, tangible or intangible, to numerical factors that could then be dissected, studied, and manipulated to arrive at a quantitative solution. In McNamara's world, no mundane human emotions such as caring or suffering could stand in the way of numbers.

Once he became secretary of defense, McNamara immediately imposed his management techniques on the military. Quantitative analysis did allow the military to make many significant improvements in its management practices. However, it also dehumanized these decisions. McNamara's techniques eventually resulted in many statistical reports being used in the Vietnam War—reports that came to symbolize the frustration of the war. Among these were the body count, kill ratios, battalion days in the field, and other figures that measured success of the various pacification programs. Though many subordinates chafed under McNamara's use of statistics to the exclusion of all other factors, Harvard Business School–trained General Westmoreland quickly became an enthusiastic advocate of the technique.

Thus, in early 1966, when McNamara first suggested a mine and wire barrier stretching all across northern South Vietnam, he found a willing disciple in General Westmoreland. Even though Westmoreland's superior, Admiral Sharp, strongly opposed the barrier because of the probable logistical problems involved in its construction and the large number of troops that would be needed to construct and defend the system, Westmoreland supported it. When this idea eventually foundered, Westmoreland came up with his own. Rather than a fence, he proposed a cleared strip of ground supported by strongpoints spaced along its length. Key terrain would be organized behind the barrier. Observation points and frequent patrols would spot any enemy crossing the open ground. Reaction forces ready to respond to any breach of the barrier would be stationed at combat bases behind the barrier. In late 1966, General Westmoreland ordered III MAF to develop plans to create such a barrier. General Walt turned over the task to General Kyle. Walt's only instruction to his subordinate was that he wanted Kyle's report to state that the barrier concept was not supported by the Marines.

General Kyle complied, stating in his report that a "mobile defense," as currently practiced by III MAF units, "would, in itself, provide an effective block to infiltration." In forwarding the study to MACV, General Walt clearly stated his views in his endorsement by emphatically noting that such a barrier "was not going to be worth the time and effort that would be put into it."

Nonetheless, on 26 November 1966, General Westmoreland forwarded to Washington his own report supporting the barrier. As recommended by MACV, the barrier would sit just south of the DMZ and extend inland from the coast for about thirty kilometers. It would be six hundred to one thousand meters wide, containing watchtowers, electronic sensors, minefields, and wire obstacles, all backed by a series of strongpoints. From the end of this barrier all the way to the Laotian border, the McNamara Line would then consist of roughly twenty defile barriers, each about a kilometer long and consisting of a minefield and wire obstacles stretching across the route blocked by the barrier.

Secretary McNamara approved this plan on 19 December 1966. He further directed that procurement of the necessary materials commence immediately. He wanted at least the eastern portion of the barrier operational by 1 November 1967. The MACV began plans to implement McNamara's directive.

The Marines and Admiral Sharp continued to voice their opposition to what was now officially called the Strongpoint Obstacle System (SPOS). In a January 1967 briefing by the 3d Marine Division, senior staff Undersecretary of the Navy Robert H. B. Baldwin was told point-blank, "We are not enthusiastic about the barrier . . ." Admiral Sharp, in a 6 February 1967 message to the Joint Chiefs of Staff, stated, "There is no indication that present operations are inadequate to cope with what has been an insignificant infiltration problem in this particular area."

Still, the barrier plan progressed as desired by McNamara and Westmoreland. By early April, the clearing of a two-hundred-meter-wide trace between Con Thien and Gio Linh had begun. When that task was completed a month later, the Marines' 11th Engineer Battalion started work to clear a five-hundred-meter perimeter around both bases. After that, the engineers would go back and widen the original trace to six hundred meters and extend it eastward from Gio Linh into the coastal floodplain. Protecting the engineers while they worked required two full Marine infantry battalions.

In June, III MAF published an operational plan outlining the SPOS concept. According to this plan, the system would be jointly manned by one U.S. regiment and one ARVN regiment. The forces would be disposed at six strongpoints, A-1 to A-6, and four battalion base areas, C-1 to C-4. Marines would be responsible for strongpoints A-3 to A-6 and base areas C-2 and C-3. An additional Marine battalion would be based at Dong Ha to serve as a reaction force.

By late summer, enemy pressure was putting a tremendous strain on the Marines involved in the SPOS. The four infantry battalions and the engineers, artillerymen, and supporting units were unable to both defend their front and construct the SPOS. It was at this point that General Cushman asked for more help. The MACV responded by ordering the 3d Brigade, 1st Cavalry Division to southern I Corps.

General Cushman told General Westmoreland that this addition would permit him to assign nine Marine infantry battalions to the SPOS. Seven battalions would support the project through protective combat roles while the other two, plus an engineer battalion, would actually build the barrier.

On 7 September, MACV asked III MAF to estimate the number of casualties expected during the building of the SPOS. Three days later III MAF estimated that in the next 30 days casualties among the troops engaged in the SPOS would be 672 dead and 3,788 wounded. As a result of this grim analysis, Westmoreland authorized a modification of the system. Construction of the obstacles would temporarily cease until the strongpoints were finished and the local tactical situation had stabilized.

Despite these concessions to the monumental task facing the Marines, progress slowed further due to heavy monsoon rains in September and October. Resources had to be temporarily diverted from the SPOS in order to keep the region's supply roads passable, a herculean effort in itself.

Even knowing of this problem and the constant headaches involved in getting timely delivery of critical construction material, General Westmoreland was still not pleased with the rate of progress on the SPOS. On 22 October, he told General Cushman that he not only found the project's construction quality to be substandard, but he didn't think that III MAF had given it the priority he felt it deserved. Further, he didn't think that the SPOS project had been properly managed. He ordered Cushman to immediately correct these deficiencies and begin better quality control.

In response, General Cushman appointed his deputy III MAF commander, Maj. Gen. Raymond L. Murray, a distinguished and highly decorated combat veteran of World War II and Korea, to head a permanent SPOS (now code-named Dye Marker) staff. Further, General Cushman advised all subordinate commands that Dye Marker was now second in importance only to emergency combat requirements. He also shifted another regiment into the area to meet increased tactical demands.

The added impetus paid off. On 10 December, Cushman was at last able to report significant progress to MACV. Bunker sites at A-4, C-2, and C-4 were done. Most of the work at the other sites was nearing completion, too. Construction had started at the combat base at Ca Lu, south of the Rockpile, and ongoing combat operations were clearing the area around A-3. The South Vietnamese were proceeding a little slower on A-1 and C-1 but were doing better.

By the end of the year all of the strongpoints and the base areas were done except A-3 and C-3, which were 70 percent complete. McNamara's Line had consumed more than three quarters of a million man days. Heavy equipment losses as a result of enemy action amounted to more than $1 million. Casualties directly attributable to the construction of the barrier were not calculated. It was expensive in every regard, and unwanted by those charged with its construction and defense, but the secretary of defense at last had his barrier.

When Operation Prairie IV began on 20 April, it was to have been a two-regiment search and destroy operation covering the same ground as the earlier Prairie operations. The new operation had barely begun when increased enemy activity changed this plan.

Besides repeatedly cutting the recently opened Route 9 in the wild country west of Cam Lo, the NVA poured rocket, mortar, and artillery fire on Gio Linh, Camp Carroll, and Dong Ha. On 8 May, the NVA launched a major ground attack on Con Thien.

Con Thien sat on a 158-meter-high hill in the middle of a red mud plain twelve kilometers north of Cam Lo and less than four kilometers from the southern edge of the DMZ. The combat base not only overlooked the DMZ but provided an unobstructed view of Dong Ha, sixteen kilometers to the southeast. This strongpoint was a vital link in the SPOS.

A battalion command group, an ARVN Civilian Irregular Defense Group (CIDG) unit, and Companies A and D, 1/4, occupied Con Thien on 7 May. They were there to provide security to the engineers working on the nearby sections of the SPOS. All had been quiet until 0255 on 8 May. At that time a green flare suddenly lit the sky south of the hill. Seconds later, the first of more than three hundred rounds of high-explosive artillery shells slammed into the base. Under the cover of this devastating barrage, two NVA battalions crept forward. At 0400, as soon as the shelling ceased, they attacked. Using automatic weapons, rocket-propelled grenades (RPGs), and flamethrowers, the determined enemy soldiers quickly breached the defensive wire in front of Company D. In the eerie light of bursting flares, the embattled Marines fought hand to hand with the intruders.

To help Company D, Company A dispatched a platoon fortified with two amphibious vehicles, a pair of jeeps, and a Duster, an army vehicle mounting twin 40mm cannons. An NVA ambush easily destroyed the Duster, one of the amphibious tractors (the other became entangled in barbed wire), and both jeeps with RPGs. Despite losing its support, the relief platoon fought through the ambush and made its way to Company D. With these new men, Company D finally threw out the enemy. By 0900 the fight was over. The attack resulted in 44 Marine dead and 110 wounded. The NVA left nearly 200 of their dead at Con Thien.

Following this attack, enemy activity increased dramatically in what the Marines were now calling "Leatherneck Square," the area cornered by Con Thien, Gio Linh, Dong Ha, and Cam Lo. The bases were bombarded daily. The 1st Battalion, 9th Marines fought a large enemy force just south of Con Thien between 13 and 16 May. Only the liberal use of supporting arms finally forced the NVA to retreat into the safety of the DMZ.

The earlier frustrations that the Marines experienced as a result of the political restrictions prohibiting them from pursuing the marauding NVA into the DMZ finally ended after this attack on Con Thien. That same day, MACV authorized III MAF to conduct ground operations in the southern half of the DMZ.

General Walt wasted no time in putting together a joint USMC/ARVN operation to exploit this new freedom. Essentially, his plan called for ground attacks into the DMZ by the 3d Marine Division and 1st ARVN Division along parallel tracks, as far north as the Ben Hai River. At the same time, SLF Alpha, BLT 1/3, would make a supporting amphibious landing in the southern portion of the DMZ just below the mouth of the river. Once all involved units reached the river, they would turn around, attack to the south on a broad front, and destroy all the enemy found between the DMZ and Route 9. A secondary objective of the sweep would be to remove any civilians found in the area who would impede the SPOS. Their removal would create a huge free-fire zone. The SLF portion of the campaign was designated Beau Charger. The ARVN called their sweep operation Lam Son 54. Operation Hickory was the code name for the 3d Marine Division's operation.

Operation Hickory

The Beau Charger portion of the combined operation began early on 18 May. Fifteen UH-34s loaded with men from Company A, 1/3, lifted off the deck of the USS *Okinawa* and headed inland. At 0800 they arrived at LZ Goose, which sat within small arms range of the north bank of the Ben Hai. As the first helicopter touched down, enemy machine-gun fire raked its entire length, killing one infantryman, wounding three crew members and three infantrymen, and destroying the craft's radios. Four other troop-carrying aircraft and two UH-1 gunships were also hit, but the entire wave got into the LZ. Within minutes the 2d Platoon was spread out around LZ Goose. Based on the pilots' reports, subsequent landings were diverted to LZ Owl, about eight hundred meters to the south.

About this time, Company D successfully completed their amphibious landing. Ninety minutes later Company B came ashore. Both of these companies, plus the rest of Company A, then double-timed toward LZ Goose, where the fighting still raged. Even after the forces linked up, the enemy wouldn't quit. Company A sent one of its platoons on a wide flanking maneuver around a tree line in an attempt to break the enemy's defenses. They were surprised by an NVA ambush. Only after a furious hand-to-hand fight were the grunts able to pull back to their perimeter. The skillful employment of gunships and air strikes eventually forced the NVA to retreat, leaving sixty-seven of their comrades dead on the battlefield.

Operation Hickory also began at 0800 on 18 May as Marines from 2/26 and 2/9, supported by tanks and ONTOs (tracked vehicles each mounting six 106mm recoilless rifles), headed north from Con Thien. At the same time, CH-46 Sea Knight helicopters carried 3/4 northwest of Con Thien into an LZ actually within the DMZ. These Marines would act not only as a blocking force to prevent any NVA from escaping to the north, but also to prevent any enemy reinforcements from heading south.

Within three hours of jumping off, the lead elements of 2/26 made contact with what ultimately turned out to be two battalions of well-dug-in NVA. The fight developed quickly as more Marines pressed forward. Within minutes the air was filled with the pop-pop of rifles, the staccato report of machine guns, the heavy booms of the tank cannons and recoilless rifles, and the sharp explosions of mortar rounds. From their deep, well-prepared bunkers, the NVA poured a veritable hail of lead on the Marines. The battalion commander and his operations officer were wounded and evacuated. Soon, the attack ground to a halt as the riflemen sought cover.

Late that afternoon, 2/9 maneuvered forward on 2/26's right flank, hoping to overrun the enemy. It didn't work. Heavy enemy fire forced them to a halt, too. With no hope of breaking the enemy's resistance, the Marines pulled back, bringing their 5 dead and 142 wounded with them.

Throughout the night 75 radar-controlled air strikes blasted the NVA's positions. Starting at 0500 the next day, an intense artillery barrage pounded the enemy defenses. At 0700 the infantry started forward in the attack. Once again the supporting arms had done a masterful job: 2/26 had overrun the enemy line by 1030. Only 34 enemy dead and 9 wounded were found. After policing the battlefield, the two battalions continued north against sporadic resistance.

In the meantime, 3/4 headed southeast from its LZ, hoping to trap any NVA fleeing from its sister battalions. Though they experienced only light contact, they did find several enemy supply caches filled with vast quantities of rice and ammo, all of which was destroyed in place.

The next two days of Operation Hickory passed quietly. Then, on 20 May, Company K, 3/9, working as a screening force to the southwest of the main forces, found the enemy emplaced in mutually supporting bunkers in a jungle-covered draw. The NVA fired first, pouring a steady stream of automatic weapons fire into the advancing troops. Because of the terrain Company K could not maneuver to get an advantage over the foe. Company L pushed forward to help them, but they, too, found they couldn't advance under the blistering NVA fire. Both companies dug in for the night, one on each side of the draw. Friendly artillery pounded the enemy throughout the night.

The next morning Company M linked up with its two sister companies and took the lead in the renewed attack. Together, the three rifle companies finally cleared the area. Only thirty-one dead NVA were found. The Marines lost twenty-six killed and fifty-nine wounded in the action.

That same day, SLF Bravo, BLT 2/3, joined the Hickory forces, landing by helicopter northwest of Gio Linh. They swept north, reaching the south bank of the Ben Hai River by midday on 22 May. Two days later the battalion turned south. It met no resistance during its movement but did uncover two extensive bunker complexes, including one made with steel-reinforced walls. The bunkers were filled with supplies; one contained more than one thousand 60mm mortar rounds.

Two other battalions, 3/4 and 2/26, swept the DMZ to the southwest, toward the mountains west of Con Thien. At the same time the 3d Battalion, 9th Marines moved northwest, sweeping through the DMZ. To the east the other Operation Hickory battalions resumed search and destroy operations south of the DMZ in Leatherneck Square.

The last major contact in Operation Hickory came on 25 May at Hill 117, about five kilometers west of Con Thien. Early that morning, Company H, 2/26, was hit by a blistering barrage of small arms fire from two enemy companies occupying mutually supporting bunkers. The fighting raged at close quarters for more than an hour before the company could pull back, evacuate casualties, and call in supporting fire. While the jets and artillery bombarded the hill, Company H maneuvered to the north. There it linked up with Company K, 3/4 (opconned to 2/26). Both companies then attacked the hill but were soon pinned down by a vicious hail of fire. Unable to maneuver, the two battered companies set in for the night, protected by a constant barrage of artillery shells ringing them and pounding the NVA positions. The day's losses were fourteen Marines killed and ninety-two wounded.

Early the next morning while reconning the area, the UH-1E helicopter containing the battalion commander, his executive officer, and the two company commanders was shot down. All four were wounded, but only the battalion commander and the commander of Company K had to be evacuated. The pending attack was delayed while the attack units were readjusted. On 27 May, Companies E and F, 2/26, now opconned to 3/4, moved against Hill 117 behind a moving wall of artillery fire. They encountered only minimal resistance and secured the hill by 1600. The next day, the 3d Battalion, 4th Marines moved west of Hill 117, sweeping deeper into the mountainous area. They met no further resistance. On 29 May, they turned back toward Con Thien.

Operation Hickory was the first large-scale allied foray into the DMZ. This effort changed the rules, signaling the NVA that they no longer had a sanctuary there. At the same time, the TAOR had been cleared of all civilians, giving the Marines complete freedom in the future use of supporting arms. The cost of these gains had been high. The Marines suffered 142 killed and 896 wounded. Enemy casualties were nearly 800 killed with 37 captured. In addition, several large stores of enemy supplies were captured, denying the NVA valuable food, ammunition, and medicine.

When Operation Hickory ended on 28 May, all participating units became part of the ongoing Operation Prairie IV. They continued their search and destroy sweeps of Leatherneck Square and the terrain southwest of Con Thien.

The only major contact of the operation occurred that same day when Companies L and M, 3/4, attacked Hill 174, about two kilometers southwest of Hill 117. The grunts had nearly conquered the hill when strong enemy forces, in previously unseen bunkers, suddenly opened fire. Using machine guns, 57mm recoilless rifles, and 82mm mortars, the NVA literally blew the Marines off the hill. It took most of the evening simply to round up all the men. After evacuating their wounded, the companies called in artillery throughout the night.

Early the next morning, Company M and a fresh Company I attacked the complex. Besides being struck by a heavy volume of enemy fire, the companies were hit by an errant barrage of their own 60mm mortar shells. Despite this, and against strong resistance, the battered Marines secured a tenuous foothold on both the western and southern slopes. Following another night of artillery bombardment, the Marines, now armed with flamethrowers and 3.5-inch rocket launchers, again went up the hill. Enemy resistance again was strong; the Marines still could not gain the hill's crest.

That night, while allied artillery blasted the top of the hill, the NVA slipped away. When the infantrymen attacked on the morning of 31 May, they met no resistance. Eight Marines had died and 99 were wounded in the fight. Only 11 NVA bodies were found.

Operation Prairie IV, the last in the series, ended on 31 May. As had the earlier Prairies, Prairie IV had hurt the enemy. By body count the NVA lost 505 soldiers. But the operation had been costly for the Marines, too: 164 Marines died during this operation with another 1,240 wounded.

The next day Operation Cimarron began as a continuation of Prairie IV, utilizing the same units in the same area. This operation lasted until 2 July and resulted in only minor contact with small bands of enemy soldiers.

While Prairie IV and Operation Hickory had raged in the eastern portion of Quang Tri Province, other Marines had been engaged in an even bloodier combat action around Khe Sanh.

First Battle of Khe Sanh

Marines who saw western Quang Tri Province for the first time were impressed with its beauty. Deep shades of green blanketed the numerous hills and low mountain peaks that dotted the area. The lush vegetation on the mountains included thick stands of vine-choked trees that stretched more than one hundred feet skyward. The lowlands were covered by fields of six- to eight-foot-high elephant grass and densely tangled bamboo thickets. Sparsely populated by nomadic bands of mountain tribes known as Bru, the jungle also served as the home to a wide variety of wildlife, ranging from miniature deer to tigers.

For years the North Vietnamese had operated in the region with bold impunity, using the area as one of its major infiltration routes into the south. The tall trees protected the enemy's trails from aerial observation. On the ground the dense grass limited ground visibility to mere meters. Only a handful of isolated U.S. Army Special Forces camps impeded the NVA's efforts.

As concern over the enemy's plans for an invasion of Quang Tri Province mounted in the fall of 1966, MACV pressured III MAF to garrison the small outpost at Khe Sanh. Although General Walt initially resisted these overtures because they were inconsistent with his strategy of controlling the populous coastal regions, he eventually relented. In the fall of 1966, III MAF garrisoned the old Special Forces base with 1/3 and a battery from 1/13.

The Marines heavily patrolled to the north, where Hill 1015, about fifteen hundred meters away, dominated the area, and to the northwest, where Hills 861, 881N, and 881S, six kilometers from the combat base, overlooked the infiltration route from the northwest. The patrols found little evidence of an enemy presence in the jungle-covered hills. As a result, III MAF reduced operations around Khe Sanh to a reconnaissance effort. In early February 1967, a single company, Company B, 1/9, supported by Battery I, 12th Marines, defended the base.

Poor weather limited Company B's activity through most of February. Then, on 25 February, when better weather finally allowed the Marines out, a squad-sized patrol came under fire just three kilometers west of the base. One Marine died and eleven were wounded before the enemy slipped away. A sweep of the area after the firefight uncovered a large supply of mortars and ammo.

The next week passed quietly. Then, on 5 March, a dozen enemy sappers probed the northern and western perimeters of the combat base. Before they could do any damage, Marines in a listening post drove them off with Claymore mines.

Based on these contacts, III MAF sent a second company, Company E, 2/9, to Khe Sanh on 7 March. The two companies expanded their patrols, paying particular attention to the Hill 861-881 complex. Although the patrols saw signs of an NVA presence, they made no contact—until 16 March.

That morning a platoon from Company E, 2/9, was returning from a night ambush mission on Hill 861. As the lead squad passed by thick stands of bamboo bordering its route, the enemy sprang an ambush. Short, accurate bursts of AK-47 fire shattered the morning calm. Six Marines fell, one dead. The rest of the platoon hurried forward. A fifteen-minute firefight ended when the unseen enemy soldiers slipped back into the jungle. The platoon then moved back about one hundred meters to a clearing suitable for a medevac helicopter. As they neared this clearing, a sudden blast of enemy fire slammed into the column. Seven Marines died in the fusillade and four were wounded. Taking cover where they could, the surviving men fought back while frantically calling for artillery fire. The heavy shells soon bombarded the enemy positions, but the NVA didn't retreat.

In the meantime, two squads of 2d Lt. Gatlin J. Howell's 2d Platoon, Company B, 1/9, operating one and a half kilometers to the east, were dispatched to help the beleaguered Marines. They, too, came under fire as they neared the trapped platoon. After calling in air strikes, the two units finally joined up. Together, they reached the hill's crest. There the able-bodied men cleared an LZ.

By 1600 the first CH-46 had landed, been loaded with casualties, and departed. Just as the second helicopter touched down, the NVA hit the LZ with mortar fire. The CH-46 made it out safely, but the ground troops suffered badly. Company E's two navy corpsmen were killed by the flying shrapnel and several Marines were injured.

After calling artillery fire on the suspected enemy mortar sites, the Marines radioed the CH-46 to return to pick up the new casualties. As soon as the helicopter touched down, the enemy again slammed a brace of mortar shells into the clearing. The helicopter again escaped unscathed, but the bursts wounded all the Marines who'd carried the other wounded to the LZ.

After this, there were not enough able-bodied men left to carry all the casualties to a defiladed location. Taking cover where they could, the Marines awaited reinforcements. A short time later, another CH-46, bringing in Lieutenant Howell's third squad, crashed on the reverse slope of the hill, injuring all its occupants. Another helicopter picked them up and carried them back to Khe Sanh. Just before dusk, a reinforcing platoon from Company E finally reached an LZ at the base of the hill. This platoon, led by Capt. William B. Terrill, the company commander, made it to the beleaguered Marines and brought the wounded down the hill for evacuation. The few remaining able-bodied men spent the night in position. The next day the enemy was gone, leaving the bodies of eleven of their comrades on the battlefield. The Marines suffered far more: nineteen were killed and fifty-nine were wounded.

With the opening of Route 9 to Dong Ha on 19 March, armored reinforcements finally came into Khe Sanh. Three heavy tanks and a section of ONTOs arrived the next day. They were soon followed by two sections of U.S. Army weapons carriers, one of which mounted dual 40mm automatic cannons. The other had quad .50 machine guns. Offsetting these gains, however, was the loss of Company E, which, because it had suffered most of the casualties during the 16 March action, returned to Dong Ha on 27 March for rebuilding.

A relative quiet descended over the Khe Sanh area for the next month. Then, on the morning of 24 April, a small patrol from Company B was ambushed three hundred meters below the crest of Hill 861. The intense blast of fire killed four men, two of whom disappeared in the thick grass. As a UH-34 helicopter arrived to carry out the two bodies, the entire crest of Hill 861 erupted in enemy automatic weapons fire. In a matter of seconds the helicopter was hit thirty-five times, but it still completed its mission.

That afternoon Capt. Michael W. Sayers, Company B's commander, arrived on the scene with a platoon of recon Marines. He ordered his other two platoons, then positioned about two thousand meters northwest of Hill 861, to change direction and hit the enemy from the rear. Before they could carry out their orders, they, too, were ambushed. Twice helicopters were called in to evacuate the wounded, but each time heavy enemy fire drove them away. The two platoons dug in for the night where they were. Captain Sayers, the recon Marines, and the twenty-two men of the other platoon pulled back to Khe Sanh. The next day they boarded helicopters and joined the two platoons to sweep the area. Company B suffered thirty casualties that day, including fourteen killed.

Captain Sayers and his Marines didn't know it but they had stumbled on the lead elements of the 325C NVA Division, whose mission was to capture Khe Sanh.

Shortly after Captain Sayers and his men departed the combat base on the morning of 25 April, Company K, 3/3, which had been scheduled to relieve Company B on 29 April, flew into Khe Sanh. Company K immediately headed to the battleground. By 1525 these Marines were attacking up Hill 861. When Company K's 1st Platoon neared the hill's crest, a brutal, grazing fire erupted from well-concealed enemy bunkers. Then, shells from mortars sited on the hill's reverse slope began dropping among the attackers. Still, the platoon fought its way upward for about another one hundred meters. It was finally forced to a halt with just ten men still on their feet. A second platoon moved to its assistance, but it, too, was soon pinned down by accurate enemy fire. The Marines pulled back and dug in for the night. The near constant rain of mortar shells and the fire from automatic weapons prevented any evacuation of casualties.

Company B had an equally rough day. Heavy fog delayed the arrival of Captain Sayers and his small force until midmorning. Once the helicopter dropped off the Marines, it loaded up with the most seriously wounded before it was driven off by incoming mortar rounds. The intense enemy fire prevented any other helicopters from coming in to evacuate more wounded. Sayers ordered a withdrawal from the ambush site. However, encumbered as it was with casualties, and ambushed by marauding NVA every few hundred meters, the fraught company made it only eight hundred meters through the jungle before it halted for the night.

Fighting continued the morning of 26 April. Company K, 3/3, battled all morning and made little progress. Burdened by their casualties, the Marines were unable to disengage. Lieutenant Colonel Gary Wilder, the commander of 3/3, who had arrived at Khe Sanh the previous day and accompanied Company K to Hill 861, ordered another reinforcing unit, Company K, 3/9, to help his trapped company. Though the two companies linked up at 1400, it took them five hours to pull back with their casualties.

The bloodied Company B started that morning by heading southwest to skirt Hill 861. They hadn't moved very far when the NVA struck again. From just five meters' distance they fired on the lead squad, cutting the point man in half with their fire. Captain Sayers and five others were also hit. No sooner had the surviving Marines started to return fire than NVA mortar rounds began falling on them. Resulting casualties were depressingly heavy. With the aid of UH-1E gunships, Sayers broke contact around noon and withdrew to the top of a nearby knoll. Medevac helicopters called in to evacuate the wounded were waved off because the NVA gunners were using them to pinpoint the Marines' position.

Around 1500 Captain Sayers radioed Lieutenant Colonel Wilder to report that he could not move any further because he had so many casualties. Wilder told him to leave his dead and move out, carrying just the wounded. Sayers responded that he had too many wounded to do that. With ammo supplies low, radio batteries weak, and no chance of a resupply, Sayers told Wilder that he would assume a defensive position and "fight until it was over."

Fortunately, that self-sacrifice proved unnecessary. Skillful use of close artillery support kept the enemy at bay, although the shells hit so close that Sayers said, "We were taking dirt from the impact." Wilder then sent a platoon from Company K, 3/9, to help Sayers. It took the rescue platoon more than four hours to hack its way through the thick jungle. Then, the united force—preceded by a moving wall of artillery fire but still hampered by the steep terrain, thick foliage, dense fog, and heavy rain, and with every man but the point man and the rear guard carrying casualties or their equipment—inched its way toward Wilder.

Not until 0500 on 27 April did the ragged column finally close on Wilder's position. Helicopters soon arrived, and by 0730 all of the casualties had been evacuated. Company B's survivors refused an offer to return to Khe Sanh in trucks. Instead, they proudly walked all the way back.

Alarmed by the intense combat, the new division commander, Maj. Gen. Bruno A. Hochmuth, plucked the SLF, BLT 2/3, from its AO north of Hue at 1200 on 26 April and rushed it to Khe Sanh. By 1600 that day, three companies—E, G, and H—plus the battalion's command group had landed at Khe Sanh and moved out to Hill 861; the fourth company, Company F, arrived the next day and remained at Khe Sanh to provide security for the base and to act as a reserve force.

That same day, Companies M of the 3d and 9th Marines replaced the battered and depleted Company K, 3/3, and Company B, 1/9.

While these forces moved into position, Marine and army artillery blasted Hill 861 all day on 27 April and into 28 April with more than 2,000 high-explosive shells. In addition, Marine aircraft dropped more than 500,000 pounds of high explosives on the target area.

The plan to defeat the NVA called for Lieutenant Colonel De-Long's 2/3 to seize Hill 861. Its attack would be supported by Lieutenant Colonel Wilder's 3/3. Once Hill 861 was taken, Wilder's Marines would turn west and attack Hill 881S from the northeast. Once that attack was under way, DeLong's battalion would move northwest to Hill 881N.

Late on the afternoon of 28 April, DeLong's men began their assault on Hill 861. Harassed only by an occasional mortar round, the Marines quickly swarmed over the hill. The NVA had pulled out, taking everything with them; the Marines found nothing of intelligence value.

Early the next morning, Wilder's battalion, consisting of Company M, 3/3, and the opconned Companies K and M, 3/9, jumped off toward Hill 881S. Just before noon, the point element of Company M, 3/9, stumbled upon an NVA platoon concealed in a draw. While Company M called for artillery fire, the other two companies bypassed the firefight, moving toward a small hill mass just north of Hill 881S. They occupied this intermediate objective at about 1900 and dug in for the night. Company M, 3/9, soon joined them in the NDP.

Early the next morning, while moving to secure 3/3's right flank, 2/3 ran into more NVA near where Company M, 3/9, had fought the day before. In a short but brutal fight, Company H, 2/3, suffered nine dead and forty-three wounded. While these casualties were attended to, Company G took over the attack. They fought for the rest of the afternoon before finally overrunning the enemy.

At 0800 that same morning, Wilder's battalion began its attack on Hill 881S. The previous evening, Marine jets had pounded the hill with 250 one-ton bombs. When they finished, the artillery took over. In the next ten hours, more than 1,300 howitzer rounds slammed into the hill. With Company M, 3/3, in the lead, followed by Company K, 3/9, the Marines made good progress, until 1030. Then, as Company M's two lead platoons reached the western end of the crest of Hill 881S, the enemy opened up. From well-concealed bunkers, the NVA poured deadly accurate automatic weapons fire on the Marines. Enemy snipers, hidden in the trees, fired on individual riflemen. Enemy mortar rounds fell among the attackers, but other NVA in bypassed bunkers opened fire from the rear. The Marines were stuck, unable to advance or retreat.

Lieutenant Colonel Wilder sent Company M's 3d Platoon and Company K to help the trapped Marines. Using close air support and helicopter gunships to suppress the enemy's fire, the relieving force reached the trapped men by 1230. Wilder then ordered the troops to disengage, but they needed several more hours before they could break contact. Even then, they had to leave behind their 43 dead in order to carry their 109 wounded with them. The heavy casualties rendered Company M ineffective as a fighting unit.

The next day, 1 May, aircraft and artillery blitzed the hill with another 600,000 pounds of ordnance. That same day, Company M, 3/3, was replaced by Company F, 2/3, the regimental reserve company. Company E, 2/9, took over reserve duty at the combat base. The assault battalions brought up their self-propelled, 106mm recoilless rifles to help destroy the enemy bunkers.

After a final artillery barrage on 2 May, Companies K and M, 3/9, headed up the hill. Facing only desultory sniper fire, the attacking Marines reached the crest of Hill 881S by 1420. Once again the NVA had fled rather than fight it out.

Lieutenant Colonel Wilder hustled his command group forward and joined the rifle companies on the newly conquered hill. Together, the Marines had a chance to closely inspect what they'd been up against. More than 250 bunkers had been built on the hill. Most were made with two layers of logs covered by as much as five feet of dirt. The larger, command bunkers had four to eight layers of logs covered with dirt. Entrances were narrow and defiladed from direct fire. Deeply buried communication wires linked the mutually supporting bunkers. Only a direct hit by a large aerial bomb could have damaged or destroyed these fortifications.

Neither Wilder nor any of his men had been prepared for this. They stood in absolute awe of any enemy capable of building this sort of network of emplacements right under the Marines' noses. Every man on that hill gained a new respect for the foe. Wilder wasted no time in passing this vital information to DeLong.

Since 28 April, DeLong's Marines had been patrolling the approaches to Hill 881N. On the morning of 2 May, they were ready go. At 1015 Company E attacked from the south, while Company G moved out from the east. Company G made contact first. After a brief firefight they pulled back to let the artillery do its job. Then, Company G started forward again, but it was soon hit by automatic weapons, small arms, and mortar fire. Company H moved up to assist its sister company, but it, too, was hit by mortars. While these two companies fought on the eastern slopes, Company E fought its way nearly to the top of the hill. Just then, a sudden, heavy rainsquall driven by forty-mile-per-hour winds lashed the area. Realizing that effective control was now impossible, DeLong had no choice but to order his companies to pull back and dig in for the night.

The early part of the night passed in relative quiet as Marine artillery dropped shells on the hill, hoping to keep the enemy at bay. It didn't work. At 0415 two reinforced NVA companies hit Company E's position. Almost before they knew it, the Marines were overwhelmed by the enemy. Vicious hand-to-hand fighting broke out. Individual Marines fought valiantly but in vain. Within minutes the enemy broke through the northeastern edge of the company's perimeter, killing or wounding everyone in the area. The NVA swarmed through the breach and occupied the Marines' bunkers. Captain Alfred E. Lyon rushed 1st Lt. Frank M. Izenour and one of his platoon's squads into the breach. The little band didn't make it very far when they were caught in the crossfire of two NVA machine guns. Izenour reported that he had several wounded and couldn't move. With no more men to send, Lyon was forced to round up eleven attached engineers and send them into the fight. The engineers bravely fired away at the enemy's flanks but were unable to do much more.

At 0700 the next morning, a platoon from Company F, 2/3, helicoptered into an LZ just outside Company E's perimeter. They quickly moved to seal the breach. A short time later Company H came in from the opposite direction. Moving toward each other the two units finally closed the gap. Once that job was done, the Marines went after the NVA hiding in the bunkers and a tree line in the middle of the position. This was close-quarters, bloody, brutal fighting. Not until 1500 was the last bunker cleared. The NVA lost 137 in this fight. The Marines lost 27 killed and 84 wounded.

After spending 4 May reorganizing, Companies E and F jumped off at 0850 the next day in a renewed attack on Hill 881N. Meeting gradually heavier fire as they neared the top of the hill, the Marines pulled back and called for support. At 1300, after air and artillery worked over the hill, the rifle companies attacked again. At 1445 the objective was at last secured. The assault companies spent the next two days futilely searching for any enemy.

The last major action in the first battle of Khe Sanh came on 9 May. Two platoons of Company F, 2/3, ran into the fleeing NVA as they moved down a ridge finger of Hill 778, about three kilometers northwest of Hill 881N. As it entered the ambush, the patrol's lead element was ripped apart by a violent fusillade of automatic weapons fire. Artillery support and the rapid arrival of Company E forced the NVA to flee. After policing the area, the Marines found 31 NVA bodies on the hill. They also discovered large piles of hastily abandoned equipment. Then a squad found the grisly remains of 203 NVA in a mass grave. The brief but tough fight cost the Marines 24 dead and 19 wounded, most of whom were hit in the opening minutes of the fight.

The first battle of Khe Sanh resulted in 940 confirmed enemy dead. Total Marine casualties were 155 dead and 425 wounded. The hill battles around Khe Sanh were one of the rare times that the NVA stood and fought. Although aggressive infantry tactics won the hill fights, artillery and close air support deserved a major share of the credit for their pinpoint accuracy and rapid response to critical situations.

The hard-won victory was tempered by controversy swirling around the newly issued M16 rifle. A plastic stocked, shoulder-fired

5.56mm weapon, the M16 was designed to replace the heavier 7.62mm M14 rifle and give each infantryman more firepower. First issued to U.S. Army troops in 1965, the weapon had not been made available to the Marines until early 1967. The Marines' first major combat test of the rifle was the Khe Sanh hill fights. Many grunts found the weapon lacking in several respects. Reports of Marines found dead beside their nonfunctioning rifles reached congressmen and senators in Washington, as well as the national press. A congressional investigation was launched. The inquiry confirmed that the M16 jammed easily if it and its cartridges were not kept immaculately clean. Obviously, these requirements could not be met under the severe combat conditions experienced in South Vietnam. As a result of the investigation, every M16 in South Vietnam was modified with a new firing chamber that was less susceptible to jamming. Despite this massive undertaking, problems with the M16 continued for more than a year until the manufacturer changed the tolerances for the chamber's components.

With the enemy threat to Khe Sanh blunted, General Hockmuth began reducing the forces in the area. The 1st Battalion, 26th Marines replaced the two battalions of the 3d Marines and assumed operational control of the TAOR. The fresh battalion was charged with denying the enemy access to key terrain areas and constantly patrolling to detect and destroy any NVA operating in the area. With a rifle company stationed on Hills 881S and 861, the patrols traveled as far as four kilometers daily looking for the enemy. These operations were code-named Crockett.

After a brief lull, enemy contact increased sharply in early June. On the sixth, the enemy attacked a small radio relay station on Hill 950, four kilometers east of Hill 861, killing six Marines. The next day a patrol from Company B was ambushed about two kilometers west of Hill 881S. First, small arms fire and mortar shells blasted the patrol, then about forty NVA charged out of the foliage. The patrol members repulsed the ground attack, but the fight lasted most of the day before a platoon from Company A arrived to help. When the enemy finally pulled out late in the day, they left behind the bodies of sixty-six of their comrades. The two rifle platoons had eighteen dead and twenty-eight wounded between them.

General Hockmuth responded by sending 3/26 to Khe Sanh on 13 June. Over the next two weeks, the two infantry battalions had numerous brief but intense contacts with small bands of NVA throughout the TAOR. However, during early July contact decreased, and Operation Crockett ended on 16 July. Nevertheless, the Marines knew that the enemy wasn't ready to give up on the Khe Sanh area.

During the month of June, Marine engineers had widened the McNamara Line between Con Thien and Gio Linh to six hundred meters. No sooner had the work been completed than the North Vietnamese decided to attack one of its strongpoints before the system became too well developed. In early July, the NVA began an offensive against Con Thien, employing extensive artillery to support their infantry. The Marine counterattack resulted in some of the deadliest fighting of the year.

Operation Buffalo

On the morning of 2 July, Company B, 1/9, now rebuilt after its fight near Khe Sanh and commanded by Capt. Sterling K. Coates, was sweeping north of the newly cleared trace about three kilometers northeast of Con Thien in conjunction with Company A, 1/9. Because the TAOR assigned to the regiment was so large, the time span between infantry sweeps of a given section sometimes exceeded two weeks. This lag did not go unnoticed by the NVA. The astute enemy began moving back into a given area as soon as the Marine rifle companies moved on. To counter this tactic, Col. George E. Jerue, the 9th Marines commander, ordered Lt. Col. Richard J. Schening to return to the same ground in which his 1st Battalion had operated less than a week earlier.

As Company B moved north along Highway 561, actually a ten-foot-wide dirt road bordered by three-foot-high hedgerows, it came under sniper fire at about 0900. Captain Coates maneuvered his command group and the 3d Platoon out to the left to flank the enemy. Increasingly heavy fire halted that movement. Coates then ordered his 2d Platoon to move to the right. To Coates's surprise it was driven back with high casualties before it had proceeded very far. As the 2d Platoon moved back on the road, enemy artillery and mortar started falling in the area. Casualties began to build.

A short distance to the west, Capt. Albert C. Slater turned his Company A to move to Coates's aid. The company made it less than one hundred meters before it ran into mines and small arms fire. Soon Slater had so many casualties that he couldn't move.

In the meantime, the fighting around Company B grew more savage. The NVA cut off Coates and the 3d Platoon. North Vietnamese soldiers then sneaked forward through the thick shrubbery and used flamethrowers to ignite the brush along the road. Marines fleeing the blaze were cut down by small arms fire or artillery bursts. Then, artillery fire dropped on the command group. Captain Coates, his radio telephone operator (RTO), two platoon leaders, the artillery forward observer (FO), and several others all died in the opening salvo. The forward air controller assumed command of the shattered company.

From the rear, the 1st Platoon tried to move forward to help the others, but it was soon halted by brutal blasts of enemy fire from both flanks. The enemy seemed to be everywhere. The platoon commander, SSgt. Leon R. Burns, called for napalm strikes as close as twenty meters to his position in an effort to hold the enemy at bay. Under this protective cover, Burns slowly pushed forward until he linked up with the remnants of the 2d Platoon.

At about 1030 Lieutenant Colonel Schening, alerted to the battle, dispatched from Con Thien a rescue force composed of four M48 tanks accompanied by a rifle platoon from Company D. He also asked Colonel Jerue for the release of Company C from security duty at the regimental CP at Dong Ha. The battalion S-3, Capt. Henry J. M. Radcliffe, and the S-2, 1st Lt. Gatlin J. Howell, who had led a Company B platoon during the Khe Sanh fights, led the reaction force out of the combat base. The small column moved down the trace without incident. As soon as they swung north on Route 561, however, they were hit by heavy enemy fire. About this same time, helicopters began landing Company C at an LZ right in front of the rescue column. Radcliffe ordered the platoon from Company D to secure the LZ. Just then an enemy artillery barrage slammed into the area. Eleven Marines fell.

Radcliffe gathered up a platoon from Company C and, with the tanks, pushed onward. About six hundred meters up the road he found Sergeant Burns. Looking at the handful of Marines around the sergeant, Radcliffe asked Burns where the rest of Company B was. "This is what's left of the company, sir," Burns replied. Radcliffe was too stunned to respond. After sending the 1st Platoon's wounded to the rear, the relief force, along with Sergeant Burns and his few remaining able-bodied men, pushed forward to recover the rest of Company B's casualties. They found so many bodies that there wasn't enough room for them on the tanks. Some had to be left behind. Lieutenant Howell was particularly bothered by the scene. He had only recently relinquished command of the 3d Platoon after leading it for eight months. Determined not to leave any of his former comrades behind, he repeatedly exposed himself to carry wounded back to the tanks. Captain Radcliffe estimated that Lieutenant Howell helped bring no less than twenty-five wounded to safety. As the pathetic column started back to the LZ, it was hit by enemy artillery and mortar fire. Then, two tanks hit mines, causing more casualties and further slowing the withdrawal. As the gruesome parade finally reached Company C's LZ, more enemy artillery shells struck. Many of the earlier casualties still awaiting evacuation were hit again. Corpsmen who braved the flying metal to rush to help the wounded fell in the blasts. In the resulting confusion about fifty wounded started making their way down the trace toward Con Thien. When they were spotted, Lieutenant Colonel Schening sent out a party to meet them and assist in their evacuation.

While all this was going on, Company A came under enemy attack, too. The first flight of medevac helicopters had just departed with some of the earlier casualties when NVA mortar shells fell on the LZ. Minutes later, enemy infantry attacked. One platoon was quickly cut off; it eventually fought its way through the enemy and joined Radcliffe's force. The remaining members of Company A fought the enemy to within fifty yards of its position before their furious fire, and supporting artillery, broke up the attack.

At 1500 Lieutenant Colonel Schening advised regiment that he had all his units engaged and had no reserve. Based on this, Colonel Jerue ordered his 3d Battalion into the fight. By 1800 three companies and the battalion command group from 3/9 were in position north of the trace. The 3d Battalion took operational control of Companies A and C, 1/9. The fresh Marines quickly attacked the NVA's left flank. This aggressive action forced the enemy back. A short time later, the survivors of Company B and the platoon from Company D pulled back to Con Thien.

A head count the next day showed that 1/9 had suffered 84 dead, 190 wounded, and 9 missing in the ambush. Most of the casualties had been from Company B. In fact, only 27 Company B Marines remained on their feet. Their heroic conduct that terrible day earned both Lieutenant Howell and Sergeant Burns a Navy Cross.

On 3 July, BLT 1/3 from SLF Alpha joined with 3/9 for the attack north to recover the remaining Marine dead and drive the enemy out of the area. The two battalions started the attack before dawn on 4 July. Almost immediately the 3d Battalion ran into heavy resistance from NVA dug in just south of Company B's battle site. The resulting fight, which lasted most of the day, involved tanks, artillery, and air support as well as infantry. Not until 1830 did the Marines finally overrun the enemy's lines. Fifteen men died and 33 were wounded in the action. Because of the unexpected heavy resistance, BLT 2/3 from SLF Bravo was committed to the fight. Helicopters airlifted it into an LZ north of Cam Lo. From there it moved north toward Con Thien.

The Marines spent 5 July recovering and evacuating Company B's dead. The next morning the rifle companies resumed their northward attack. The BLT 2/3 was hit first. Three kilometers south of Con Thien, a well-dug-in NVA force dropped a barrage of mortar shells on the Marines. Attacking aggressively across the brush-clad terrain, the battalion lost 5 dead and 25 wounded before driving away the enemy.

To the northeast of Con Thien, 1/3 and 3/9 were harassed by sporadic enemy artillery and mortar fire as they advanced toward the DMZ. At the zone's southern edge the two battalions halted to set up a night defensive position. Company A, 1/9, and the survivors of Company C were sent about 1,500 meters to the northwest to guard the force's left flank. Once his men had dug in, Captain Slater sent a patrol north to the Ben Hai River to watch for any enemy activity.

A short time later the patrol excitedly reported that they had spotted a force of more than 400 NVA fording the Ben Hai and heading right for Company A. Slater hurriedly ordered the patrol back. He then passed the word to his Marines. Everyone dug deeper, checked and rechecked their weapons, and waited.

About this time, a heavy and accurate artillery barrage ripped into the main force. The artillery shells fell like rain in a thunderstorm. In a relatively short period nearly 600 shells hit 3/9 and about 1,000 landed on 1/3.

While the enemy artillery pounded the two battalions, the 400-man force of NVA infantry ran smack into Captain Slater's Marines. When they closed to 150 meters of his perimeter, Slater gave the order to open fire. The initial onslaught of heavy fire caught the NVA by surprise. They scattered, some running right into the Marines' lines. Soon, however, they reorganized themselves and swarmed all around Slater's position. Fire discipline born of intense training and their well-constructed bunkers gave the Marines the upper hand. The NVA probed from all directions but couldn't breach the company's perimeter. A few enemy soldiers crept close enough to heave grenades into the friendly lines, but individual Marines hunted down and killed these intruders. Slater also skillfully employed his artillery support, dropping shells to within 50 meters of his position.

Faced with an impregnable position, the NVA began withdrawing just before midnight. Small arms fire and an occasional grenade harassed the Marines throughout the night, but they had held against a far superior force. When patrols left the perimeter at first light, they found 154 NVA bodies scattered around their position. Only 12 Company A Marines had been wounded. Captain Slater's gallant leadership that night earned him a Navy Cross.

While Slater's company fought its lone battle, the rest of what was later identified as the 90th NVA Regiment hit the two battalions. Throughout the night of 6–7 July, NVA infantry assaulted the main force's positions. The Marines responded with every bit of supporting arms at their disposal, including flare ships, attack aircraft, helicopter gunships, naval gunfire, and all available artillery. Unable to penetrate the tightly defended perimeter, and repeatedly battered by the intense bombardment, the NVA began retreating at about 2130.

The next morning the Marines policed the battlefield. Assessing the damage done to the NVA was extremely difficult due to the extensive destruction caused by the supporting fire. The enemy dead had been badly damaged by the high explosives. Only by counting canteens could an estimate of the number of enemy soldiers killed during the fight be made. In all, the Marines claimed eight hundred dead NVA.

Though they had suffered incredible losses, the NVA weren't defeated. All day on 7 July, NVA artillery and rockets pounded the Marine positions. Large-caliber, long-range artillery pummeled Con Thien. One shell tore into 1/9's command bunker. Among the eleven killed was Lieutenant Howell. Among the eighteen wounded was Lieutenant Colonel Schening. He had the dubious distinction of adding a fourth Purple Heart to the ones he'd already collected for wounds received in World War II and Korea. Enemy ordnance also rained on the Marine base at Dong Ha. So intense was the bombardment that the 9th Marines were forced to move their headquarters from Dong Ha to northeast of Cam Lo to escape the shelling.

The last significant action of Operation Buffalo came on 8 July, southwest of Con Thien. After reaching the combat base following its northerly sweep, BLT 2/3 had turned west, then south. Soon afterward Company G discovered an enemy bunker complex. After calling in air strikes and artillery, the Marines quickly overran the enemy, killing thirty-one NVA and losing two of their own.

About a kilometer to the southwest, Company F engaged another enemy force that same afternoon. Initially, one of the company's patrols had had a brief fight with what appeared to be a small band of NVA stragglers. However, the enemy's firing continued to build. First Lieutenant Richard D. Koehler then led the rest of his company into the attack, thinking that his superior firepower would overwhelm the enemy. He was wrong. No sooner had he arrived on the scene than enemy 82mm mortar shells started dropping among the grunts. Koehler called for help. Once again the timely arrival of Marine close air support saved the day. When the fight was over, Company F counted 118 dead NVA on the battlefield. However, 14 Marines were killed and 43 were wounded in the fight.

The Marines ended Operation Buffalo on 14 July. The NVA's plans to capture Con Thien had failed, but it had been a vicious battle. Enemy losses were recorded as 1,290 killed against 159 Marines killed and 345 wounded.

* * *

Immediately following Operation Buffalo, III MAF ordered a sweep of the southern half of the DMZ. Dubbed Hickory II, the operation involved two Marine battalions and three ARVN battalions. There was little contact, and Hickory II ended on 16 July.

As soon as Hickory II ended, Operation Kingfisher began in the same area; it employed the five battalions then making up the 3d and 9th Marines. Only minor contacts occurred through 27 July. Then, on 28 July, the 2d Battalion, 9th Marines—accompanied by a platoon of M48 tanks, three ONTOs, three tracked amphibious vehicles, and engineers—entered the DMZ. Though the tanks provided additional firepower, they also hampered the battalion's movement—the huge armored vehicles were restricted to existing trails because of the thick underbrush that covered the area. The column would have to return south using the same route it had taken north. Also, a wide bend in the Ben Hai River placed the river north and west of the battalion; a tributary to the east meant that the operation was confined to a wide V. As the Marines prepared their night laager sites just south of the Ben Hai, NVA units were already moving into previously prepared positions behind them.

After sweeping the area surrounding its NDP on the morning of 29 July, the battalion was ready to head back south at about 1000. Company E had the point. It was followed by Command Group Alpha, the Headquarters & Supply Company, Command Group Bravo, then Companies F, H, and G. An airborne forward air controller turned lazy circles overhead as the battalion started out.

At 1115 the enemy blew up a 250-pound bomb buried in the road. The blast wounded five men. While they were being treated, some engineers discovered another bomb and soon destroyed it.

The explosion triggered a fury of enemy fire. Rifles, machine guns, 60mm and 82mm mortars, and RPGs slashed into the column. The devastating enemy fire quickly fragmented the column into platoon- and company-sized segments. The tanks and tracked vehicles became a liability in the rough terrain. The NVA gunners repeatedly pounded the vehicles with antitank rockets. Infantrymen ended up protecting the tanks instead of the other way around.

Not until late in the afternoon did Company E and a portion of the battalion forward command group escape the killing ground. At

1830 they linked up with Company M, 3/4, which had been sent
from Con Thien to help the embattled column.

By this time the isolated segments of the column had withdrawn
into individual perimeters. Many units were intermingled, and there
was no central control. Burdened by numerous casualties, most of
the segments could not move. They had no choice but to dig in for
the night where they were. Though marauding bands of NVA harassed the column all night, accurate Marine artillery prevented any
major attacks. By dawn the enemy had slipped away. At first light,
medevac helicopters were finally able to enter the battle site. It took
them a long time to remove all the casualties. Twenty-three men were
dead and 251 were wounded; 32 enemy bodies were found.

On the morning of 21 July, an 85-vehicle convoy departed Dong
Ha for a routine resupply run on Route 9 to Khe Sanh. As the convoy traveled west, a rifle platoon from Company M, 3/3, began a routine road sweep on Route 9 just west of Ca Lu. After covering about
five kilometers, the point man spotted and fired on an enemy soldier. Concealed NVA answered with a violent burst of fire. The platoon went to the ground.

The 3d Battalion headquarters immediately dispatched the rest
of Company M to rescue its platoon. At the same time, the convoy
was halted at Ca Lu. It took the rest of the day for Company M to
reach the convoy's ambushed platoon and help it disengage.

Over the next two days, rifle companies from the 26th Marines
at Khe Sanh and the 3d Marines cleared the enemy from positions
alongside Route 9 west of Ca Lu. The grunts not only found and
killed enemy soldiers emplaced along the route, but they uncovered
numerous mines rigged with trip wires in the tall grass bordering
the road.

The convoy finally and uneventfully completed its journey on 25
July. There was one more major convoy to Khe Sanh in the next two
weeks, but then III MAF shut down the route. Sending trucks along
it was far too dangerous. Not until April 1968 would the road be reopened. Until then the troops at Khe Sanh would be dependent
upon aerial resupply for survival.

The next several weeks passed in relative quiet, with only small-
scale fighting. As September began, the North Vietnamese increased
their activity to coincide with the South Vietnamese elections. From

positions within the DMZ, the enemy unleashed a heavy volume of artillery shells and rockets onto the various Marine bases. Hardest hit was Dong Ha, which took hundreds of rounds on each of the five days prior to the election. On election day itself a rocket barrage destroyed Dong Ha's ammo storage dump and the bulk fuel farm and damaged seventeen helicopters. As a result of this attack, Marine helicopters were no longer based at Dong Ha. Instead, they operated out of Phu Bai or Marble Mountain near Da Nang until a new facility was completed at Quang Tri City, which was out of range of the enemy gunners.

During September and into October, the NVA gunners focused their attention on Con Thien. Almost daily a minimum of two hundred artillery rounds pounded the forward combat base. On 25 September more than twelve hundred high explosive shells blasted the base.

The enemy's infantry forces also aggressively attacked the Marines during this period. Less than two kilometers south of Con Thien, a strong NVA force ripped into 3/4 on 4 September, causing heavy casualties. Three days later, and three kilometers farther south, a company of 3/26 was ambushed as it moved through tall elephant grass. Unable to see the enemy, the Marines pulled back to link up with supporting M48 tanks. As they waited for medevac helicopters, they were hit by a deadly accurate mortar barrage. Scattering in a wild retreat, the company was not reorganized until nightfall.

On 10 September, the NVA launched a bold, daylight human wave assault against the weakened 3/26 as it moved off its night laager site. Heavy fighting raged at close quarters for most of the morning before the enemy was beaten off. With its ranks badly depleted by the more than two hundred casualties it suffered in these two fights, the battalion was sent back to Phu Bai for rebuilding. The much-used 2d Battalion, 4th Marines replaced it.

By the time 2/4 was assigned to guard a key bridge north of strongpoint C-2 on 10 October, and after a month of almost daily combat, 2/4's "foxhole strength" had been reduced to 462 men from 952. The badly depleted rifle companies of 2/4 could barely man the positions around the important bridge left behind by the departing full-strength BLT 2/3.

The first few days passed quietly. Then, at 0125 on 14 October, Company H, manning the southwest quadrant formed by the east-west river and the north-south road, detected an enemy force approaching its position. An ambush squad in front of the company quickly and easily repulsed the NVA. But the enemy wasn't done. At 0230 mortar shells fell on Company G, occupying the northwest quadrant. Then RPGs, flashing brilliantly out of the night, slammed into a vital M60 emplacement, destroying it, and opened a breach in Company G's perimeter. The NVA quickly poured through the opening. Running amok through the company's position, the enemy soldiers overran the CP, killing the company commander, three platoon leaders, and the artillery FO. A replacement company commander was hustled forward from the battalion staff. He made it about halfway to his new command before he was killed by marauding enemy soldiers. With little in their way, the enemy pressed forward to the battalion CP, located at Company G's rear.

Closing to within grenade range of 2/4's CP, the attackers killed the entire forward air control team and the battalion medical chief. Lieutenant Colonel James W. Hammond hurriedly moved the remnants of his command group across the stream into Company H's lines. From there Hammond ordered Company F, holding the northeast quadrant, into the melee.

By 0330 the counterattack by Company F, helped by the arrival of aerial gunships, had pushed back the NVA. At first light, Company F, joined by Company E, chased the enemy from the battleground. When the attack was over, at least twenty-four NVA bodies were found around the bridge. Marine casualties were twenty-one dead and twenty-three wounded. Later that day, 2/4 was pulled back to Dong Ha for a rest while 3/3 took its place.

Ten days later, 2/4 returned to the field. Its mission was to sweep north along the west side of Route 561, moving toward 3/3, which still held the positions around the bridge. Though 2/4 did not find the enemy, the hump through the heavy brush greatly slowed the battalion. As night approached it was still about one kilometer south of the bridge. Hammond ordered his battalion to stop where it was. He then called for an ammunition resupply. It was a risky decision, because the inbound helicopters would reveal his location to any lurking enemy. But Hammond figured that he could unload the ammo before the NVA pinpointed his position. Unfortunately, he was wrong.

The helicopters brought ammo and other items in far greater quantities than the men could move. Because the helicopters were unable to return to remove the excess materiel, the battalion would have to stay in position.

All was quiet until 2330, when ten NVA artillery rounds slammed into the battalion's NDP. The battalion executive officer was killed and Lieutenant Colonel Hammond was badly wounded in the blasts. The battalion S-3, Capt. Arthur P. Brill, who had just given up command of Company H the day before, quickly took over the battalion. He called for medevac choppers to evacuate the casualties. After the injured were unloaded at Dong Ha, Lt. Col. John C. Studt, the 9th Marines S-3, jumped aboard one of the UH-34Ds. He was 2/4's new commanding officer and wanted to get to his men. Despite the enemy fire and a developing layer of fog, the gutsy helicopter pilot flew Studt out to his new command.

Once Studt had reorganized his battalion, now numbering less than four hundred men, he ordered Company F to guard the ammo pile until it was picked up. The rest of the battalion started out toward its original objective. By 1300, without further incident, the 2d Battalion, 4th Marines reached their destination. No sooner had the war-weary Marines dug in than a handful of enemy 60mm mortar rounds landed in the battalion area. An hour later, a heavier mortar barrage fell on the hard-pressed Marines. That was soon followed by bursts of small arms fire from the west and northwest. One helicopter called in to evacuate the resulting casualties was shot down, and a second was badly damaged.

Worried about the ability of his depleted battalion to hold its position through the night, Lieutenant Colonel Studt radioed for help. The 9th Marine headquarters dispatched two companies from 3/3, still holding at the C-2 bridge. They joined Studt's battalion just before dusk.

Studt also ordered Company F to blow up the ammo pile and rejoin the battalion. Try as they might, the engineers couldn't detonate their charges. Because the pile was visible from the NDP, Studt then ordered the company to leave the ammunition and move to him. Company F arrived at the NDP just after the 3/3 companies.

From dark until 0200 the next morning, Studt's Marines experienced almost constant ground attack from mortar-supported NVA infantry. Fortunately, the deep fighting holes dug by the experienced Marines limited their casualties. Accurate friendly artillery fire, as it had so many times in the past, prevented the NVA from overrunning the besieged perimeter.

At dawn, on 27 October, 2/4 retreated southward. The able bodied struggled to carry all the dead and wounded with them. Harassed by enemy rocket, mortar, and artillery fire all the way, 2/4 finally closed on C-2 that afternoon. From there it returned to Dong Ha, where it once again went into a reserve role. Lieutenant Colonel William Weise took command of the battalion there. After having the companies' first sergeants verify casualties against the muster rolls, Weise found that his battalion had an effective strength of just more than three hundred men. It had been a rough few weeks for the battalion known as the "Magnificent Bastards."

Operation Kingfisher ended on 31 October. The scoreboard listed 1,117 enemy dead against the Marines' 340 dead and 1,461 wounded. Unfortunately, the losses did nothing to lighten the enemy's attacks on Con Thien. Daily barrages of artillery, rocket, and mortar fire, enemy infantry attacks, and miserable weather made the "Hill of Angels" a dreadful place to be that fall.

Not all of the 3d Marine Division's activities took place along the DMZ. Because it lacked the manpower to effectively operate throughout its TAOR, the division had been forced to ignore several enemy base areas in the southern portion of Quang Tri Province. In the fall, though, III MAF ordered General Hockmuth to clear one of these neglected areas, the Hai Lang Forest south of Quang Tri City. To clear this home of the 5th and 6th NVA Regiments, General Hockmuth selected the two battalions of the 1st Marines, which had recently been opconned to his division.

Operation Medina began on 11 October, when UH-34Ds carried the men of 1/1 and 2/1 into clearings deep in the thick forest. After sweeping the area around their LZs, the two battalions started moving northeast toward where the SLF, BLT 1/3, held blocking positions. Company C of BLT 1/3 had actually been the first unit to come in contact with the enemy during this operation. Helicopters had carried the SLF to its blocking position on the afternoon of 10 October. After digging in, the riflemen settled down to wait for the enemy to be driven into them. They didn't wait very long. At 0330 on 11 October, the NVA launched a ground assault against the company's night perimeter. Nearly two hours of heavy, close-quarters fighting passed before the NVA withdrew.

At 1500 the next day, Company C, 1/1, was pushing through the dense foliage when its point element bumped into a ten-man NVA squad. In the initial exchange of rifle fire, several Marines were wounded. The casualties were pulled back to a small clearing where the rest of the company had already set up defensive positions. Just after the casualties had been evacuated, three full NVA companies suddenly slammed into Company C from two directions. The fighting raged at close quarters all across the clearing. Hand grenades flew back and forth as the adversaries battled at arm's length. One NVA grenade landed among members of the command group who were clustered behind a fallen log. Corporal William T. Perkins, a combat photographer attached to Company C, shouted, "Grenade!" and flung himself on the missile. The ensuing blast killed him, but those around him survived. Perkins was posthumously awarded the Medal of Honor, the only combat photographer ever to be so honored.

The fighting around the clearing continued until dusk, when Company D arrived to help. Together, the two companies finally scattered the attackers. Eight Marines were killed and thirty-nine were wounded in the fight. The Marines later found the bodies of forty NVA in the jungle surrounding the clearing.

The NVA avoided further contact after this fight. In their subsequent sweeps the Marines found and destroyed several abandoned base camps. Operation Medina ended on 20 October, when BLT 1/3 returned to the control of the SLF. The two 1st Marine battalions remained in the Hai Lang Forest on Operation Osceola, continuing their search for the elusive NVA.

In early November, the 3d Marine Division made several changes in its subordinate units' operational responsibilities. The 9th Marines would conduct a new series of sweeps dubbed Operation Kentucky, in Leatherneck Square. To the west, the 3d Marines opened Operation Lancaster in the Camp Carroll–Rockpile–Ca Lu area. The operations around Khe Sanh were renamed Scotland and placed under the control of the 26th Marines. The 1st Amphibious Tractor Battalion conducted Operation Napoleon along the coast between the Cua Viet River and the DMZ. The 4th Marines continued to cover the approaches to Hue in Operation Neosho. The 1st ARVN Division operated east of Highway 1 adjacent to the 1st Amphibious Tractor Battalion.

The nature of the war in South Vietnam exposed all levels of Marines to danger. This was dramatically illustrated on 14 November, when the UH-1E carrying General Hockmuth was shot out of the sky seven kilometers northwest of Hue. Hockmuth and five other Marines aboard the aircraft were killed.

On 28 November, Maj. Gen. Rathvon Mc. Tompkins arrived from the United States to take over the 3d Marine Division. A thirty-two-year veteran, Tompkins had earned a Navy Cross as a battalion commander during the fighting on Saipan during World War II. After being briefed on the situation facing his new command, Tompkins expressed dissatisfaction with the system of constantly shifting battalions from one regiment's control to another as the tactical situation dictated. However, he opted not to do anything to change the system, which had been in place for more than two years.

Most of the combat that the Marines experienced in Quang Tri Province in the last two months of 1967 consisted of small-unit actions around the SPOS. On 30 November, 2/9 had fifteen killed and fifty-three wounded during a fight against a well-entrenched NVA company four kilometers northeast of Con Thien.

Company F, 2/4, was operating as a security force for engineers constructing strongpoint C-4, on the coast two kilometers north of the Cua Viet River. Early on the afternoon of 10 December, two platoons from the company became embroiled with a company of NVA hiding in a fishing village situated in the coastal sand dunes. Unable to break free, the platoons from Company F were reinforced by two platoons from Company B of the 1st Amphibious Tractor Battalion. Despite this help, the Marines remained engaged throughout the night.

At dawn the next day, believing that the NVA had withdrawn, the composite force started out of the village in a driving rain. It hadn't gone very far when it was again attacked. Another company from the 1st Amphibious Tractor Battalion was rushed into the foray. In addition, a company of ARVN infantry from strongpoint A-1, two and a half kilometers west, was moved into position to trap the NVA from behind. Before the ARVN could advance, however, the NVA hit the Marines again. Attacking from three sides, the enemy force also pounded the perimeter with mortars. Forced to tighten their perimeter, the Marines directed artillery and naval gunfire to within fifty meters of themselves. About this time, the ARVN company appeared on the horizon to the west. As soon as the NVA spotted it, they started pulling back north to the DMZ. As the composite force headed south to C-4, it discovered a large enemy supply cache dug into nearby sand dunes. Now the Marines understood why they had been attacked in the first place.

As 1967 ended, the major problem facing III MAF was the continued NVA threat to invade Quang Tri Province from across the DMZ. In addition, intelligence sources reported that two NVA divisions, the 325C and 304th, had moved into the Khe Sanh area from Laos.

Though General Westmoreland had been very positive about the conduct of the war during a visit to the United States in September, by December he had somewhat tempered that optimistic outlook. Because he saw Khe Sanh as the keystone of the American position in South Vietnam, Westmoreland ordered III MAF to reinforce the base in preparation for a big fight. General Cushman, in turn, directed General Tompkins to send another battalion to the distant combat base.

In a message to the Joint Chiefs of Staff on 20 December, Westmoreland declared, "I believe the enemy has already made a crucial decision to make a maximum effort [in the Khe Sanh area]."

The next six weeks would prove that the MACV commander was correct, but only partially so.

Chapter Four
1968 (3d Division)

3d Marine Division

Several hours after dusk on 2 January 1968, six men wearing Marine uniforms casually emerged from the twilight and approached the concertina wire barrier at the western end of the Khe Sanh combat base. For several minutes they stood there, outside the wire, talking among themselves. Occasionally, one of the six gestured to a bunker inside the combat base.

Unsure what action to take, the nearby American sentries waited patiently; they expected the figures to cross back to the friendly side of the wire any minute. When they didn't, one sentry issued a challenge. Suddenly, the six men froze in silence. They hesitated a moment too long. The still night air was shattered by the sharp reports of an M16 rifle. The sentry emptied a full magazine into the shadowy figures. Five fell, dead. As Marines raced to the scene, the sixth man, obviously badly wounded, ripped a map case from one of the corpses. Before the sentry could fire again, the figure limped into the nearby brush and disappeared.

The reaction squad found a bonanza of documents on the corpses. The evidence indicated that the men were an NVA regimental commander and members of his staff. For base and 26th Marines commander Col. David E. Lownds, the incident confirmed his worst suspicion: the enemy was planning a major assault on Khe Sanh. General Westmoreland agreed wholeheartedly.

Westmoreland had returned to the United States in mid-November 1967 filled with optimism. A recent MACV intelligence analysis had identified the early fall of 1967 as the crossover point for the North Vietnamese Army—that statistical moment when the enemy's battlefield losses exceeded his ability to replace them. In his war of attrition Westmoreland smelled victory. Consequently, his briefings to President Johnson were exceptionally encouraging. He told his commander in chief that he could "foresee the possibility of the start of an American withdrawal." In a well-publicized address to the National Press Club in Washington on 21 November, Westmoreland told the assembled correspondents, "We have reached an important point where the end begins to come into view. . . . Whereas in 1965 the enemy was winning, today he is certainly losing." Significantly, he did not say that the United States was winning.

General Westmoreland, schooled in the grand strategies of massive land battles as experienced in Europe in both world wars, was eager for a decisive military victory, one that would force the enemy to his knees. He became convinced that his nemesis, the brilliant strategist Gen. Vo Nguyen Giap, was planning to repeat his stunning 1954 victory over the French at Dien Bien Phu. When Westmoreland reviewed his battle maps, he could see only one likely target for Giap: Khe Sanh. The general had this to say about Khe Sanh: "Were we to relinquish the Khe Sanh area, the North Vietnamese would have an unobstructed invasion route into the two northernmost provinces from which they might outflank our positions south of the demilitarized zone—positions which were blocking North Vietnamese attacks from the north."

Since the brutal fighting of the previous April, the area around the Khe Sanh combat base had been relatively quiet. As a result, only the 1st Battalion, 26th Marines garrisoned the combat base. Throughout the summer and fall, their daily patrols had found few signs of enemy activity. Then, in early December, intelligence sources reported that North Vietnam was funneling a large quantity of men and materiel into the Khe Sanh area. Based on this, Westmoreland instructed III MAF to strengthen the combat base. At 1400 on 13 December 1967, General Cushman ordered General Tompkins to put a second battalion at Khe Sanh. The 3d Battalion, 26th Marines had only recently returned to Dong Ha after being sent south to Hue to recover from its August mauling. Tompkins ordered Lt. Col. Harry L. Alderman to move his battalion to Khe Sanh immediately. By 1900 that same day, three of 3/26's rifle companies were at the combat base; the fourth would make the trip the next day.

After the 2 January incident, Westmoreland became obsessed with the notion that Giap planned to capture the combat base. Convinced that the war's definitive battle would be fought in this isolated region, the general ordered a major buildup for I Corps. Two more Marine battalions arrived at Khe Sanh: 2/26 on 16 January (making the 26th Marines the only regiment in I Corps to operate with all of its organic battalions) and 1/9 on 22 January. General Lam, the ARVN corps commander, contributed the 37th Ranger Battalion to the base. By the time the buildup was over, Khe Sanh was defended by five infantry battalions, three batteries of 105mm howitzers, a battery each of 4.2-inch mortars and 155mm howitzers, six 90mm gun tanks, ten ONTOs, two U.S. Army M42 armored vehicle Dusters mounting twin 40mm cannons, and two U.S. Army M50s with quad .50-caliber machine guns. Sheer congestion prevented more troops from cramming into the base.

General Westmoreland shifted other resources north. The lead elements of the U.S. Army's 1st Cavalry Division (Airmobile) arrived at Phu Bai on 17 January. Within a week the rest of the talented and experienced division had arrived on the scene. On 22 January, it opened Operation Jeb Stuart to protect the western approaches to Hue. That same day the first part of the U.S. Army's famed 101st Airborne Division arrived at Quang Tri City. The Korean Marine Corps brigade also moved north, as did two tough ARVN divisions. By mid-January, half of all U.S. combat troops—nearly fifty maneuver battalions—were concentrated in I Corps.

General Westmoreland wanted this battle as much as he had desired anything in his entire army career. The decisive defeat of the North Vietnamese Army would be the capstone of his twenty-five years of service to his country. He would bring victory to South Vietnam through victory at Khe Sanh.

Khe Sanh

Colonel Lownds had arrived at Khe Sanh with the 1st Battalion of his 26th Marines in the late summer of 1967. Since that time enemy contact had been light. Nonetheless, a flurry of activity began in mid-October as MACV ordered improvements to the Khe Sanh Combat Base in preparation for Westmoreland's long-hoped-for cross-border strike into Laos. Engineers rebuilt the airfield. Supplies and ammunition flowed into the base for stockpiling.

In the meantime, signs of an enemy presence increased. Bru tribesmen and their families appeared around the base in increasingly large numbers, indicating that something or someone had forced them from their jungle villages. Sniper fire harassed the Marines holding the hilltop outposts surrounding the combat base. The daily patrols around the perimeter of the base found fresh shoe prints near the concertina wire; some cleverly concealed cuts in the wire were found and repaired.

When 3/26 arrived in December, Lownds sent these Marines to the northwest to Hills 881N and 881S. The scene of much heavy fighting in the spring of 1967, this hill mass was the area's dominant terrain feature. It was also the Americans' westernmost position in South Vietnam. Company I, 3/26, dug in on Hill 881S. One kilometer to the east, Company K took up residence on Hill 861, which overlooked the base's airfield.

When 2/26 arrived on 16 January, Lownds sent it north to outpost Hill 558, just east of Hill 861. From there it could guard against any enemy infiltration down the Rao Quang River, which ran from the hill down past the base. These troops could also help their comrades on Hill 861, if the need arose.

After the 2 January incident, tension built around the base. Lownds and everyone else knew that the enemy was going to hit; it was only a matter of when. Then, to confirm Lownds's suspicions, and raise his anxiety, allied intelligence reported that the 325C NVA Division had been spotted about twenty kilometers northwest of the combat base. Within reinforcing range to the northeast were two regiments of the 320th NVA Division. If that weren't enough to whet Lownds's appetite, word soon came that a third division, the 304th, and a Front Headquarters were sited just across the border in Laos.

"They are going to attack," Lownds told his staff officers during a 10 January briefing, "and we are going to inflict a heavy loss on them."

Still, there was no overt sign of the enemy. The dense jungle blanketing the region made it very difficult to detect enemy units. Besides regular combat patrols from his line companies, Lownds depended on small recon teams to be his eyes and ears. The highly trained, eight-man recon units helicoptered daily into the remote reaches of western Quang Tri Province to search for the enemy. Silently, carrying a minimum of equipment, their faces streaked with green greasepaint, the recon Marines stealthily searched the steep hillsides, deep ravines, and wide valleys for any evidence of the enemy. No matter where they looked, though, they found nothing. Until 17 January.

Early that morning, a team was hit while patrolling the south slope of Hill 881N. The patrol leader and his RTO were killed and several others were wounded in the sudden blaze of small arms fire. The survivors fell back, frantically radioing for help. By chance, a platoon from Company I was patrolling nearby. After ordering his men to drop their packs, 2d Lt. Thomas Brindley led his platoon on the run to the team's aid. Once on the scene, Brindley called in medevac helicopters for the dead and wounded. When that was handled, the young lieutenant pulled back. Not another shot had been fired.

Two days later, another patrol from Company I returned to the scene of the ambush. Colonel Lownds had ordered a search for a missing radio and some classified radio call sign sheets. About one hundred meters south of the site, the patrol's point man suddenly fired. Not fifteen meters away, an enemy soldier dropped into the underbrush. As the point man dove for cover, the enemy soldier's comrades filled the air above him with hot lead. The patrol leader, 2d Lt. Harry F. Fromme, immediately radioed for supporting mortar fire. As the 81mm mortar shells crashed through the tangled canopy of vegetation, the patrol pulled back. Fortunately, no one had been hit.

Under the direction of their tireless commander, Capt. William Dabney, the men of Company I had turned their position on Hill 881S into a virtual fortress. Multiple concertina wire barriers surrounded the encampment. Hundreds of Claymore mines—antipersonnel weapons mounted on stubby tripod legs—had been aimed along likely avenues of attack. The camp fairly bristled with heavy weapons, including machine guns, recoilless rifles, mortars, and three 105mm howitzers. It would take a massive attack by a determined enemy force to overrun Company I's camp.

But Dabney didn't want any surprises. He had to know what was going on north of him. He asked Lownds for permission to take his whole company on a sweep of Hill 881N. Lownds approved the request. On the afternoon of 19 January, one hundred men from the combat base were helicoptered to Hill 881S to take up the slack while Company I was gone.

At 0500 on 20 January, Dabney led the 185 men of Company I out of their perimeter and toward Hill 881N. A thick layer of milky-white fog covered the area like a taut blanket. The swirling mist cut visibility to mere feet. Though the men had walked this land many times before, they inched forward cautiously, all their muscles tight in anticipation of a burst of enemy fire. No one knew what awaited just a feet away behind the curtain of moisture. In four hours Company I had moved but five hundred meters. Finally, by around 0900 the sun had baked away the fog. Now, Dabney had his eyes back. The whole company picked up the pace, moving forward with confidence.

The company advanced in two columns several hundred meters apart along parallel ridgelines. Lieutenant Brindley led the right-hand column, proceeding up a treeless ridgeline pointed right at the top of Hill 881N. In a similar column to the left, Lieutenant Fromme led his platoon uphill. Behind him came Dabney and his command group. Trailing them was a forty-five-man reserve platoon led by 2d Lt. Michael H. Thomas. A barrage of 105mm howitzer shells preceded the Marines up the hill in an attempt to flush out any waiting NVA. It didn't work.

Suddenly, automatic weapons fire ripped into Lieutenant Brindley's column. The point man dropped heavily on the trail. The other Marines dove for cover. From his position with the left column, Dabney ordered Fromme to move forward and outflank the NVA firing on Brindley. The young lieutenant had barely started his men moving when a single burst of enemy machine-gun fire ripped into the platoon. Twenty men dropped. Fromme hastily radioed for a medevac. When the CH-34 appeared overhead, a stream of NVA machine-gun fire from a ridge farther west sliced into the craft. Trailing flames, the chopper slammed into the earth just in front of Fromme. Only one crew member survived the inferno.

In the meantime, Brindley had bombarded the enemy positions

facing him with volley after volley of artillery fire. Then, in the best Marine Corps tradition, he personally led an attack straight up the hill. Urging his men forward, the young officer overcame stubborn resistance to throw the enemy off the hill. Though Brindley's gallantry earned him a Navy Cross, it was awarded posthumously; he died in the final charge.

When Dabney heard this, he sent his executive officer forward to take command of Brindley's platoon. He then ordered Lieutenant Thomas to take his reserve platoon from the left ridge to reinforce what remained of Brindley's platoon. Accompanied by Dabney, Thomas and his men hastily crossed the five hundred meters of open ground. A short time later they were digging in around the hilltop. When Thomas learned that eight members of Brindley's platoon had been badly wounded and left isolated on the ridge's eastern slope, he immediately leaped from his hole to go to their rescue. He took all of five steps before he was cut down by a blast of AK-47 fire. His platoon sergeant then went to the aid of the isolated Marines, carrying several of the badly wounded men to safety.

From his fighting hole Dabney directed supporting fire on the enemy's positions. At his command, high-speed jets streaked earthward to unleash tons of bombs or gallons of napalm on the NVA. When he ordered it, batteries of powerful howitzers miles away sent high-explosive shells slamming into the hill above him. On his cue, the mortars, recoilless rifles, and cannon on Hill 881S added their voices to the cacophony of terror that surrounded Hill 881N. By 1730, with seven dead and thirty-five wounded on his hands, Dabney realized that he didn't have the strength to continue the fight. He ordered a withdrawal back to Hill 881S. In short order the ragged column of Marines, staggering under the weight of the casualties, headed to the security of their compound.

Dabney had no way of knowing it, but his company had just engaged in the opening fight of what would prove to be the longest, most controversial battle of the Vietnam War.

At the same time that Captain Dabney was maneuvering his platoons against Hill 881N, Company B, 1/26, tasked with guarding the combat base's perimeter, accepted the surrender of an NVA defector along the base's eastern end. Lieutenant La Than Tonc proved to be a veritable gold mine of information. He confirmed the presence of the 325C and 304th NVA Infantry Divisions around Khe Sanh. He pinpointed the location of the 320th Infantry Division as being near the Rockpile; from there it intended to attack Camp Carroll. The talkative NVA defector further revealed detailed plans for attacks on Hills 881S and 861 and the combat base itself that very night.

Lieutenant Tonc's information was so detailed and so precise that many Marine intelligence officers doubted him. However, Colonel Lownds, General Tompkins, and General Cushman all elected to believe him. Not only did his information coincide with other data available to III MAF intelligence analysts, but the Marines had nothing to lose by acting on his information.

So Colonel Lownds ordered Captain Dabney and Capt. Norman J. Jasper, Jr., the Company K commander on Hill 861, to prepare for the attacks. Lownds also passed the information to the U.S. Army Special Forces troops stationed at Lang Vei, about nine kilometers farther west along Route 9.

As darkness fell, Marine artillerymen at the combat base registered their cannon one last time; they wanted to be able to deliver accurate supporting fire to the infantry as fast as they could. On the surrounding hills, individual Marines checked their weapons, placed grenades within easy reach, filled a few more ammo magazines, put out trip flares, and settled in for a long night. They were as ready as they could be.

At thirty minutes past midnight on 21 January, the first of several hundred NVA rockets, mortar shells, and RPGs slammed into Hill 861. A short time later, bursts of heavy machine-gun fire peppered the hillside. Deep in their bunkers, the Marines of Company K gripped their weapons and prayed.

At 0100 more than 250 NVA soldiers climbed up Hill 861's steep southwest side. Despite the defensive fire, the enemy soldiers blasted a path through the perimeter wire. Within minutes they had poured into Company K's position. Captain Jasper took three hits in the fight's opening minutes. Unable to continue, he turned over command to his executive officer. The ferocious attack drove the Marines out of their prepared positions to higher ground on the hill's crest.

One kilometer to the west, Company I watched the battle in fascination. Anticipating an attack on his own position, Captain Dabney and his men could only wait for it to begin. After several hours of quiet, Dabney decided that the enemy wasn't coming for him that night. He ordered his mortars to fire in support of Company K.

On Hill 861, Company K's surviving Marines still fought on. Despite the battering they'd been taking all night, at 0500 they counterattacked. Down the enemy-filled trenches they charged. In hand-to-hand, no-holds-barred fighting, the plucky Marines retook their hill. Colonel Lownds relaxed when he received the good news. He issued orders to ready the medevac helicopters and round up replacements for Captain Jasper's battered command. He wanted the CH-46s in the air as soon as the morning fog lifted. He'd barely finished giving these orders when the NVA launched a volley of rockets from the slopes of Hill 881N.

On Hill 881S, Captain Dabney and his men watched in awe as dozens of 122mm rockets streamed over their heads toward the combat base. Seconds later they hit. Explosion after explosion erupted all over the base. The steel matting covering the airstrip was ripped to shreds, the waiting helicopters were flung about like toys, bunkers collapsed, tents were blown away, and zinging steel shards tore human flesh.

Worst of all, though, was the loss of nearly all of the Marines' ammo stores. One of the first rockets landed right in the middle of the ammo dump. A colossal explosion rocked the entire eastern end of the base as the bulk of fifteen hundred tons of munitions went up. Flaming debris and unexploded shells rained down all over the base. To make matters worse, drums of aviation fuel erupted, sending rivers of flame flooding into the ammo dump.

In the midst of this holocaust, Marine gunners frantically searched for any sign of the enemy rocket sites but without avail. Thick fog cloaked the slopes of Hill 881N, masking the enemy locations. With the glowing duds from their own dump raining down on them, the artillerymen could only fire random barrages into the fog, hoping that they would hit the enemy.

Enemy shells slammed into the combat base all day. Fires burned everywhere, sending thick columns of black smoke skyward. Because the airstrip was reduced to just two thousand feet of usable runway, only six cargo planes made it in that day. They brought in just 24 of the 160 tons of supplies that Lownds needed every day to keep his regiment going.

To compound the problems, at 0630, NVA infantry attacked the ARVN troops garrisoning Khe Sanh village, just a few kilometers to the west of the combat base on Route 9. Though the ARVN and their American advisers kept the enemy at bay, Colonel Lownds was too busy to send them any help. Late that afternoon he ordered the village evacuated.

With the enemy now between Khe Sanh and the U.S. Army Special Forces camp at Lang Vei, and with Route 9 to the east still held by the NVA, the 26th Marines were truly cut off. The world's attention began to focus on their little plot of ground.

Almost from the moment the siege at Khe Sanh began, the Marines' position there had been compared to the French situation at Dien Bien Phu a decade earlier. There, in the mountainous region north and west of Hanoi, the French Expeditionary force commander had used his paratroopers as bait to draw out what he believed were the ragtag forces of rebel general Vo Nguyen Giap. Giap's forces proved to be anything but ragtag. His peasant army outfought France's finest troops. Against all odds, Giap delivered supplies and ammunition to the remote battlefield. From the surrounding high ground, Giap's artillery loosed a torrent of shells on the French garrison. Finally, on 7 May 1954, after a fifty-six-day siege, the surviving French paratroopers surrendered. With that event, the First Indochina War ended in a victory for Ho Chi Minh's forces.

American commanders from Colonel Lownds to President Johnson began comparing Khe Sanh to Dien Bien Phu. There were many similarities: both were remote sites with little strategic value, both could be shelled by direct observation, both depended on aircraft for resupply, and both were defended by elite troops.

But there were differences, too—important differences. Dien Bien Phu sat in a valley surrounded by high peaks occupied by enemy troops. Khe Sanh sat on a high plateau, and the nearby hilltops were held by Marines. The French had no artillery to support them from the outside. The Marines at Khe Sanh not only had their own artillery but a battery of powerful U.S. Army 175mm guns at Camp Carroll. Dien Bien Phu was completely isolated with no hope of overland relief. Route 9 to Khe Sanh could be opened if necessary. The French commander had just two hundred aircraft of all types to support his troops and the garrison could be resupplied only via parachute drop. In a major contrast, General Westmoreland had thousands of aircraft of all types, from observation helicopters to B-52 bombers, available to support Khe Sanh. It was this massive force that gave Westmoreland the confidence to seek the battle. In fact, he wanted the enemy to attack. Then he could destroy him.

Not everyone shared Westmoreland's optimism. In Washington, a clearly nervous President Johnson demanded hourly situation reports. He became so absorbed in the tactical situation at Khe Sanh that he wandered into the White House situation room at all hours of the day or night to learn the latest of the siege.

Most of the news from Khe Sanh was not good. Because the helicopters based there drew enemy mortar fire as soon as they turned over their turbines, Colonel Lownds decided to move the craft to Quang Tri City, thirty minutes east. But it didn't make much difference. The rotary-winged craft were still like mortar magnets.

As soon as the fog cleared on the morning of 22 January, the first resupply helicopter touched down on Hill 881S. Seconds later a pair of 120mm mortar rounds slammed into Company I's position. Huge chunks of jagged metal flew across the hill. Five men died and 15 were wounded badly enough to be medevacked. In just two days Dabney's company had been whittled down from 185 to 123.

With the enemy pressing him, Lownds asked for reinforcements. Though additional troops would strain the logistics pipeline, Khe Sanh had to have them. At midafternoon on 22 January, the nearly 1,000 members of 1/9 boarded C-130s at Camp Evans near Hue. A short time later they were forming up along Khe Sanh's airfield. After sorting out their gear, they marched west out of the base. Not quite two kilometers later they were digging in around a small hill that had served as a rock quarry. The western approaches to the Khe Sanh combat base were now secure.

For some time General Westmoreland had been growing weary of the Marines. Ever since their arrival in South Vietnam in March

1965, they had resisted his plans for victory. Both III MAF commanders had objected to his orders to carry the war to the wild reaches of the interior of South Vietnam; they believed that the war would be won among the populous coastal regions. Senior Marine commanders had been reluctant to establish a combat base at Khe Sanh in 1967, feeling that it did nothing to solidify their position. And they had not had any enthusiasm for the construction of the "McNamara Line" south of the DMZ.

With more than twenty U.S. Army battalions now operating in I Corps, Westmoreland decided that it was time to put the army in charge. On 25 January, he ordered the opening of an MACV forward headquarters in I Corps. The Marines were outraged. General Tompkins called the move "a slap in the face. The most unpardonable thing Saigon ever did."

General Westmoreland ignored the protests. That same day he began planning for the relief of Khe Sanh. Operation Pegasus would be an army show. The heliborne 1st Cavalry Division (Airmobile) would reopen Route 9 by leapfrogging down its length. Westmoreland ordered the cavalrymen to move from Phu Bai to Quang Tri City to prepare for the operation.

While all this was going on, the weather over Khe Sanh cleared. As a result, enemy activity decreased during the last days of January. Colonel Lownds used the lull to repair the airstrip and rush in supplies. The C-130s could now land without interference from enemy artillery. On 27 January, reinforcements in the form of the 37th ARVN Ranger Battalion arrived. The jaunty, red beret-crowned little soldiers took up positions in trenches two hundred meters east of the base. The outlook was improving for the men at Khe Sanh.

Then the Tet Offensive erupted.

Beginning prematurely in the morning hours of 30 January, well-coordinated attacks by Viet Cong and North Vietnamese Army forces were launched all across South Vietnam. That morning and the next, thirty-six of forty-four provincial capitals were attacked. Five of six autonomous cities were hit. Every major airfield was bombarded by mortars. Sixty-four district capitals were soon battling for survival. Even the massive U.S. embassy complex in downtown Saigon was nearly overrun by enemy attackers.

Just about the only major allied base that was not hit in the opening round of the Tet Offensive was Khe Sanh. None of the five NVA divisions reported to be in western Quang Tri Province joined in the offensive. Westmoreland believed he knew why.

Referring to the countrywide attacks, General Westmoreland said, "This is a diversionary effort to take attention away from the north, from an attack on Khe Sanh." The MACV commander was still convinced that the NVA had Khe Sanh as their main target.

The only thing the Tet Offensive brought to Khe Sanh was the return of bad weather. There were no massive bombardments, no human wave attacks against the combat base or its outposts. Instead, the dense fog reappeared. Still, the allied combatants waited in nervous anticipation for an attack. Then, on 2 February, one well-placed enemy rocket tore into the U.S. Army communications bunker. The explosion killed four soldiers and temporarily cut off the base from the outside world. After this, quiet returned for several days—until the night of 4 February, when highly classified electronic sensors detected a large body of people moving toward Hill 881S. Carefully plotting the enemy's probable route over the rugged terrain, the Fire Support Control Center (FSCC) at Khe Sanh picked a target box north of Captain Dabney's position. On signal, five hundred high-explosive artillery shells shredded the designated site. Even though there was no evidence that their aim had been accurate, when no enemy ground attack materialized against Company I, the men of the FSCC congratulated themselves.

A short time later, at 0400 on 5 February, NVA sappers blasted apart the barbed wire perimeter protecting Company E, 2/26, on Hill 861 Alpha, a spur of Hill 861. The follow-up enemy mortar barrage killed seven Marines. Volleys of well-aimed RPGs knocked out several key automatic weapons positions. The enemy infantry then poured through the torn wire. The defenders gave ground in the face of the bold attack, but the assault faltered as the enemy soldiers stopped to loot the abandoned Marine positions. Company commander Capt. Earle G. Breeding coordinated massive volumes of supporting artillery fire from both Camp Carroll and Khe Sanh, further disrupting the enemy's attack. Still, the NVA pressed on. By 0500 they held one fourth of the hill.

Demonstrating a tenacious fortitude, Breeding launched a counterattack. Using knives, rifle butts, grenades, and bare fists, the men
of Company E blew through the NVA. By dawn the Marines had recaptured the lost ground. One hundred nine enemy bodies littered
the area.

Though periodic bombardments continued to pound the combat base over the next few days, the main action now shifted west to
the Special Forces camp at Lang Vei.

Sitting alone at the end of Route 9 since Khe Sanh village had
been lost on 21 January, the Green Berets were not overly concerned
about their perilous situation. After all, the very nature of their duty
required them to exist in isolated surroundings. Plus, Lang Vei was
one of the best built and defended Special Forces camps in all of
South Vietnam. Its combat bunkers were well constructed with reinforced concrete and thick timbers. Besides the 18 Special Forces
soldiers, the camp roster included some 300 members of the Civilian Irregular Defense Group and 160 Montagnards in a Mobile
Strike Force. The camp's defenders were well armed with more than
a dozen mortars, six recoilless rifles, two .50-caliber machine guns,
thirty-nine Browning automatic rifles, two M60 machine guns, light
antitank weapons, and more than half a million rounds of ammunition. And the Marine artillery at Khe Sanh could be called on for
support. The camp commander, U.S. Army captain Frank C.
Willoughby, felt that he had enough strength to hold off a full enemy regiment.

At dawn on 6 February, NVA mortar shells began dropping on the
camp. The pounding lasted more than an hour, but there were few
casualties. The heavily reinforced bunkers proved their worth. Later
that same day the NVA ambushed a routine patrol operating less
than one kilometer west of the camp. The Green Beret leading the
patrol was captured.

At about 2000 that night, sentries heard the unmistakable sound
of diesel engines approaching the camp. Willoughby radioed
Colonel Lownds to ask for a test of his artillery support.

At forty-two minutes past midnight on 7 February, perimeter
guards along Lang Vei's southeast quadrant frantically radioed the
command bunker. "We've got tanks in the wire!"

At least seven NVA light tanks supported by NVA infantry were tearing through the camp's wire barrier. Willoughby called Khe Sanh for artillery support, then raced outside the command bunker to join the fight.

Though the Green Berets and their indigenous forces fought valiantly, they were no match for the NVA. At 0300 Willoughby radioed Colonel Lownds to execute the long-established relief plan. He declined.

Colonel Lownds thought that sending a Marine company down Route 9, as called for in the original relief plan, was now plainly suicidal. An alternative plan to use helicopters to evacuate the Americans from the base was also abandoned as too risky due to the presence of enemy tanks. Plus, Lownds felt that the combat base was next on the enemy's list, and he didn't want to weaken its defenses.

By late afternoon on 7 February, Lang Vei was gone. Of the nearly 500 defenders, 325 were lost. Only 14 of the 24 Americans survived, and 11 of those were wounded; among them was Captain Willoughby.

General Westmoreland was greatly disturbed by the loss of Lang Vei. He issued orders directly to General Cushman to send helicopters to pick up survivors of the disaster. The Marines' failure to respond to the Lang Vei debacle depleted Westmoreland's remaining confidence in them. Two days later he sent his deputy, army general Creighton W. Abrams, Jr., to I Corps to oversee the deployment of troops in northern I Corps.

Oblivious to the politicking of their senior commanders, the Marines at Khe Sanh endured another heavy shelling beginning at 0400 on 8 February. Hundreds of enemy rockets, artillery shells, and mortar rounds relentlessly pounded the combat base and its outlying positions. Particularly hard hit was Company A, 1/26, holding a spur of ground near the rock quarry occupied by 1/9. At 0420, after a violently brutal shelling, NVA infantry charged the positions held by one of Company A's platoons. Easily rolling over the shell-shocked Marines, the NVA quickly knocked out one bunker after another. After a counterattack retook the position at 0900, twenty-five of the fifty-two defending Marines were found dead; of the rest, all but one had been wounded.

As February progressed, life at the Khe Sanh Combat Base assumed a tense routine. Along with the heavy gray fog that draped the base every morning, the round-the-clock bombing and shelling filled the air with a thick red dust that cast an eerie pall over the base. Smoke from burning fires contributed to the dense haze. The debris scattered throughout the base as a result of the enemy bombardments gave it the appearance of a shantytown.

Though actual contact with enemy soldiers was scarce, the Marines at Khe Sanh knew that their foe was still out there in the fog because every day at least one hundred enemy shells, mortars, or rockets fell on the base and its outposts. Every day men were killed or wounded. By early February, 10 percent of the base's defenders had become casualties. Though other soldiers in earlier wars had endured more intense artillery barrages, the shelling of Khe Sanh wore heavily on the Marines' nerves because of its persistence and their inability to halt it. Despite their best efforts to destroy NVA artillery positions with numerous B-52 bomber strikes, they never succeeded in silencing the deadly weapons.

Some Marines responded to the constant shelling with defiance. Every morning Captain Dabney held a flag-raising ceremony on Hill 881S. He would holler, "Attention to Colors." Every ragged Marine at the outpost then stood at attention. Accompanied by a bugled "To the Colors," a tattered and torn American flag was raised on a radio antenna. About halfway through the ceremony the distinctive *thunk* of the first NVA mortar shell leaving its tube on Hill 881N would be heard. The experienced combatants knew that they had just twenty-one seconds to finish the ceremony before the shell, and those following it, fell to earth. As soon as the bugler finished his tune, everyone would dive for cover. An instant later, the shells would erupt across the hilltop.

Supplying the troops at Khe Sanh proved to be a bigger problem than initially anticipated. The persistent fog frequently reduced visibility to zero-zero conditions, forcing the pilots of the air force C-123s and C-130s to descend to a landing using only their flight instruments. As a result, they had to fly a precise path as prescribed by the ground radar control operators. It was thus simple for the NVA to set up their antiaircraft guns directly below the flight path and pepper the unseen cargo planes as they passed overhead in the fog. The enemy gunners couldn't miss.

If the air force planes made it onto the runway, they instantly became huge, attractive targets for the NVA artillery and mortar gunners. To reduce vulnerable time on the ground, a pilot typically taxied his plane back down the ramp at a fast pace while the cargo crew rolled one-ton pallets out the craft's open tailgate. If all went well, the last pallet left the plane just as the pilot turned back on the runway for his takeoff. In the final seconds before the plane began its takeoff roll, a mass of bodies would rush up from the trenches bordering the airstrip and race for the open tailgate. Marines who were rotating home, the walking wounded, corpsmen carrying casualties on stretchers, and visitors to the base all scrambled to board the plane before the tailgate closed. Then, with engines screaming, the plane would rush down the runway, lift off, and almost immediately disappear in the fog.

Three minutes was the typical length of time that a cargo plane stayed on the ground at Khe Sanh. Still, during the last half of February, only fifty planes made it into the base. The rest of the badly needed supplies arrived by parachute.

Since 20 January, any patrols departing the combat base had been limited to a distance of a few hundred meters or line of sight. On 25 February, Colonel Lownds decided to send out a twenty-nine-man patrol from Company B to search for a small mortar that, for several days, had been hammering their positions with uncanny accuracy. For this first foray beyond line of sight, the Marines were heavily armed, each man carrying at least five hundred rounds of ammo and a half dozen grenades. They were to follow a precisely prescribed route so that artillery and mortar support could respond instantly.

Soon after leaving, the patrol leader, 2d Lt. Don Jacques, spotted three enemy soldiers casually walking along a dirt road just south of the base. Overly anxious to tangle with some live NVA after more than a month of fighting phantoms, Jacques and his patrol galloped after the enemy soldiers. It was a trap, a deadly trap.

The patrol bounded across the road and right into an ambush. A violent sheet of automatic weapons and rifle fire tore into the Marines. They fell in clumps, their screams rising above the weapons' roars. Lieutenant Jacques frantically radioed for help. A fifty-man relief force raced out of the base. As soon as the Marines reached the road, the NVA sprang another, more powerful ambush. Machine-gun fire, RPGs, and mortars drove the relief force to the ground. Casualties were very heavy.

With his rescuers pinned down, Jacques pleaded for more help. The rest of Company B got ready to go. Colonel Lownds said no. He had no desire to feed more forces into the NVA killing machine. He ordered air strikes and artillery to hit the enemy positions while the survivors withdrew as best they could.

It took more than three hours for all the living Marines to return to the combat base. Lieutenant Jacques was not one of them. Twenty-five Marine bodies remained outside the base. They would stay there until the siege was lifted.

Although General Westmoreland continued to feel that Khe Sanh would be the decisive battle he desired, by this time others were starting to openly disagree. Members of MACV's senior staff began to realize that the siege of Khe Sanh had, indeed, been a feint, designed to tie down huge numbers of American troops in remote regions while Giap's main forces struck South Vietnam's vital cities. On 6 March, after a detailed study of all the available intelligence material relating to Khe Sanh, even General Westmoreland reluctantly concluded that the enemy had abandoned its plan of capturing the combat base. Three days later, Westmoreland so advised President Johnson.

The next day it was revealed to the public that General Westmoreland had requested 206,000 additional troops for service in South Vietnam. America was stunned. For weeks Westmoreland had been proclaiming the great victories his troops had achieved over the enemy as a result of their foolhardy Tet attacks. Khe Sanh had come to symbolize American resolve against the wily foe. Surely, total victory could not be far off. But no, said the general. He expected major enemy attacks in Quang Tri and Thua Thien Provinces. None of the enemy divisions reported to be around Khe Sanh had yet been committed to the fight. Instead, they were poised for a full scale invasion across the DMZ. Only with more troops could he meet this threat and defeat the North Vietnamese Army. As the political repercussions from this unexpected request reverberated across the country, President Johnson made several significant decisions regarding the war in South Vietnam. Among them was his 23 March announcement that General Westmoreland would soon be coming home. The NVA greeted this news by pumping 1,109 artillery shells onto the Khe Sanh combat base.

Two days later General Westmoreland traveled to Washington, D.C., to brief President Johnson on his plans for the relief of the siege. The general told his commander in chief that he believed it was politically imperative to break the siege with a massive demonstration of America's military might. The improving weather would permit a display of force just like Westmoreland had experienced in World War II. It would be the biggest land battle of the war. Westmoreland told the president that more than thirty thousand men would take part in Operation Pegasus. The major component would be the army's 1st Cavalry Division. The airmobile cavalrymen would leapfrog down Route 9, establishing a series of mutually supporting firebases as they headed toward Khe Sanh. Heavy bombardments would precede the division's movement, softening up the enemy's positions. Then the cavalrymen would swoop down, surprising and overwhelming the enemy defenders. It was a meticulously planned, multifaceted operation, just like those of World War II.

The senior Marine commanders were wary of the relief effort. They had not wanted to hold Khe Sanh in the first place and then had been severely criticized for not defending it well. General Cushman was adamant when he told MACV that he did not want an "implication of a rescue or breaking of the siege by outside forces."

To maintain that posture, Company B, which had suffered 185 casualties, including 50 dead, during the siege, attacked out of the base early on the foggy morning of 30 March. Their stated objective was the recovery of the 25 bodies left behind from Lieutenant Jacques's patrol. Advancing with the protective cover of a double box of artillery that dropped shells just 75 meters from them, Company B's men made it to the dirt road without problems. When the artillery fire moved on, the Marines fixed bayonets and prepared for their attack. On signal they charged across the road.

Just then, the enveloping fog lifted.

The startled enemy responded by dropping dozens of mortar shells right on the Marines. One exploded smack in the middle of the command group, killing the RTO, the artillery FO, and the heavy-mortar FO. The company commander, Capt. Kenneth W. Pipes, though hit by shrapnel, urged his men onward. Using flamethrowers, grenades, satchel charges, and cold steel, the vengeful Marines destroyed one enemy bunker after another. By noon it was over. The Marines killed 115 NVA in the fight.

The dead Marines of the lost patrol were recovered. Their remains had been undisturbed.

At 0700, on 1 April, the 1st Marines attacked west down Route 9 from Cam Lo. At the same time, the 1st Cavalry Division (Airmobile) sent its infantry-laden helicopters to the site of their first LZ. No resistance was met by either force. But none had been expected. The charade was simply for the cameras and the politicians.

Over the next week, the cavalrymen slowly continued their westward advance. On 8 April, they linked up with a patrol from Khe Sanh. There was no joyous celebration of the occasion. The Marines were adamant that they had not been rescued from anything. As far as they were concerned, the enemy threat had ended before Operation Pegasus began.

On 11 April, Westmoreland, who had made a special trip to Washington for the occasion, stood alongside President Johnson on the White House lawn as he triumphantly announced the linkup between the army and the Marines. And, he noted, the Marine engineers had once again opened Route 9 between Dong Ha and Khe Sanh.

A few days later, Colonel Lownds turned over command of his regiment to his replacement, Col. Bruce Meyer. For his sustained outstanding leadership during his eight months at Khe Sanh, Lownds was awarded a Navy Cross.

The battle for Khe Sanh ended where it began. Three companies of 3/26—Companies K, L, and M; more than five hundred men—would attack Hill 881N. The enemy-occupied hill had been a thorn in the Americans' side for more than eighty days; when the 3d Battalion was finished with the hill, it would be cleared of enemy soldiers.

In the eerie, fog-enshrouded, early morning hours of Easter Sunday, 14 April, the riflemen moved to their jump-off positions. For some of the men it was the first time in weeks they'd been out of their trenches. With ragged uniforms and sallow faces, the Marines waited patiently to exact their revenge.

The bombardment of Hill 881N began at 0400. From the combat base and Camp Carroll, dozens of howitzers blasted the hill with 8-inch, 105mm, 155mm, and 175mm shells. Marine jets roared earthward to unleash a frightening array of high-explosive aerial bombs and napalm canisters. From Hill 881S, recoilless rifles, mortars, and .50-caliber machine guns paid back the enemy-held hill for all the pain and suffering it had inflicted during the siege.

At 0540 the infantry started forward. A short time later scout dogs raised the first alert. Quick bursts of rifle fire attested to the deaths of the enemy soldiers manning the outposts. Resembling a colony of swarming ants, the Marines clawed their way through the enemy's defenses, stopping only long enough to blow away any enemy soldiers they found. Seized by a blood lust, some men repeatedly plunged their sharpened bayonets into dead bodies, unable to be restrained by either their sergeants or their officers.

By noon the assault companies had reached the top of the hill. The mopping up of small pockets of resistance continued for several hours. By 1430 Hill 881N belonged to the Marines. Their casualties were surprisingly light—6 killed and 32 wounded; 106 North Vietnamese were killed.

The III MAF had hoped to abandon Khe Sanh right after Hill 881N was captured. Westmoreland vetoed that idea. The combat base was too big a symbol to close so soon after the fighting. The 26th Marines, however, were removed from the base. They moved east to take up positions along the DMZ.

General Cushman continued to press for the closing of Khe Sanh. He argued that the new base at Ca Lu, west of the Rockpile, not only gave the Marines a presence in northwest Quang Tri Province but was out of the range of the enemy artillery in Laos. It was also easier to supply and not susceptible to fog. At last Westmoreland concurred. He insisted on one restriction: the combat base could not be closed until after he had turned over command of MACV to his successor.

Thus, on 17 June, six days after Westmoreland departed the country, the new MACV commander, Gen. Creighton W. Abrams, Jr., signed the order authorizing the abandonment of Khe Sanh.

That very day the dismantling began. The Marines slashed sandbags, blew up bunkers, filled in trenches, tore up runway matting, packed up all possible materiel, and blew up what they couldn't move. When the base was unrecognizable, a well-guarded truck column started east down Route 9. Along the way the troops destroyed the bridges and tore up the roadway where they could.

By the end of June, the Khe Sanh Combat Base was no more.

The rest of the 3d Marine Division had not been idle while the 26th Marines fought at Khe Sanh. The year began with Operation Checkers, transferring the few remaining 3d Marine Division infantry battalions that were still holding positions west of Hue up to Quang Tri Province. When that was done, on 10 January, General Tompkins moved his headquarters to Dong Ha from Phu Bai. A division rear remained at Phu Bai for several more months but was eventually relocated north to Quang Tri City.

During Tompkins's tenure, operational names changed from being used to identify individual timed operations to identifiers for specific TAORs. As a result, the division's combat operations continued for indefinite periods, not beginning and ending with the rapid-fire specificity of the search and destroy era of previous years. Thus, as 1968 began, the 9th Marines were still conducting Operation Kentucky, started on 1 November 1967, in the Leatherneck Square area.

At the mouth of the Cua Viet on the South China Sea sat Camp Kistler, home of the 3d Marines. About ten kilometers inland, a branch of the Cua Viet, the Bo Dieu, flowed past the 3d Marine Division headquarters at Dong Ha. Just north of this confluence, the Cua Viet turned south and eventually ran past Quang Tri City. The bulk of supplies for Dong Ha and Quang Tri City were moved down these waterways by U.S. Navy utility craft assigned to Task Force Clearwater. Thus, this vital link had to be kept open.

In a periodic sweep of the land bordering the waterway, SLF Bravo, BLT 3/1, began Operation Saline on 30 January by attacking north from the Cua Viet just a few kilometers inland of Camp

Kistler. Almost immediately the Marines ran into stiff resistance from the 803d NVA Regiment near My Loc, just north of the river. Though 3/1 overcame the enemy, the fight confirmed a division intelligence summary that the NVA were establishing positions north of the Cua Viet from which they could interdict river traffic.

To keep the NVA off balance, General Tompkins had planned a thrust into the DMZ in the late spring. These plans were interrupted when it was learned that the 320th NVA Division was moving south toward Dong Ha adjacent to Route 1. Although it was not known if the NVA planned to actually attack the base or were more intent on cutting off its supplies by disrupting river traffic, the 3d Marines went out to meet the 320th before the NVA did either.

Battle for Dong Ha

The opening contact with the 320th NVA Division came early on 29 April. Two battalions of the 2d Regiment, 1st ARVN Infantry Division bumped into the NVA seven kilometers north of Dong Ha. As the fight raged on and it began to look as if the ARVN were beaten, General Tompkins dispatched part of his division reserve from Cam Lo, ten kilometers to the west, to help them. Task Force Robbie, consisting of a rifle company from 1/9 and a tank company from the 3d Tank Battalion, made it just three kilometers east of Cam Lo before being ambushed by a strong NVA force. After losing eleven dead, twenty-nine wounded, and four tanks, TF Robbie limped back to Cam Lo.

Surprised at the viciousness of the ambush, General Tompkins ordered 3/9 to counterattack the next day, 30 April. To backstop the ARVN still engaged along Route 1, Tompkins ordered the 3d Marines to send a rifle company to guard a bridge on Route 1 a few kilometers north of Dong Ha.

Colonel Milton A. Hull, 3d Marines commander, currently had three battalions opconned to his regiment: the 1st Amphibious Tractor Battalion, which operated just inland of the South China Sea on the north side of the Cua Viet; 1/3, which was operating south of the river; and BLT 2/4, SLF Alpha, which operated north of the Cua Viet between the 1st Amphibious Tractors and the 2d ARVN Regiment to the west. Colonel Hull ordered Capt. James E. Liv-

ingston to take his Company E, 2/4, to the bridge from its position
in Nhi Ha, a deserted hamlet about four kilometers north of the Cua
Viet. Livingston and his men were carried by UH-34 helicopters to
their new position north of the bridge on the afternoon of 29 April.

Early the next morning, Company H, 2/4, while on routine patrol, was surprised to find NVA in the village of Dong Huan, a small
hamlet set on an unnamed tributary of the Cua Viet where it turned
south, and less than one kilometer above the Bo Dieu. The NVA were
already much farther south than was originally thought. A brief firefight erupted, with both sides exchanging short bursts of fire. Then,
as the Marines watched, other NVA fired a 57mm recoilless rifle at
two U.S. Navy utility landing craft (LCUs) moving on the Bo Dieu.
An instant later, the lead boat rocked as two shells ripped through
its thin sides. The boats whipped into a U-turn and sped back to
Dong Ha.

As soon as he got this news, battalion commander Lt. Col. William
Weise ordered Company H to attack Dong Huan from its position
in the hamlet of Bac Vong to the north. At about the same time, the
U.S. Navy halted all further river traffic between Camp Kistler, Dong
Ha, and Quang Tri City. The enemy had achieved his objective with
just a few well-placed shots.

The little peninsula between the Bo Dieu and the unnamed tributary to the north contained five hamlets laid out along an extended V. At the upper end of the right arm was Dong Huan.
Roughly five hundred meters south, at the tip of the V and on the
north bank of the Bo Dieu, sat An Lac. Five hundred meters up the
left arm was the largest of the five hamlets, Dai Do. A few hundred
meters farther northwest was Dinh To, and just past that hamlet was
Thuong Do.

Given the NVA's propensity for setting up situations where they
were dug in and their foe was in the open, Weise realized that he
had to secure Dai Do, directly to the west. He thus ordered Company
F to maneuver on Company H's right flank. Its objective was a cemetery just to the east of Dai Do.

Even though Company F hadn't yet moved into position, Company H nonetheless launched its attack at about 1400 on 30 April.
As the last pair of F-4 Phantom jets unleashed their five-hundred-

pound bombs and napalm canisters on Dong Huan, and the supporting artillery fired its final salvo, the company arose and, advancing on line, headed for the hamlet.

Enemy resistance was immediate, fierce, and at close range. Advancing through thick vegetation crisscrossed by hedges more than three meters high, the Marines were fired on by NVA from only two meters away. The crackling of AK-47s built slowly to a crescendo as enemy soldiers recovered from the bombardment. Popping up from spider holes hidden in the hedgerows, the NVA fired left and right. Hand-to-hand fighting erupted as NVA soldiers grappled with surprised Marines. Grenades tossed by both sides exploded in thundering crashes, felling Marines and killing NVA trapped in their holes. In the opening minutes of the attack the company commander, Capt. James L. Williams, went down with shrapnel wounds. As he lay bleeding in the dirt, his executive officer quickly assumed command.

Despite the heavy resistance, Company H pressed on. The fighting was at close quarters and deadly, but by 1430 the Marines had advanced through Dong Huan. Exhausted but pumped with adrenaline, they gazed across open paddies at An Lac to the south and Dai Do to the west. With some thirty dead NVA behind them, Lieutenant Colonel Weise gave Company H permission to return to its jumping-off point. There the Marines set up a night defensive position and evacuated their casualties.

At about the same time that Company H reached Dong Huan, Company F finally started moving toward Dai Do. The company commander, Capt. James Butler, had been delayed because he'd been trying to get a smoke screen laid around Dai Do. Because Company H had priority on the available artillery, his company would have to move across the five hundred meters of open ground completely exposed. Riding atop four amtracs, the Marines were hit as they neared the hamlet. At about 1430 RPGs flashed out from Dai Do, crashing into the amtracs, their explosions spilling Marines into the tall grass. This first barrage of RPGs damaged two amtracs and caused a number of casualties. After finally getting some artillery to fire on the hamlet, Butler sent two platoons forward. As they neared the first hedgerow, located about one hundred meters east of Dai Do, the enemy infantry let loose. The sudden roar of AK-47 fire drowned out the artillery explosions. The deadly sheet of automatic weapons fire dropped men all along the line. Those who could helped the wounded pull back to the rest of the company, now clustered around the amtracs.

After another artillery barrage tore into the hamlet, Company F's Marines rushed forward again. This time their tenacity allowed them to secure a tenuous toehold in northwest Dai Do. Determined to maintain that position, Weise wanted Company G to reinforce Company F. Colonel Hull told him there weren't enough helicopters available to transport them in time. Weise then appealed for the return of Company E from division control. Hull responded that not only was he working on that, he was also giving Weise Company B, 1/3. Weise ordered Company B to attack and secure An Lac.

From its position south of the Cua Viet near Camp Kistler, Company B, 1/3, boarded amtracs for the trip up the river. At about 1615 the vessels neared the beaches fronting An Lac along the Bo Dieu. In a scene resembling a World War II island beachhead assault, a withering hail of enemy fire raked Company B as its members poured out of the amtracs. The company commander died in a flurry of AK-47 fire just minutes after stepping ashore. A platoon leader and platoon sergeant died, too. In the first five minutes ashore, seven Marines were killed and fourteen were seriously wounded, including the company gunnery sergeant. Weise had had no idea that the NVA had that much strength in An Lac.

Using F-4 Phantoms from both the Marine Corps and air force, naval gunfire, and artillery, Weise pounded An Lac for the next thirty minutes. Only then could Company B, with just one surviving officer, secure its beachhead. Weise then ordered the company to dig in for the night, evacuate its wounded, and carry out a resupply.

In the meantime, Captain Butler, concerned about a counterattack against his company's weak positions in Dai Do, radioed Weise to request permission to pull back and link up with Company H for the night. Although Weise hated to give up hard-won ground, he gave his okay. It took until dark to complete the retrograde movement, but Company F finally straggled into Dong Huan with just fifty-five effectives. Together with Company H, they spent the night of 30

April–1 May secure behind a wall of artillery and mortar fire. Company B, 1/3, spent a similar night at An Lac.

Because of the beating that Company B, 1/3, had taken that day, Lieutenant Colonel Weise decided to commit his Company G to the fight. From its position ten kilometers northeast of the battleground, Company G was ordered to proceed immediately to An Lac, move through Company B, and attack Dai Do in the predawn darkness.

Adequate transportation still could not be secured, so Company G did not arrive at An Lac until about 0945 on 1 May. When all its men were ashore, Weise ordered the company commander, Capt. Jay R. Vargas, to move his Marines around Company B to the right, then attack northwest toward Dai Do across seven hundred meters of open ground. Companies F and H would support Vargas from Dong Huan as he drove into the hamlet.

While Vargas prepared his company for the attack, Dai Do was pounded with napalm and bombs from Marine Phantoms and Skyhawks. At the same time, NVA artillery batteries north of the DMZ were blasting Dong Huan and An Lac. The noise was tremendous with all the explosions and the screams of low-flying jets. Men had to shout at one another to be heard above the din.

Supported by two tanks, Company G jumped off at about 1300. Advancing with two platoons forward, the company made it about one third of the way across the open ground before the NVA opened fire. The 3d Platoon, on the left, was particularly hard hit. A 12.7mm machine gun played havoc with the advancing Marines. Its deadly rounds cut men down like an invisible scythe. Just then, enemy mortar and artillery rounds tore into the area, throwing towering geysers of dirt skyward. Ignoring the lethal danger, Vargas boldly ran to the stalled platoon. Under his urging the advance resumed. By 1500 Company G was in Dai Do.

Heavy, close-quarters fighting raged as the Marines moved through the hamlet. Enemy soldiers seemed to be everywhere, popping up from spider holes, from under haystacks, from trench lines behind hedgerows, and from inside the abandoned huts. But Vargas's men routed them out one by one with ruthless efficiency.

Company G had just barely reached the far side of Dai Do when the NVA counterattacked. Aerial observers excitedly reported scores of enemy soldiers pouring out of Dinh To and headed right toward Dai Do. Though supporting fire blasted the enemy formations, by 1630 they were seriously pressing Vargas's company. He had no choice. He ordered a withdrawal. As the Marines retreated they couldn't believe what they were experiencing. The NVA were so close that they were being killed at pistol range and in hand-to-hand combat. Some North Vietnamese soldiers were so pumped up that they actually ran right past the withdrawing Americans.

Vargas and about forty-five of his men dropped into a deep drainage ditch that ran along Dai Do's northeastern edge. The heavy volume of fire that the small but determined force put out finally halted the enemy's momentum. At the same time the forward artillery controllers were on their radios desperately calling for more supporting fire. Within minutes their pleas were answered. The heavy 105mm shells were soon crashing down less than fifty meters from the ditch.

Now, greatly concerned for Company G's survival, Lieutenant Colonel Weise ordered Company B, 1/3, into the fight. Mounted on amtracs, what remained of the battered company started for Dai Do about 1730. At the same time, Company E, 2/4, was finally released from division control. Captain Livingston immediately started his men on the two-kilometer march to An Lac. Along the way marauding bands of NVA scouts repeatedly fired on them, killing several Marines. But by 1900, Company E was in An Lac.

At 1745, while still less than halfway to Dai Do, Company B was blasted off its amtracs by RPGs and automatic weapons fire. Among those grievously wounded was the new company commander, who'd taken command but a few hours earlier. Unable to proceed, with tracer rounds snapping just inches over their heads, the survivors of Company B began pulling back to An Lac. They dragged their wounded with them; the dead stayed in the field. Four hundred meters to the north, Captain Vargas and his forty-five surviving Marines dug in for the night. Besides their own weapons, they had the support of artillery to hold the determined NVA at bay.

Before first light on 2 May, Company E was up and ready to go. Captain Livingston ordered, "Fix bayonets." It was very satisfying to him to hear the distinct click of the edged weapons locking into place on 150 rifles. Because of a communication problem, Company E moved toward Dai Do without the benefit of a rolling barrage of artillery to keep down the enemy's heads. Still, only occasional pops from a sniper's rifle interrupted the advance. Then, in a blur of confusion, the NVA let loose with everything they had when the Marines were just 150 meters short of the hamlet. From the hedgerows along Dai Do's south edge, small arms, automatic rifle, and RPG fire slammed into Company E. Livingston and his command group dove behind one of numerous burial mounds dotting the open area. Eighteen RPGs exploded around them in the next few minutes. Company E was pinned down.

From his position on the northeast edge of Dai Do, Captain Vargas tried to relieve the pressure on Company E by leading his forty-five men in an attack through the hamlet. Soon, the NVA shifted their fire to meet this new threat. With less fire coming his way, Captain Livingston then rallied his men and led them forward to the hamlet's edge. Dead NVA littered the ground everywhere, but there were plenty of live ones left and they weren't giving up easily. Marines used grenades and M79 grenade launchers to clear enemy positions. The fighting was brutal but the Marines pressed forward, meter by bloody meter.

At 0914 Captain Vargas advised Lieutenant Colonel Weise that he had linked up with Livingston. They were digging in on Dai Do's northwestern edge. Before Weise could respond, NVA mortar shells fired from Dinh To began dropping among the Marines. During the fifteen-minute barrage, Weise was ordered by Colonel Hull to continue the ground attack into Dinh To. Weise was incredulous but had no choice. Realizing that Companies E and G were in no shape to launch another full-scale attack, Lieutenant Colonel Weise turned to Company H.

Just before 1000, Company H left its positions in Dong Huan and moved through Dai Do's western edge. Using fire and maneuver tactics, two of its platoons made it into Dinh To under relatively light enemy fire. As the two platoons started through the hamlet, the NVA suddenly counterattacked. Within minutes Company H was in serious trouble.

Seconds later Captain Livingston, who'd been monitoring Company H's progress on the radio, called Weise: "I'm going to help Hotel. They're really fixing to get in trouble. I'll go get 'em." Without waiting for a response, Captain Livingston took the seventy able-bodied men left in his company on the attack. Charging through the enemy fire, Livingston led his men right through clusters of NVA bypassed by Company H. They were killing the enemy on the run. Some NVA fled, actually trotting along with Livingston's Marines before they were shot down.

Once Company E tied in with Company H, the two companies resumed the attack on Dinh To. Initially, they made good progress, but then the NVA counterattacked yet again. A sudden increase in enemy fire signaled their intention. From as close as twenty-five meters the NVA cut loose with an awesome display of firepower. The noise rose to an ear-shattering roar as weapons of every caliber spewed hot lead. Under tremendous pressure the Marines were forced back. Bravely defying the enemy's onslaught, Livingston stood in the open, firing a rifle at the crew with a 12.7mm machine gun. The NVA got lucky before Livingston did. A heavy slug from the automatic weapon tore into his thigh, sending him sprawling. As two other wounded men helped him to safety, he turned over command of Company E to a rookie lieutenant.

The two battered companies retreated all the way back to Dai Do. There they evacuated their seriously wounded and loaded up on more ammo.

At this time Lieutenant Colonel Weise arrived in Dai Do with more orders from Colonel Hull. Impossible as it seemed, 2/4 was to immediately launch yet another attack into Dinh To. Calling upon what remained of Companies F and G, Weise ordered them to clear Dinh To. The renewed assault kicked off at 1550. It was a bloody failure.

Through a misunderstanding of orders, Company F did not provide Vargas's company with adequate support. Rather than advance in trail behind Company G, from where it could pass through Vargas's company to exploit any weak spots, Company F moved on their right flank, in the open fields east of the hamlet. As a result, the entrenched NVA easily flanked the two companies. Then, at 1645 the NVA, displaying incredible reserve strength, counterattacked once again.

To the shock of the Marines, the NVA seemed to be everywhere. Dozens of enemy soldiers poured out of the nearby brush. Wearing pith helmets and firing their AK-47s from their hips, they raced forward. Vargas's depleted platoons retreated right past the ditch he was using as a command post. Lieutenant Colonel Weise and his command group, who'd joined Vargas just a few minutes earlier, fought as riflemen. Weise blazed away with an M16, picking off enemy soldiers as easily as hitting targets on a firing range. Then, the attacking enemy soldiers were alongside the ditch. In rapid succession Weise was hit by enemy rifle fire, and the battalion sergeant major was killed by the shrapnel from an exploding RPG.

Intent on saving his commander, Captain Vargas valiantly risked his own life to carry Weise rearward to an evacuation point. Vargas then returned to his embattled company. Using an AK-47, he fired away at the enemy while he helped the wounded rearward. An RPG explosion knocked him down as it tore a chunk of flesh from his leg. Still, he fought on and got his casualties headed to safety. All around him Marines and North Vietnamese soldiers grappled in death struggles. Vargas himself killed an enemy soldier with his knife.

Despite these heroics, the Marines were forced back. By 1800 Companies F and G were in Dai Do. All four companies of 2/4 dug in there for the night. The Marines spent a nervous night as the NVA probed their positions throughout the dark hours. More than a dozen enemy soldiers were killed as they sneaked forward to try to throw grenades into the friendly positions.

It had been a brutal three-day fight for 2/4. At the end of 2 May, Company E had forty-five men left, Company F fifty-two, Company G thirty-five, and Company H sixty-four.

That night, Colonel Hull ordered the rest of 1/3 to land at An Lac on the afternoon of 3 May. They would then renew the attack through Dinh To and into Thuong Do, the next village north.

The new attack went off as planned. By 1500 two companies of 1/3 had entered Dinh To. Although they encountered some resistance, it was apparent that the NVA had pulled out the night before. By 1800, 1/3 had swept through Thuong Do. All that remained was to tally up the losses.

The BLT 2/4 was credited with 537 enemy dead. The battalion

suffered 81 dead and 397 wounded. For that, they had prevented the 320th NVA Division from attacking the Dong Ha combat base.

For their incredible heroism during this violent three-day fight, Captains Vargas and Livingston were awarded the Medal of Honor. Lieutenant Colonel Weise received a Navy Cross.

Though battered, the 320th NVA Division was not down. Pursued by 1/3, on 5 May, the NVA stood and fought at Som Soi, one kilometer north of Thuong Do. The Marines lost fifteen killed and sixty-four wounded before the NVA broke contact. The next day the division recrossed the DMZ into North Vietnam to lick its wounds.

Shortly after the battle for Dong Ha, the 3d Marine Division received a new commander. Major General Raymond G. Davis transferred to the post from duty as deputy commander, Provisional Corps, Vietnam. A soft-spoken, diminutive Georgian, Davis had been a Marine since 1938. He fought his way across the Pacific during World War II, storming beaches from Guadalcanal to Peleliu. During the latter battle he earned a Navy Cross for his personal valor as a battalion commander. In 1950, during the disastrous Chosin Reservoir campaign in North Korea, he again demonstrated incredible courage when leading a battalion against the fanatical Chinese. This time his reward was a Medal of Honor.

Upon taking charge of the 3d Marine Division, Davis made a number of significant changes. One of the first was the restoration of unit integrity. As much as tactically possible, battalions organic to a specific Marine regiment would operate under the control of their parent regiment. No longer would a regimental commander have operational control of a conglomerate of battalions, and rifle companies, from a variety of other regiments. This move not only restored command cohesiveness but greatly improved morale as units developed a sense of belonging.

The most significant change that General Davis made involved improving the mobility of his ground forces. Fortunate to have assumed command at the time when divisional helicopter assets peaked, Davis ordered his regimental commanders to adopt the airmobile tactics used so successfully by the U.S. Army's 1st Cavalry Division. This change not only resulted in the more effective use of helicopters to move rifle companies rapidly about the battlefield, but it also increased the use of fire support bases.

A fire support base (FSB) is a forward artillery position on a key terrain feature. Normally collocated with an infantry battalion CP, the FSB can usually be adequately defended by one rifle company or less. The battalion's other rifle companies then fan out from the FSB under the protective umbrella of the artillery. A given FSB would be occupied only as long as it was needed for the current tactical situation. Once its usefulness had passed, an FSB could be quickly abandoned.

General Davis wasted no time in putting these new concepts to use. In late May, intelligence sources reported that the 308th NVA Division had entered South Vietnam south of Khe Sanh. From there it could strike at either Quang Tri City or Hue. To thwart this movement, General Davis established TF Hotel under Brig. Gen. Carl W. Hoffman. Two fire support bases, Loon and Robin, were blasted out of the jungle about eight kilometers south of Khe Sanh.

Following five days of preparatory air strikes and artillery fire, on 2 June, elements of 2/4 airlifted into FSB Loon and 1/1 into FSB Robin. Both units then advanced north, hoping to drive any lurking NVA into the waiting rifles of 2/3, positioned just south of Route 9. Over the next ten days, the attacking battalions uncovered numerous abandoned enemy positions but few live NVA. On 12 June, the units linked up, having made few actual contacts. The day after the two battalions set off, the rifle companies of 1/4 occupied FSBs Loon and Robin. They spent the next three days aggressively patrolling the jungle around their bases. They, too, found nothing.

Then, at dawn on 6 June, the NVA attacked Companies C and D at FSB Loon. Although the fight lasted several hours, the attackers were easily repulsed. The enemy tried several more ground attacks against the FSBs, but by 19 June the 308th NVA Division had turned around and returned to Laos.

This first use of mountaintop fire support bases by the Marines had gone well. General Davis would not only vastly expand their use throughout his division but would return to this same area in less than eight months to conduct another major operation.

Heavy enemy shelling of both Camp Kistler and Dong Ha during June resulted in the launching of Operation Thor on 1 July. This operation was unusual because it was designed to destroy the enemy artillery positions in the southern portion of the DMZ by the massive application of aerial bombs and artillery. Infantry units would then follow up. Marine, navy, and air force aircraft—including B-52 bombers from Guam, 2 U.S. Navy cruisers and 6 destroyers, and 118 pieces of army and Marine artillery—poured thousands of tons of high explosives into the target area over a seven-day period. It was one of the largest and most concentrated bombardments of the entire war.

As the eastern infantry arm of Operation Thor, Colonel Hull sent his 3d Marines attacking north from the Cua Viet on 5 July. Enemy contact developed almost immediately as 1/3 fought the NVA at Lai An, a hamlet ten kilometers north of Dong Ha. Over the next few days, the grunts found the NVA in nearly every hamlet they entered.

To the west, in the Operation Kentucky AO, elements of the 9th Marines aggressively patrolled the area north and east of Con Thien. The Marines and NVA clashed every day in sharp, but short, engagements.

On 17 July, the 3d Marines, 9th Marines, and 2d ARVN Regiment were helicoptered into LZs along the southern edge of the DMZ. Then, in a movement reminiscent of Operation Hickory in 1967, they attacked to the south, their objective being to clear the land of the enemy all the way to Route 9. Faced with this formidable onslaught, the NVA simply disappeared into the rugged terrain. The most significant action of the operation came on the first day, when 3/9 fought a well-entrenched NVA company on a ridgeline about ten kilometers northwest of Camp Carroll. Working with close air support from A-4s and F-4s, the infantrymen overran the enemy position by nightfall. On 31 July, Operation Thor ended. The month-long campaign resulted in the destruction of dozens of enemy fortifications and the capture of significant quantities of supplies.

Reinforcements for the overworked 3d Marine Division arrived on 31 July in the form of the 1st Brigade, 5th U.S. Infantry Division (Mechanized). Because the terrain east of Highway 1 to the coast and between Dong Ha and Gio Linh was ideally suited for mechanized infantry operations, III MAF put the army brigade there.

Quang Tri Province was relatively quiet in early August. Consequently, on 26 August, the 1st Marines returned south to 1st Marine
Division control as the 1st Brigade, 5th U.S. Infantry Division (Mechanized) expanded its TAOR. The army unit now had control of both
the Kentucky and the Napoleon/Saline tactical areas.

In late August, the 3d Marine Division's nemesis, the 320th NVA
Division, again slipped across the DMZ. The NVA were trying to penetrate Quang Tri Province via a more westerly route, traversing the
rugged, mountainous terrain north of Route 9 between Cam Lo and
the Rockpile. Though the enemy division had lost nearly four thousand men in battles with the Marines in April and May around Dong
Ha, they were still spoiling for a fight. General Davis's Marines gave
it to them.

Various elements of the 3d Marine Division met each of the
320th's three regiments as they made their way south from the DMZ:
the 64th NVA Regiment north of Cam Lo; the 52d NVA Regiment
west of the Rockpile; and, finally, the 48th NVA Regiment north of
the Rockpile. General Davis's enhanced mobility techniques proved
to be effective. Encounters with the enemy were exploited to their
fullest by the rapid insertion of Marine infantry supported by FSBs.
Full battalions were helilifted into LZs that advanced progressively
farther north, thus blocking the enemy's withdrawal routes and causing its units to break into smaller groups, complicating the NVA's already weak command and control functions.

Units of Col. Robert H. Barrow's 9th Marines spent the period of
15–22 August chasing the 64th NVA Regiment around the area
southwest of Con Thien. During this same period, 3/3 swept the
Mutter's Ridge area. Actual contact was infrequent, but vast quantities of supplies were uncovered and destroyed. In early September,
the 3d Marines' other two battalions arrived on the scene. Moving
east from Mutter's Ridge, they passed through Helicopter Valley,
finding and destroying numerous rocket sites, ammo caches, and
bunkers. On 3 September, without a major contact, they returned
to Camp Carroll.

On 26 August, both 1/9 and 2/9 were inserted by UH-34 helicopters into the rugged, jungle-covered terrain west of the Razor-

back. The 2d Battalion made strong contact almost immediately as it secured positions on the high ground near their LZ. After that, there was very little action, and no enemy supplies were discovered.

Action then shifted back to Mutter's Ridge as 3/3 slammed into the 52d NVA Regiment north of the Razorback on 3 September. Both 1/3 and 2/3 were rushed into positions to the north and west to block the enemy's escape routes. In a series of sharp engagements over the next week, the Marines of 1/3 killed 48 enemy soldiers.

The riflemen of 2/3 made major discoveries of enemy supply caches during their patrols. Among their finds were 390,000 rounds of ammo, 4,000 pounds of TNT, and 3,400 mortar rounds. To their west, the members of 3/9 killed 209 NVA during the second week of September and uncovered a regimental supply area. They captured 10,000 mortar rounds, 13,000 hand grenades, and hundreds of 107mm, 122mm, and 140mm rockets.

On 16 September, Colonel Barrow opened FSB Winchester on a hilltop west of the Razorback. Commanding six battalions (including 1/4, 2/26, and 2/3, besides his three organic battalions), Barrow was determined to destroy the 320th NVA Division once and for all. Heavy fighting began that same day when the SLF, BLT 2/26, went into an LZ north of FSB Winchester. The Special Landing Force men were severely pounded by enemy mortar rounds all day as they struggled northward in the heavy jungle. Both 2/9 and 3/9 made strong contact over the next few days as they swept west of FSB Winchester trying to take the pressure off of 2/26.

The NVA continued to be a menace in the Mutter's Ridge area, too. In two days of fighting, beginning on 18 September, elements of the 3d Marines accounted for 155 dead NVA.

As the fighting continued over the next few weeks, the Marines moved rapidly back and forth across the battlefield in a dizzying display of airmobile effectiveness, thwarting the 320th's every effort to move farther south. As the end of September neared, it became apparent that the enemy was attempting to retreat back north. To block that movement, Barrow sent 1/9 and 1/4 into the DMZ near the banks of the Ben Hai River. As the two battalions then swept south, they captured several prisoners, who confirmed the low morale of the enemy soldiers facing them. Continuing south, 1/9 uncovered a mass grave containing the remains of 168 enemy soldiers, attesting to the deadly effectiveness of artillery and aerial bombardments.

On 1 October, 2/26 replaced 1/4 in the field with 1/4 returning to patrol around the new Vandegrift Combat Base near Ca Lu. Because of dwindling enemy contacts, 1/9 was removed from the field a few days later, too. Then, on 4 October, supported by the massive 16-inch guns of the battleship USS *New Jersey*, 2/26 reversed direction and attacked north into the DMZ. Much to their surprise, the Marines found that the NVA had recently constructed a road that ran east along the south bank of the Ben Hai for several kilometers before turning south and terminating less than two kilometers from the southern boundary of the DMZ.

The road was well built in a corduroy fashion, though the North Vietnamese laborers left plenty of trees standing to conceal their handiwork from the allies' prying aerial eyes. The enemy-built road even crossed the Ben Hai at three different locations. The fords had been built up with rocks and gravel to make underwater bridges that defied detection.

As the incredulous Marines patrolled the road, they found several sophisticated base camps complete with thatched huts, underground bunkers, and well-stocked kitchens. Numerous, mutually supporting fighting positions ringed each location. All the camps were destroyed. On their second day of moving along the road, the men of 2/26 discovered two recently abandoned 152mm artillery positions. Though they later found several tracked vehicles capable of towing the artillery pieces and several caches of shells and could hear diesel engines in the distance, the Marines never did find the enemy guns.

Because of needs elsewhere, the Special Landing Force, 2/26, was pulled out of the DMZ on 16 October. The 1st Battalion, 3d Marines continued the mission but had no better luck. By 26 October, all units were out of the DMZ, and operations against the 320th NVA Division were terminated. For the third time since April, the enemy division had failed to achieve a victory against the 3d Marine Division. Enemy losses were put at 1,585 killed. The various Marine units involved in the operations had 182 killed while turning back the division.

* * *

In an attempt to further the cause of peace in South Vietnam, President Johnson told the nation on 31 October that he was halting all air, naval, and artillery bombardments of North Vietnam. Only in direct retaliation to enemy attacks would allied artillery be permitted to fire across the DMZ. Although the North Vietnamese announced three days later that they would participate in the stalled peace talks, the members of the 3d Marine Division weren't happy. After all, if the North Vietnamese Army did the same as they had done during other olive branch–inspired truces, they'd simply use the bombing halt to build up their forces along the DMZ. And the division would be the ones to fight the revitalized enemy forces.

The last two months of 1968 were relatively quiet along the DMZ. The 4th and 9th Marines conducted operations around Khe Sanh but found few signs of the enemy. The last named operation of the year was Dawson River, conducted by the 9th Marines west of Dong Ha. From its beginning on 28 November to the end of the year, only sixty enemy soldiers were killed during the operation. Marine losses were three killed and forty wounded.

Because of the increased mobility of his forces, coupled with the abandonment of Khe Sanh, General Davis decided that the artillery base at Camp Carroll was no longer needed. On 28 December, the base was closed.

When 1968 began, Quang Tri Province was one of the most threatened provinces in South Vietnam. As the year ended, it was one of the calmest.

Marines from BLT 3/9 wade ashore at Red Beach 2, 8 March 1965.

Members of Company E, 2/4, move off of LZ White during Operation Starlite, August 1965.

Mortarmen advance to a new position during Operation Double Eagle, January 1966.

Marines from 3/9 fire on enemy positions near the Ky Lam River south of Da Nang during Operation Georgia, May 1966.

The Rockpile from the northwest perspective, with the Razorback in the background.

A Marine helicopter delivers supplies to the top of the Rockpile.

An M-60 machine gun crew provides covering fire during the assault on Mutter's Ridge, October 1966.

Marines of Company A, 1/9 observe an air strike during Operation Prairie II, March 1967.

Marines of 3/7 duck from the rotor wash of a departing helicopter, near Da Nang, November 1967.

Accompanied by an M-48 tank, Marines of 1/4 advance toward the Ben Hai River during Operation Hickory, July 1967.

Armed with an M-60, a Marine bravely fires on an enemy position during the fighting for Hue, February 1968.

Marines patrol battle-scarred Hill 881S, near Khe Sanh, February 1968.

Wounded in the fighting near **Dai Do**, May 1968, a Marine is rushed by his buddies to a medevac helicopter.

During Operation Allen Brook, August 1968, members of the 27th Marines patrol near Go Noi Island.

Marines of 2/5 cordon off a Vietnamese village during Operation Meade River, November 1968.

Company B, 1/3, patrols along Route 9 near Khe Sanh, February 1969.

Marines of 2/26 board a CH-46 to respond to an enemy sighting near Da Nang, February 1970.

Members of a Kingfisher patrol exit a CH-53 helicopter atop Charlie Ridge, southwest of Da Hang, April 1970.

Weary members of Company H, 2/5, after returning from a patrol on Go Noi Island, May 1970.

Marines of Company B, 1/7, advance up a hill in the Thu Bon River Valley, Operation Pickens Forest, August 1970.

Fire Support Base Ross, summer 1970.

Members of 1/7 cross a
river south of Da Nang,
summer 1970.

Members of a CAP unit question a woman suspected of aiding the Viet Cong, 1971.

Marines from 2/1 exit a CH-46 helicopter southwest of Da Nang during Operation Scott Orchard, April 1971.

Chapter Five
1968 (1st Division)

1st Marine Division

On 30 January 1968, as the evening sun disappeared below the western horizon beyond Hue, Vietnam's ancient imperial capital and the nation's cultural center, North Vietnamese soldiers bivouacked in the mountains to the north and west prepared to move into the city. The uniquely Vietnamese Tet holiday, the advent of the lunar new year, was in full swing. For more than a week, scores of Viet Cong agents had been making their way into Hue, safely hidden among the thousands of others traveling home for the national holiday. In the predawn hours of 31 January, the agents would attack predesignated targets, which would ease the way for the NVA to pour into the city, capture it, and expel the hated American imperialists.

North Vietnam's senior military leader, Gen. Vo Nguyen Giap, had planned this masterful stroke for years. He had cleverly drawn the allied forces away from South Vietnam's population centers by sparring with them in the wild country's border regions. Now the cities and district capitals lay vulnerable to his forces. Before the Americans could react, the NVA would have taken their objectives. The South Vietnamese government and its allies would be forced to negotiate for a reunification of the country.

As the evening grew darker, the NVA soldiers began moving. Proceeding confidently down well-marked trails, the long column of enemy troops closed on Hue. Though units of the 1st ARVN Infantry Division guarded the approaches to the revered city, only one column of the NVA force was detected. A patrol west of the city stayed hidden as two battalions of enemy soldiers filed past. The patrol commander then radioed his observations to division headquarters in the Citadel in Hue, but no further action was taken.

By 0300 the enemy forces were in place. Situated in strategically located attack positions ringing the city, the NVA awaited the signal to begin. A barrage of rockets was timed to crash into the city at 0330. Inside the city, members of various VC units stood ready.

More than five thousand enemy soldiers waited nervously for the rockets to flash across the night sky. As the seconds ticked slowly by, they checked their weapons or demolition charges one last time. In mere hours they would emerge victorious in their decades-long struggle for independence. The years of sacrifice and hardship would be over, and they would be free of foreign interference.

The appointed time came and went. There were no flashing streaks of light, no explosions, nothing. What had gone wrong?

Then, at 0340, a salvo of NVA 82mm mortar shells erupted on the tile roof of a building near the MACV compound. Seconds later a barrage of 122mm rockets exploded right in the compound's courtyard.

The opening shots of the most ferocious battle of Giap's much-vaunted Tet Offensive had been fired. The Americans in the compound had no idea of what was going on.

As 1968 began, elements of the 1st Marine Division were shifting northward as part of Operation Checkers. The purpose of this operation was to relieve the 3d Marine Division of the responsibility of guarding the western approaches to Hue. To that end, the 1st and 5th Marines moved into Thua Thien Province from their TAORs around Da Nang. Operational control for this movement rested with Brig. Gen. Foster C. LaHue, the 1st Marine Division's assistant commander, with headquarters at Phu Bai.

As part of the shifting of U.S. Army units into I Corps in mid-December, the 11th Infantry Brigade moved into Duc Pho, at the southern tip of Quang Ngai Province. This allowed the 1st Battalion, 5th Marines to move to Phu Loc, north of the Hai Van Pass above Da Nang. In early January, MACV moved the 1st Cavalry Division (Airmobile) and the 2d Brigade, 101st Airborne Division (Airmobile) into Quang Tri and Thua Thien Provinces. When these changes were finished, General Cushman would have three U.S. Army and two U.S. Marine Corps divisions, plus assorted ARVN and allied units, operating under his III MAF.

On 13 January, the 1st Marine Division opened TF X-ray at Phu Bai. Essentially a division forward headquarters, TF X-ray had tactical responsibility for the AO from the Hai Van Pass to just north of Hue. Its specific mission was to protect the combat base at Phu Bai, screen the western approaches to Hue, and keep open the portion of Highway 1 that ran through its AO. Two days later, 2/5, under Lt. Col. Ernest C. Cheatham, Jr., arrived and took over tactical responsibility for the Phu Bai TAOR. Over the next few days the headquarters elements of both the 1st Marines (Col. Stanley R. Hughes) and the 5th Marines (Col. Robert D. Bohn) set up residence at Phu Bai. Despite its multiple missions, TF X-ray controlled only three understrength infantry battalions: 1/1, 1/5, and 2/5. Although a variety of other units passed in and out of TF X-ray's control as they moved north and south on Route 1 as part of Operation Checkers, none were around long enough to perform any tactical missions.

The other units of the 1st Marine Division remained deployed around the vital Da Nang area. Division commander Maj. Gen. Donn F. Robertson's headquarters was on Hill 327, three kilometers west of the city and just behind Red Beach, where the Marines had first come ashore nearly three years earlier. The three battalions of the 7th Marines guarded the western and southwestern approaches to Da Nang. Two battalions operating under control of the 5th Marines, 3/5 and 2/3, worked the area south of Marble Mountain between Route 1 and the sea.

Though III MAF had no way of knowing it, its shuffling of units played right into Giap's hand.

Giap's master plan for expelling allied forces from South Vietnam and reuniting the two countries was called the "General Offensive–General Uprising." The first phase of the plan was to pull allied forces away from the populated coastal region. This process began in the summer of 1967 with the intense pressure placed on Con Thien. It continued in the fall with tough fights around Dak To in the Central Highlands, at Loc Ninh north of Saigon, and, in late January 1968, at Khe Sanh. General Westmoreland responded to the enemy's initiatives by shifting his forces to the hot spots. With the stronger American forces removed to South Vietnam's interior, North Vietnam began the second phase of its master plan by infiltrating its forces past the weaker ARVN units guarding the country's

cities. There they awaited the signal to commence the General Uprising. North Vietnam's leaders sincerely believed that the citizens
of the south would join in an uprising once they realized that the
NVA and VC were capable of destroying the allies and ejecting the
Saigon government.

The General Uprising was scheduled to begin on the most revered
of all Vietnamese holidays—Tet. The centuries-old, week-long, lunar
new year celebration was not only a cherished Buddhist holiday but
also a national patriotic festival. So important was Tet to the Vietnamese people that for years all sides of the conflict had observed a
cease-fire during this period. A three-day cease-fire from 30 January
to 1 February had been agreed upon for the 1968 Tet celebration.

Battle for Hue

A major target of the Tet Offensive was the city of Hue. One of
the most beautiful cities in all of Asia, Hue was a unique and interesting blend of Vietnamese and French culture, Buddhist and
Catholic shrines, and ancient and modern architecture. A sophisticated center for advanced learning as well as remembrances of tradition and ancient values, Hue was the acknowledged cultural hub
of South Vietnam.

Hue was actually two cities. Hue was thoroughly modern south of
the Perfume River, which flowed through the city from the southwest to the northeast on its way to the South China Sea ten kilometers to the east. Complete with a university, government buildings,
a country club, a prison, and a vast residential area, south Hue was
known for its tree-lined streets and numerous shops.

North of the river sat the Citadel, copied from the Imperial City
in Peking. Construction of the three-square-kilometer Citadel was begun by Emperor Gia Long in 1802. With French help and money,
the massive project was completed eighteen years later. Defended by
a wide moat and six-meter-high, earth-filled masonry walls that
ranged up to seventy-five meters in thickness, the Citadel contained
an entire city. The Imperial Palace, home to ancient Vietnam's
rulers, was located at the south end of the Citadel. The palace's walls
were two to five meters high and measured seven hundred meters
per side. Complete with block after block of row houses, parks, vil-

las, shops, an airstrip, and government buildings, the Citadel was a camera-toting tourist's dream. It would be a rifle-toting infantryman's nightmare.

Though it straddled the vital Highway 1, Hue had never before been seriously threatened by enemy forces. This tranquillity was undoubtedly a measure of the reverence that both sides held for the city. In fact, very few ARVN units, and no American units, were stationed around Hue. Although the 1st ARVN Infantry Division did have its headquarters in the northeast corner of the Citadel, none of its infantry battalions operated near Hue. In fact, as Tet approached, more than half the division personnel had been granted leave for the holiday.

Though Marine supply convoys passed through Hue every day, their closest base was at Phu Bai, ten kilometers south on Highway 1. This was primarily a headquarters and support facility. There were no U.S. combat units in place at Phu Bai.

The only real U.S. military presence in Hue was the MACV compound. A variety of U.S. Army officers, U.S. Marine Corps officers, and Australians, who all served as advisers to the 1st ARVN Infantry Division, as well as permanent party U.S. Army enlisted men, called the compound home. When they retired on the evening of 30 January, they had no idea that their compound would become the focal point of the battle for Hue.

Although primitive communications caused a few enemy units to begin their attack a day early, the main Tet Offensive erupted across South Vietnam during the early morning hours of 31 January. Every major city, nearly every provincial capital, dozens of lesser towns, and most military bases came under attack. Even the U.S. embassy building in Saigon, as well as MACV headquarters at Tan Son Nhut air base, did not escape the enemy's fury. Though these attacks were deadly for both attacker and defender alike, the enemy forces were defeated in a matter of days. The attack on Hue was different. Because of its revered status, the enemy planned to capture the city in one swift blow. According to the plan, once the city's population realized the superiority of the NVA and VC, they would immediately join forces against the Americans. The resulting victory would be celebrated with patriotic parades for years to come.

The enemy allocated more than five thousand soldiers to achieve this important victory. Three independent NVA regiments—the 4th, 5th, and 6th—plus the 12th NVA Sapper Battalion, a rocket battalion, and a variety of local Viet Cong units were committed to the capture of Hue. Over the previous weeks they had slipped down the Ho Chi Minh Trail and made their way through the rugged jungle until they closed on Hue. By the evening of 30 January, they all were in position.

One of the first rockets to hit the MACV compound blew up a jeep parked right outside Marine major Frank Breth's room. When the vehicle's full gas tank went up, the explosion collapsed the building's roof on top of Breth. With a deep gouge in his head, the former commander of the 3d Marine Division rifle company struggled for several minutes to free himself from the debris. Breth, the division's liaison officer to the ARVN 1st Infantry Division, could hear small arms fire crackling around the compound's closed gates. Quickly dressing and grabbing his M16, he made his way to the roof of the compound's main building.

By the time Breth reached the rooftop, other Marines and soldiers had started firing on an NVA sapper platoon rushing the compound's main gate. As Breth watched, satchel charge–carrying enemy soldiers dodged among the trees lining Highway 1. Someone yelled, "Shoot! Shoot! They're coming down the road! Shoot!"

With that, everyone on the roof opened fire. Breth sprayed a full clip from his M16 on a group of enemy soldiers. One fell in a crumpled heap. As he slammed another magazine into his smoking weapon, the men around him tossed grenades into the street. The sharp cracks of their explosives filled the night air.

Still, the enemy pressed forward. The Marine security guards in a bunker alongside the gate filled the air above the street with bullets, but one sapper slipped close enough to flip a grenade into the bunker. It detonated, killing all three Marines.

In an observation tower looking over the compound, a U.S. Army specialist poured M60 machine-gun fire onto the sappers. Then an RPG hit the tower. The soldier's legs were nearly torn off in the explosion. Reacting to the man's screams for help, another Marine officer, Capt. James Coolican, ignored the enemy fire to climb the twenty-five-foot tower and carry the man down to safety. Then, armed with an M79 grenade launcher, Coolican climbed back into the observation post. From there he plopped away at the enemy sappers still milling around in the street.

Under this deadly accurate fire, and with nearly a dozen of their comrades sprawled dead in the street, the rest of the NVA fled into the night. Some set up shop in the upper floors of nearby buildings. From there they harassed the compound with bursts of fire and an occasional RPG. But the attack against the MACV compound was over. Around the city, though, it was another story.

While the MACV compound was under attack, other NVA troops rushed into Hue. At the same time, the Viet Cong guerrillas who'd earlier infiltrated the city emerged from the shadows. Within a few hours they had occupied all of the city's major buildings and most of its neighborhoods. They also swarmed into the Citadel, easily overcoming the handful of ARVN sentries. Within a short time it was over. Except for the small area in the northeast corner held by the headquarters troops of the 1st ARVN Division, both the Citadel and the Imperial Palace were in the enemy's hands. A fifty-four-square-meter NVA flag soon fluttered from a pole outside the Citadel's southeast wall. The NVA intended the banner to serve not only as a symbol of their triumph but as a rallying beacon for Hue's citizens who wanted to join the rebellion against the foreigners.

The desperate radio call for help from the surrounded MACV compound slowly made its way through channels until it arrived at the Phu Bai Combat Base. With dozens of other panicky messages pouring into TF X-ray headquarters about enemy attacks throughout the TAOR, this one was nearly overlooked. But then, III MAF specifically ordered TF X-ray to send reinforcements into Hue.

The message gave General LaHue no idea what was actually happening in Hue, so he assumed that it was merely a local diversionary attack. As a result, he ordered just one company to reinforce the MACV compound and find out what was going on.

Company A, 1/1, was the last of Lt. Col. Marcus J. Gravel's battalion to pass through Phu Bai. Following a two-month stint along the DMZ opconned to the 3d Marine Division, the battalion was returning to the Da Nang area as part of Operation Checkers. Three quarters of Capt. Gordon D. Batcheller's Company A had arrived at Phu Bai early on 30 January; his fourth platoon had missed the last helicopter the evening before and was still at Quang Tri. The company was supposed to spend 31 January at Phu Bai being refitted. But that didn't happen. Instead, they were rousted out of their bunks at first light on 31 January.

The operations officer of 1/1 ordered Batcheller to move south on Highway 1 to meet up with an ARVN unit operating in the area. Boarding trucks, the members of the rifle company set off. A cold, dreary fog greatly reduced visibility, but they soon arrived at the rendezvous site. When the ARVN guide did not show, Batcheller radioed Phu Bai for further instructions. To his surprise he was ordered to abandon that mission. Now he was to head north and link with a U.S. Army unit north of Hue.

Company A reboarded the trucks and reversed direction. A short time later, after the company passed through Phu Bai, Batcheller's orders were changed again. The battalion CP directed him to the MACV compound. No one knew for sure what was going on there. Batcheller was to find out and let Phu Bai know. As Company A drove north, the fog thickened, and visibility was reduced to a few hundred meters. The veterans in the company noted the absence of civilians along the road. Usually the highway was packed with traveling South Vietnamese. Now, at the height of the Tet holidays, there was no one around. The sense of unease climbed drastically.

When Batcheller's truck neared the southern outskirts of Hue, he noticed four stopped M48 tanks ahead in the haze. After he came up behind them, he saw what had halted them—the charred carcass of an ARVN M41 tank. Batcheller learned that the tanks were on their way to Quang Tri City. Both commanders immediately agreed to join forces. After crossing the An Cuu Bridge over the Phu Cam Canal, which formed Hue's southern boundary, the column approached a built-up commercial area with two-story wooden buildings flanking the highway. Batcheller, who had shaved his head to display his ferociousness, stopped the column and ordered his men out of the trucks and onto the tanks. He and his RTO climbed aboard the first M48. Then Batcheller gave the signal to go. Driving as fast as they could, the tanks roared through the area. The Marines poured a hail of M16 and M60 fire into the buildings as they raced past them.

Batcheller's tank cleared the gauntlet and entered a traffic circle. Just then a brace of RPGs flashed out of the fog and slammed into the tank. The deep explosions threw bodies everywhere. Batcheller found himself sprawled, unwounded, in the roadway. He saw his corpsman lying dead. His RTO was missing. Around him others were firing in the direction of the unseen enemy. Observing another wounded man in front of the tank, Batcheller bolted forward to help him.

He had just started pulling the man behind the tank when a burst of enemy machine-gun fire tore into them. The casualty died instantly. Batcheller was flung off the road into a tangle of concertina wire running along the pavement. Blood poured from at least three holes in his body. He hollered for his men to stay back, then collapsed. As soon as his men learned of Batcheller's dilemma, Company A's progress halted.

Back at Phu Bai, Lieutenant Colonel Gravel hastily organized a reaction force. Besides himself and his command group, he mounted up the attached Company G, 2/5. Captain Charles Meadows loaded his 160-man company aboard trucks. Around noon, under low clouds and a light drizzle, the convoy headed north toward Hue.

Around 1300 Gravel's column came upon Company A, still pinned down and fighting. Gravel quickly had the casualties evacuated. He helped cut Batcheller free of the wire and saw him rearward. Then, under intermittent fire, the combined column of tanks and Marine infantry started forward again. Fighting every meter of the way, the lead elements of the column finally entered the compound around 1500. Once the rest of the column gained the MACV compound, Gravel dispersed them. The riflemen fanned out and took up positions around the compound as far out as the Perfume River.

A short time later, TF X-ray, reflecting a total lack of knowledge of the situation in Hue, ordered Company G to join the 1st ARVN Division headquarters in the Citadel. Lieutenant Colonel Gravel was incredulous. He desperately tried to get the foolish orders changed by explaining what was going on, but his efforts were to no avail; the orders had come directly from III MAF in faraway Da Nang.

Shortly after 1600 Captain Meadows led Company G out of the MACV compound. He turned right, or northwest, and headed straight up Highway 1 toward the Nguyen Hoang Bridge over the Perfume River. As the lead platoon crested the arched center of the four-hundred-meter-long span, an enemy machine gun that was dug in at the far end of the bridge raked them with fire. Ten Marines went down. One brave corporal then charged forward. Single-handedly he killed the five-man crew and destroyed the enemy weapon. After the casualties were evacuated, Meadows started his company forward again.

After crossing the bridge, the Marines turned left, paralleling the Citadel's southeast wall and the river. A short distance later the lead squad came to Thuong Tu Gate, one of eight ornamental gates allowing access to the inner Citadel. Meadows planned to advance up the gate road the two kilometers to the 1st ARVN headquarters. The NVA had other plans.

No sooner had the first platoon started up the street than the defending NVA unleashed a storm of fire. Machine-gun fire, B40 rockets, grenades, and small arms fire tore into the riflemen. Ducking for cover in the shops lining the street, the Marines fired back. The roar of M16s, M60s, AK-47s, and RPG machine guns filled the sodden air. Soon the sharp crack of exploding grenades and mortar shells added to the din. Several times the Company G grunts tried to push forward, but as hard as they tried they couldn't penetrate the NVA line of defense.

It took another two hours of heavy fighting before Meadows could pull his company back to the bridge. Not until 1900 did they reach the safety of the MACV compound. Of the 150 Marines who started out three hours earlier, only 100 were still on their feet.

Because of Lieutenant Colonel Gravel's detailed reports, TF X-ray finally began to understand what was actually happening in Hue. To keep the chain of command intact, on the morning of 1 February, control of operations south of the Perfume River inside Hue was given to Col. Stanley R. Hughes's 1st Marines. The 5th Marines had tactical responsibility for all operations outside of the city. The

ARVN would retain responsibility for the Citadel. At the same time, TF X-ray ordered Gravel to relieve ARVN forces still holding out west of the MACV compound in the Thua Thien Provincial Prison. When they finished that, they were to liberate the adjacent Thua Thien Province administration building.

Though TF X-ray viewed this movement as a relatively simple one-kilometer advance, Gravel saw it as an eight-block battle through solid enemy forces. Besides that, his Marines had no experience and little training in city fighting.

Not since the fight to retake Seoul, South Korea, in September 1950, had the Marines engaged in house-to-house combat. Seoul had been tough, but the North Korean soldiers holding the capital had had little taste for extended combat and yielded easily. The NVA and VC occupying Hue had no intention of just fading away. The Marines would pay dearly in blood for every step they took down Hue's tree-lined boulevards. Enemy forces would have to be blasted from each building; in some cases the fighting would be room by room. Taking advantage of Hue's numerous courtyards and walled estates, the NVA and VC would ambush the Marines every step of the way.

Captain Meadows's remaining Marines found that out when, at 0700 on 1 February, they began their attack toward the prison. Enemy reaction was so strong that it took them several hours just to cross Highway 1 in front of the MACV compound and advance one block. Even the support of several of the M48 tanks didn't help. In fact, Meadows regarded them as a liability, because they drew volleys of RPG fire.

Besides the enemy fire, other factors hampered the Marines. Bad weather in the form of cold temperatures, low ceilings, and near constant rain reduced aerial support. Most important, though, was ARVN I Corps commander Lt. Gen. Hoang Xuan Lam's order prohibiting use of artillery and air strikes so that civilian casualties and damage to the city would be kept to a minimum.

While Company G was stalled in its attack less than two blocks from the MACV compound, the first reinforcements for Gravel's little command arrived. Company F, 2/5, commanded by Capt. Michael P. Downs, had been abruptly pulled out of a field south of Phu Bai the day before. The Marines spent the night at the combat base, resupplying themselves, replenishing their ammunition stocks, and eating a hot meal. At 1500 on 1 February, they boarded CH-46s at Phu Bai. A short time later, the first elements of Company F touched down at an LZ in Doc Lao Park, along the river just north of the compound. No sooner had they assembled than Lieutenant Colonel Gravel ordered them to reinforce Company G.

The fresh troops managed to extend the advance toward the prison about one more block before the intense enemy fire halted them, too. In less than two hours, Company F had taken fifteen casualties, including four dead. By 1800 both companies had recovered their casualties and returned to the compound. It had been a long, deadly day with absolutely nothing to show for the effort.

Late that same day, Lt. Col. Ernest C. Cheatham, Jr. was ordered by TF X-ray to take to Phu Bai his 2/5 command group and his Company H from their positions about eight kilometers to the south. Once at Phu Bai, he was told that Company H had been assigned to Gravel's 1/1; they'd be trucked into the MACV compound the next morning. As for Cheatham and his headquarters group, TF X-ray had no assignment for them. Cheatham reacted with disbelief at the pandemonium and confusion that reigned at Phu Bai.

The riflemen of Capt. George R. Christmas's Company H, 2/5, boarded trucks early on the afternoon of 2 February. In addition to Christmas's men, the convoy carried a couple of dozen members of Company A, 1/1's missing platoon that had been stranded at Quang Tri City. Protection for the convoy came in the form of two U.S. Army M55 quad .50 trucks and two U.S. Army M42 tracked Dusters packing dual 40mm gun cannons. After numerous delays due to the persistent low clouds that hampered supporting helicoper operations, Christmas (whose father-in-law was Col. David Lownds) finally received departure clearance at 1417.

The trip was completely uneventful until the convoy entered the built-up area less than half a kilometer south of the MACV compound. From rooftop and second- and third-story windows, enemy soldiers raked the convoy with a blistering fire. Complying with Captain Christmas's orders, the truck drivers instantly floored their accelerators and raced up the road. Individual Marines fired straight up at the enemy soldiers leaning out of windows to drop grenades in the trucks.

The lead truck had nearly run the gauntlet when a command-detonated mine exploded right in front of it. The truck crashed headlong into the crater, spilling men onto the road and blocking it. The rest of the convoy ground to a halt.

As they had been ordered, the Marines immediately jumped from their trucks, set up positions, and laid a base of suppressive fire on every NVA gun position they could see. The heavily armed army trucks crept forward, the gunners firing their lethal weapons into the surrounding buildings. The 40mm cannons of one Duster nearly halved a three-story building with their vicious fire. Small groups of grunts stormed into several buildings, wiping out the NVA holed up inside.

Faced with this deadly response, the surviving enemy soldiers fled. Christmas and his men then reboarded their trucks and resumed their movement. By 1530 they had entered the compound.

For the Marines already in Hue, 2 February began with a loud bang. Enemy sappers blew up the Nguyen Hoang Bridge over the Perfume River. Traffic between south Hue and the Citadel was cut off.

At last starting to grasp the situation in Hue, TF X-ray scaled back the day's objectives. Company F, 2/5, was assigned the task of clearing out and securing several enemy-occupied buildings that abutted the MACV compound. Company A, 1/1, and Company G, 2/5, were ordered to take possession of Hue University's main building. Located northwest of the compound and south of the river across Highway 1, the two-and-a-half-story building built around a courtyard dominated the entire area. No sooner had the Marines crossed Highway 1 than they were pounded by enemy fire from several quarters. Mortar shells and heavy machine-gun fire erupted from the Citadel, forcing the Marines to seek cover. At the same time, small arms fire from enemy troops emplaced in the university sliced into the ranks of the attackers.

Inch by bloody inch, determined to take their objective, the two companies crept forward. Finally, just before 1500 the first squads of Company G entered the building's ground floor and began the difficult job of clearing each room.

Around 1600 Company H, 2/5, and the stragglers from Company A, 1/1, left the MACV compound and entered the fray at the university building. First Lieutenant Ray Smith, a relatively recent arrival in South Vietnam, took command of Company A from the company's gunnery sergeant, who'd been leading the rifle company ever since Captain Batcheller had been wounded three days earlier. The fresh Marines joined their buddies in searching each room of the huge building for any lingering enemy.

At 1815 the NVA counterattacked, hitting both the university and Marine positions around the LZ at Doc Lao Park, on the south bank of the Perfume River. Intense fire from the Citadel and from buildings west of the university poured onto the Marines' positions. One M48 tank was badly damaged by a 75mm recoilless rifle round. When the firing finally died down four hours later, one Marine was dead and twenty-one were wounded.

Unbelievably, that evening TF X-ray ordered Company F, 2/5, to launch a night attack toward the prison and eject any enemy they found there. As foolhardy as the order was, Captain Downs personally led two of his platoons down the tree-lined boulevard running along the university's south side. The lead platoon had just passed the university when the enemy sprang its ambush. The sudden cracking and popping of small arms fire echoed off the nearby buildings. With Captain Downs shouting in order to be heard, his brave men sprinted forward to pull wounded buddies to safety. Within minutes one Marine was killed and sixteen were wounded. After the casualties were pulled to cover, Captain Downs ordered his weary men back to the compound.

The seriousness of the situation in Hue finally became apparent to TF X-ray on the morning of 3 February. General LaHue ordered Col. Stanley R. Hughes, the 1st Marines commander, to enter the city and take charge of the newly created Hue City Task Force. Accompanying the convoy was Lieutenant Colonel Cheatham, who'd been sitting frustrated in Phu Bai while three fourths of his battalion fought in Hue. Also aboard the trucks were infantry replacements and a large number of rear echelon troops going forward to the depleted rifle companies as infantrymen.

Encountering sporadic rifle fire during its trip, the convoy entered the compound at 1300. Colonel Hughes immediately set up his CP and took command of all units on the south side of the Perfume River. Under his control Hughes had the three companies of 2/5—

F, G, and H—under Lieutenant Colonel Cheatham; Lieutenant Colonel Gravel's depleted battalion consisting of Company A, 1/1; and a provisional company consisting of one platoon of Company B, 1/1, and several dozen cooks and clerks who'd been sent to the front lines to fight.

Colonel Hughes, a taciturn commander who'd earned both a Navy Cross and a Silver Star in World War II, wasted no time in issuing attack orders. Cheatham's stronger battalion would attack to the southwest through Hue, with the meandering Perfume River anchoring their right flank. Gravel's one-and-a-half-company battalion would hold positions on Cheatham's left flank. When they reached the Phu Cam Canal, which formed Hue's southwest border, they'd swing left, or east, and clear out any remaining enemy forces.

At 1545 on 3 February, Companies F and H stepped off the attack, with Company G in reserve. Lieutenant Colonel Cheatham's plan called for one platoon to suppress the enemy's fire from the target building with a continuous blast of its own fire while a second platoon launched a ground attack. A third platoon remained in reserve, ready to assist where needed. Cheatham planned to clear one building at a time until all of the day's objectives had been taken. Although the dreary weather continued to restrict aerial support, the Marines had one advantage they'd lacked on previous days: ARVN I Corps commander General Lam had lifted all restrictions on fire support south of the river.

Captain Christmas sent some of his men to the roof of the university. From there they could fire down on the buildings forming the public health complex, Company H's objective which was immediately behind the university across Ly Thuong Kiet Street. Unfortunately, as soon as these men made their presence known, the NVA across the street unleashed a violent barrage of small arms and rocket fire on them. Within minutes, six of the ten Marines were hit. Everyone scrambled off the roof.

On the ground, Christmas's 2d Platoon pressed its attack against the complex. With a veritable storm of enemy fire pouring down on them, Captain Christmas called for smoke. Though the smoke provided an effective screen, the NVA fired right into them anyway. The attack bogged down. About then, one of the M48 tanks clanked up

Truong Dinh Street, which ran perpendicular to Ly Thuong Kiet and parallel to the university's south side. As soon as the tank stuck its nose onto Truong Dinh, NVA gunners peppered the behemoth with green-tracered .51-caliber machine-gun rounds. With the colorful rounds ricocheting around the intersection, the tank hammered out a response with its .50-caliber weapon. The orange tracers sped toward the suspected site of the enemy weapon. Almost immediately the green tracers stopped. Before the watching Marines could cheer, an RPG swooshed toward the tank and exploded smack on its front. Seconds later, with its diesels roaring, the tank backed down the street out of the fight.

"Hell," said one disgusted Marine. "All I've got for protection is my flak jacket."

Despite the vehicle's disappearance, it did do some good. During the machine-gun duel, several squads of Marines crossed the street and entered the complex. Fighting room to room with M16s and grenades, they had cleared the enemy stronghold by 1900. Thirty minutes later, though, Captain Christmas ordered them to pull back. As much as he hated to give up the hard-won building, he couldn't leave his men dangling out there by themselves.

Captain Downs's Company F faced a two-and-a-half-story building surrounded by a black wrought-iron fence mounted on a white knee-high masonry wall. They could see NVA machine guns in sandbagged upper-floor windows of the treasury building. As the Marines moved into attack position, a .51-caliber machine gun on their left flank began firing down Ly Thuong Kiet Street in front of them. Under a barrage of covering mortar fire, several squads started across the street. They made it about halfway before they were cut down in a hail of fire. The rest of the afternoon was spent recovering the casualties.

After a bone-chilling but uneventful night, the two companies resumed their attack at 0700 on 4 February. Both companies instantly encountered the same level of stubborn resistance they'd met the day before. The attack remained stalled until the gunner of a 106mm recoilless rifle mounted on a Mechanical Mule (a flat-bedded, self-propelled carrier about the size of a jeep) pulled his weapon right into the street in front of Company H. Firing down Ly Thuong Kiet

Street in the direction of the .51-caliber machine gun, the gutsy young lance corporal fired several rounds in its direction. His shells not only destroyed the nest, but the weapon's back blast created such a cloud of dust that Company H's lead platoon was able to use this cover to dash across the street. A short time later the public health complex once again belonged to Captain Christmas's Marines.

Lieutenant Colonel Gravel's small battalion joined the attack on 4 February. Moving down Tran Cao Van Street, which paralleled Truong Dinh Street, on Company F, 2/5's left flank, Company A, 1/1, and the provisional Company B blasted their way forward building by building using 3.5-inch rocket launchers to rout out the die-hard defenders. Lieutenant Smith's company made good progress until it reached the Jeanne d'Arc Girls High School, just east of the intersection of Tran Cao Van and Ly Thuong Kiet Streets. There, a well-entrenched NVA force stopped the company cold.

During the five days that Company A had been fighting in Hue, Sgt. Alfredo Gonzalez had repeatedly demonstrated exceptional heroism and leadership. Though only twenty-one, he had taken command of his platoon when its leader was wounded and evacuated. Repeatedly displaying extraordinary courage day after day, Gonzalez was an inspiration to all who saw him.

When Company A stalled at the girls' school, Gonzalez grabbed an armload of light antitank weapons (LAWs), similar to the enemy's RPGs. Stationing himself at a second-story window in the one school building that Company A occupied, Gonzalez fired his weapons into enemy-held rooms across the inner courtyard. When the NVA revealed themselves, other Marines cut them down. Finally, the deadly game caught up with Gonzalez. Members of an NVA RPG team spotted him in an open window. They fired a B40 rocket right at him. Gonzalez posthumously received the only Medal of Honor awarded for the month-long fight in Hue.

By stopping Gravel's battalion, the NVA also halted Company F, 2/5. Despite the heroic efforts of individual Marines, the tenacious defenders of the treasury building facing Captain Downs's men refused to give up. About this time, Maj. Ralph J. Salvati, the battalion executive officer, arrived on the scene. Though his duties normally kept him in the rear handling the administrative details of the bat-

talion, Salvati was eager to get in the fight. His Vietnam tour was ending soon, and he'd experienced no combat. This might be his last
chance. After witnessing the stalled attack on the treasury building,
Salvati approached Captain Downs and Lieutenant Colonel
Cheatham with an idea. Though it was far-fetched, the two combat
leaders agreed to try it. Salvati headed to the rear. He soon returned
in a jeep loaded with four E8 gas launchers. This area-saturation device fired sixty-four 35mm tear gas projectiles in four five-second
bursts of sixteen projectiles each.

Assured that all the Marines had gas masks, Major Salvati prepared
his weapon. Right at noon he fired the device. Twenty seconds later
the treasury complex was covered in a cloud of gas. A blast from a
106mm recoilless rifle tore apart the wrought-iron front gate. A split
second later a squad of Marines burst from cover and entered the
grounds. Though hampered by the sight-restricting gas masks, they
blew their way into the building using hand grenades and tear gas
grenades. Once inside, they rushed from room to room, clearing
each one by tossing in a grenade, then following up the blast with a
burst of M16 fire. In short order the building was free of the enemy.

After hunting down and killing the few remaining NVA holding
out on the treasury grounds, Company F also occupied the post office buildings next door. With Company H's conquest of the public
health complex, the Marines had made substantial progress in gaining control of the city. Rather than attack again during the few remaining daylight hours, the Marines dug in for the night along Le
Dinh Duong Street, the next street west.

Late on the afternoon of 4 February, a truck convoy from Phu Bai
entered the MACV compound. Having survived the heavy volume
of fire from enemy soldiers emplaced along Highway 1, the truck drivers were not looking forward to the return trip. They needn't have
worried. At 1940 the NVA blew up the An Cuu Bridge over the Phu
Cam Canal. Highway 1 was closed.

With little rest after being harassed by the NVA all night,
Cheatham's Marines renewed their attack at 0530 on 5 February. This
time all three companies were on the line, Company G having
moved to the right flank along the river. Resistance was lighter than
expected and all three companies made good progress, advancing

one full block beyond Le Dinh Duong Street. Lieutenant Colonel
Cheatham decided to keep going forward as long as he could. He
believed that the enemy was reeling under his rifle companies' persistent attacks and he didn't want to let up. At 0900 Captain Christmas's Company H attacked toward its next objective—the Hue Central Hospital complex, a vast network of buildings occupying more
than two square blocks.

The enemy commander may have conceded a full city block that
morning, but that's all he was giving up. As soon as Company H
stepped off in its attack, NVA soldiers, emplaced in the hospital buildings, opened fire with an incredible array of small arms, machine
guns, and B40s. To the left, Captain Downs's Company F fared no
better.

For more than four hours the two sides exchanged ordnance without either making any gains. Then, following a heavy 81mm mortar
barrage from Company G, a squad of Company H rushed across the
street, killed eight NVA, and seized an outlying hospital building. A
short time later some Company F Marines used a 106mm recoilless
rifle to blow the NVA out of a building in front of them. The bodies
of four freshly killed enemy soldiers lay among the rubble. A few
dazed survivors staggered into a nearby building as the Americans
rushed forward.

In the meantime, Lieutenant Colonel Gravel's badly weakened
battalion was still bogged down in the heavily defended Jeanne d'Arc
complex. Adding to their problems was the fact that Colonel Hughes
had taken away Company A's strongest platoon to garrison outposts
around the MACV compound. The 1st Battalion, 1st Marines by this
time consisted of just five woefully understrength rifle platoons. Even
an M48 tank's 90mm cannon couldn't help this battered force take
its objective.

Suddenly, at 1300 the NVA counterattacked, hitting both Company H, 2/5, and Company A, 1/1. Captain Christmas's Marines responded with everything from M16s and M60s to 106mm recoilless
rifle rounds, driving back the attackers. Lieutenant Smith's Marines
responded in a similar manner but were helped by the tank. Fifteen
rounds from its massive 90mm gun blew the enemy attackers out of
the street.

After taking a few hours to replenish its ammo supplies, Cheatham's battalion renewed its attack shortly after 1500. This time Captain Meadows's Company G slipped to the left to cross in front of Company H, attacking southward right into one of the hospital's main buildings. Chasing the defenders from ward to ward, Meadows's men finally secured the building. After another ninety minutes of close-quarters fighting, the surviving NVA fled. The entire hospital complex belonged to the Marines. In searching the complex the Marines found piles of bloody, still-damp bandages littering the operating rooms, revealing that dozens of wounded enemy soldiers had recently been treated.

While Company G finished securing the hospital complex and evacuated its more than two dozen casualties, Company H jumped off to seize a large building just south of the hospital. With Companies F and G blocking any escape routes, the defending NVA fought like cornered animals. They poured a devastating barrage of small arms and RPG fire into Captain Christmas's men. When his lead platoons bogged down, Christmas twice braved the concentrated enemy fire to cross a wide expanse of open ground to check on the men. Then he climbed aboard the rear deck of a supporting M48 tank and guided it forward. Directing its cannon fire while others fired tear gas canisters into shattered windows, Christmas helped reduce the building. When the fight was over, more than twenty-five dead NVA littered the ground, and Captain Christmas had earned a Navy Cross.

At 1830 Cheatham ordered his battle-weary rifle companies to halt and dig in for the night. It had been a hard, but successful, day. Just a little more than a block away was the regiment's original objective: the prison and the provincial administration complex. North Vietnamese soldiers and Viet Cong guerrillas had raised the flag of the National Liberation Front (NLF) on the flagpole in front of the administration building on 1 February. Its continued display both infuriated and inspired the Marines. Cheatham and his company commanders agreed that 6 February was the day the rebellious banner had to come down.

The three companies of 2/5 began their drive toward the prison at 0700 on 6 February. All three immediately ran into stiff resistance.

An awe-inspiring array of weapons greeted the advancing riflemen; B40 rockets, mortar shells, AK-47s, and machine guns rained a hail of death on the Marines. Particularly hard hit was Company F. As its 2d Platoon moved along a wall just outside the hospital complex, the enemy caught its command group in a deadly cross fire. In a blistering barrage of small arms fire, the group was cut down. In seconds, four men were killed and five were wounded.

Meanwhile, at the Jeanne d'Arc school to 2/5's left rear, Company A and the provisional Company B, 1/1, were still stymied in their efforts to defeat the stubborn NVA. For most of the morning of 6 February, they'd been battling an enemy force for possession of a large church just south of the school. After pounding the once beautiful structure with 106mm recoilless rifle fire, machine guns, and mortar rounds for more than fifteen minutes, Smith's Marines charged headlong into the church. The fight was over a few minutes later. Thirty dead NVA littered the once hallowed place.

Around 1100 the remaining NVA defenders suddenly and unexplicably abandoned the Jeanne d'Arc campus. Gravel's two battered rifle companies thoroughly scoured the grounds for any remaining foe. Once convinced that the NVA had indeed withdrawn, the Marines hustled down Tran Cao Van Street to catch up to 2/5.

Cheatham's companies had spent most of the morning attacking a number of NVA-occupied buildings around the prison. Using explosive charges to blow holes in the block walls surrounding the residential backyards, the grunts scurried forward yard by yard. Enemy soldiers, emplaced in the upper floors of nearby buildings, poured a deadly hail of fire on the Marines as they moved forward. Only sheer guts and determination sustained them. By 1300 all three companies were closing in on the main prison building. Supporting weapons—primarily 106mm recoilless rifles, the 90mm cannons of the M48 tanks, and 81mm mortars—had been pounding the prison for nearly three hours.

Covered by Company F, Company G attacked at 1405. Ten minutes later it had breached the prison's outer wall. The rest of the prison fell quickly. Surprisingly, the NVA had caved in. Only one Marine was slightly wounded in the final attack. Thirty-six NVA were killed and eight wounded enemy soldiers were captured. Captain

Meadows's men found an impressive arsenal of weapons stashed in the prison. Among the weapons were American rifles of World War II vintage and a wide variety of explosives.

As Company G secured the prison complex, Captain Christmas's Company H veered to the right to attack the Thua Thien provincial administration complex, which sat east of the Perfume River on Le Loi Street. Using the same tactics employed by the other two companies, Company H unleashed a ferocious barrage of supporting fire on the administration building as, on signal at 1425, the 1st Platoon charged straight at the main building's front door. Barging through the doorway, the lead riflemen threw grenades left and right. The sharp explosions were followed by prolonged bursts of M16 and M60 fire. As the dust settled, the Marines chased the NVA down the long corridors, tossing grenades into every room they passed. Suprisingly, most of the NVA managed to flee unharmed. Only four enemy bodies were found in the building.

When Captain Christmas got the news, he immediately radioed Lieutenant Colonel Cheatham. "The building's ours, sir. We're gonna run up the American flag."

This was a politically sensitive area. Strictly speaking, Captain Christmas should have turned over the Thua Thien provincial administration buildings to the ARVN and continued the fight. But no red-blooded American Marine commander could have watched his men die to capture a target, then just walk away. Turning to his gunnery sergeant, Christmas said, "We've been looking at that damn North Vietnamese flag all day, and now we're gonna take it down." With snipers' bullets smacking into the ground around them, Christmas and GSgt. Frank Thomas, accompanied by a squad of riflemen, dashed toward the flagpole. At the base of the pole Thomas pulled an American flag from beneath his flak jacket. Earlier that day two resourceful Company H riflemen had sneaked back to the MACV compound and stolen the American flag flying over it.

Now, as two men lowered and removed the NLF flag, Gunny Thomas affixed the Stars and Stripes in its place. At 1603 Old Glory was snapping in the breeze. To those who witnessed the impromptu ceremony, it was every bit as inspiring as the flag-raising on Mount Suribachi on Iwo Jima twenty-three years earlier that had brought the U.S. Marine Corps everlasting glory.

Though several more days of heavy fighting remained before all of Hue south and east of the Perfume River would be declared secure on 11 February, the capture of the administrative headquarters essentially broke the back of the NVA. Those who remained were desperate, fighting for their lives, unable to mount any serious offensive attacks or flee. They could only wait for the Marines to hunt them down and kill them. In the meantime, the major action shifted north of the Perfume River to the Citadel.

Since the beginning of the battle for Hue, the struggle to wrest control of the Citadel from the enemy had been an ARVN show. Our allies were desperate to save face by achieving a victory on their own. General Ngo Quang Truong, 1st ARVN Division commander, had started the fight to retake the revered national site with just his headquarters troops and one rifle company. Over the next forty-eight hours, from their positions outside the city, the division's infantry battalions fought their way into the Citadel. Eventually, Truong had fifteen battalions at his disposal, including three ARVN airborne battalions, three Vietnamese Marine Corps battalions, and two ARVN Ranger battalions. North Vietnamese troops consisted primarily of the 4th and 6th Regiments, although elements of several other regiments slipped into the Citadel from Khe Sanh as the fighting there waned.

Despite having numerical superiority, the ARVN were not able to make much headway in destroying the NVA. The enemy forces had not only burrowed deeply into the tightly packed urban buildings, but they were able to infiltrate reinforcements and supplies into the Citadel right to the end. In addition, poor weather hampered the use of U.S. air support. By day four of the battle for the Citadel, the ARVN forces had become demoralized. Displaying their usual lackluster leadership abilities, the battalion commanders essentially decided to remain in place and hold down casualties.

Completely frustrated by his troops' unwillingness to tangle with the NVA, General Truong finally appealed to III MAF for help. On 10 February, General Cushman sent a message to General LaHue to move a Marine battalion to the Citadel.

On that day, the 1st Battalion, 5th Marines was spread out along Highway 1 between the Hai Van Pass and Da Nang. Charged with protecting the vital roadway, the widely dispersed rifle companies of

1/5 had been fighting the NVA and VC almost constantly since the Tet Offensive began. So heavy had the fighting been that even the battalion headquarters at Phu Loc had been attacked several times. In fact, the battalion commander was severely wounded and evacuated on 1 February. Major Robert H. Thompson, a staff officer with III MAF, took command of the battalion the next day.

At midnight on10 February, while in the middle of a rain-swept field west of Phu Loc and in contact with an enemy force that his Marines had been chasing all day, Major Thompson was ordered by 5th Marine headquarters to immediately return to Phu Loc. Incredulous, Thompson explained his situation. Too bad, came the reply, move out. Obeying orders, Thompson saddled up his Marines and began the nine-kilometer hike back to Phu Loc. Slogging across drenched fields, fording cold, fast-moving streams, and lashed by wind-driven rainstorms during the entire march, Thompson had his men at Phu Loc just after dawn.

Events moved rapidly that morning. At 0830 on 11 February, 1/5 was ordered to Phu Bai, where control of the battalion would pass to Colonel Hughes's 1st Marines. Helicopters and trucks ferried the battalion to Phu Bai. At 1045 CH-46s carried two platoons of Company B right into ARVN headquarters in the Citadel. Heavy enemy fire prevented the rest of the company from landing. Though anxious to join their buddies, the remaining members of the battalion boarded trucks. Company A and the rest of Company B, accompanied by five M48 tanks barged up from Da Nang, entered the Citadel late on 11 February. Companies C and D would make the trip the next day.

Once inside the Citadel, Thompson was given his mission. His battalion was to secure the complex's northeast wall (the Citadel's four corners were oriented north, east, south, and west), allowing the ARVN to complete its drive to the Imperial Palace, which sat along the southeast wall. Troopers from the 1st ARVN Airborne Task Force currently held the positions, which were about one kilometer southeast of General Truong's headquarters. Thompson's men would relieve the paratroopers in the morning. Once settled, they would then attack straight down the remaining fifteen hundred meters of the wall. The ARVN's left flank would thus be well protected.

Most of Thompson's men were used to fighting their war in the bush, away from any urban areas. Their first few nights in the Citadel were tense. Surrounded by houses, gardens, stores, buildings two and three stories high, and paved roads littered with abandoned vehicles, the riflemen felt out of their element. The near-constant, bone-chilling rain added to their misery. Sounds from the enemy's portion of the Citadel echoed off the brick and masonry walls. The Marines didn't know what the morning would bring; they only knew it would be tough.

At 0800 on 13 February, Capt. James J. Bowe led his Company A, 1/5, down Dinh Bo Linh Street, paralleling the northeast wall; it was headed for the positions held by the ARVN airborne. Fifteen minutes later, and fully two hundred meters north of the ARVN, hidden NVA unleashed a vicious ambush. An onslaught of AK-47 rifle fire, B40 rockets, and mortar rounds slammed into the column of unsuspecting Marines. Within minutes, Company A was devastated. Badly wounded were thirty Marines, including the executive officer, the company gunnery sergeant, and Captain Bowe, who'd taken over only two days earlier. Two men were killed.

The survivors scrambled for cover among the nearby buildings, pulling the wounded with them. Then, minutes after the fight began, it was over. Company A, effectively destroyed as a fighting unit, spent the rest of the morning caring for its casualties. As Major Thompson ordered Company C to move forward from its reserve position, he wondered how the NVA could possibly have maneuvered behind the ARVN.

They hadn't. As soon as the ARVN paratroopers learned the previous afternoon that the Marines were going to relieve them, they pulled out. The NVA simply swept in behind them, occupying the ARVN's positions. They waited for dawn and the unwary Marines.

Just after noon, Thompson sent his assault companies forward again. No sooner had 1st Lt. Scott Nelson's Company C started forward than the NVA let loose. An earsplitting barrage of small arms and automatic weapons fire, accompanied by volleys of RPGs, tore into the riflemen. Emplaced in buildings overlooking the company's planned route, the enemy soldiers could fire on the Marines from every direction.

At first confused, Company C's veterans quickly responded. Learning to clear rooms with a well-tossed grenade followed by a full clip of M16 fire, the riflemen advanced building by building.

On a parallel avenue to the east, Company B, commanded by Capt. Fern Jennings, attacked down the base of the wall. Accompanied by three M48 tanks, the infantrymen cleared several nests of enemy soldiers from atop the wall. They, too, learned urban fighting lessons on the job. The men learned never to enter a doorway or crawl through a window without first clearing the way with a hand grenade. The lessons were hard learned but indelible.

By 1445 both companies had broken through the NVA—or, more probably, the enemy had pulled back. The two units were in place along Mai Thuc Loan Street, which ran from the Dong Ba Gate to the north corner of the Imperial Palace.

Major Thompson requested artillery fire throughout the night to help soften up his battalion's objective for the next day. The request was granted, but the fire was not as effective as it could have been. Because the batteries were at Phu Bai, they had to fire their destructive shells right at the attacking infantry rather than over their heads, as they normally did. Also, the proximity of the venerable Imperial Palace, off-limits to all but small arms fire, narrowed the target box. There was little margin for error.

As confined as it was, this artillery fire was all the support available to Major Thompson. The continued poor weather, with low ceilings and restricted visibility in fog, kept airplanes and helicopters on the ground. For the most part then, the fight to clear the Citadel would be a rifleman's war.

At 0800 on Valentine's Day, Companies B and C attacked abreast, with Company D in reserve. Initially, they made good progress. Then sniper fire erupted. That quickly built into a cacophony of small arms that drove the Marines to cover. Particularly troublesome was a nest of NVA around the Dong Ba tower. So closely mingled were the foes that Thompson could not use his supporting weapons. He had to order the rifle companies to temporarily withdraw so they would be clear of the impact area. By the time this maneuver was finished, it was late enough in the day that Thompson ordered his rifle companies to dig in for the night; he'd continue the artillery bombardment through the night. Late in the afternoon a rare break in the weather allowed Marine F-4s to drop their bombs on the targets, too. The enemy positions were soon engulfed in explosions and napalm, but nobody on the ground believed that the positions were completely destroyed.

Captain Myron Harrington's Company D was given the mission of neutralizing the tower. Upon arriving in Hue two days earlier, the company had been opconned to Lieutenant Colonel Cheatham's 2/5. It spent the intervening time sweeping the southeast bank of the Perfume River, clearing the area of any remaining die-hard NVA. Late in the afternoon of 14 February, Company D was returned to Major Thompson's control. By 1800 the company was in the Citadel.

At dawn on 15 February, Companies B and C slipped to the right to make room for Harrington's fresh company along the wall. All three companies jumped off at 0800. Companies B and C easily crossed over the rubble in front of them and retook all the ground they'd given up the previous afternoon. On the left, though, it was a different story.

As Company D neared the Dong Ba tower it ran into a hornet's nest. Enemy soldiers, huddled in bunkers and pillboxes, fired every conceivable weapon in their arsenal. The noise of the battle reached a deafening roar as grenades crashed and rifles fired. Orders had to be shouted several times before they could be heard. Two weapons that helped the Marines were the World War II–vintage 3.5-inch rocket launcher, "bazooka," and the company's 60mm mortars. Both weapons fired point-blank at the enemy, blowing him into oblivion.

Helped by the deadly blasts from the 90mm cannon mounted on an M48 tank, which could barely squeeze down the narrow streets, a rifle squad finally made it to the top of the wall. Leaping forward over mounds of rubble, the squad closed in on the tower. Below it other Company D Marines pressed forward, too. Finally, at 1630 the grunts on the wall, following a blistering 60mm mortar barrage, captured the tower. At street level the rest of the company captured the Dong Ba Gate. Twenty-four dead NVA were pulled from the tower's rubble. Marine losses were six dead and thirty-three wounded and evacuated. (Casualties were so high that unless a wound put a man down, he stayed in the fight after being treated.)

The NVA counterattacked the tower at 0430 the next morning. Behind a wall of deadly accurate mortar fire, enemy soldiers sneaked close enough to drive off the defending Marines with grenades and B40 rockets. Captain Harrington responded instantly. Firing his .45-caliber pistol at point-blank range, he led his CP Marines in the assault. Using M16s, M60s, M79 grenade launchers, and hand grenades, the two sides slugged it out in the predawn darkness. By first light the tower was back in Company D's possession.

The next day dawned clear. For the first time since the battle for Hue began, air support could be routinely scheduled throughout the day. Following an early morning barrage including air, naval gunfire, artillery, and organic mortars, the three badly worn rifle companies pressed forward. Instantly, the enemy responded. A barrage of small arms fire and B40 rockets lashed the Marines. The battle was a rifle squad's war. Small teams of brave young men would ignore the hail of enemy fire to charge into a target building. Rushing from room to room, throwing grenades before them, the riflemen would clear the building while another squad moved to the next one. Many of the enemy riflemen were dug in in spider holes located at the base of buildings and courtyard walls. Marines had to attack each one, dropping in grenades to kill the defenders. Meter by meter the Marines fought their way forward, slowly but surely closing in on the Citadel's southeast wall. On 16 February, Thompson's battalion suffered a dozen dead and forty-five wounded.

The brutal fighting continued unabated the next day. To many of the riflemen each day was the same. Attack at dawn, rout out the enemy, treat casualties, attack again. As 1/5 squeezed the enemy into an ever smaller perimeter, the NVA turned more vicious. Each strongpoint had to be reduced with close-quarters fighting. No sooner had one strongpoint been taken than the enemy would open fire from another. On 17 February, 1/5 suffered 12 dead and 55 wounded and evacuated. They claimed 24 dead NVA.

By this point the 1st Battalion, 5th Marines was running out of steam. In just five days of fighting it had suffered 47 killed, 240 seriously wounded, and at least 60 wounded but not evacuated. Company A fielded roughly 70 men, Company B had about 80, and Companies C and D only a few more each. Although replacements routinely arrived during the battle, too often they were chewed up by the killing machine of Hue before their squad leaders could even learn their names. Some replacements arrived in Hue directly upon completion of their infantry training at Camp Pendleton, California. As evidence of the rapid rate of attrition, there were Marine KIAs found still wearing their stateside fatigues and boots.

The NVA was not only a formidable foe, but the terrain favored the defense. The Citadel was a densely packed community of thick-walled masonry houses. Narrow streets and tight alleys severely restricted the use of armor and heavy weapons. Courtyard walls enclosed nearly every house. Thick hedgerows lined many of the streets. Often it was hard to see much past twenty-five meters. Continued poor weather not only restricted air support but the cold rain hampered the troops. Artillery was available, but the close-quarters fighting severely reduced its effectiveness. And ammo for every weapon was low.

Because of all this, Major Thompson chose 18 February to rest his Marines. His men would use the day to clean weapons, stock up on ammo, have minor wounds treated, and eat. Many of the frontline infantrymen hadn't had a meal in one and a half days.

As expected, when the rifle companies resumed their attacks the next day, they found that the NVA had used the twenty-four-hour lull to strengthen their fighting positions. Even if they were a fresh battalion, the men of 1/5 would have had a tough time. Weakened and weary as they were, Thompson's men faced a near impossible task. Each enemy position had to be taken by direct frontal attack. There was no other way. With the rifle companies inching their way toward the Citadel's southeast wall, artillery fire and air support had to be curtailed. The target area was simply too small.

As the Marines pressed farther southeast, they came under increasingly heavy and accurate fire from enemy automatic weapons emplaced atop the Imperial Palace. Forbidden to fire on the sacred structure with anything heavier than their small arms, they felt helpless. Finally, Company C peeled off a platoon to protect its right flank. By the end of 19 February, 1/5 was just three blocks from its objective, the Thuong Tu Gate, the same place that Company G, 2/5, had been so badly chewed up three weeks earlier.

That same day, General Truong sent two of his companies to support 1/5. They took up positions on the battalion's right flank. This not only reduced Thompson's battle front but put the ARVN in position to attack the Imperial Palace when the time came. Task Force X-ray had decided that, for face-saving political purposes, capture of the Imperial Palace would be an ARVN-only show.

Pressed by his superiors to end the fight, at his nightly meeting on 20 February, Major Thompson told his company commanders that he wanted to punch through the last NVA defensive positions with a surprise night attack. Although all his commanders agreed with the concept, Thompson quickly realized that they weren't enthusiastic about it. Then 1st Lt. Patrick D. Polk said that his Company A, which had been in reserve the last few days, would do it.

Major Thompson assigned Polk the mission of taking a large multistory government building about three hundred meters in front of them and just inside the Thuong Tu Gate. Capture of this building would deny the enemy an unobstructed view of the battalion advance.

At about 2300 on 20 February, Company A's depleted 2d Platoon, accompanied by Polk and an 81mm forward observer, crept forward. To their complete amazement, they crossed the entire distance without encountering any enemy soldiers. By 0300 on 21 February, the platoon had not only occupied the large target building but several smaller outbuildings, as well.

In the half-light of predawn, Lieutenant Polk spotted two groups of NVA moving toward the courtyard surrounding the building. Anxiously, the FO called for a fire mission. Just minutes later a brace of 81mm mortar shells dropped from the cloudy skies right in the midst of the unsuspecting foe. This barrage was followed by several tear gas rounds. With the irritant creating confusion among the enemy soldiers, members of Polk's patrol sniped away. By the time the gas cleared, nineteen enemy soldiers lay dead on the debris-filled street.

When news of Polk's success reached the other companies, they reacted with renewed vigor. It was morale boosting to learn that the enemy could be beaten at his own game. Inspired by this news, 1/5 had taken all of the northeast wall by the end of the day.

That same day, reinforcements arrived in the form of Company L, 3/5. By late afternoon, Capt. John Niotis's fresh Marines were in position atop the northeast wall. The next day they'd attack down the southeast wall toward the Imperial Palace. Also on 22 February, Company B, 1/5, was pulled out of the line for rest and rebuilding. The company had just sixty-one effectives, most of whom had at least one minor wound.

Company L started down the Citadel's southeast wall early on 23 February. Almost immediately heavy enemy fire halted them. Below them to their right, Companies C and D tried to penetrate the remaining NVA defensive line, but they, too, had little luck. Heavy automatic weapons fire from the Imperial Palace kept the Marines from gaining much yardage that day.

While the Marines battled on, the ARVN I Corps commander, General Lam, finally lifted the restrictions on the aerial bombardment of the Imperial Palace. When 24 February dawned clear, Marine jets blasted the palace. Immediately, the NVA defenses started to crumble.

Unknown to the Marines, the enemy commander had finally permitted his forces to begin withdrawing from the Citadel on 22 February. Under the cover of darkness during the previous few nights, the NVA had been infiltrating past the ARVN forces holding the western portions of the Citadel. Except for the last-ditch defenders, the battle for Hue was nearly over. The one major obstacle to victory was the Imperial Palace.

Forbidden by III MAF and the ARVN from entering the Imperial Palace, Major Thompson's Marines halted in place while an elite company of 1st ARVN Division soldiers stormed the palace. Under sporadic fire, they entered the complex. A short time later they were followed by troops of the 2d Battalion, 3d ARVN Regiment. The South Vietnamese troops swept through the complex, killing the few remaining NVA. In a few hours it was over; the revered Imperial Palace was finally back in friendly hands.

Early on 25 February, soldiers of the 2d Battalion, 3d ARVN Regiment made the final assault down the southeast wall toward the flagpole. Since 31 January the NLF banner had taunted Marines and ARVN alike. The ARVN commander of 2/3 offered to let Major Thompson's Marines capture the flagpole. Thompson politely refused. As badly as he may have wanted to strike the enemy battle standard, he was under strict orders not to touch it.

Beginning at 0500 the ARVN started toward the flagpole and they easily overran the few defending NVA. By 0730 the flag of the Republic of South Vietnam again fluttered from the pole. Inside the Citadel, Marine and ARVN troops routed out the last of the NVA from the southwest corner. At 1700 on 25 February, the Citadel was declared secure. The next day the battle for Hue was officially ended. A short time later the 1st Marines were temporarily detached from the 1st Marine Division and sent north. There they participated in Operation Pegasus, opening Route 9 from Ca Lu west. The 5th Marines returned to operations south of Phu Bai.

The final tally of casualties put known enemy dead at 5,113, with another 89 captured. United States Marine casualties were officially set at 147 killed in action and 857 wounded seriously enough to require evacuation.

When the battle ended, the city that everyone believed was immune from the war lay ruined. Although the South Vietnamese government immediately launched a rehabilitation program designed to provide food, clothing, and shelter to the hapless residents of Hue, it would take years of effort before the city regained any of its former luster.

However, the real tragedy of this fight lay in the great loss of civilian lives—not just the civilians caught in the cross fire of warring factions, but those murdered by the Viet Cong. Among the enemy units infiltrating Hue prior to Tet were special execution squads. At the start of the Tet Offensive they systematically rounded up thousands of Hue's elite. Using detailed lists titled "Enemies of the People," the VC picked up most of Hue's leading businessmen, government officials, foreigners, politicians, military officers, artists, intellectuals, teachers, and students—anyone who posed any threat to their plans. The captives were marched off, never to be seen again. By most estimates about five thousand citizens were murdered by the VC. No one has ever been held accountable for this crime.

Other elements of the 1st Marine Division fought the NVA and VC during the Tet Offensive, too. Da Nang itself was hit by several 122mm rocket attacks in the offensive's opening days. The enemy missiles damaged several U.S. Marine facilities but, fortunately, caused few casualties. In the predawn darkness of 30 January, VC sappers attacked the ARVN I Corps headquarters just east of the air base. The ARVN headquarter troops managed to hold off the enemy until U.S. Marine military police from the air base arrived. Fighting together in the dark, the allies repulsed the enemy, killing more than a dozen.

The 2d NVA Division had planned to participate in the attack on Da Nang, but Marine recon teams picked up their movement while they were still in the mountains west of An Hoa. The recon teams called in air strikes and artillery missions. Then, division headquarters dispatched 3/5 and 2/3 to follow up the bombardments. Faced with this formidable force, the remaining NVA melted back into the mountains.

Since the opening days of the Tet Offensive, General Westmoreland had been under considerable pressure from Washington to quickly contain the enemy. To do so, he requested the immediate deployment of an additional 206,000 troops. Though this call for reinforcements shocked both Washington and the American public, and would have far-reaching political ramifications for the U.S. effort in South Vietnam, for III MAF it meant the addition of another Marine regiment to its order of battle.

When the 27th Marines was alerted for movement to the war zone, two of its battalions, the 2d and 3d, were stationed at Camp Pendleton in California and one was afloat in the Pacific. The regiment's 2d Battalion arrived at Da Nang by air on 17 February. Three days later, 3/27 landed at Da Nang. The 1st Battalion, 27th Marines was at sea on a training exercise with the Hawaii-based 1st Marine Brigade when word came to go to Da Nang. The Marines arrived in South Vietnam on 28 February.

The deployment of the 27th Marines was planned by MACV to be temporary; General Westmoreland felt that it could be released in no more than four months. The new arrivals were assigned a TAOR along the coast south of Marble Mountain and north of Hoi An. This freed the 5th Marines to concentrate its efforts in the area from the Hai Van Pass north to Phu Bai. Accordingly, it opened Operation Houston on 26 February with 2/3 and 3/5 to sweep the area adjacent to Highway 1.

Continued concern about the Marine commands' ability to effectively control the tactical situation in I Corps finally prompted General Westmoreland to open an MACV subheadquarters at Phu Bai. He appointed his hard-charging deputy, Gen. Creighton W. Abrams, Jr., as the commander of MACV-Forward on 9 February. Abrams would directly oversee III MAF and the soon-to-be-formed Provisional Corps, Vietnam. Neither General Cushman nor his subordinates were pleased with this move.

Additional reinforcements for III MAF arrived on 19 February in the form of two U.S. Army airborne brigades—the 101st Airborne Division's 1st Brigade and the 82d Airborne Division's 3d Brigade—directly from the United States. Both units were assigned to the 101st Airborne Division, which was operating north of Hue. With these additions, MACV decided that control of five-plus scattered divisions was too great a span. Accordingly, on 10 March, Lt. Gen. William B. Rosson, the former commander of I Field Force, Vietnam, was given command of the newly created Provisional Corps, Vietnam. Marine major general Raymond G. Davis was appointed his deputy. The Provisional Corps assumed operational control of the army's 1st Cavalry Division and 101st Airborne Division, as well as the 3d Marine Division. Operational control of the Provisional Corps was, in turn, given to General Cushman. With the activation of the Provisional Corps, the MACV-Forward headquarters was inactivated, and General Abrams returned to Saigon. On 15 August 1968, the Provisional Corps would be redesignated XXIV Corps, with an army general in command.

To keep pressure on the enemy, the 1st and 2d Battalions, 7th Marines began Operation Worth on 12 March, twenty kilometers southwest of Da Nang. It soon became apparent that the NVA had a full division in the operational region. The enemy forces seemed to be concentrated in the Go Noi Island area, a delta west of Hoi An formed by the meanderings of the Ky Lam River and bisected by Highway 1 and a bermed railroad.

Eager to tangle with the enemy, Col. Reverdy M. Hall ended his 7th Marines' Operation Worth and began Operation Allen Brook on

4 May. On that morning, CH-46s carried 2/7 into LZs along the western edge of Go Noi Island. Proceeding eastbound, the rifle companies encountered only light resistance for the first four days. Then, enemy resistance picked up as they neared Xuan Dai, a hamlet just south of the river and west of the bermed railroad. The Marines fought for most of 9 May, making generous use of air and artillery support before they overran the defenders. Eighty dead NVA attested to the viciousness of the fighting.

On 13 May, 3/7 replaced 2/7, reversed direction, and started sweeping back to the west. Two days later the battalion found the enemy in bunkers in Phu Dong, two kilometers west of Xuan Dai. It took most of the day for the rifle companies to clear the hamlet.

Following that fight, the 7th Marines passed control of Operation Allen Brook to the 27th Marines. The fresh regiment's 3d Battalion air-assaulted into LZs two kilometers west of Phu Dong. Almost immediately it encountered strong enemy forces. Heavy fighting raged for the next ten days as the Marines steadily moved westward toward An Hoa.

Once removed from the Allen Brook operation, the 7th Marines opened Operation Mameluke Thrust on 18 May. This new operation focused on the area west and south of Da Nang, known to the Marines as Happy Valley.

The dual operations screened the enemy's avenues of approach to Da Nang throughout the summer. In the Go Noi Island TAOR, the two infantry battalions assigned to the 27th Marines, 1/26 and 1/27, maneuvered back and forth in search of the enemy. Though most days passed without any contact, when the Marines did find the foe the fighting was vicious.

In early June, General Robertson relinquished command of the 1st Marine Division to Maj. Gen. Carl A. Youngdale. A Marine since 1936, Youngdale brought his considerable combat experience from both World War II and Korea to his new post.

The 5th Marines assumed responsibility for Operation Mameluke Thrust in mid-July. It shifted the operation's focus south to An Hoa. The 2d and 3d Battalions, 5th Marines pushed east out of An Hoa on 16 August, sweeping toward positions held by 2/7 (Special Landing Force Bravo). On day two of the sweep, 200 enemy soldiers were pushed into 2/7's position; 50 of them were killed in the subsequent fighting.

The 27th Marines ended Operation Allen Brook on 24 August. Tallies for the campaign showed 1,017 enemy killed. Marine casualties were 172 dead and 1,124 wounded.

Despite the best efforts of the Marines involved in these twin operations, the enemy again managed to maneuver to within striking distance of Da Nang. In the early morning hours of 23 August, the 402d VC Sapper Battalion, charging behind a cloud of mortar shells and rockets, overran the Popular Forces detachment guarding the Cam Le Bridge over the Song Cau Do south of Da Nang. However, before the enemy could exploit its victory, Company C, 1st Marine MP Battalion came roaring up in trucks and jeeps and took positions on the north end of the bridge. Fighting valiantly, the policemen stopped the VC from crossing the bridge. Later that morning, Company A, 1/27, attacked the enemy from the south. Squeezed between the two forces, the sappers broke contact and fled.

In early September, the 1st Marines, which had been operating with the 3d Marine Division along the DMZ, returned to the Da Nang TAOR. This, in turn, permitted the 27th Marines to begin preparations for its return to Camp Pendleton. The regiment's 2d and 3d Battalions began their redeployment on 10 September; the movement was completed six days later. The 1st Battalion completed its move to Hawaii a few days later.

In late September, the NVA attacked a U.S. Army Special Forces camp at Thuong Duc. Situated in a picturesque river valley in central Quang Nam Province, the Green Beret camp had long been an irritant to enemy forces intent on traversing the area. On 28 September, enemy infantry struck two of the camp's outposts. The quick response of Marine A-6As broke up the attack before the NVA could do further damage.

To help stabilize the tenuous situation, on 6 October, General Youngdale authorized the 7th Marines to launch Operation Maui Peak. With the enemy holding the high ground on three sides of the camp, any overland relief force would be prone to ambush by the NVA. The Marines responded to this often-used NVA tactic by setting a trap of their own. A relief column would head down Route 4 toward the camp to fix the enemy in place. Then, helicopters would bring other Marines behind the NVA in strength.

By noon on 6 October, the overland force, 2/5, had indeed slammed into fortified enemy positions six kilometers east of Thuong Duc. Meanwhile, 2/7 and two battalions of ARVN soldiers landed unopposed at LZ Vulture, five kilometers northwest of the camp. Landing Zone Sparrow, five kilometers southeast of the camp, proved to be too well protected by enemy antiaircraft fire for 3/5 to land. Instead, 3/5 diverted to an alternate LZ five kilometers farther east.

In the meantime, the column easily pushed through the enemy roadblocks. The next day the column attacked an NVA force emplaced on Hill 163, just east of the camp. It finally cleared the hill on 8 October. The other Marine and ARVN battalions encountered only minor resistance as they swept the high ground overlooking the camp. The NVA tried to retake Hill 163 on 12 October, but Company E, 2/5, easily repulsed the attackers. With the Special Forces camp once again secure, Operation Maui Peak came to an end on 19 October; 28 Marines died in the operation and 100 were wounded.

The ongoing operation Mameluke Thrust was closed out a few days later, on 23 October. The Marines claimed 2,728 enemy killed versus 267 dead of their own and 1,730 wounded.

At the beginning of November, the South Vietnamese government began the Le Loi, or Accelerated Pacification, Program. It was designed to restore within the rural population by 31 January 1969 the pre-Tet level of security. As an active participant in Le Loi, the 1st Marine Division decreased its search and destroy operations and focused on village cordons designed to promote area security. Essentially, the tactics were the same as the County Fair operations that had been used by the Marines since they had been in-country.

The most successful of the 1st Marine Division's Le Loi sweeps was Operation Meade River, begun on 20 November. Meade River's target area, known to the grunts as Dodge City for its shoot-'em-up atmosphere, was twenty kilometers south of Da Nang. Long a hotbed of VC activity, Dodge City was forty square kilometers of hostile terrain. A lowland dotted with rice paddies and swamps, Dodge City was honeycombed with camouflaged caves and tunnels. Eight villages were spaced across the area. Marine intelligence estimated that elements of three NVA regiments—the 36th, 38th, and 368B—called Dodge City home. In addition, one hundred named VC operated a tight infrastructure within the target area.

Operating under control of the 1st Marines for Operation Meade River were six infantry battalions: 1/1; 2d and 3d Battalions, 5th Marines; 3/26; BLT 2/26 from SLF Alpha; and BLT 2/27 from SLF Bravo. The Marine commanders knew that in order for the cordon to be effective it had to be put into place rapidly. Underscoring the superb coordination that existed between the air and ground forces, the Marine helicopter squadrons responded with precision and speed. On the morning of 20 November, in the Marines' largest airmobile operation of the war, 76 helicopters ferried 3,500 Marines into 47 different LZs in just two hours. Truck convoys hauled other Marines, ARVN, and Korean soldiers to their positions. Before the enemy could react, more than 7,000 allied troops had encircled them in a 30-kilometer cordon so tight that there was one three-man fire team positioned every 15 meters.

Once in position, the Marines eventually evacuated 2,600 civilians to an interrogation center operated by the ARVN. There the civilians were fed, given needed medical attention, screened, and issued new ID cards. So effective was the sweep that 71 of the 100 known VC cadre were picked up and held.

The Marines spent each day of the operation searching for bunkers and tunnels. When enemy positions were found, supporting arms were called in to blast them. Initially, the fighting was light as small bands of enemy soldiers tried to slip through the cordon at night. As the cordon shrank, however, enemy resistance stiffened. Desperate NVA and VC soldiers boldly attacked the Marines closing in on them. Once again working with superb coordination, Marine riflemen, air support, and accurate artillery fire decimated the last ditch defenders.

Operation Meade River ended on 9 December. Enemy losses were 841 killed and 182 captured. The Marines lost 107 killed and 385 wounded.

As a follow-up to the successful Operation Mameluke Thrust, Operation Taylor Common began on 7 December. Controlled by Task Force Yankee, six infantry battalions from the 3d and 5th Marines poured into the area north of An Hoa known as the Arizona Territory. Once they completed the sweep of that long-hostile area, the Marines planned to penetrate the high ground to the west and southwest. This area, known as Base Area (BA) 112, was believed to be the home of the 21st and 141st NVA Regiments.

Operation Taylor Common continued into 1969. The major result of the operation up to the end of 1968 was the establishment of a secure supply line all the way from Da Nang to An Hoa.

The fourth year of U.S. Marine Corps involvement in the war in South Vietnam is easily divided into two distinct halves. In the first half of the year the enemy launched several strong offensive operations, primarily focused on I Corps' two northern provinces. The brutal combat that followed sent the enemy reeling.

The NVA tried to return to the offensive in August, particularly around Da Nang, but was once again soundly beaten. As a result, he pulled his major units back across the border into their sanctuaries. Rather than pursue victory through costly large-scale attacks, the enemy resorted to small-unit assaults combined with mortar and rocket attacks on major bases and population centers.

The casualty figures reflect the change in enemy tactics. Marine records show 40,144 enemy killed in the year's first six months; 22,093 were claimed for the last half. Marine casualties fell by nearly 50 percent in the second half of the year, too. The first six months of 1968 showed 3,057 Marines killed and 18,281 wounded. In the second half, 1,561 Marines died and 11,039 were wounded.

The Marines didn't know it at the time, but the Tet Offensive marked the beginning of the end for U.S. involvement in South Vietnam's civil war. With General Abrams replacing General Westmoreland, and the new U.S. president elected in November 1968 pledging to end the war, its intensity would never again reach the height of previous years.

Chapter Six

1969

The faint, distant buzz of the CH-46A helicopters gradually built as the flight of four neared the Laotian border west of Khe Sanh. Growing steadily louder, the noise became a deafening roar as the aerial machines hovered over the thick jungle. While the other three helicoters kept a wary eye peeled for any sign of North Vietnamese troops, one Sea Knight at a time dropped into various clearings. As the aircraft hung suspended a few feet off the jungle floor, the camouflage-suited members of the 3d Reconnaissance Battalion leaped to the ground. In less than a minute, the men were unloaded and melting into the dense surrounding jungle. Within five minutes, the entire platoon was on the ground.

Wordlessly, the well-trained jungle fighters fanned out. Moving without a sound, and using only hand signals, each team carefully reconned the area around its assigned LZ. Only when each team leader was completely satisfied that his LZ was free of enemy soldiers did he break the silence. He spoke the appropriate code word into his radio's microphone, indicating to headquarters that the LZ was cold. Each team then broke down into two-man teams, which took up key positions around their respective LZs. Keeping two-hour watches throughout the night, the team members would guard their LZ from any marauding NVA until the infantry arrived the next day. It was a hell of a way to spend New Year's Day.

At dawn the next morning, a fleet of CH-46As brought in the 1st and 2d Battalions of Col. Robert H. Barrow's 9th Marines, 3d Marine Division. As the Marine riflemen bailed out of the aircraft, the recon teams boarded them. Their work in Operation Dawson River West was over. Thanks to their clandestine efforts, the rifle battalions landed safely without the need for a prelanding artillery or aerial bombardment. Their unannounced arrival just might give them an advantage over any NVA lurking in the area.

After being joined by a battalion of the 2d ARVN Regiment, which took up positions just south of Route 9 on 2/9's right, or south, flank, the rifle companies began their searches of the area. Though the operation continued for three weeks, the Marines saw few live enemy soldiers. They did, however, uncover several caches of the enemy's supplies. Among the booty was a large quantity of equipment, arms, and ammunition that had obviously been taken from the overrun U.S. Army Special Forces camp at Lang Vei nearly a year earlier.

During the operation, Marine patrols probed as far north as fifteen kilometers above Route 9, then back east toward Vandegrift Combat Base. Very few casualties were suffered by either side during Operation Dawson River West, but the effort did confirm that the enemy had not reestablished a presence in the Khe Sanh area. As Colonel Barrow reported, "If there was ever a piece of ground in the western part of Quang Tri Province that was searched out thoroughly, [it] was that operation."

Unfortunately, few of the year's other operations would prove to be as placid.

The fifth year of U.S. involvement in the civil war in South Vietnam would prove to be one of change and transition. Though the basic objective of the war—helping the South Vietnamese government retain control of its country and population against assaults by the insurgent Viet Cong and North Vietnamese Army regulars—remained unchanged, the methods of achieving that goal were being reevaluated. Even though North Vietnam's 1968 Tet Offensive had failed militarily, essentially eliminating the Viet Cong as a viable opponent, the political ramifications of the countrywide attacks had forced the U.S. government to turn away from enhanced American participation in favor of Vietnamization, or military self-sufficiency for the ARVN.

Facing the political realities, General Abrams's new strategy placed greater emphasis on population security and improving South Vietnam's armed forces to the point where they could finally shoulder the majority of offensive operations themselves. General Abrams's new "one-war" strategy not only integrated all aspects of the conflict but also totally phased out General Westmoreland's war of attrition. In all operations, mobility and flexibility were to be emphasized, allowing existing plans to be rapidly modified to meet a changing tactical situation.

Late in 1968, the South Vietnamese Joint General Staff issued two documents setting forth the strategy for the conduct of the war in the upcoming year. The first was the 1969 Pacification and Development Plan. This document presented for the first time the strategy, concept, priorities, and objectives to guide the total pacification effort.

The second document was the Combined Campaign Plan, which provided basic guidance for all Free World forces in the conduct of military operations in 1969. In the I Corps tactical zone, allied forces were to continue offensive operations to reduce the infiltration of NVA forces into Quang Tri Province and to destroy enemy base areas. In addition, major population centers such as Hue, Da Nang, and Quang Ngai were to be protected from enemy attack. Pacification efforts with the Marines' CAP teams would continue in the populated coastal areas surrounding the major cities.

Tactically, the Marines planned to rely more heavily on the temporary fire support base concept initiated in 1968 as opposed to tying down large numbers of men protecting permanent base camps. This way, infantry units could leapfrog into enemy territory by helicopter, secure a mountaintop for engineers to prepare for the arrival of supporting artillery, then move deeper into the surrounding AO, all the while staying within range of the artillery. Once that area was secure or the operational sweeps were completed, everyone would move on to begin the process anew at a different location. Fire support bases could be up and running in a matter of hours and abandoned even more easily. In fact, the shorter their life span, the less chance the enemy could organize an attack against them.

A major command change occurred, too. Lieutenant General Herman G. Nickerson replaced General Cushman on 26 March. Cushman returned to Washington and was eventually appointed commandant of the Marine Corps. Nickerson was well versed in the Vietnam War. As the commander of the 1st Marine Division from

October 1966 to May 1967, Nickerson had witnessed the difficult
early days of the war. But now he had an even tougher task in protecting his men during the final days of the war.

While the troops of the III MAF conducted their combat operations under these new guidelines and with a new commander, America's leaders were making political decisions that would have a major impact on the troops' lives and the conduct of the war in South
Vietnam. Forced to accept the reality that the United States could
not win this war in the traditional military meaning of the word,
newly elected president Richard M. Nixon decided to withdraw
from the fight by gradually reducing U.S. forces in South Vietnam.
Among the units to be included in the initial drawdown was the 3d
Marine Division. Its departure from the combat zone during the
summer and fall of 1969 signaled the beginning of the end of the
war for the United States.

But, of course, the average Marine grunt fighting to survive his
thirteen-month tour in the war zone knew little, if anything, about
these political maneuvers. He knew only that his war continued unabated.

1st Marine Division

The primary mission of the division in this transitional year was
the defense of Da Nang and its environs. Secondary tasks included
providing security for construction crews that were improving Highway 1 and providing personnel for a variety of pacification efforts,
including the CAP program. The 1 million South Vietnamese living
in and around Da Nang, combined with the region's varied terrain,
made the 1st Marine Division's job extremely difficult. Besides the
inherent danger of the daily patrols, the Marines had to contend with
a civilian population not entirely unsympathetic to the Viet Cong.

To conduct his war, Maj. Gen. Ormond R. Simpson, who had
taken command of the division on 20 December 1968, had four infantry regiments at his disposal. North of Da Nang, securing the vital Hai Van Pass and portions of Highway 1, was the 26th Marines.
The 7th Marines operated in the scrubland and mountains to the
west of Da Nang. To its south, the 5th Marines' AO included An Hoa
and the inhospitable Arizona Territory, a rice paddy–dotted region

infested with the enemy. South of Da Nang, the 1st Marines conducted operations around Dodge City, Go Noi Island, and the coastal lowlands. Separate batteries of the 11th Marines supported the infantry regiments.

As the year began, three battalions of the 5th Marines and the SLF Bravo, BLT 2/7, were engaged in the continuation of a major operation that began on 7 December 1968.

Operation Taylor Common

Of particular concern to both MACV and III MAF in late 1968 was a major NVA staging area identified as Base Area 112. Located in the rugged mountains southwest of An Hoa, BA 112 provided training and logistical facilities for the NVA forces threatening the area between Da Nang and Tam Ky. Among the enemy units that intelligence sources identified as occupying part of BA 112 were the Front 4 Headquarters and Headquarters Military Region 5, which controlled NVA and VC activities in Quang Nam, Quang Tin, and Quang Ngai Provinces, plus the 21st Regiment, 2d NVA Division, and the 141st NVA Regiment. Faced with this lucrative a target, MACV urged III MAF to conduct an operation in the area.

Accordingly, the 1st Marine Division activated Task Force Yankee under assistant division commander Brig. Gen. Ross T. Dwyer, Jr., on 4 December. As planned, Operation Taylor Common would have three phases. First, elements of TF Yankee, in conjunction with ARVN units, would conduct clearing operations from the Liberty Bridge south to An Hoa. Next, a series of fire support bases would be opened southwest of An Hoa along the approaches to BA 112, leading to the penetration of the base area by the infantry elements. Finally, once the base area was cleared, task force units would conduct recon operations farther west in order to interdict enemy infiltration routes from Laos.

The deep roar of CH-46 helicopter rotors echoed over the rice paddies north of An Hoa as all four companies of BLT 2/7 headed for their LZ in the Arizona Territory on the morning of 7 December. In short order the four rifle companies were spreading out from the landing zone, ever alert for any sign of the enemy. Fortunately, there were none.

Once established on the ground, the battalion headed northeast. Across swollen streams and mucky rice paddies, and through thick tree lines, the riflemen advanced, searching for the foe. Meanwhile, elements of the 5th Marines started their search and clear sweeps from the Liberty Bridge to An Hoa. Although enemy contact was light and sporadic during this phase, the Marines did take casualties. A number came from booby traps, but more, including five deaths, came from friendly fire. Regrettably, this problem would plague the maneuver elements throughout the operation.

On 9 December, TF Yankee was augmented by the 1st and 3d Battalions, 3d Marines, on loan from the 3d Marine Division. General Davis had made the battalions available because Operation Taylor Common was the 1st Marine Division's first "high-mobility" operation—a concept developed and fostered by General Davis—and he thought that Simpson's division would benefit by having some experienced battalions around.

Phase Two of Taylor Common opened on 11 December, when 3/5 landed on Hill 575, about ten kilometers southwest of An Hoa, and established FSB Lance. Once the supporting artillery battery was in place, the rifle companies of 3/5 fanned out from the fire support base in clearing operations. Over the next week, this pattern was repeated as other TF Yankee units established FSB Pike (2/5), two kilometers northwest of Lance, and FSBs Spear (1/3) and Mace (3/3) to the southwest.

With four rifle battalions now on the ground along the eastern edge of BA 112, the search and destroy operations began in earnest. Although actual contact with enemy forces over the next two weeks was sparse, the Marines did uncover and destroy a number of enemy base camps, hospitals, supply facilities, and even an enemy POW camp. All of the facilities were unoccupied, because the enemy had fled westward.

For the men of the 1st Marine Division, this campaign in the mountains was vastly different from what they had experienced so far in the war. Most of the men had not operated in the mountainous, triple-canopied jungle. One rifleman later noted, "The density of the woods, the vines, the jungles; it's really thick and it's nagging and tiresome to work in, and everything is against you."

The final phase of Operation Taylor Common began on New Year's Day 1969, when 3/5 established Combat Operations Base (COB) Javelin about seven kilometers west of FSB Mace, at the western edge of BA 112. (A combat operations base was similar to a fire support base but did not include artillery.) Two weeks later, 1/3 secured Hill 508, six kilometers north of COB Javelin, and set up FSB Maxwell.

Using helicopters to drop into select LZs, the infantry companies fanned out on search missions from their bases. From COB Javelin 3/5 advanced generally southward, leapfrogging from one new combat operations base to another. At the same time, the rifle companies of 1/3 advanced on a parallel axis north and west of Maxwell. As before, any actual contact with the enemy was light. Most of the time the action involved a platoon or less of fleeing NVA holding rearguard positions. However, several large arms caches were found, including one that contained several dozen 122mm rockets, thousands of mortar rounds, and several dozen smaller rockets.

While the mountains west of An Hoa were being prowled, other units swept the eastern area of the Taylor Common AO. On 10 February, BLT 3/26, Special Landing Force Bravo, was deployed to the Arizona Territory, relieving an ARVN ranger group. From the time those seaborne Marines touched down, they were tracked and pursued by relentless NVA snipers. Any halt in their march resulted in sniper rounds and an occasional rifle grenade shattering the quiet. Not until 26 February were they able to extract some revenge. Company L, 3/26, cornered a platoon of NVA in an abandoned hamlet. Though the enemy force peppered the Marines with fire from two .50-caliber machine guns, high-explosive bombs from supporting Marine F-4B Phantom jets blew the NVA to pieces. The grunts advanced, easily overrunning the remaining defenders. Seventy-five NVA bodies were found scattered throughout the area.

By mid-February, BA 112 had effectively been neutralized. Brigadier General Samuel Jaskilka, who had replaced General Dwyer as commander of TF Yankee on 14 February, ordered all Taylor Common forces except Companies L and M, 3/5, to return to An Hoa by 16 February. Because of increased enemy activity along the DMZ, both battalions of the 3d Marines immediately returned to Dong Ha.

No sooner had the rifle companies returned to the An Hoa area than the enemy attacked it. In the early-morning darkness of 23 February, a barrage of enemy mortar rounds slammed into the base's northeast corner. This was followed by a ground assault that penetrated the base's perimeter defenses. Once inside the base, the sappers used long bamboo poles to fling explosive charges into the ammunition dump. A series of sharp explosions destroyed most of the dump and threw hot rounds for hundreds of meters. While some Marines ignored the danger to battle the fires, others chased the intruders. Not until well after dawn was the last sapper hunted down and killed. To prevent any future attacks on An Hoa, 2/5 was deployed to Liberty Bridge. There its rifle companies took up positions that screened the base.

To the west, enemy pressure against the two companies remaining in BA 112 increased in late February. Almost nightly, Companies L and M were hit by mortar barrages and ground assaults. In the pitch-black darkness just after midnight on 1 March, FSB Tomahawk, the westernmost base, was attacked. Four Marines in a listening post first heard the enemy moving toward them in the thick jungle. As they radioed a warning to the fire support base, a satchel charge flew out of the jungle toward their position. Private First Class Daniel D. Bruce, a mortar man from the Headquarters and Service Company, 3/5, caught the explosive device in mid-air, then shouted a warning to his buddies as he leaped from the bunker. Intent only on protecting his fellow Marines, Bruce held the device to his body as he ran into the jungle. Before he could dispose of the charge, it exploded. Bruce absorbed the full and deadly blast, but his buddies survived to fight off their attackers. Bruce would receive a posthumous Medal of Honor for his valor.

As a result of these frequent attacks, the rest of 3/5 returned to the western region of BA 112 on 28 February. It had been there but a few days when General Jaskilka, reacting to the continued pressure against An Hoa, ordered the battalion to withdraw. Planned as a one-day operation, the withdrawal turned into a three-day fighting disengagement.

Late on 3 March, Company M, while on a final patrol northeast of FSB Tomahawk, was suddenly hit by a heavy blast of small arms and automatic weapons fire from a well-entrenched enemy force. Three Marines died in the opening seconds. The bodies of two of them could not be recovered due to the intensity of enemy fire. The company commander called for artillery fire and air support. The jets managed to drop a few bombs before darkness forced the aircraft to depart. The artillery pounded the enemy positions throughout the night. The next day one body was retrieved, but surprisingly intense enemy fire prevented Company M from recovering the remaining corpse. A third recovery attempt was made on 5 March; however, after losing two more men whose bodies also could not be recovered, Company M pulled back into defensive positions. At the same time, operations were under way to close FSBs Tomahawk and Maxwell. Helicopters extracted the artillery from Tomahawk and, late on 5 March, the last of the infantry. Low clouds, however, delayed the closing of Maxwell.

On 6 March, Company M made another attempt to recover its dead. Despite the hundreds of artillery rounds that had pounded the enemy, once again their fire proved too intense. Rather than risk more casualties, Company M finally withdrew. (Sometime later a force recon patrol recovered the three bodies.) The rugged terrain, bad weather, enemy fire, and the burden of carrying their wounded slowed the company. They didn't reach FSB Maxwell until well after dark, too late to be airlifted to An Hoa. After enduring frequent probes throughout the night, the weary Marines of Company M were finally pulled out on 7 March, still under sporadic sniper and mortar fire.

The next day Operation Taylor Common was closed down. The three-month operation cost the Marines 183 killed and 1,487 wounded. Of these casualties, 27 dead and 386 wounded were the results of booby traps; 26 were killed and 103 were wounded by errant friendly fire. Enemy casualties exceeded 500 dead. Although the Marines captured huge quantities of enemy arms and supplies, forcing the NVA out of Base Area 112, as soon as they departed the AO, the enemy began returning. Such was the war in South Vietnam.

While the 5th Marines conducted Operation Taylor Common, the 7th Marines conducted Operation Linn River south of Hill 55, which sat about twenty kilometers south of Da Nang and just north of Route 4. The operation's purpose was to cordon and sweep a ten-square-kilometer area in support of the Le Loi, or the Accelerated Pacification Program.

The operation began at midday on 27 January when 1/7 headed east along Route 4 from its base adjacent to Hill 65. Once the Marines arrived in the objective area, the Marines of 2/26 would join up with them and participate in the cordon. Although little enemy action was expected, four CH-46D helicopters carrying members of 2/26 were badly damaged by small arms fire on 29 January as they hovered over LZ Owl waiting to land. The rest of the lift had to be postponed while replacement aircraft were rounded up. By late that afternoon all units were in position and the initial cordon was established. The next morning, the two battalions began their sweeps. Enemy contact consisted primarily of the Marines engaging fleeing bands of NVA and VC. Although only fifty-three enemy were killed in the two-week operation, the real success came in the relocation of hundreds of endangered Vietnamese to government resettlement villages and the destruction of numerous enemy bunkers and fortifications.

As February began, evidence of an enemy buildup around Da Nang increased. Marine patrols throughout what was now called the "Da Nang Vital Area" found numerous signs of the enemy's presence. On 8 February, Company L, 3/7, uncovered a cache of 122mm rockets hidden along the banks of the Song Yen, fourteen kilometers south of Da Nang. Two kilometers to the west, another 3d Battalion patrol uncovered thirteen 140mm rockets hidden in a well.

A week later Company D, 1/7, found an enemy platoon in bunkers twenty kilometers southwest of Da Nang. Under the protective umbrella of a well-coordinated artillery barrage, the riflemen launched an assault. As the deep booms of the 155mm shells faded, they were replaced by the sharp cracks of M16s and the deep-throated bursts of M60 machine-gun fire. It was over sooner than anyone expected. The NVA suddenly pulled out, leaving the bodies of sixteen of their comrades crumpled in the foliage. Wise to the way of the enemy, the company commander left a squad-sized ambush in the area. The rest of the company noisily withdrew. Soon after dusk the enemy returned to reoccupy the bunker complex. The squad leader sprang the ambush. Two Claymore mines erupted in sharp explosions, spraying thousands of death-causing steel ball bearings across the ambush site. Then the Marines blazed away with their M16s and M60s. When it was over, fourteen more NVA soldiers had died.

Additional evidence continued to mount that the enemy was up to something. That was proven true on 23 February, the first day of Tet. Early that morning, NVA rockets and mortars fell out of the sky and tore into Da Nang. Lucky hits destroyed an ARVN ammo dump and a 450,000-gallon fuel storage area adjacent to the air base.

While the 122mm rockets rained havoc on Da Nang, enemy infantry units slipped out of the hills and moved into positions to attack allied installations and disrupt the approaches to the city. Just after midnight, Company K, 3/1, detected enemy soldiers approaching the Song Cau Do bridges south of the city. Seizing the initiative, the grunts, along with Company D, 1st Marine MP Battalion, attacked the still-unassembled enemy units. The fight was short but deadly. The combined unit killed forty-seven and captured eleven before the rest broke away. A little later, the CP of the 2d Battalion, 1st Marines, a short distance away, was attacked by nearly one hundred Viet Cong. Proving that all Marines are first and foremost riflemen, the headquarters clerks drove them off, incurring only light casualties while killing seventeen VC.

So pervasive were the enemy attacks that a squad of sappers managed to close on the 1st Marine Division headquarters complex, sited on Hill 327 west of Da Nang. Fortunately, security personnel repulsed these satchel charge–carrying VC before they did any damage. Then, just to the northwest, the headquarters compound of 2/7 came under a similar attack. Again, headquarters Marines rose to the challenge. Even though the enemy actually breached the defensive wire at one point, the plucky clerks rallied and drove back the enemy. When dawn came, the Marines had lost eighteen killed and eighty wounded in the two futile attacks, but they had slain more than seventy-five of the enemy.

The most serious threat to Da Nang, however, came from the west. The 141st NVA Regiment launched a three-pronged attack with their ultimate objective being the 1st Marine Division headquarters. Company M, 3/7, spoiled the attack when one of its night ambush squads trapped an enemy force west of Hill 10, just a few kilometers southwest of Hill 327. The small band of Marines killed ten NVA and captured a number of weapons in the fight. Later, another Company M squad spotted forty more NVA milling about in the same general area. An accurate artillery barrage dispersed this enemy group. Dawn revealed that this had been an 82mm mortar company. Besides a pair of mortars, the NVA left behind a dozen dead and their wounded first sergeant. He later confirmed that a major offensive had been launched.

As dawn broke, Lt. Col. Francis X. Quinn, the commander of 3/7, committed the rest of his Company M in an attempt to halt the advancing NVA. That wasn't enough. The enemy aggressively pushed forward, engaging the Marines in close-quarters combat. Quinn was forced to send in the rest of his battalion to blunt the attack.

The fighting raged into 24 February. Several times Company L attacked portions of the enemy regiment entrenched in thick bamboo groves along the Song Tuy Loan. Despite repeated air strikes and artillery barrages, the Marines couldn't pry the NVA loose. After taking heavy casualties, including its company commander, Company L was forced to withdraw and regroup. On 26 February, Company M and the two effective platoons of Company L returned to the attack. Despite more air strikes employing both napalm and five-hundred-pound bombs, artillery, and a tear gas barrage, the Marines still could not dislodge the NVA. Not until the morning of the twenty-seventh, under the cover of another tear gas blanket, did Company M finally manage to drive a wedge deep into the enemy's lines. Fanning out left and right, the Marines rolled up the enemy's lines. By the time the fight was over, the enemy regimental commander was a prisoner and more than two hundred dead NVA were scattered among the elephant grass.

Although other patrols continued to encounter a few stray bands of NVA throughout early March, the main Tet attacks against Da Nang were effectively blunted on 23 February by Quinn's battalion.

The captured commanding officer of the 141st NVA Regiment proved to be a gold mine of information. He revealed a great deal about the NVA's infiltration routes into the Da Nang area from Laos. Based on this, General Simpson decided to launch an attack into the hills southwest of Da Nang.

Operation Oklahoma Hills

Lying just north of Base Area 112, the scene of the recently concluded Operation Taylor Common, were the new areas of focus, known to the Marines as Charlie Ridge and Happy Valley. Charlie Ridge, and its northern neighbor Worth Ridge, were both high, narrow ranges cut by deep ravines and gorges and covered by multi-canopied tropical jungle. Happy Valley, to the west of Worth Ridge, was carpeted with dense underbrush and elephant grass growing more than seven feet high. Any movement through the area would thus be severely restricted. As Col. James B. Ord, commander of the 5th Marines, noted: "The enemy always has the advantage of operating in the jungle. You only get a point-to-point contact. You cannot maneuver on a broad front . . . your observation is limited and your fields of fire are limited . . . it is difficult to make use of supporting arms. And this being the case, we have no advantage."

General Simpson selected Col. Robert L. Nichols's 7th Marines to conduct Operation Oklahoma Hills. As finally planned, two battalions would attack westward along Worth and Charlie Ridges. A third battalion would secure the southern flank to prevent enemy forces from moving into or out of the area. This preparatory portion of the operation began on 21 March when Lt. Col. John A. Dowd's 1/7 headed west along Highway 4 from FSB Rawhide (Hill 65) to take up these blocking positions. At Hill 52, ten kilometers west of FSB Rawhide, Dowd's men set up FSB Mustang. Soon Battery K, 4th Battalion, 11th Marines had set up shop.

The operation officially commenced on 30 March when 2/7 moved west from Hill 10 to the approaches of Worth Ridge and 3/7 started down Charlie Ridge from its jump-off positions at Hill 40, four kilometers south of Hill 10. This opening move was unique because the Marines moved into the area of operations by foot under the cover of darkness. After starting off at 2000, by early the next morning the advancing columns were well into the jungle. As Capt. Paul K. Van Riper of Company M, 3/7, said, "The NVA had no idea that we had moved that far and no idea of our location." It was very satisfying to be one up on the enemy for a change.

The next morning, members of 3/26 were delivered by CH-46s into the western end of Happy Valley. By the end of the day they had been joined by a battery of 4.2-inch mortars from 1/13. Fire Support Base Robin was officially opened.

On 1 April, the efforts of Operation Oklahoma Hills received an unexpected boost when two enemy soldiers were taken. A recon force working deep within the tangled jungle captured a senior sergeant from the 141st NVA Regiment. Later that day, Company K, 3/7, took as prisoner an officer from the 31st NVA Regiment. Both captives provided information pinpointing the specific locations of their units' respective base camps. Colonel Nichols immediately opted to act on this information, altering his plan in order to exploit the new intelligence. He ordered the infantry battalions to rapidly move to the identified base campsites, bypassing other suspected enemy camps. At the same time, he initiated planning to have the battalions later reverse direction and search the bypassed areas.

From FSB Robin, Lt. Col. Edward W. Snelling's 3/26 moved southeast toward Hill 1166 and the base camp of the 141st as rapidly as the rugged, broken terrain permitted. Unfortunately, the Marines' movement was no secret: small groups of NVA harassed the column as it struggled through the dense vegetation. At the same time, 3/7 pushed forward along Charlie Ridge from the east, hoping to catch the NVA while they still occupied the camp. Despite the inhospitable terrain, by late afternoon of 7 April the lead companies of both battalions had reached their respective objectives on either side of the deep ravine holding the 141st NVA Regiment's base camp.

At first light the next morning, Company L, 3/26, eagerly crept down the steep hill into the ravine. Company K, 3/7, held its position on top of the ravine, prepared to block any enemy escape attempt. As soon as Company L reached the bottom of the gorge, it found the first base camp—it was empty. A little farther in the dense jungle the Marines found a well-equipped dispensary. The point squad had just entered the jungle on the other side when a flurry of AK-47 rounds snapped through the foliage. The Marines hit the ground. Responding instinctively, they sprayed the jungle before them with hundreds of rounds from their M16s. Then silence returned. A quick recon revealed that the enemy attackers had fled, apparently intent only on buying time to make good their comrades' escape.

That afternoon Company I, 3/26, made it to the bottom of the ravine. The two rifle companies spent the next few days thoroughly searching the area and its numerous offshoot canyons. Small bands of stay-behind NVA soldiers harassed the Marines almost constantly but could not keep them from uncovering a number of base camps.

Colonel Nichols described one camp as made up of bunkers "reinforced with logs, eight to fifteen inches of dirt, then another layer of logs. [Some had] a trap door and a subterranean space below that, providing additional individual protection. Each generally accommodated eight to ten soldiers . . . tunnel complexes connected these. Very careful preparations were made to ensure that cookhouses were well camouflaged, and smoke conduits, to abort any evidence of smoke coming through the jungle, had been laid throughout."

In the meantime, Lt. Col. Neil A. Nelson's 2/7 advanced along Worth Ridge to the area that the prisoner pinpointed as holding the base camp of the 31st NVA Regiment, about five kilometers east of the 141st NVA Regiment's base camp. As Company E stealthily approached the area on 11 April, the point platoon took a burst of heavy machine-gun fire. The Marines deployed, slugging it out with the enemy. Again, the foe was a relatively small stay-behind force. It was easily destroyed, and the Marines entered the NVA camp. It quickly became obvious that this was a large camp, larger than the others; more than two hundred structures were hidden in the thick foliage. The riflemen were surprised, but very grateful, that the camp was abandoned.

The next several days passed in relative quiet as both base camps were thoroughly searched. Although a considerable quantity of documents and other items of great intelligence value were uncovered, enemy contact had evaporated by 15 April. As a result, four days later 2/7 was ordered to return to the Da Nang area to fill the void left by 1/26, which had returned to duty as part of the Special Landing Force. The 1st Battalion, 51st ARVN Regiment would take the place of 2/7.

Once the exchange of forces was completed, Operation Oklahoma Hills shifted into its second phase. The participating battalions were given specific zones in which to search for the enemy. The 3d Battalion, 7th Marines essentially reversed direction and retraced its route along Charlie Ridge, looking for any bypassed enemy positions. The 3d Battalion, 26th Marines concentrated its search in the vicinity of the 141st NVA Regiment's base camp. Colonel Nichols wanted to make sure that all enemy facilities making up this camp were uncovered and destroyed. Once that was accomplished, 3/26 was pulled out of the AO on 2 May.

While these searches continued, enemy activity picked up in the AO's southern portion. The 1st Battalion, 7th Marines, still holding its blocking positions, was advised of the movement of a large force of enemy soldiers north out of the Arizona Territory. Lieutenant Colonel Dowd had his three companies set up a series of platoon-sized ambushes on the north side of the Song Vu Gia. Sure enough, on the evening of 21 April, an ambush squad from Company C spotted a group of men moving west to east along the river's south bank. Captain Joseph M. Romero quickly alerted the other company commanders of the intruders.

At 1945 a squad from Capt. James W. Huffman's Company B, about three kilometers downriver, saw a handful of NVA emerging from the thick foliage on the south bank. The enemy squad appeared to be inspecting a long, wide sandbar that hugged the river's southern edge. Wisely ordering his men to hold their fire, Huffman quickly moved several of his outlying platoons closer to this site. He also ordered his 3d Platoon, three hundred meters upriver, to turn its .30-caliber machine gun toward the enemy soldiers. Then he alerted his supporting artillery.

About thirty minutes later the first group of enemy soldiers slipped back into the vegetation. All was quiet for another thirty minutes. In their ambush positions hidden deep in the wild hedgerows bordering the north bank, Huffman's riflemen waited nervously. The jungle's night sounds only added to their anxiety.

Then, without a sound, a force of some two hundred NVA materialized across the river. Clustered in platoon-sized groups of about forty men, the first carried a number of small, round, woven boats.

The enemy scurried across the sandbar and entered the water. Using light-enhancing starlight scopes, Huffman's men watched as four or five of the North Vietnamese entered each little tub. Then, guided by a pair of men, the boats floated across the water. About twenty-five NVA remained on the sandbar.

As soon as the boats reached midriver, Huffman called the artillery battery for an illumination round. Seconds later the shell burst overhead, bathing the jungle in a brilliant white light. Huffman's Marines opened fire with all they had. The sound of dozens of M16s and M60s firing, the machine gun chopping out rounds, and mortar and artillery shells exploding nearly drowned out the screams of the panicked enemy soldiers. They jumped from their boats, taking to the water in mostly vain attempts to escape the killing field.

Unfortunately, the illumination rounds were not continuous. As darkness again blanketed the river, many of the enemy escaped. Still, the bodies of fifty-seven enemy soldiers, clad in fresh, new uniforms, were found in the river or along its banks the next morning. Two of Huffman's men received slight wounds.

Huffman requested LVTs that morning so he could cross the river. Following an air strike by F-4s at 0900, Company B boarded the amphibious vehicles and chugged across the water. Sweeping to a depth of several hundred meters on the south bank, the Marines found fourteen more enemy bodies. Numerous blood trails provided evidence that a large number of casualties had been carried away.

Anxious to follow up this successful action, Colonel Nichols planned a quick thrust into the northern portion of the Arizona Territory to find the enemy. Once permission to operate in their AO was received from the 5th Marines, 1/7 prepared for the operation. On the night of 29 April, Companies B and D, accompanied by Lieutenant Colonel Dowd and his battalion command group, crossed the Song Vu Gia.

At first light the force began moving southeast. Almost immediately Captain Huffman's company, on the right flank, was hit by a fusillade of small arms fire. While they tried to extract themselves from the ambush, the rest of the column wheeled to the northeast to face two more NVA companies. The fighting was fierce as the well-emplaced enemy force battered Dowd's men with small arms and mortar fire. The thick, nearly impenetrable jungle greatly reduced the Marines' ability to effectively fight back or use air and artillery support. Finally, once Company B disengaged, the force reversed direction and attacked back toward the river. There they pivoted left to continue their drive along the south bank of the river. The two infantry companies fought side by side throughout that day and into the next, calling air strikes and artillery onto each succeeding tree line.

On the morning of 1 May, the rifle companies of Lt. Col. Thomas E. Bulger's 3/1 moved overland from the Liberty Bridge area and took up blocking positions west of Dowd's force. Not long after Dowd's two companies renewed their attack, they bumped smack into an unmovable NVA force. Struggling forward against the near constant blaze of enemy fire, the Marines had gained only two hundred meters by noon. As a result, 3/1 began an attack to the east, catching the NVA by surprise. By the end of the day, less than a kilometer of tangled jungle separated the two battalions.

Responding to the ever changing tactical situation, the two battalion commanders agreed that Dowd's force would hold its position the next day while 3/1 attacked toward them. Bulger's Marines pushed off at 0600 on 2 May. To their disappointment the NVA had sneaked away during the night. The two battalions linked up early that afternoon. Both then began a drive to the northeast. They reached the south bank of the Song Vu Gia without further significant contact. By nightfall both units had crossed to the north side of the river.

The foray into the Arizona Territory had cost nine Marines their lives and sixty more had been wounded. The NVA casualties were set at sixty killed. This proved to be the last significant enemy contact of Operation Oklahoma Hills. By 12 May, only one Marine battalion, 3/7, remained in the operational area. One ARVN unit, 1/51, worked with them.

For some time NVA POWs had mentioned in their interrogations that the Ken Valley was a major arms and ammunition storage depot. A number of prisoners reported traveling to this valley, twenty-five kilometers west of the 141st NVA Regiment's base camp area, to pick up rockets that were eventually launched on Da Nang. After a period of relative calm from 12 to 20 May in the Oklahoma Hills AO, Colonel Nichols decided to shift his forces westward to exploit this information. On the morning of 21 May, a fleet of the new CH-53 Sea Stallion helicopters deposited Marines from Company L in the Ken Valley. Subsequent airlifts brought in Company M and the 51st ARVN's recon company. The three units then fanned out in different directions. Over the next five days, the allied companies conducted a thorough search of the valley. They found no evidence of a major enemy presence. On only two occasions were enemy soldiers spotted. On 25 May, all units were extracted.

Over the next few days, the Marines of 3/7 spent their time closing down the principal fire support bases used in the operation. On 29 May Operation Oklahoma Hills ended. In all, 44 Marines were killed and 439 were wounded seriously enough to require evacuation. More significant, however, was the large number of nonbattle casualties, 456 in all. The vast majority of these were broken bones, sprains, and serious lacerations caused by falls in the rugged, slippery jungle terrain.

For several years the VC and NVA had used the areas south of Da Nang and east of the Liberty Bridge as staging areas for attacks into the coastal lowlands between Da Nang and Hoi An. Known to the Marines as Dodge City and Go Noi Island, these two staging areas had been the focus of a number of earlier operations, the most recent being Operation Meade River in December 1968. Although all these operations were considered successful, the enemy maintained the same pattern he had used in earlier encounters—withdraw his forces when pressed, then reenter the area after the friendly forces moved on. Ridding these two areas of enemy troops once and for all became a major goal of the 1st Marines during the last half of 1969.

Intelligence agencies estimated that Dodge City and Go Noi Island harbored between seven and nine enemy battalions. Total enemy strength was estimated at between twenty-five hundred and three thousand, the majority of whom were North Vietnamese Army regulars. These enemy soldiers not only regularly sniped at and harassed friendly forces but were quite capable of attacking allied installations in strength. The 1st Marine Division headquarters decided that it was time to clear the region of enemy forces, once and for all.

Operation Pipestone Canyon

In mid-May, General Simpson was briefed by Col. Charles S. Robertson, commander of the 1st Marines, on a campaign designed to deny the enemy continued safe haven in the two areas. In his briefing Colonel Robertson stressed that Operation Pipestone Canyon was a natural sequel to Operations Taylor Common and Oklahoma Hills.

As planned, the operation would begin with two battalions, BLT 1/26 from SLF Alpha, and 3/5, attacking eastward into the operational area. Designed as a feint, these two battalions would then establish blocking positions. Once this had been accomplished, five battalions (1st and 2d Battalions, 1st Marines; 37th ARVN Ranger Battalion; and the 1st and 4th Battalions, 51st ARVN Regiment) would attack southward into and through Dodge City, then on into neighboring Go Noi Island. This movement would be executed in coordination with two Korean Marine Corps battalions holding positions on the southern edge of the AO. The effort would be a true allied operation.

The contiguous areas of Dodge City and Go Noi Island lay ten to twenty kilometers south of Da Nang and six to twenty kilometers west of Hoi An. The combined area was bordered on the west by the south fork of the Song Vu Gia; on the north by the Song Ai Nghi, Song Lo Tho, and Song Thanh Quit; on the east by Route 1; and on the south by the Song Thu Bon, Song Ba Ren, and Song Chiem Son. A north-south railroad berm bisected the area. Most of the land was flat, but it was covered with rice paddies, thick brush, tangled hedgerows, and vast expanses of tall elephant grass. Nearly two dozen villages and hamlets dotted the region.

The morning of 26 May opened with a blistering bombardment of the AO's western region. Heavy 8-inch shells from the offshore USS *Newport News* and artillery fire from the cannons of 1/11 ripped into the terrain with an explosive fury. Following this bombardment, the members of Lt. Col. George C. Kliefoth's 1/26 and Lt. Col. Harry E. Atkinson's 3/5 stepped off on their eastward attack. The first few days of the movement resulted in only minor contact. However, as the Marines moved closer to Dodge City and Go Noi Island, enemy resistance picked up. By midafternoon on 30 May, the two battalions had set up their blocking positions just west of the railroad berm.

They had killed sixteen NVA but lost a total of ten dead and more than a hundred wounded. All of the friendly casualties had been caused by mines or booby traps.

The next day the five allied battalions stepped off from their positions on the Song Lo Tho. The southward attack was preceded by an intense artillery and naval gunfire bombardment. As concussion waves rolled over the waiting riflemen, they hoped that the bursting shells would not only get the enemy soldiers but would detonate any mines and booby traps waiting for them. Soon after crossing the river, the lead rifle platoons started uncovering well-built bunker complexes generously salted with booby traps. These brutal devices would become even more prevalent the deeper the infantrymen drove into enemy territory. Actual enemy contact during the first few days, however, was light. All the evidence indicated that the enemy troops were fleeing to the south and west, toward the blocking force. Then, on 2 June, enemy resistance suddenly stiffened. Company G, 3/5, was hit by a shower of enemy mortars as it approached a small bunker complex. The company commander quickly ordered up a pair of the accompanying M48 tanks. After the armored giants had pumped more than a dozen deadly 90mm shells into the heart of the enemy position, the riflemen attacked. The tanks had done their job well. Only a handful of enemy soldiers resisted the Marines. In minutes it was over. Seven NVA lay dead and one wounded enemy soldier was captured.

Three days later the attackers reached the Song Ky Lam, which divided Dodge City from Go Noi Island. With the second phase of Pipestone Canyon over, the attacking forces paused to resupply and reposition themselves for the third phase. During this interim period Marine jets pounded Go Noi Island with an unrelenting fury. More than 750,000 pounds of high-explosive bombs chewed up the ground in front of the attackers.

The new phase began on 10 June. While General Simpson and the new 1st Marines commander, Col. Charles E. Walker, watched from a command post atop Hill 119 just south of Go Noi Island, twenty-two helicopters carried in Marines from 2/1 and a force of Korean Marines. The CH-46s touched down unmolested in two LZs on the southern edge of Go Noi Island. Once formed, the combined

force began sweeping north. That same afternoon the rifle companies of 1/1 began moving eastward from the Liberty Bridge area.

Once again, enemy contact proved light. The Viet Cong and NVA
were scattering, breaking into small groups and sneaking past the
advancing attackers to head south into the Que Son Mountains.
Occasional brief firefights did break out, but these were mostly the
futile efforts of small stay-behind forces. A number of prisoners were
taken, but they were primarily wounded or nearly starved enemy
soldiers.

By 13 June, the major sweeps had been completed. While the allied battalions established company-sized AOs, the Provisional Land
Clearing Company moved into eastern Go Noi Island. Equipped with
a wide variety of bulldozers and tractors, the provisional company
began plowing up eastern Go Noi. Able to clear 250 acres at a time,
the company would eventually level more than eight thousand acres
on the island, denying the enemy a major sanctuary.

While the bulldozers turned the soil on eastern Go Noi Island, the
1st Battalion, 1st Marines turned its attention to the western portion
of the island. At dawn on 19 June, Company C headed west from the
railroad berm. Within a short time the deep *karumph* of an exploding booby trap shattered the morning. That one was soon followed
by a second, then a third, then a fourth. It seemed that whichever
way the Marines moved, the enemy had sown an explosive device.
To reduce the frustration of dealing with these hidden killers, the
battalion peppered its forward areas with artillery and an aerial bombardment. Infantry units took to riding atop tanks. But there was no
way to completely avoid the antipersonnel devices. Only a constant
state of awareness could combat the deadly mines.

After sweeping to An Quyen, 1/1 was replaced by 2/1 on 21 June.
Determined to clear western Go Noi of the enemy, the fresh Marines
conducted daily search and clear operations. As had the Marines
before them, the men of 2/1 found few enemy troops but many
booby traps.

Company G had it particularly tough. Fifty-nine of the seventy
dead and wounded that it suffered during this period resulted from
booby traps and mines. As Capt. Frank H. Adams pointed out, the
threat of death or injury from these devices severely demoralized the

troops. "It gets to the point," he said, "where each individual says, 'They put them out there, we have got to sweep . . . ultimately I'm going to hit one.' When you get to that point, as a leader you're lost."

After a particularly bad day with booby traps, Adams had to pull his company off the line to give them a pep talk. It went surprisingly well. He finished up with a prayer and returned to the sweeps. The upturn in morale made him tremendously proud to be a Marine.

By late June, General Simpson had decided that eastern Go Noi would be permanently occupied. The 3d ARVN Battalion, 51st Regiment, and the 1st Battalion, Korean Marine Corps would occupy two new combat bases that covered the eastern portion of Go Noi. At least one U.S. Marine rifle company would patrol the island's western half.

For the rest of June and into early July, enemy activity waned in the Pipestone Canyon AO. Then, intelligence reports indicated that the enemy had returned to eastern Dodge City. On 14 July, elements of 2/1 air-assaulted into four landing zones in that area. As the troop-laden CH-46s came into the LZs, all took heavy enemy fire. Seven were hit and one was forced to make an emergency landing; fortunately, it was near a Korean Marine position. At two of the LZs the enemy fire was so strong that the helicopters were forced to divert to alternate landing zones. This caused a one-hour delay in establishing a cordon around the abandoned village of Tay Bang An, which was believed to harbor the enemy.

Once the Marines were in position, aerial observers reported seeing nearly fifty enemy troops moving around the village. By mid-morning all four companies of the battalion had engaged the enemy. Company F had the hardest time, losing two dead and seven wounded to machine-gun fire and RPGs as they neared the village's western edge. The fight to defeat the enemy continued into the next day. Fleeing enemy soldiers reportedly tried to break out through the part of the cordon held by Company G, but they were easily repulsed. The next day sweeps of the village and its environs failed to uncover any sign of the foe. As a result, late on 17 July, the battalion was pulled out.

The Marines continued their sweeps and patrols of various zones of the Pipestone Canyon AO throughout the rest of the summer.

During this time actual contact with the enemy was limited. Most of the friendly casualties still resulted from booby traps. Enemy sightings did pick up in late September. To eliminate them, several companies from 1/1 were rushed into the Dodge City area north of Route 4 on 25 September. Again, though the grunts uncovered numerous bunkers, only a few enemy soldiers were spotted. After four generally fruitless days of patrolling the area, the battalion pulled out.

This frustrating pattern continued until Operation Pipestone Canyon officially ended on 7 November. Though no major combat action had occurred, the campaign did drive the VC and NVA out of Dodge City and Go Noi Island. The land clearing operations transformed Go Noi Island from a heavily vegetated tract into a barren wasteland, free of tree lines and other cover long used by the enemy to conceal his movements across the island. The participating forces claimed 852 enemy dead and 58 captured. Marine casualties numbered 71 killed and 600 wounded, the vast majority of which were caused by booby traps.

While the 1st Marines were involved with Operation Pipestone Canyon, the 5th Marines defended the large, broad plain north of the An Hoa Combat Base known to the Marines as the Arizona Territory. The activities of the regiments' maneuver battalions varied according to their mission. The 1st Battalion, 5th Marines held no fixed positions in the Arizona Territory but rather continually moved about in company-sized formation, patrolling, setting up ambushes, and looking for the enemy. The 2d Battalion manned positions guarding the vital Liberty Bridge and conducted constant patrols of the surrounding area. The 3d Battalion normally operated in the regiment's eastern area, where it aggressively patrolled the northern tier of the Que Son Mountains.

Throughout May and into early June, enemy contact in the Arizona Territory was light. Then, at dawn on 7 June, NVA sappers attacked the An Hoa Combat Base. Shortly after midnight a dozen 82mm mortar rounds fell out of the sky, erupting with sharp explosions across the base. As the base's defenders raced to their fighting positions, the NVA sappers sprayed the base with automatic weapons fire, RPGs, and B40 rockets. The sappers focused their assault on two sectors, breaking through the defenses in both places. The victory didn't last long. Responding rapidly, An Hoa's defenders rushed forward, attacking the sappers before they could exploit their breakthrough. It was nearly dawn before the pop-pop of M16s ended, but the sappers were thrown back. In all, nineteen NVA died and two were captured. No Marines were killed and only three were lightly injured.

That same night, a force from the 90th NVA Regiment attacked the night defensive position held by Company A and Lt. Col. William J. Riley, Jr.'s battalion command group about six kilometers west of An Hoa. Attacking the NDP from three directions, the enemy soldiers drew close enough to toss hand grenades into the Marines' bunkers. Hard pressed, the defenders had to call on aerial gunships to stop the attackers. A search of the ground around the NDP at first light turned up eleven dead and three wounded NVA. Though the enemy had been unsuccessful in their drive to overrun the Marines, they continued to harass them throughout the day with mortar fire and sniper rounds.

Despite the beating they'd taken, the NVA weren't done. In another attempt to throw the Marines out of the Arizona Territory, they hit Company A and Riley's command group again the next morning. In the predawn darkness, enemy sappers crept close to the unit's NDP and poured a heavy volume of small arms fire at the Marines. Before the enemy could close on the perimeter, preregistered artillery was called up. Under a barrage of high-explosive rounds, the attackers fled.

While relocating that same afternoon, Company A came under heavy enemy fire from .30- and .50-caliber machine guns. Following an air strike on the enemy positions, Capt. Phillip H. Torrey ordered his men into the attack. Not only did the NVA respond with intense machine-gun fire, but they now added mortars to the din. Despite this, Torrey's lead platoon battled forward. Defying a withering fire, it gained a toehold on the southern edge of the enemy's perimeter. The Marines battered the well-emplaced NVA with automatic weapons fire, rockets, and small arms fire for more than an hour and a half before being called back because of darkness. Torrey reorganized his company and settled down for the night, but Marine air and artillery kept up their fire until dawn.

After a heavy barrage the next morning, Company A, reinforced by a platoon from Company C, resumed the attack. Fighting raged for several hours, but the determined Marine riflemen persevered. When the fight ended, more than eighty dead NVA were scattered across their position. Documents found in several bunkers revealed that the site was a battalion command post defended by two rifle companies.

While Company A inventoried the spoils of its victory, Company B, a short distance away, was hit by heavy enemy fire. Reacting quickly, the Marines attacked. Charging boldly across three hundred meters of open rice paddies, the grunts overran the enemy position, killing seventy-five NVA and capturing a large number of weapons.

Undeterred by the beatings they had taken, the NVA continued to hit Riley's battalion. Over the next four days they rarely passed up an opportunity to strike, using mortars, RPGs, and small arms fire. Gutsy as they were, however, the enemy never seriously threatened Riley's units. Fire superiority in the form of aerial bombardment and massed artillery barrages prevented the NVA from overrunning any of Riley's rifle companies. Indeed, the enemy lost nearly one hundred more dead, whereas the Marines' casualties were a handful of wounded.

As a result of these losses, enemy activity subsided beginning on 12 June; however, just after midnight on 17 June, the NVA struck again. Two full companies hit the battalion's night position. In a fight that lasted more than five hours, the Marines, again well supported by air and artillery, held off the attackers, who finally retreated at dawn. Riley's men found more than thirty enemy bodies around their position in the morning.

After having lost more than three hundred men in ten days, the enemy withdrew from the Arizona Territory. The tired men of 1/5 had their first uneventful night in nearly two weeks.

On 18 July, Col. William J. Zaro realigned the battalions of his 5th Marines in preparation for a new operation. Two companies of the 1st Battalion relieved the 2d Battalion at Phu Lac (6) east of the Arizona Territory while the other two companies moved to the An Hoa

Combat Base. There they relieved the 3d Battalion. Named "Durham Peak," the new campaign would introduce Marines into Antenna Valley and the adjacent Que Son Mountains, about ten kilometers south of An Hoa. Rising from the lowlands of Quang Nam Province like a row of jagged stakes, the Que Sons tower more than nine hundred meters. Carpeted with a single canopy of jungle foliage and densely packed undergrowth, the range is cut by uncountable deep ravines. Intelligence reports indicated that enemy forces fleeing Dodge City and Go Noi Island were setting up in the rugged mountains. Besides his own 2d and 3d Battalions, Colonel Zaro would also have operational control of 2/1 for Durham Peak. South of the AO, units of the Americal Division took up blocking positions.

Following a prepping of the area by 105mm howitzers and the 5-inch guns of the USS *Boston,* Marines of 3/5 alighted from their CH-46 helicopters at LZs in the southern portion of Antenna Valley. The next day, 2/1 helilifted into three LZs at the base of the Que Son Mountains. The 2d Battalion, 5th Marines remained at An Hoa, acting as reserves for the operation.

As the rifle companies of 2/1 pushed south into the formidable mountain chain, they immediately began finding evidence of a recent enemy presence. Bunkers, hooches, supply caches, and fresh graves were found nearly everywhere the Marines looked. Enemy resistance was light, at least initially. As the battalion pushed farther into the mountains, however, enemy contact increased.

A platoon from Company H took heavy sniper fire on 25 July as it moved up a ridge finger leading to the peak of Hill 845. Enemy snipers on a rock ledge about one hundred meters above them plunked away at the Marines, dropping several with well-placed rounds. The platoon pulled back as an orbiting OV-10 Bronco loosed a barrage of rockets at the ledge. The snipers scattered. The next day another platoon from Company H returned to the area. An estimated company-sized unit of NVA ambushed them as they neared the battle site. The enemy was dug in along one side of the route of march. Because the dense foliage restricted visibility, the enemy aimed right along the ground, hitting the Marines in the lower legs. As they lay writhing on the jungle floor, an NVA sharpshooter shot them in the head or back. Six Marines were killed and sixteen were wounded before the platoon could pull out of range.

In the confusion of the fight the platoon's exact position could not be determined. Artillery was fired at the supposed enemy location but proved to be nearly a kilometer off. Rescue efforts faltered. While a medevac helicopter waited, it was shot down. A platoon of Marines had to be diverted from the original rescue attempt in order to secure the crash site. Finally, though, the lost platoon was located. The relieving force held off the enemy while the casualties were pulled to safety through the trees. Then the two platoons moved out to join the rest of the company near the summit of Hill 845.

Though the companies continued to aggressively patrol the rugged mountains, this contact proved to be the only significant one of Operation Durham Peak. In order to stir the pot further, Colonel Zaro brought 2/5 into the operation on 31 July, but its patrols turned up only a few sick NVA stragglers. By 7 August, Colonel Zaro had decided to end the operation. Over the next week, the maneuver elements were pulled out of the field. Operation Durham Peak ended on 13 August.

One of the major tasks facing the 7th Marines in the last half of 1969 was the manning of the Da Nang Anti-Infiltration System (DAIS). Similar to the McNamara Line south of the DMZ, the DAIS was started in June 1968. As directed by III MAF, this barrier was to be built at the outer edge of the Rocket Belt, a semicircle surrounding Da Nang whose twelve-thousand-meter radius was the maximum range of the enemy's most powerful rockets. Just like the McNamara Line, the Da Nang barrier was to be a five-hundred-meter wide cleared belt of land containing two parallel barbed wire fences, concertina wire, observation towers, and minefields. And, just like the ill-advised McNamara Line, the Da Nang barrier would never be completed.

But that didn't mean it would be ignored. Both the 2d and 3d Battalions, 7th Marines were assigned to defense and construction duties on the barrier in June 1969. And there was much work to be done. The DAIS had fallen prey to divided responsibility, the lack of manpower, unavailable material, and poor defensive coordination plans. As a result, older sections of the barrier were in a state of disrepair. In some places the brush had completely overgrown the cleared areas. Very few of the electronic sensors had been installed.

The clever local farmers capitalized on this by cutting numerous shortcuts to their rice paddies through the barrier. Faced with these violations of the barrier, both battalions focused the majority of their attention on revitalizing it.

While its sister battalions were so occupied, the regiment's 1st Battalion concentrated on maintaining a presence along Route 4. Constant squad- and platoon-sized patrols paid frequent dividends as the Marines caught roving bands of VC and NVA moving at night. This intense but low-key patrol and sweep activity continued throughout July and into August.

The relative quiet of recent weeks was shattered on the night of 11–12 August. Not only the 7th Marines, but every major unit in the 1st Marine Division AO was hit by enemy rockets or mortars. Most of these bombardments were followed by a ground assault. The heaviest fighting occurred in the Arizona Territory, where Lieutenant Colonel Dowd's 1/7 found itself in a three-day brawl reminiscent of 1/5's June fight.

At 0415 on 12 August, a listening post from Company D and an ambush squad from Company B both opened fire on a force of two dozen enemy soldiers moving between their adjoining positions. When the enemy responded with a heavy volume of small arms fire, the two patrols pulled back to their respective company's positions. An eerie quiet then descended upon the four-company NDP. Alert to the threat of the enemy's presence, Dowd's men maintained a constant vigil. Then, measured bursts of heavy small arms fire sprayed the company's positions. The generous use of preplanned artillery kept the NVA at bay, preventing them from massing for a ground attack against any one company. A dawn sweep of the nearby area uncovered more than fifty dead NVA and more than two dozen weapons.

Unwilling to concede the area to the enemy, Dowd sent his companies in pursuit. Company C found them first. The NVA were emplaced in bunkers in a nearby village complex. The fight raged for several hours, with neither side able to gain the upper hand. Finally, at 1330 Dowd ordered Company D to move up and join the attack. The two companies engaged a determined foe in a slugfest that raged for several more hours. By late afternoon, the resolute Marines had broken through the enemy's main trench line and routed the remaining defenders. As artillery chased the fleeing NVA, Dowd's battle-weary companies dug in for the night. The next day they would count 145 dead NVA in the battle area.

Reinforced by Company L, 3/7, and Company I, 3/5, Dowd continued his pursuit of the NVA on 13 August. Around noon the four attacking companies again became embroiled with the enemy. The resulting seven-hour fight was a near duplicate of the previous day's action. The two sides battled from mere meters away. When they could, artillery and air support lent their massive firepower to the battle. By the time the fight ended, seventy-five NVA were dead. Five Marines were killed and another thirty-three were wounded. Lieutenant Colonel Dowd was one of the dead. His posthumous Navy Cross citation noted how he had been struck down while advancing to the site of the heaviest fighting.

Undeterred by the severe losses they'd taken, the NVA tried one last time to beat the Marines. Just after midnight on 14 August, the NVA launched an attack on the command post of Lt. Col. Frank A. Clark, the new battalion commander. Using a full array of defensive weapons, Clark's headquarters Marines easily beat back the attack. A dozen dead NVA were found around the perimeter the next day. It had been a tough three days for the enemy. The 1st Battalion, 7th Marines killed more than 225 members of the 90th NVA Regiment, forcing it to withdraw from the battlefield.

Within hours of this engagement, Col. Gildo S. Codispoti received orders from III MAF and division headquarters to take his 7th Marines 55 kilometers south to the Que Son Valley. This southward expansion of the 1st Marine Division's TAOR would be a permanent one. The regiment began the move on 15 August and finished the relocation by the twenty-third.

The U.S. Marines had been battling the NVA and VC in the strategic Que Son Valley since 1965. In 1967, as the III MAF moved its forces north to meet enemy pressure along the DMZ, the region came under the operational control of the U.S. Army's Americal Division. On 20 August 1969, the army handed back to the Marines the responsibility for that portion of the Que Son Valley lying to the north of the Song Ly Ly. The two major bases that the 7th Marines inherited were LZ Baldy, at the intersection of Route 1 and Highway 535, where Codispoti set up his headquarters, and FSB Ross, at the village of Que Son, sixteen kilometers to the west. Within days of their arrival, the members of the 7th Regiment would be involved in some of the heaviest fighting of the year.

On 21 August, Colonel Codispoti was asked to lend assistance to the American's 4/31. This battalion had been embroiled with the 1st VC Regiment and the 3d NVA Regiment, a component of the Marines' old nemesis, the 2d NVA Division, for several days. In heavy fighting in the shrub-covered hills northeast of Hiep Duc, the soldiers had killed more than three hundred enemy but still were unable to advance. That afternoon Companies F and G, and a forward battalion command group of 2/7, left FSB Ross and headed west along Highway 535, actually a narrow dirt road running west from Route 1 to Que Son. Early on the morning of 22 August, the two companies completed a sweep of Hill 441, which sat north of Phu Binh (3) at the northern edge of the Marines' route. Moving as fast as the enervating one-hundred-plus-degree heat allowed, by the morning of 23 August, the two rifle companies had set up blocking positions stretching more than fifteen hundred meters across the valley floor. West of them, the U.S. soldiers were moving east, sweeping the enemy before them.

So far, the Marines' only casualties had come from the oppressive heat. At midday, patrols from both companies set out to reconnoiter the terrain to their front. On the left, or south flank, Company F found nothing. On the right, however, the squad-sized patrol from Company G came under deadly sniper fire as it moved across a small hill mass running off Hill 441. In short order, three Marines were killed. Company G sent a platoon to attempt to recover the bodies, but it was unable to do so. So accurate was the sniper fire that anyone who tried to reach the bodies was immediately a target. Even when Company H arrived as reinforcement late in the day, the enemy fire was too intense to effect a recovery. Not until the next morning could the three bodies be recovered.

On the morning of 25 August, the three companies of Lt. Col. Marvin H. Lugger's 2/7 moved out to the west to effect a linkup with the 31st Infantry. Almost immediately they came under heavy fire from what proved to be two NVA regiments. On the right, Companies G and H ran into a brutal wall of deadly fire, took heavy casualties, and had to pull back. They spent the rest of the afternoon recovering and evacuating their casualties. On the left, Company F suffered a vicious pounding from enemy mortar, RPG, and automatic weapons fire. Lugger's command group suffered, too, as enemy soldiers swarmed out of the tall elephant grass. They closed to fifty meters before hastily ordered air strikes burned the foe with napalm.

Company F was locked into a close-quarters battle on the left flank. Despite five-hundred-pound bombs dropped by screaming, low-altitude jets, the beleaguered company couldn't pull back without abandoning its casualties. Lugger had no choice but to call in his Company E to help.

Enemy tracers slashed colorful swatches across the darkening skies as CH-46s ferried the fresh rifle company into Company F's position. While AH-1G Cobra gunships raked the enemy positions with massive volumes of firepower, Company E helped gather up the casualties, organize a column, and head to Lugger's CP.

Though night had fallen, daring medevac helicopter pilots ignored the continued enemy fire to evacuate the casualties. Then, as the battered and exhausted survivors of the two companies collapsed around the CP, the enemy dropped a barrage of heavy mortar rounds right on them.

Lugger noted, "It was a very grim lesson we learned. After an intensive fight, there is a tendency for people to let down because they feel they have given their all."

The barrage killed four and wounded twenty-six. Once those casualties were handled, the wiser Marines hurriedly dug in.

Despite this pounding, Lugger received new orders a short time later. His battalion would advance two kilometers west to complete the linkup with 4/31. As soon as it was light enough on the morning of 26 August, Lugger started his men forward. The advance didn't last long.

While Companies G and H easily secured the high ground on the right flank, Companies E and F ran into a firestorm of enemy resistance. A blistering hail of small arms and mortar fire forced both companies to the ground. The Marines barely advanced six hundred meters. Ordered to continue the advance regardless of the cost, Lieutenant Colonel Lugger brought Company G over from the right flank to help. The NVA spotted the movement and turned their mortars on the advancing companies. Before it had covered half the distance to Companies E and F, Company G had been shattered by the exploding rounds.

With all forward movement of 2/7 blocked, Colonel Codispoti ordered Lugger to hold his positions. While 2/7 consolidated its positions and handled its casualties, Lt. Col. Ray G. Kummerow's 3/7 came into LZ West, on the high ground south of 2/7, on the afternoon of 26 August. That same evening Lt. Col. Joseph E. Hopkins replaced Lieutenant Colonel Lugger as commander of 2/7.

Kummerow's battalion started for Hopkins's position before darkness cloaked the valley. As they neared 2/7's reported position, Kummerow's Marines were surprised to find its rifle companies already pulling out and headed back to FSB Ross. Quickly adapting to the unexpected tactical change, Kummerow's battalion dug in for the night at 2/7's farthest point of advance. At dawn the next day, the new battalion entered the North Vietnamese Army's meat grinder.

Company L, on the right flank, was cut up by heavy automatic weapons fire from well-dug-in NVA. Suffering numerous casualties, the company was unable to move. Kummerow ordered Company K to push through the pinned-down company and continue the attack. In a series of violent assaults, Company K's Marines rolled over the entrenched NVA, killing thirteen and capturing several enemy machine guns. The intensity and violence of the attack is attested to by the valor of individual Marines who overcame tremendous odds to achieve their goals. One of the enemy machine guns was captured by LCpl. Jose Jimenez. He aggressively attacked the enemy position, killing a number of NVA. Despite the fact that several other enemy machine guns now concentrated their fire on him, Jimenez continued his single-handed attack. His bold actions caused the destruction of one more enemy emplacement before he was cut down in a hail of small arms fire.

Not far from Jimenez, Pfc. Dennis D. Davis charged another enclosed NVA bunker. He raced across ten meters of open ground and jumped atop the bunker. Just as he shoved a grenade into an aperture in the bunker, he was gravely wounded by fragments from an enemy grenade. Despite this, Davis then entered the position and used the enemy's weapons to fire on a nearby NVA position. Later, he pulled a wounded Marine to safety and used that casualty's weapon to charge yet a third position. He was cut down before he reached it.

Second Lieutenant Richard L. Jaehne ordered his platoon to join the attack. Almost immediately one of his platoons was ripped by bursts of deadly fire from an enemy machine gun. As his men hunkered down alongside a paddy dike, Jaehne crawled forward while slugs from the automatic weapon whizzed by within inches of his head. From behind a dike he tossed several grenades at the machine-gun nest. Then he pushed up from the dike and dashed forward. Blazing away with his .45-caliber pistol, the young officer killed those North Vietnamese who had survived his grenades. Minutes later he was severely wounded by a burst of small arms fire, but he refused to give up his command.

When Cpl. Clarence H. St. Clair saw Lieutenant Jaehne fall, he immediately ordered the members of his squad forward. They laid down a base of fire that allowed corpsmen to reach the officer and patch him up. When St. Clair noticed an enemy position spraying rounds across the battlefield, he low-crawled toward it. His well-placed grenades destroyed the weapon but not before a burst of enemy fire ripped into his body. Undaunted, St. Clair started inching his way toward a second enemy position but immediately became the target for other NVA weapons. He died just meters from his objective.

Jimenez received a posthumous Medal of Honor, and Davis and St. Clair posthumous Navy Crosses; Lieutenant Jaehne lived to receive his Navy Cross. The gallant actions of these men and others allowed Kummerow's battalion to effect a linkup with the 31st Infantry before dusk on 27 August. Over the next several days, Colonel Codispoti deployed his forces north of Hiep Duc into the rugged Que Son Mountains in pursuit of the NVA. Although the troops found numerous signs of an enemy presence, few NVA soldiers were spotted. Later, intelligence sources revealed that the enemy units had fled west rather than north and thus evaded the pursuing Marines.

The 7th Marines spent the rest of 1969 patrolling various areas of the Que Son Valley. Though they found and fought the enemy on numerous occasions, the resulting battles never reached the intensity or frequency of those experienced in August. The continued presence of the Marines greatly limited the enemy's control of the rich valley, but, as in the past, it would prove to be but a temporary reprieve.

On 15 December 1969, the division received a new commander: Maj. Gen. Edwin B. Wheeler replaced General Simpson. A Marine since 1941, Wheeler had first experienced combat as a member of the famed Marine Raiders in World War II. He later saw service during the Korean War as an infantry battalion commander. During 1965 he commanded the 3d Marines in the Da Nang area. In June 1969, he had returned to South Vietnam to serve as the deputy commander of the XXIV Corps.

3d Marine Division

As 1969 began, the combat elements of Maj. Gen. Raymond G. Davis's division were spread all across Quang Tri Province. In the province's far western reaches, the 9th Marines patrolled the area north of Khe Sanh in the ongoing Operation Scotland II. The 4th Marines had responsibility for the central region of Quang Tri Province, patrolling the rugged mountains north of the Vandegrift Combat Base in the Kentucky AO. One battalion of the 3d Marines operated farther east, just below the DMZ; the regiment's two other battalions were opconned to the 5th Marines in Quang Nam Province for Operation Taylor Common.

Although all elements of the division conducted offensive operations in January, enemy contact was light and scattered. At mid-month, General Davis received intelligence information regarding increased enemy activity in a remote area of Quang Tri Province. The Song Da Krong Valley sat in the far southwest corner of the province, about thirty kilometers south of Vandegrift and just north of the A Shau Valley. A major enemy infiltration route entered South Vietnam through the Song Da Krong Valley via Route 548 (Route 922 in Laos). Marine and air force reconnaissance and attack aircraft sighted as many as one thousand enemy trucks a day using the high-

way. The volume of antiaircraft fire directed at the snooping reconnaissance planes confirmed the enemy's presence. The intelligence
reports concluded that the NVA were stockpiling materiel as they
moved eastward through the Da Krong and A Shau Valleys toward
Hue and Quang Tri City.

The 3d Marine Division operations staff developed a three-phase
campaign to counter this threat. In phase one, the 9th Marines and
its supporting artillery battalion would leapfrog into the AO via a series of mutually protective fire support bases. In phase two, the regiment's infantry elements would conduct extensive patrolling
around the fire support bases. The final phase would be a conventional three-battalion attack into the objective area.

On 18 January, 3/9 began phase one by opening FSB Henderson,
about ten kilometers southeast of Vandegrift. In rapid succession
over the next week, the other battalions established a series of fire
support bases running farther south: Tun Tavern, Shiloh, Razor, Dallas, and finally, southernmost Cunningham on 25 January.

Operation Dewey Canyon

After a majority of the regiment deployed into the AO, the operational code name was changed from Dawson River South to Dewey
Canyon. The terrain in the operational area was as rugged as any experienced by the Marines in the war. Thick, nearly impenetrable jungle growth cloaked jagged mountains that stretched to more than
one thousand meters above sea level. Trees towered hundreds of feet
above the ground, and the lower levels were choked with dense foliage that limited visibility to less than three meters. The jungle would
prove to be as difficult a foe as the North Vietnamese.

The second phase was kicked off on 25 January when the rifle
companies of the 2d and 3d Battalions, 9th Marines pushed out
from FSBs Razor and Cunningham to clear the surrounding areas.
Once that mission was accomplished, the two battalions would take
up positions along the Da Krong, which ran roughly east to west just
south of FSB Cunningham. The 3d Battalion would hold the eastern flank while the 2d held the west; the regiment's 1st Battalion
would move into the center position once the other two battalions
were in place.

The patrolling Marines immediately began making contact with small bands of NVA. One led to the discovery by Company M, 3/9, of a sophisticated four-strand communications wire. A special Marine and army intelligence team tapped into the wire and immediately began intercepting NVA communications. Company F, 2/9, stumbled on a well-equipped 150-bed hospital situated along the Song Da Krong. Complete with eight permanent buildings, the complex was well stocked with surgical instruments, medicine, and foodstuffs. Evidence indicated that the hospital had been abandoned less than 24 hours earlier.

The Co Ka Leuye ridge straddled the border of Laos and South Vietnam at the southwestern edge of the AO. The boundary actually ran down the middle of the promontory that soared steeply 1,500 meters above sea level, allowing anyone on its top to casually stroll between the two countries. Because its height gave an excellent view into either country, it was an important site. However, the steepness of its sides made scaling it impractical for heavily laden infantrymen—until 31 January.

Captain David A. Hitzelberger's Company G, 2/9, had been patrolling the jungle south of LZ Dallas since 26 January. The menacing Co Ka Leuye ridge towered over the company the entire time. To Hitzelberger the peak resembled a jagged tooth. When the battalion ordered him, on 31 January, to scale the ridge, he reacted with stunned disbelief. "You've got to be kidding," he responded to the radioed message.

No, they weren't. The importance of the high ground as an observation post could not be overly stressed. Company G would have to scale the peak. After scouting the ridge's approaches, Hitzelberger selected the northeast side as the most promising—it was only a 35 percent grade.

As the company prepared for its climb, the thickening clouds began releasing rain. The now muddy terrain made the climb even more difficult. Hitzelberger organized climbing teams that would scurry uphill, pulling ropes behind them. Once a team had tied a rope around a stout tree, other Marines would use it to pull themselves uphill. In the meantime, the climbing teams moved farther uphill, securing another length of rope. In this slow, laborious manner the two hundred men of Company G gained the summit at dusk. They found a mountaintop covered by dense jungle. "You couldn't see anything, the foliage was so thick," Hitzelberger said. "There were no signs that anyone had used the top for anything. It was virgin territory."

Over the next two days, the already bad weather continued to deteriorate. Heavy rains, alternating with drizzle and fog, dropped the ceiling to zero and vastly cut visibility. Most of the time Company G was above a thick layer of gray rain-filled clouds. Unable to observe anything, Hitzelberger received orders to abandon the peak.

Late on the morning of 5 February, Hitzelberger sent a reinforced fire team down the ropes first to provide security for the following platoons. As the Marines descended the slippery slope, they spotted enemy soldiers flitting among the trees below them. They weren't trying to hide. They were waiting for the Marines to get closer.

A short distance downhill the NVA opened fire. From behind trees and well-camouflaged positions, about thirty enemy soldiers fired bursts of small arms and automatic weapons fire at the fire team. Reacting quickly, Hitzelberger sent a platoon into the foray. While they slipped and slid downward, Hitzelberger sent a second platoon to the left to flank the enemy. As it approached the battle site, several RPGs swooshed out of the jungle. The rockets erupted in sharp crashes that sent sizzling shards of jagged metal flying everywhere. Several Marines dropped. The quick pop-pop of rifle fire announced the presence of more enemy riflemen.

A company corpsman rushed forward, ignoring the enemy fire, intent only on treating the casualties. As he cared for the wounded, an enemy rifleman drew a bead on him. The corpsman fell, hit several times.

From behind a nearby boulder, LCpl. Thomas P. Noonan watched in horror as blood spurted from the corpsman's neck wound. Concerned only with saving his friend, Noonan ignored the heavy volume of fire to squirm downhill to him. With torrents of rain washing across his face, Noonan slid next to the wounded man and started pulling him to safety. Digging his heels into the soft earth, Noonan struggled to tug the man behind a nearby tree. Hit once, Noonan flopped over backward. Shaking off the shock and pain, he continued his self-appointed task. He'd nearly reached his goal when he was shot again. This time he didn't get up.

While this drama played out, Hitzelberger had his remaining platoon maneuver farther to the left. From this position the Marines crept up a small ravine that led directly to the enemy's positions. Breaking through the NVA's defensive line, the platoon drove off the enemy. A check of the area turned up two enemy bodies. Company G suffered five dead and eighteen wounded in the skirmish. Lance Corporal Noonan's gallant conduct brought him a posthumous Medal of Honor.

The thick canopy of trees and worsening weather prevented helicopters from evacuating the casualties. They'd have to be carried out. Using improvised stretchers, Hitzelberger's men started down the ridge. The pace was agonizingly slow due to the rugged terrain and bad weather. More than half the company was needed to carry the stretchers down the steep, slippery slope. As darkness descended on the jungle, Hitzelberger called for flare ships. Every time a flare dropped below the clouds, the tattered column would surge forward forty to fifty meters. In this manner the company proceeded until 0200 the next morning when they halted for a brief rest.

At dawn, Hitzelberger had his men moving. They were headed for a rendezvous with a reinforcing platoon from Company E. The terrain continued to present incredible obstacles. "At times the stretcher cases were moving up and down slopes in excess of seventy degrees," Hitzelberger said. "We had to use up to ten men to carry a stretcher, and it would take us over thirty minutes to move one stretcher case over one bad area."

At 1400 Company G began the most difficult phase of its journey. Over the next few hours, the able-bodied men used ropes to lower the stretcher cases and walking wounded down a steep cliff face. In the driving rain the casualties were carefully lowered to where the relief platoon waited with medical supplies and the first food that Company G had in three days. Once the linkup was made, the force still had a thirty-six-hour hike to the Da Krong. As the company reached the river, a pair of brave CH-46 pilots descended through the clouds to pick up the casualties. Then the combined unit set out for LZ Dallas, finally reaching it late on 8 February. Battalion commander Lt. Col. George C. Fox called Company G's ordeal "a tremendous performance in leadership and discipline."

The continued heavy rain, alternating with drizzle and fog, kept most helicopters on the ground. As a result, the 9th Marines commander, Col. Robert H. Barrow (a future commandant of the Marine Corps), had ordered all units to hold in place as of 4 February. Not until 10 February did the weather clear sufficiently to allow helicopters to resupply the ground troops and move them into position to begin phase three. Unfortunately, the week-long weather delay not only cost the 9th Marines its momentum but also allowed the NVA to strengthen its positions.

The final phase of Operation Dewey Canyon began early on the morning of 11 February when 3/9 crossed the Song Da Krong. The battalion's objectives were Hills 1228 and 1224, the dominant hill masses separating the Song Da Krong Valley from the A Shau Valley, about eight kilometers to the southeast. The next day, the 1st and 2d Battalions crossed the river, too. Each battalion would move generally south until it reached the Vietnamese-Laotian border.

Almost immediately the Marines ran into the NVA. In fact, the 1st Battalion bumped right into a force of enemy preparing for a ground assault on FSB Erskine. Heavy fighting raged for several hours before the NVA withdrew, leaving behind twenty-five dead. On the east, Company M lost two Marines in repulsing a ground attack that cost the NVA eighteen dead. Company C fought a day-long skirmish on 13 February against NVA dug in along its route of march. That evening the enemy hit Company C's night defensive position but did not break through.

All the involved infantry units found their foe to be well disciplined and determined. Most NVA held to their positions until killed. Enemy snipers tied high in treetops fired at close range or dropped grenades on Marines passing beneath them. At night, NVA sappers probed and harassed the Marines' NDPs. It was obvious that the NVA were doing all they could to keep the Marines from tampering with their vital supply bases.

The rifle companies continued their sparring with the enemy as they pushed farther south through the thick, triple-canopied jungle. Company K was particularly hard hit on 16 February, when North

Vietnamese forces attacked it from both the front and the rear. Under a barrage of RPGs, rockets, and automatic weapons fire, the company responded with a formidable array of artillery and air strikes. The results were seventeen dead NVA and only a handful of wounded Marines. A still-weak Company G fought a running battle with an enemy company all day on 17 February; the encounter cost five Marines and thirty-nine NVA their lives.

Determined to hurt the invaders of their sanctuary, the North Vietnamese sent a reinforced company against FSB Cunningham early on the morning of 17 February. Weighed down with high explosives, sappers slipped through the perimeter wire and wrecked havoc inside the base. Not only was one howitzer of the 2d Battalion, 12th Marines destroyed in the attack, the enemy also knocked out the fire direction center. Before the enemy sappers were hunted down and killed, four Marines died and forty-six were wounded in the three-hour fight. The bodies of thirteen sappers were found inside the base, and another thirty-seven lay outside.

In the meantime, the regiment's maneuver elements were nearing the east-west–running border and Highway 922. The closer they came, the stiffer the enemy resistance grew. Particularly hard hit was the 1st Battalion. On the morning of 18 February, Company A fought a pitched battle with NVA ensconced in reinforced bunkers dug into a heavily forested ridgeline. Following air and artillery strikes, the grunts finally overwhelmed the force, killing thirty NVA while losing one Marine. The next morning, Company C moved through Company A and continued the advance. On the twentieth, it encountered another fortified enemy position. After pummeling the hillside with all available supporting arms, the infantry attacked. When the fight ended, seventy-one dead NVA were added to the operation's body count; five Marines died and twenty-eight were wounded.

Using rotation tactics, Company A resumed the lead. Almost immediately it slammed into yet another dug-in enemy force. When that fight ended, seventeen NVA were dead; one Marine was killed and two were wounded. During these various actions the rifle companies also captured a considerable quantity of enemy weapons and equipment. Among the trophies were two 122mm field guns, the largest taken in the war, a five-ton prime mover, several trucks, and tons of ammo.

On 20 February, to the west of the 1st Battalion fights, two 2d Battalion units finally reached positions that overlooked Route 922 and the international border. The men of Companies E and H could actually see enemy convoys moving on the dirt road below them.

Until now, the allies had been forbidden from crossing the international border. Although U.S. Army Special Forces and Marine recon teams had run clandestine cross-border operations for years, political considerations had kept any major infantry units from crossing the border. Now, as the NVA freely moved his forces across the border under the watchful eyes of the Marines, it was obvious to all involved that something would have to be done about that policy.

General Davis sent the request to cross into Laos to III MAF, who, in turn, forwarded it to MACV. General Abrams said no.

However, on the afternoon of 21 February, Capt. David F. Winecoff, commander of Company H, 2/9, received a classified message authorizing him to conduct an ambush on Highway 922. Taking just two platoons, Winecoff personally led them downhill. By midnight they were in place in the thick brush that lay between the dirt road and a paralleling stream. At 0230 on 22 February, a convoy of eight enemy trucks entered the kill zone. Winecoff opened the ambush by firing his Claymore mine. With a loud roar and a cloud of inky black smoke, thousands of steel balls shredded the second truck and its occupants. An instant later a cacophony of M16 and M60 fire exploded from the brush. As Winecoff said, "Everybody had been waiting a long time and the excitement was keen."

The firing continued for several minutes. An eerie quiet then descended on the jungle road as Winecoff waited for the dust to settle. He then signaled his men to inspect the convoy. Eight dead North Vietnamese were found; three of the trucks were completely destroyed. Not a single Marine was injured. Satisfied with their work, Winecoff ordered his platoons back into the jungle. By midmorning, they had rejoined the rest of the company on the top of the ridge.

Once Winecoff was safely back inside South Vietnam, word of his cross-border incursion swiftly made its way up the chain of command.

Permission to expand operations in Laos against enemy forces using Highway 922 was sought by III MAF. Faced with the realities of the tactical situation, General Abrams reluctantly agreed, although he restricted the efforts to this small portion of the border. Also, he imposed gag orders on any public discussion of the incursions.

Before the 2d Battalion could move back into Laos, though, heavy fighting erupted in the 1st Battalion's area. On the morning of 22 February, the 1st Platoon of Company A fought a quick battle with an NVA squad dug in on a hillside. When the skirmish was over, the company commander, 1st Lt. Wesley L. Fox, sent a detail to fill canteens at a nearby creek. No sooner had the twenty-man detail reached the water when it suddenly came under intense machine-gun and mortar fire. Lieutenant Fox immediately recalled the detail and sent the 1st Platoon forward in an attack.

After advancing just a short distance through the thick jungle, the platoon ran smack into a reinforced NVA company occupying well-prepared, mutually supporting bunkers. As the Marines maneuvered forward, NVA machine guns, RPGs, and mortars emplaced on a ridgeline behind them suddenly opened up. Unable to use air support because of the bad weather or artillery support due to the close proximity of the enemy, Fox knew that he had to maintain the momentum of the attack. Quickly advancing to the front, he personally led his remaining platoons in a spirited assault.

A few minutes later, Fox's command group was devastated when an enemy mortar round landed in their midst. Everyone except the executive officer, 1st Lt. Lee R. Herron, was killed or wounded. Herron immediately took over for the mortally wounded 2d Platoon leader while Fox, despite painful wounds, continued in command of the company. His grunts fought valiantly in the bitter, close-quarters combat that followed. Fox himself destroyed several enemy positions and was wounded twice more before the fight ended. The results of what would prove to be the last major engagement of Operation Dewey Canyon yielded 105 dead NVA and more than two dozen automatic weapons captured. However, the victory came at a high price. Company A suffered 11 killed and 72 wounded; in all, more than half the company were casualties. For their personal valor,

Lieutenant Fox received a Medal of Honor, and Lieutenant Herron, who did not survive the fight, received a Navy Cross.

Five days later, Company D, operating several kilometers east of where Company A fought, uncovered one of the largest enemy weapons and ammo caches of the year. Near the base of Hill 1044 the Marines found more than 600 rifles, 60 machine guns, 14 mortars, 15 recoilless rifles, 19 antiaircraft guns, and more than 100 tons of ammunition. It took the men two days to catalog and destroy the cache.

The 3d Battalion made substantial finds, too, as it moved east and south. On 18 February, Company L discovered a cemetery containing the remains of 185 NVA, most of whom had been buried in June 1968. Three days later, in the Tam Boi Mountain complex astride the border, Company M found a well-equipped maintenance facility containing repair pits, a front loader, several complete engines, and a huge supply of fuel. On the twenty-third, the battalion came upon several damaged 122mm field guns, a prime mover, and vast quantities of ammo near Hill 1228. Further exploration revealed a headquarters and administrative facility composed of 11 huge tunnels. Extending up to 250 meters into the solid rock, the cross-connected tunnels contained extensive repair shops, storage facilities, and even a hospital. The latter had been evacuated so rapidly that one patient was actually abandoned in midoperation.

In the meantime, once General Abrams had given his reluctant approval, 2/9 was ordered back into Laos. According to the plan, Company H, followed by Companies E and F, would push eastward along Highway 922, forcing any NVA into the waiting 1st and 3d Battalions. Neither Captain Winecoff nor his men were excited at the news, but on the night of 24 February, they obediently set up another ambush along Highway 922. Before too long they opened fire on six NVA, killing four. At dawn Company H headed eastward. Winecoff's riflemen killed another eight enemy that day and captured a 122mm field gun and two 40mm antiaircraft guns. Two Marines were killed and seven were wounded in that firefight. Later the same day, the NVA ambushed one of Company H's flanking patrols, killing three Marines and wounding five. One of the dead was Cpl. William D.

Morgan, who earned a Medal of Honor by deliberately sacrificing his life to allow two of the wounded men to be pulled to safety.

The three companies continued their rapid-paced trek, covering five kilometers in five days and killing forty-eight enemy soldiers. As they neared the South Vietnamese border, enemy resistance all but disappeared. On 3 March, the battalion was airlifted out of Laos back to the Vandegrift Combat Base. In accordance with General Abrams's dictates, all references to the incursion were withheld from the official record. To sustain the deceit, the families of casualties were informed that their loved ones' injuries had occurred in South Vietnam. Even Corporal Morgan's parents were presented their son's posthumous Medal of Honor with a citation stating that the action had taken place "southeast of Vandegrift Combat Base."

Once the 2d Battalion was removed from the AO, the extraction of the other units, and the closings of the numerous fire support bases, began. Originally scheduled to be completed by 7 March, the extractions were slowed by extremely bad weather. Not until 18 March was the last part of the 1st Battalion pulled out of FSB Cunningham. Final results for Operation Dewey Canyon tallied 1,617 enemy killed and huge quantities of supplies, weapons, and munitions destroyed. The 9th Marines lost 130 killed and 920 wounded. But, for those losses the Marines greatly disrupted the enemy's presence in this border region and blocked his ability to move on major civilian and military targets to the east.

As the 9th Marines finished up Operation Dewey Canyon, the 4th Marines, under Col. William F. Goggins, initiated Operation Purple Martin in northwest Quang Tri Province on 1 March. Evidence indicated that the 246th NVA Regiment was moving south of the DMZ on a broad front through this area.

The first encounter with the 246th came on 2 March when Company C, 1/4, clashed with the NVA as the Marines attempted to reoccupy LZ Mack, on a hilltop north of the Elliott Combat Base (formerly the Rockpile). Lashed by enemy mortars, Company C was reinforced by Company L, 3/4, that afternoon. The two companies, handicapped by dense fog and a steady drizzle that eliminated any air support, withdrew under heavy pressure. After consolidating their defensive positions, the two rifle companies waited for the weather to clear before attacking again.

The rain didn't hold back the enemy. Over the next three days, the NVA bombarded the units with a near continuous barrage of mortar fire, sniper fire, and nightly ground attacks. Fifteen Marines died in these assults. Finally, on the afternoon of 5 March, with clear weather and following an extensive air and artillery bombardment of the objective, the two companies moved on LZ Mack again. Battling a fiercely determined, well-dug-in enemy, the Marines, amply supported by artillery, finally succeeded in clearing the LZ of the NVA. The Navy Cross was awarded to four members of the company: 1st Lt. Karl A. Marlantes, the executive officer; 2d Lt. Thomas E. Noel, a rifle platoon leader; and two enlisted men, George V. Jmaeff and Yale G. Allen, the latter posthumously. These awards were the most given to a single rifle company in one action during the war.

Fifteen kilometers to the west, Company G, 2/4, on 9 March, engaged yet another enemy unit while moving near the site of abandoned LZ Catapult. As the company approached the LZ, which overlooked an extensive enemy trail network north of the old Khe Sanh Combat Base, NVA resistance toughened. Using snipers, ambushes, and Claymore mines, the determined foe worked hard to halt the Marines. Over the next two days, Company G fought a nearly continuous running battle with the enemy. On the morning of 11 March, the NVA counterattacked with small arms, grenades, and RPGs. Fighting raged as close as five meters before the enemy line broke and Company G finally claimed LZ Catapult. Littering the hilltop were two dozen NVA corpses. The Marines lost four killed and thirteen wounded.

Action shifted eastward on 13 March when Company M, 3/4, moved northwest of LZ Mack to resecure LZ Sierra. Abandoned in January, LZ Sierra had been used by the NVA to mortar LZ Mack, two kilometers away. Advancing through a hail of enemy small arms fire, Company M cleared LZ Sierra, losing ten dead and thirty-five wounded against twenty-three NVA dead.

The next morning, Company I moved through Company M to assault the high ground to the north. Just after Company I departed, the NVA counterattacked Company M. Calling upon the dependable howitzers of the 3d Battalion, 12th Marines, the Marine infantry beat off their attackers. After Company I took its objective, the NVA disappeared from the area. The companies of the 3d Battalion then moved north to establish landing zones along the DMZ.

In order to secure his regiment's western flank, Colonel Goggins ordered his 1st Battalion to assault abandoned FSB Argonne. Built on Hill 1308 about twenty kilometers northwest of the former Khe Sanh Combat Base, FSB Argonne sat just two kilometers from the Laotian border. The base thus offered excellent observation into Laos and the nearby portions of the Ho Chi Minh Trail. Battalion commander Lt. Col. George T. Sargent planned to land one company on the fire support base and two others in the valley north of Hill 1308.

Company D, 1/4, assaulted into a hot LZ atop FSB Argonne on the morning of 20 March. Earlier that morning, the NVA defenders had downed a UH-1E carrying a preassault recon team into the LZ. Though Company D received only sporadic enemy fire as they poured out of their CH-46Ds, resistance increased steadily as they fanned out across the fire support base. As they neared the crest of Hill 1308, vicious blasts of enemy automatic weapons fire from well-constructed bunkers halted their progress. Unswerving in the face of such heavy fire, the Marines used fire and maneuver techniques to destroy one bunker after another. Lieutenant Colonel Sargent, who'd been on the first helicopter, personally led a group of Marines in an attack on an enemy machine gun. Hurling grenades, he killed the weapon's gunners and cleared a path across the LZ. Not until dark was the last enemy fortification destroyed. Company D lost six killed and eleven wounded in securing FSB Argonne. The Marines found fifteen dead NVA scattered amidst the ruined bunkers.

Due to the heavy fighting on FSB Argonne, Lieutenant Colonel Sargent delayed his other two companies' assault into the northern valley until the next day. At 0815 on 21 March, a dozen NVA 82mm mortar rounds suddenly slammed into Argonne. Among the four killed in the blast was Lieutenant Colonel Sargent, who would receive a posthumous Navy Cross for his personal gallantry and skillful leadership; another dozen Marines were wounded. Later, as a medevac helicopter carried out those casualties, more mortar rounds fell, killing three more Marines and wounding another eleven.

As a result of these attacks, Company A was diverted from its planned sweep north of FSB Argonne and sent west to search for the enemy mortars. On 28 March, Company A, after repeated skirmishes with small bands of NVA, finally swept through a bunker complex guarding the crest of Hill 1154, just inside the Laotian border. Though the Marines didn't find any mortar tubes, harassment of the friendly positions on FSB Argonne ceased.

In the meantime, Colonel Goggins dispatched Company C to reinforce FSB Argonne. On 23 March, the new battalion commander, Lt. Col. Clair E. Willcox, sent Company B six kilometers northeast of FSB Argonne to establish FSB Greene and, finally, open the northern part of the operation.

With all the maneuver elements of his regiment at last established in the AO and their initial objectives secured, Colonel Goggins ordered his battalions to begin sweeping their areas. The infantry companies spread out, methodically searching the jungle for the NVA. Their efforts proved futile. Only an occasional contact was made with small bands of NVA. Even when the patrols moved into the DMZ, very few North Vietnamese were found. Throughout April the 4th Regiment searched in vain for the enemy. By the end of the month it was apparent that the NVA had fled to their cross-border sanctuaries. On 25 April, Goggins ordered his infantry companies to withdraw from the DMZ. Once safely out of NVA mortar range, the Marines dug in. From these new positions they could still send patrols north into the DMZ as needed.

Colonel Goggins ended Operation Purple Martin on 8 May, when intelligence sources indicated that the 246th NVA Regiment had indeed moved back into Laos. During the operation the 4th Marines killed more than three hundred members of the enemy regiment while losing less than two dozen of their own.

While the 4th Marines were engaged in the far northwestern reaches of Quang Tri Province, the 3d Marines opened a campaign in the area south of Khe Sanh known as the Vietnam Salient. Just west of the Dewey Canyon AO, the Vietnam Salient poked south into Laos for twenty kilometers. Intelligence sources reported that the NVA, after being halted along Route 922, were using the area to penetrate Quang Tri Province. Marines had entered the salient twice before, in June and September 1968. This time the 3d Marines, recently returned to Quang Tri Province after fighting in Operation Taylor Common with the 1st Marine Division, were tapped to clear the salient.

The tactics of this operation, named "Maine Crag," would follow the pattern of Operation Dewey Canyon. First, fire support bases reaching successively deeper into the salient would be established. Then, infantry patrols would clear the area around each fire support base before leapfrogging farther south. This time, though, the Marines would be supported by a U.S. Army task force and an ARVN regiment.

In preparation for the operation, 2/3 airlifted into FSB Hawk, just south of Route 9 and about halfway between the Vandegrift Combat Base and Khe Sanh, on 10 March. That same night they began a rare overland trek to FSB Snapper, seven kilometers to the southwest. "It was a moonless night," recalled battalion commander Lt. Col. James J. McMonagle. "There were quite [a few] streams to cross and a heck of a lot of elephant grass. It was really amazing how they [the point company] were able to find this place going through elephant grass at that time of evening." The next morning, McMonagle's men searched the nearby area but found no sign of the enemy.

Operation Maine Crag officially began on 15 March when 2/3 started an overland push from Route 9 south into the salient all the way to FSB Saigon, which overlooked Route 616. For the first few days, the Marines encountered only occasional snipers. Then, on 18 March, a patrol from Company G ambushed a convoy of enemy trucks moving along Highway 616. The next day the company ambushed seven NVA soldiers sent out to check on the convoy.

On 20 March, three companies of 1/3 helilifted into FSB Saigon. These fresh Marines headed southwest to block Route 616 to the west of 2/3. McMonagle's battalion then worked its way eastward along the road. On the twenty-first, Company H uncovered a large cache of foodstuffs, including more than 350 tons of rice.

This proved to be the only major success of the operation. Though the maneuver elements of Operation Maine Crag thoroughly searched their AO, and even extended eastward into the old Operation Dewey Canyon AO, enemy contact was limited to occasional sniper rounds and a few mortar shells fired from Laos. Several more supply caches were uncovered and the foodstuffs extracted. By the end of April, the 3d Marines had been relocated to the central portion of Quang Tri Province, where they took up positions below the DMZ to begin Operation Virginia Ridge.

During this period the command of the 3d Marine Division changed. After eleven months as the division's commander, Maj. Gen. Ray Davis's tour was coming to an end. Davis's tenure had done wonders for the division, putting it on the move and driving it deep into enemy-controlled territory, where the Marine infantry kept the NVA off balance. Davis's replacement, Maj. Gen. William K. Jones, took command on 15 April. A decorated veteran of the bloody World War II island battles of Tarawa and Saipan, as well as Korea, Jones completely agreed with Davis's mobility philosophy and saw no need to institute any change.

Despite the success of the 9th Marines during Operation Dewey Canyon, the enemy quickly returned to the area. Aerial reconnaissance confirmed that the NVA were repairing Route 922. Long-range recon patrols reported the presence of two NVA infantry regiments, the 6th and the 9th, as well as supporting units, including artillery, in the area. Headquarters XXIV Corps responded to this news by ordering a major campaign in the region. The 3d Marine Division would return to the southern Da Krong Valley and the U.S. Army's 101st Airborne Division (Airmobile) would operate in the adjacent A Shau Valley. The operation was code-named "Apache Snow."

The 1st and 2d Battalions, 9th Marines were assigned the task of occupying the lower Da Krong Valley to prevent any NVA from slipping away from the A Shau Valley via Route 922. Operation Apache Snow began for the Marines on 10 May when 1/9 airlifted into Operation Dewey Canyon's old FSB Erskine, overlooking Route 922. Sporadic enemy fire greeted the incoming Marines. One troop-laden helicopter was shot down, killing seven and injuring five men. At the same time, 2/9 landed at FSB Razor, another old Dewey Canyon site.

The rifle companies of the two battalions immediately fanned out to search for the enemy. It soon became apparent that there were no major NVA units operating in this AO. Contact with enemy forces was limited to brief engagements with small bands of enemy soldiers.

The companies of 1/9 vigorously patrolled Route 922 and the surrounding mountains but found only a few NVA.

While members of the 9th Marines were wishing they could find the enemy, members of the 101st Airborne Division wished they hadn't. Soon after they entered the A Shau Valley, the soldiers encountered the NVA on Hill 937, known locally as Dong Ap Bia and soon nicknamed by the soldiers "Hamburger Hill." The 101st's fight to drive the enemy off Hill 937 lasted more than a week and engulfed five battalions. The American soldiers prevailed but at a cost of more than three hundred casualties, including forty-four dead.

Operation Apache Snow ended for the 9th Marines when the two battalions returned to Vandegrift Combat Base on 27 May.

In January 1969, a new administration took office in Washington, D.C., and with it came a new direction for the war in Southeast Asia. President Nixon had campaigned on a promise to end the war in South Vietnam. Although he had no specific plan to do so then, by the time he took the oath it was obvious that no solution could be found in a negotiated settlement. Nixon's only other option was to begin the withdrawal of U.S. troops and turn over the war to the forces of South Vietnam.

After a complete and careful review of the entire military situation, and a visit with South Vietnam's leaders, Secretary of Defense Melvin Laird recommended that fifty thousand Americans be pulled out of South Vietnam in the latter half of 1969. Included for redeployment in this first stage was the 3d Marine Division.

Operation Keystone Eagle

The MACV selected the 3d Marine Division to be part of the initial redeployment because it could return to Okinawa, it would be replaced by the well-disciplined 1st ARVN Division, and, thanks to the heroic efforts of the officers and men of the division, Quang Tri Province was one of the most secure in the country.

According to the schedule developed by MACV planners, one infantry regiment (along with its supporting air, artillery, and other units) would depart South Vietnam for Okinawa on 1 July 1969; a second regimental landing team (RLT) would leave on 1 August, a third on 1 September, and, finally, all remaining division personnel by 30 September.

Because the 9th Marines were currently acting as the division reserve and were not occupying a fire support base, they received the distinction of being chosen as part of the first increment, code-named Operation Keystone Eagle. Included with the infantry units would be the artillery of 2/12, the 3d Antitank Battalion, 1st Amphibious Tractor Battalion, Company C, 3d Tank Battalion, and the 1st Searchlight Battery. To accompany the RLT, the 1st Marine Air Wing would release one jet and one helicopter squadron along with an assortment of other, smaller supporting units.

Though the designated units would be departing South Vietnam, the men making up those units at redeployment time would not necessarily be the ones who had earlier been carried on each unit's roster. Instead, III MAF instituted a program of shifting individual Marines who had neared the end of their thirteen-month tour into the redeploying units, while the deploying unit's members with more time to serve were transferred to outfits not being redeployed. This shifting of personnel was called "mix-mastering."

Since returning from Operation Apache Snow at the end of May, the 9th Marines had been involved in two other operations. Cameron Falls had begun on 29 May as the regiment searched for the 304th NVA Division in the mountainous region south of the Vandegrift Combat Base, near the upper reaches of the Da Krong. After setting up FSB Whisman on 30 May, the regiment's 2d Battalion was hit by an NVA ground attack during the early morning hours of 1 June. Fortunately, the Marines' well-ingrained habit of stringing defensive wire, digging fighting holes, setting out Claymore mines and trip flares, and digging bunkers as soon as they arrived paid off. The attack was quickly repulsed, at the cost of two Marines and nineteen NVA killed.

After that fight, the 2d Battalion started a sweep to the northeast along the Da Krong while 3/9 proceeded southeast from FSB Shepherd, five kilometers to the north. The two battalions hoped to trap an NVA force reported to be on Hill 824. After moving through rugged terrain consisting of triple-canopied rain forest and four-meter-high elephant grass, the two Marine columns converged on

Hill 824. On 5 June, Company H, 2/9, was ambushed by a well-dug-in force on the southern banks of the Da Krong. Intense fighting at close quarters raged for nearly twelve hours before the Marines broke through the enemy's defensive line. Upon policing the immediate area, battalion members found a sophisticated network of bunkers, caves, and living quarters and a wide variety of supplies.

Continued patrolling by the two Marine battalions in their AOs over the next two weeks failed to turn up any other large groups of the enemy. Operation Cameron Falls ended on 23 June, when the participating units were shifted farther west to participate in a new operation.

Acting on intelligence reports that enemy units had infiltrated the area south and east of the old Khe Sanh Combat Base, 3d Marine Division headquarters created a joint task force to deploy Marine, army, and ARVN units into the area. Operation Utah Mesa began on 12 June, when 1/9 moved onto FSB Bison northeast of Khe Sanh. The 3d Battalion, 2d ARVN Regiment occupied nearby FSB Quantico. While these units swept west, three companies of U.S. Army mechanized infantry would advance west along Route 9.

The NVA reacted to this intrusion by launching a series of night attacks against the allied units. The first came against Company B, 61st U.S. Infantry on 18 June. Before dawn that day, the NVA hit the soldiers' night defensive position located just east of Lang Vei. After breaking through the perimeter, the NVA swarmed over the NDP, fighting the soldiers at close quarters. The NVA pulled out at dawn, leaving forty-one bodies behind. The U.S. Army units lost eleven killed and fifteen wounded.

A few hours later, a recon patrol from Company C, 1/9, was ambushed three kilometers southeast of Khe Sanh. The fight started when the NVA raked the patrol with .50-caliber machine-gun fire, instantly killing three Marines. The patrol's survivors then attacked, destroying the enemy machine gun. Soon joined by the remainder of Company C, the riflemen assaulted the enemy's defensive line, driving them southward into a wall of artillery fire.

Two days later, after having continued their westward push, the allied force was hit again. In three separate ground attacks the NVA assaulted the combined NDP of Company D, 1/9, and Company B,

1/61. Though they had to call in air strikes, artillery, and helicopter gunships, the Marines and soldiers held, killing twenty-seven NVA.

On 23 June, 1/9 was pulled out of the field and returned to Vandegrift Combat Base. There, the battalion's equipment was upgraded and its personnel was mix-mastered. On 12 July, the battalion moved to Da Nang. Two days later, the unit boarded the USS *Paul Revere* and sailed for Okinawa.

The two remaining battalions of the 9th Marines continued their operations near Khe Sanh. Enemy contact was an almost daily event. Not only were small bands of determined NVA encountered during the day, but the enemy probed the Marines' NDPs nearly every night. One unit, Company K, 3/9, was hit on two successive nights, 24 and 25 June. Though the fighting was hard and raged for hours, the Marines held.

On 2 July, the NVA struck FSB Spark south of Khe Sanh, where 2/9 was headquartered, with a flurry of 82mm mortar rounds. The barrage wounded more than forty Marines. Four days later Operation Utah Mesa ended when both battalions were pulled back to the Vandegrift Combat Base to prepare for redeployment.The second major unit of the 3d Marine Division to be pulled out of the war zone was 2/9 on 1 August. It was followed by 3/9 on 13 August. In all, nearly eighty-four hundred Marines moved to Okinawa in this first increment of America's withdrawal from South Vietnam.

With only two regiments remaining in the 3d Marine Division, tactics changed from multibattalion search and destroy operations to company-sized ambush and patrol operations. Fortunately, the heavy damage inflicted on the North Vietnamese Army units operating in Quang Tri Province in 1968 and the first half of 1969 greatly reduced their ability to conduct large-scale attacks on allied installations.

As July began, the 3d Marines were engaged in Operation Virginia Ridge in the area northwest of Dong Ha and below the DMZ. The rifle companies of 1/3 concentrated their efforts around Mutter's Ridge and in the Helicopter Valley area. To the southwest, 2/3 was spread thin covering the Khe Gio Bridge outside Dong Ha, protecting Route 9, and patrolling southwest of Dong Ha. The northern portion of the Virginia Ridge TAOR was the responsibility of the regiment's 3d Battalion. These Marines held the fixed positions from Alpha 4 to Cam Lo.

Combat action during Operation Virginia Ridge was mostly limited to brief encounters with small bands of NVA infiltrating south from the DMZ. Increased use of several types of new seismic intrusion devices planted along likely routes provided the Marines with an early warning system. Once the devices were activated, artillery barrages could be called in on preselected target areas. Often, too, CS gas crystals were sown along these routes to deny their use to the enemy.

When the 9th Marines redeployed, the operational area of the 3d Marines was extended westward. Regimental commander Col. Wilbur F. Simlik ended Operation Virginia Ridge on 16 July and immediately replaced it with Operation Idaho Canyon to include the new TAOR.

During the beginning stages of Operation Idaho Canyon, enemy activity continued to be small in scale and brief in duration. However, toward the end of July, the NVA became much bolder. On 25 July, Company I, 3/3, was suddenly bombarded with 60mm mortar rounds, RPGs, and small arms fire as it patrolled a few kilometers west of Charlie 2. Responding with artillery and air strikes, the Marines killed more than twenty NVA. Two days later, in what might have been a retaliatory attack for the beating it took at the hands of Company I, the enemy hit the night laager site of Company K. The platoon of NVA damaged the three tanks that had been operating with Company K and killed three Marines before being driven off. At first light, only two enemy bodies were found, though a large number of blood trails and drag marks disappeared into the nearby brush.

The action then shifted westward. While patrolling about seven kilometers north of the Rockpile on 7 August, Company F, 2/3, came upon two well-dug-in NVA companies. Though supported by air and artillery, Company F's repeated attacks against the enemy's positions were unsuccessful. Suffering six killed and more than twenty wounded, Company F was reinforced at dusk by a platoon from Company A, 1/3. The next morning, the combined unit resumed the attack. Meeting only light resistance, it took the enemy's position. The defenders had fled, leaving behind the bodies of forty-six of their comrades.

Quiet reigned over the area for the next two days, then the enemy hit Company E's 3d Platoon, which was protecting the battalion's 81mm mortar platoon at a position several kilometers to the northwest of Company F's fight. Attacking with grenades, satchel charges, and small arms fire, the fanatical NVA swarmed over the NDP. They immediately focused on the command post, peppering it with a multitude of explosive charges. As a result, communication with the beleaguered force was lost for more than an hour, forcing the supporting artillery to cease firing its barrages. Though the enemy was finally driven off, the attack cost the Marines thirteen dead and fifty-eight wounded; the enemy lost seventeen.

Simultaneously, Company E's 1st Platoon, dug in less than a kilometer to the south, was struck by a heavy ground and mortar attack. Barely able to hang on, the Marines were able to beat back their attackers only with the timely arrival of air support. Nineteen enemy bodies were later found; the 1st Platoon suffered six killed and seventeen wounded.

As a result of this battering, Company E was pulled out of the field for rest and rebuilding; Company A, 1/3, replaced it. Also, Colonel Simlik issued orders for his regiment that prohibited all but company-sized NDPs within five kilometers of the DMZ; individual platoons were forbidden to establish night laager sites within that zone. General Jones thought that this was such an effective way to reduce unnecessary casualties that he extended the order division-wide. To keep the NVA from pinpointing a unit's position, Jones further ordered units to move at least one kilometer per day. Though this order immediately became unpopular, it did help keep down the casualty rate during the division's final months in South Vietnam. General Jones also banned all independent platoon operations.

Following Company E's ordeal, another lull of several weeks occurred before activity in the AO increased again. On 28 August, Company B, 1/3, began a five-day-long series of engagements as it moved toward Mutter's Ridge. Early that morning, despite taking all the necessary and required precautions, the company was hit by a particularly violent RPG, hand grenade, and small arms attack. When the

NVA sappers killed a platoon leader and breached the perimeter, Capt. Gerald H. Sampson raced through heavy enemy fire to rally the battered grunts. Leading them in a counterattack, he restored the torn perimeter. He was killed a short time later. Sampson's gallantry resulted in the award of a posthumous Navy Cross, the last for a 3d Division Marine.

Over the next four days, Company B fought a number of short but sharp fights with enemy troops trying to block their progress to Mutter's Ridge. The last engagement came on 1 September as the company finally crested the long-fought-over ridge. Four enemy snipers were killed before the Marines took the top of the hill.

This pattern of quiet followed by a flurry of enemy attacks continued for the next several weeks. Nearly every company of the regiment was hit at least once. Planning for more aggressive operations against the enemy was under way when, on 19 September, division headquarters ordered the 3d Marines to cease all further offensive operations and prepare for redeployment from South Vietnam. As a result, Operation Idaho Canyon ended that same day. Unlike the 9th Marines, who moved to Okinawa, the 3d Marine Regiment would be returning directly to the United States. On 6 October 1969, the 3d Marines departed South Vietnam for Camp Pendleton in California.

An interesting episode occurred during the regiment's redeployment that clearly illustrated the frustration of fighting a political war. Because it was reported that President Nixon desired to greet the returning Marines at the El Toro Marine Corps Air Station in southern California, Colonel Simlik was ordered to personally lead a contingent of his men back to the States. "We wiped the mud off our boots and took one hundred fifty men down to the air base at Da Nang," Simlik said.

Somehow the supply people rounded up new helmets, starched fatigues, and spit-shined boots. Simlik recalled, "We practiced getting on and off a 707 for three days so we would look sharp for the president. And so we flew back to the States, changing into our new uniforms fifteen minutes from El Toro. Of course, the president was not there; Undersecretary of the Navy John Warner was. It was a strange war indeed."

Because Colonel Simlik had not completed his tour, he reboarded the 707 for a return trip to Dong Ha.

When the 9th Marines were pulled out of South Vietnam in July, the 4th Marine Regiment was engaged in Operation Arlington Canyon. The AO for this operation included the valleys and mountains northwest of Vandegrift. The 4th Marines' operation was, in fact, very similar in character to the adjacent 3d Marines' operation—numerous company-sized sweeps intent on blunting any enemy infiltration into the area.

During most of the summer, enemy activity in the Arlington Canyon AO, and the adjacent Georgia Tar AO to the south, was very light. Only occasional contact with small bands of recon-type NVA forces was experienced. The Marines spent many days humping the rugged terrain searching for the enemy, only to be frustrated as their efforts repeatedly failed.

As the division worked on plans for its redeployment, the 4th Marines received orders to destroy any of its fire support bases that were unwanted by either the U.S. Army units replacing them or the ARVN. In addition Colonel Goggins was ordered to destroy all the fire support bases in the vicinity of Khe Sanh. Goggins was also told to prepare for the closing of the Vandegrift Combat Base and Ca Lu. He assigned 1/4 to these tasks.

In the Arlington Canyon AO, 2/4 conducted frequent patrols to locate and destroy the enemy units known to be operating in the area. Unfortunately, the division's rules of engagement severely handicapped the patrols' effectiveness. For example, all patrols within three kilometers of the DMZ were now completely prohibited. The rifle companies still had to move one klick per day; regardless of the ruggedness of the terrain or the adversity of the weather, the companies still had to move. Not only did this rule greatly tax the infantrymen, the accomplishment of the one kilometer movement frequently became a goal unto itself. Companies were often forced to rush along their assigned route of march in order to "make their klick," paying little heed to signs of the enemy.

On 20 August, all offensive operations within the Arlington Canyon AO were halted. The main fire support base, Russell, northwest of the Rockpile, was ordered leveled. When that was completed on 22 August, Operation Arlington Canyon officially ended. The campaign had resulted in just twenty-three enemy dead and eight weapons recovered. Marine casualties were ten killed and twenty-three wounded.

With a shrinking TAOR, the 4th Marines now concentrated their activities in the vicinity of Mutter's Ridge. Intelligence sources indicated that the 9th NVA Regiment had reinfiltrated the area after the 3d Marines left. The rifle companies of 2/4 vigorously patrolled the region but made contact only once.

On 26 September, Company G was hit by a mortar and ground attack at its NDP at LZ Dixie Pete three kilometers north of the Rockpile. Unable to obtain artillery support due to confusion over map coordinates, company commander 1st Lt. William H. Stubblefield rallied his men to fight off the attack with their M16s and M60s. Not until just before dawn was the hard-pressed company successful in repulsing its attackers. A first-light sweep of the perimeter revealed a number of blood trails but no bodies. Company G lost two killed and fifty-nine wounded in the fight.

The regiment's 1st Battalion received orders on 1 October to dismantle the Vandegrift Combat Base. When that task was completed, the battalion moved to Quang Tri to prepare for redeployment to Okinawa. On 22 October, the battalion boarded ships at Cua Viet and sailed east.

The 2d Battalion, 4th Marines was now not only responsible for the security of the Elliott Combat Base and Khe Gio Bridge on Route 9 but also for conducting all offensive operations north of the highway all the way to the DMZ. On one such patrol, the regiment experienced its last engagement of the war. On the night of 9 October, 2d Lt. Danny G. Dennison's 3d Platoon, Company L was hit by a surprisingly strong ground attack at its hilltop position a few kilometers northeast of Elliott. Two enemy platoons struck the NDP with grenades, satchel charges, and automatic weapons fire. Dennison said, "Three men moved up to the main part of the wire throwing Chicoms [grenades] and satchel charges. To the left of the CP a ten-man engineer detachment moved up." Almost immediately, two of the Marines' machine guns were destroyed. The NVA exploited this loss by breaching the platoon's perimeter and swarming over their ammo dump, destroying it. A reaction platoon arrived from the Khe Gio Bridge, about two kilometers away. With their help Dennison's men threw the enemy out of their perimeter. At dawn, Marine air support pounded the NVA and they fled, leaving ten dead bodies strewn around the Marines' position. Friendly casualties were eight dead and seventeen wounded.

On 22 October, 2/4 was ordered to Quang Tri. One company remained at Elliott to destroy that combat base. The entire battalion sailed for Okinawa on 6 November.

The last infantry battalion of the 3d Marine Division remaining in South Vietnam was 3/4. Since early October, the battalion's rifle companies had been protecting the Dong Ha Combat Base and patrolling along the Cua Viet River. On 2 November, they received word to cease all combat operations and prepare for redeployment. Two weeks later the battalion moved to Da Nang. There they boarded ships on 24 November and sailed for Camp Courtney on Okinawa the same day.

The end of 1969 saw Marine strength in South Vietnam at a little less than fifty-five thousand. Sandwiched between the massive Tet fighting of 1968 and the major de-escalation of American involvement in the war that occurred in 1970, the year 1969 marked a major change in U.S. policy in South Vietnam. Overall, it was a successful year: the Marines consolidated their positions and continued to pursue both combat and pacification goals. The next year would witness a further reduction in the Marines' presence in the war zone as the Nixon administration continued to fulfill its pledge of turning over more of the combat load to the South Vietnamese.

Chapter Seven
1970–71

First Lieutenant William R. Purdy leaned out the open side door of the UH-1E Huey helicopter. From one thousand feet above the flat, sandy terrain about six kilometers south of Da Nang, the commander of Company A, 1/1, kept a sharp lookout for any sign of enemy soldiers. This was the second try at a new tactic that the division planners called "Kingfisher" patrols.

These were offensive patrols, designed to seek out and initiate contact with the enemy. A typical Kingfisher patrol consisted of a reinforced rifle platoon embarked on three CH-46D Boeing Sea Knight helicopters, four Bell AH-1G Huey Cobra gunships, a command UH-1E Huey, and a North American OV-10 Bronco carrying an aerial observer. Launched at first light, the Kingfisher patrols hoped to catch the enemy when his night activities were ending and he was returning to his camps. If one of the observers spotted the enemy or any sign of him, the Sea Knights would land and disgorge the riflemen while the Cobras hovered protectively nearby waiting for a call to action. In the meantime, the Bronco circled overhead, alert for any targets for the supporting artillery. If a significant contact developed, the empty CH-46s could ferry in the rest of the company to help.

The first Kingfisher patrol had been run just a few days earlier, on 2 January 1970. Though the rifle platoon had landed twice, no contact developed. Now, four days later, Purdy launched again. At about 0730 the lieutenant spotted several men squatting next to a thatched hut. As he signaled the Huey's pilot to drop down for a closer look, Purdy noted a number of cooking fires. This was certainly worth investigating, he decided.

As the three Sea Knights settled over the LZs, a flurry of small arms fire ripped into the crafts. There was no doubt now who the men were. In fact, the Kingfisher patrol was setting down in the middle of a company of Viet Cong. One of the infantryman said, "We dropped down on their breakfast table."

Purdy explained, "We landed directly on top of people. They were running right beside the windows of the chopper . . . we got a couple of kills right out of the choppers."

After rushing from the CH-46Ds, Purdy's men quickly organized and attacked by fire teams and squads. Caught completely by surprise, the enemy broke and ran in all directions. They had prepared strong fortifications to withstand a ground attack but were totally unprepared for an assault out of the sky. Purdy said, "We were fighting from their positions. Every berm we came to, all we had to do was drop our rifles on it and start firing."

As the VC fled across the flatlands, the Cobras swooped in, tearing apart the enemy with their machine guns and grenade launchers. Farther out, artillery shells burst, blocking other escape routes. No matter which way the enemy ran, hot steel was waiting for him.

When the fight ended about 0900, fifteen enemy bodies were scattered in the dirt around the LZs. The Cobras claimed another ten. Purdy's men suffered no casualties. They did take one prisoner and captured two weapons, more than a dozen grenades, and a good quantity of documents. It was a very satisfied platoon of Marines who reboarded the Sea Knights for the flight back to Da Nang.

The war that the U.S. Marines in South Vietnam faced as the new decade began was, in many respects, far different from the war of five years before, or even one year before. After the departure of the 3d Marine Division, the focus of Marine operations became Quang Nam Province. Within that province the Marines were primarily concerned with the Da Nang TAOR.

The III MAF had started 1969 with nearly eighty thousand Marines under its command. As 1970 began, Marine Corps personnel numbered just about fifty-five thousand. To replace the deployed Marines, MACV repositioned a number of U.S. Army units in I Corps. The 1st

Brigade, 5th Infantry Division took up positions along the DMZ, and the 101st Airborne Division spread out through Thua Thien Province. These two units made up the U.S. Army's XXIV Corps, which remained under the operational control of III MAF. To the south in Quang Tin and Quang Ngai Provinces, the Americal Division continued to hold the southern reaches of the corps' zone. This U.S. Army division operated under III MAF's direct control.

The tempo of the war had changed as well. With the continued emphasis on Vietnamization, the large multibattalion operations that had been the norm as recently as eight months before were now a relic. Besides not having the manpower to conduct such campaigns, the Marines were no longer encountering the enemy in the large formations of the past. Indeed, as 1969 ended, contact with enemy units larger than platoon size rapidly diminished. The war was now one of ambushes, brief skirmishes, rocket and mortar attacks, and, worst of all, booby traps. These devious devices caused the majority of casualties in the final months of Marine operations in South Vietnam.

Despite the drawdown of its forces, III MAF still had a mission assignment. According to the allies' Combined Campaign Plan for 1970, the Marines were to continue their mobile operations against the enemy while screening the civilian population from attack. However, to achieve this objective, the 1st Marine Division would have to make do with one less infantry regiment.

On 15 December 1969, President Nixon announced that fifty thousand more American troops would be pulled out of South Vietnam by 15 April 1970. Though MACV originally advised III MAF that it would be contributing two full regimental combat teams to this phase of the drawdown, the number was ultimately reduced to one. General Nickerson selected the 26th Marines to be part of the Operation Keystone Blue Jay withdrawal. After being relieved of responsibility for the defense of Khe Sanh in April 1968, the 26th Marines had operated south of the DMZ in central Quang Tri Province. When the 3d Marine Division was designated to be part of the initial American redeployment, the regiment was transferred to the 1st Marine Division. As 1970 began, the regiment was holding down positions north and west of Da Nang.

Among the supporting units that would leave with the 26th Marines were its artillery unit—the 1st Battalion, 13th Marines—and most of the 1st Tank Battalion and the 3d Amphibious Tractor Battalion. The 1st Marine Air Wing would send out one group headquarters, three jet squadrons, and one helicopter squadron.

The units participating in Operation Keystone Blue Jay began withdrawing from combat in late January. As the 26th Marines left the field, the neighboring 1st Marines extended its TAOR northward to take over the 26th's positions. In mid-February, the supporting units began boarding ships for the trip to Camp Pendleton. Between 11 and 19 March, the 26th Marines departed South Vietnam. When the regiment arrived in California, it was deactivated.

With the reduction of III MAF to less than 43,000 officers and men, it became obvious to MACV that it was now impractical for the larger XXIV Corps to remain subordinate to III MAF. Although General Nickerson recognized the need to streamline his headquarters staff, he and other senior Marines feared that any change in their command structure could result in the disruption of the long-cherished Marine air-ground team concept. Headquarters, U.S. Marine Corps fully supported General Nickerson in his concerns. In every discussion involving a headquarters consolidation, Marine Corps commandant Gen. Leonard F. Chapman, Jr., insisted that as long as a Marine division and air wing remained in South Vietnam, there would be a Marine headquarters over them.

Ever sensitive to interservice rivalries, General Abrams issued a directive in mid-February that established the relationships among the various American commands in South Vietnam. The MACV directive placed XXIV Corps in command of all U.S. troops in I Corps. However, it defined III MAF as "a separate command subordinate to and under the operational control of XXIV Corps" but exercising control of all Marine ground and air units in I Corps. Generals Chapman and Nickerson were happy with this compromise.

Working together, the staffs of III MAF and XXIV Corps agreed on 9 March 1970 as the date to exchange roles. Besides the reassignment of the control of various units, for example, the Americal Division would now operate under XXIV Corps. A change of headquarters locations was needed. The III MAF agreed to turn over its headquarters complex at Camp Horn, east of Da Nang, to XXIV Corps, and the army would abandon its facilities at Phu Bai. Searching for a new headquarters site, III MAF settled on the soon-to-be-abandoned Camp Haskins, home of the navy's Seabees, on Red Beach north of Da Nang. In five years, the Marines had now come full circle, returning to the site of their original 1965 landing.

All the changes went according to plan, and on 9 March 1970 the transfer of command responsibility was completed. On the same day, General Nickerson turned over command of III MAF to Lt. Gen. Keith B. McCutcheon. No stranger to the war in South Vietnam, General McCutcheon had commanded the 1st MAW in 1966–67. The III MAF (Marine air wing) that McCutcheon took over had about forty thousand Marines on its rolls, a reduction of nearly fifteen thousand since the first of the year.

An unfortunate accident cut short the tenure of division commander Maj. Gen. Edwin B. Wheeler. On 18 April 1970, his command helicopter crashed while he was visiting a 1st Marines LZ. Wheeler suffered a badly broken leg in the accident and had to relinquish his command. His replacement was Maj. Gen. Charles F. Widdecke, who arrived from Washington on 27 April. Widdecke, who had earned a Navy Cross in World War II, also had a great deal of experience in the Vietnam War, for he had commanded the 5th Marines in 1966. He would remain in command of the 1st Marine Division until its redeployment in April 1971.

All these command changes had little impact on the Marine grunt humping the rice paddies and mountains surrounding Da Nang. His view of the war was limited to the terrain around him. All he knew was the tedious routine of daily patrols and ambushes that more often than not produced zero results.

Its mission of protecting Da Nang gave the 1st Marine Division a TAOR of more than thirteen hundred square kilometers of territory. Though tasked with defending the Da Nang Vital Area, the division was not responsible for the defense of the city itself. The division's TAOR began just outside the Da Nang Vital Area with the newly created Northern and Southern Sector Defense Commands (NSDC and SSDC).

With the redeployment of the 26th Marines, the 1st Marines shifted north to assume responsibility for the area from the Hai Van Pass south to just north of Hill 55. The 5th Marines' TAOR was the region around the An Hoa Combat Base and the land paralleling the Song Thu Bon. The 7th Marines' TAOR stretched from the coastal plains south of Hoi An westward into the still-hostile Que Son Valley.

To deal with the wide variety of responsibilities it held, the division headquarters' staff divided combat operations into three categories. Category I operations were focused on populated areas where the NVA and VC had direct contact with the population. These were primarily cordon and search activities where villages were sealed off and any VC were hunted down and killed or captured. Included in this category were all CAP programs.

Category II operations covered small-unit patrols and night ambushes usually conducted in the vicinity of hamlets and villages. The goal of these operations was to interdict bands of marauding NVA and VC preying on the South Vietnamese citizens. The vast majority of Marine Corps operations in 1970–71 fell into this category.

Category III was reserved for multicompany, and the increasingly rare multibattalion, operations conducted away from population centers. These operations would be aimed against enemy main force units and their base camp areas. Only a few Category III operations were conducted during the Marines' final months in the war zone.

A major concern of the 1st Marine Division continued to be the Da Nang Anti-Infiltration System (DAIS), the physical barrier similar to the McNamara Line south of the DMZ. The barrier's effectiveness in notifying the responsible unit of any marauding NVA/VC had never been good. By early 1970, it had gotten even worse. False signals were sent more often than real ones, and the real signals were usually South Vietnamese peasants or their livestock crossing the barrier. Though most Marines regarded the DAIS as an expensive waste of the taxpayer's dollar, they still had to respond to reports of enemy sightings.

One tactic developed to respond rapidly was the Kingfisher patrols. Lieutenant Purdy's Kingfisher patrol on 6 January and several others were reasonably successful. But the enemy soon grew wise to the new tactic. They altered their movement to ensure that they were under cover by first light. As a result, the effectiveness of the Kingfisher patrols rapidly diminished, and by mid-March they were rarely used.

Although the 1st Marines launched no named operations in the first half of 1970, it did conduct an occasional Category III operation. Typical of these was the one conducted by 1/1 from 15–27 April in the Charlie Ridge region. Although the area had been left essentially untouched since Operation Oklahoma Hills in early 1969, the NVA had returned to the area, honeycombing the mountains with headquarters, supply caches, and base camps. Though concealed by the jungle, these areas were also well protected by mutually supporting bunkers, tunnels, and caves.

In fact, the enemy had sown the area so thickly with camps that they could easily move to another one if an occupied camp was threatened. One defector told his interrogators, "The people in the base camp do not worry about allied operations. Forewarning of an attack is obvious when [the allies] conduct air strikes, artillery fire, and when helicopters fly in the area. When an operation takes place in the vicinity of the base camp, the people simply go farther back into the mountains and return when the operation is over."

The operation began on 14 April when Company C, 1/1, humped into the Charlie Ridge area along a well-used VC trail. Two days later FSB Crawford was set up on Hill 502, about twenty kilometers southwest of Da Nang and south of Company C's route of march. On 17 April, three opconned rifle companies (A and B, 1/5, and Company L, 3/5) helicoptered into three separate LZs west and south of the fire base. Once on the ground the riflemen began a thorough search of their assigned areas.

As the defector had predicted, the NVA chose not to fight over the area. Instead, they simply melted away. Only an occasional sniper round broke the silence of the jungle. A few enemy mortar rounds fell on Company B's perimeter on the night of 18 April. A probe of Company A's lines four nights later was quickly ended with a few well-tossed hand grenades.

Though actual enemy contact was rare, signs of the enemy's presence were everywhere. Almost immediately upon jumping from their Sea Knights, the ground troops started uncovering bunkers, huts, tunnels, caves, and small auxiliary base camps. On 24 April, the point man for Company B spotted a commo wire partially buried in the jungle floor. The company followed it and soon came into a large enemy base camp. Their entrance into the camp was immediately followed by the sharp crack of AK-47s. With enemy rifle rounds whizzing past them, the Marines assaulted the estimated platoon-sized force. Dashing forward among the trees, they quickly forced the withdrawal of the enemy rear guard. The company lost one man in the attack, but two NVA were killed, including one who proved to be the executive officer of the 102d Battalion, 31st NVA Regiment.

The company set about searching the camp but soon were called off. The CO was told that the enemy base camp actually lay in the AO of the neighboring 51st ARVN Regiment, who were not partici-pating in this operation. Rather than let the Marines have any credit for their success, the local ARVN commander was angrily insisting they depart.

The base camp discovery proved to be the only major find of the operation. After a few more days of scouring their AOs, the rifle com-panies were pulled out. They claimed thirteen enemy killed against two dead and five wounded of their own, plus ten base camp sites uncovered and nearly one hundred weapons captured.

The TAOR of the 5th Marines began just south of Charlie Ridge. It included the formidable Arizona Territory, the An Hoa Basin, the Liberty Road and Liberty Bridge, and the Go Noi Island–Dodge City AO.

Though Go Noi Island had been scoured by the 1st Marines and Republic of Korea Marines in 1969, VC guerrillas maintained a strong presence in the region. The rifle companies of 2/5 constantly conducted recon patrols of Go Noi Island searching for bands of the enemy. On the night of 11 March, the enemy found the Marines. Staff Sergeant Allan Jay Kellogg was leading a small patrol from Com-pany G through heavy foliage along a stream bank when the patrol was ambushed. Unleashing an intense fusillade of small arms fire, the NVA pinned down the small force. In the darkness, an enemy soldier crept up close enough to flip a grenade into their midst. It glanced off Kellogg's chest while he was tending to a casualty. Rather than duck for cover, the noncommissioned officer dropped on the lethal missile and absorbed its violent blast with his own body. Miraculously, Kellogg survived the explosion, although he was badly wounded. Ignoring the intense pain from his massive injuries, he continued in command of his patrol and extracted it from the ambush. After recovering from his wounds, Kellogg was awarded a well-deserved Medal of Honor.

Although the enemy seldom initiated offensive actions during this period, they did occur. On 8 May, Company G, 2/5, was guarding the vital Liberty Bridge. Early that night, the enemy struck with 60mm and 80mm mortar shells and B40 rockets. While the Marines hunkered down in their reinforced bunkers, an enemy infantry company crept close to the perimeter and under the protection of the exploding missiles, penetrated it. The grunts responded bravely. Ignoring the falling shells erupting around them, they went after the enemy soldiers. Soon the VC were pulling back. Calling in pre-registered artillery fire, the company finally broke up the attack, suffering twenty-one wounded in the process. At dawn, battalion headquarters launched a quick reaction force to search for the attackers. A platoon from Company E soon found them headed south for the Que Son Mountains. The heliborne Marines landed in front of the enemy, blocking their escape route. In the ensuing firefight, ten enemy soldiers died before the rest broke into small bands and fled the area.

In August 1969, the 7th Marines had assumed responsibility from the Americal Division for the northern half of the much-fought-over Que Son Valley. The regiment permanently garrisoned only three bases in its TAOR: LZ Baldy, FSB Ross, and FSB Ryder, located on a hilltop in the Que Son Mountains overlooking the valley. The 7th Marines' three battalions rotated between the three areas so as to block enemy infiltration routes into the Que Son Valley.

In early January, the Americal Division, operating to the south of the 7th Marines, passed along information that the 409th VC Local Force Battalion had moved north from their usual area in Quang Tin Province. United States Army intelligence felt that the enemy might be targeting FSB Ross.

In anticipation of such an event, 1st Battalion, 7th Marines commander Lt. Col. Charles G. Cooper pulled two platoons of 1st Lt. Louis R. Ambort's Company B in from the field to the fire support base on 5 January. At first light the next morning, they'd patrol to the south trying to intercept the enemy. Besides artillerymen and support troops, Company A was also at FSB Ross that day. They were not normally stationed there either but were transitioning on their way to civilian pacification duty.

As night fell, heavy monsoon clouds rolled in from the nearby mountains. By dark, a major storm was dumping sheets of rain across the valley, cutting visibility to less than three meters. The crafty NVA used the downpour to sneak up to the perimeter wire. Working carefully, the estimated six, five-man sapper teams cut through the barbed wire strands without alerting the perimeter guards. Wearing only shorts and head bandanas, but heavily laden with high explosives, the sappers spread out across the base.

At 0130 on 6 January, several NVA mortar rounds suddenly fell on the base. The explosions not only roused the Marines but confused the sappers, who did not know of the mortar attack. With their own shells killing and wounding them, the enemy infiltrators still attacked. They hurled explosives into bunkers, huts, offices, and vehicles. Several sleeping Marines were killed in their bunks without knowing what had hit them. Others scrambled around in the darkness, frantically searching for helmets, flak jackets, and weapons. Once equipped, they splashed through the mud to reach their fighting bunkers. Some bumped right into the sappers and were cut down. Others made it to their positions and started firing on the enemy troops outside the wire who were supporting the sappers.

In the driving rain and confusion, five enemy sappers made it all the way to the battalion headquarters area. The attackers put the mortar batteries' counterfire radar system out of action with a well-placed grenade. They also blew up Company A's headquarters with a satchel charge just seconds after the company commander and his chief clerk fled the building.

Quickly overcoming the initial confusion, the Marines rallied. After hunting down the infiltrators, the defenders sealed off the breached perimeter. Supporting artillery and mortar fire threw a wall of hot shrapnel around the base.

By 0330 the fight was over. Medevac helicopters were called in to evacuate the casualties. In all, the Marines lost thirteen killed and sixty-three wounded. A dawn sweep of the base's outer defenses by Company B turned up thirty-eight enemy dead, three prisoners, and a large quantity of rifles, ammo, and explosives.

That same day, Ross's permanent residents began strengthening the base's defensive positions. More concertina wire was strung, deeper bunkers were dug, more movement sensors were emplaced, and a forty-foot tower mounting a 106mm recoilless rifle and a night vision device was built. One artilleryman summed up the new attitude: "No matter where you are and no matter how secure you may feel, you have to retain the capability of fighting hand to hand. . . ."

Less than six weeks later, Company B again became embroiled with the NVA. At 0930 on 12 February, the company's 2d Platoon was moving east along the south bank of the Ly Ly River about seven kilometers southeast of FSB Ross. Without warning an enemy machine gun fired on the column from its front. No one was hit, but before the platoon could react, another enemy machine gun off to their right, or south, opened up. The platoon leader sent a squad to handle this new threat while the rest of the platoon went after the first weapon. As the squad broke through the heavy brush along the river and entered a small rice paddy bordered by tree lines, the NVA cut loose with a heavy volume of small arms fire. Immediately, two Marines fell dead; a third lay badly wounded. The two survivors were pinned down, unable to reach the wounded man or pull back. A relief squad from the platoon was hit as soon as it reached the paddy. Now the platoon leader turned the remainder of his men south to attack the enemy emplaced in the tree line.

The platoon had fallen victim to a well-executed NVA trap. Squeezed between the river on one side and the NVA on two more, and with casualties lying exposed as bait, the 2d Platoon could not do much. Lieutenant Ambort tried to maneuver his other platoons around the western edge of the paddy, but every time one of his Marines moved, the well-placed enemy fired on him.

Lieutenant Colonel Cooper brought in reinforcements. Company C landed by helicopter on the north bank of the Ly Ly west of the battlefield and pushed east. Two companies of the American Division's 3/21 attacked from the southeast and east. At the same time, Marine artillery began falling on the enemy-held tree lines. Under this cover, the 2d Platoon was finally able to gather up its casualties and retreat about three hundred meters west. From this position medevac helicopters carried out the dead and wounded at about 1300.

By now, Company C had started its attack. Under this pressure the NVA pulled out, leaving behind four dead. Company C killed two more in the subsequent chase but lost four of their own before night-fall at last ended the fight. Company B had nine dead and eight wounded, making it a bad day for the battalion. (One week later, members of Company B participated in one of the few cases of atrocity visited upon South Vietnamese civilians by U.S. Marines. On the night of 19 February, Lieutenant Ambort exhorted a five-man "killer team" to "get some damned gooks tonight" on their ambush patrol. Entering the nearby hamlet of Son Thang (4) later that evening, the patrol murdered five women and eleven children. Subsequently, Ambort was removed from command for his role in the incident and given nonjudicial punishment. Four of the enlisted men were eventually tried by courts-martial; two were convicted and sentenced to jail and the other two were acquitted.)

After this fight, actual contact with the enemy decreased significantly. However, mortar and rocket attacks on FSB Ross and the nearby district capital of Que Son increased throughout the spring. Enemy sappers avoided a second attack on FSB Ross, instead focusing on Que Son. One particularly strong attack came on 6 May. Supported by a diversionary mortar attack on FSB Ross, VC ground forces hit Que Son. The local Regional Forces managed to hold the enemy at bay, but only the arrival of a quick reaction force of Marines from FSB Ross finally turned the tide. The defenders claimed twenty-seven enemy dead, but five Marines were wounded along with fourteen Regional Forces' soldiers and seventy-four civilians.

To keep the enemy off balance in the Que Son Mountains, the 7th Marines had a battalion actively scouring the rugged terrain. During late May and early June, this assignment belonged to 3/7. On their patrols the grunts found several unoccupied base camps and small caches of weapons, but enemy resistance was limited to booby traps—until the rifle companies started moving south out of the mountains into the valley.

On 12 June, the 1st Platoon of Company I took sniper and automatic weapons fire as it moved down a ravine toward the valley floor northwest of FSB Ross; three Marines were wounded and evacuated. A short time later, a heavy volume of automatic weapons and RPG fire suddenly tore into the platoon from three sides. Accurate return fire and a barrage of supporting artillery rounds sent the enemy fleeing. Fortunately, no Marines were hit in this exchange. The platoon then wisely altered its route of march to one that was less objectionable to the local VC.

That same evening Company I's 2d Platoon set up its night defensive position in the thick underbrush on the valley floor. All was quiet until, suddenly, three NVA casually strolled into the platoon's camp. Instantly realizing their mistake, the enemy soldiers turned and fled before the equally surprised Marines could bring their M16s to bear. Starting out in pursuit, the platoon discovered that it had inadvertently set up its NDP just fifty meters from a comparable NVA position. The thick foliage had prevented either side from knowing the other was there. Scattered return fire met the Marines as they chased the enemy, but the NVA were soon swallowed up by the dense underbrush and the coming of darkness.

The next day, all of 3/7 assembled in the Que Son Valley and headed for LZ Baldy. Though just nine enemy soldiers were killed during this operation, regimental headquarters considered it a success because it kept the enemy off balance in this oft-contested region.

The 7th Marines accounted for more than half the division's enemy contacts during the first half of 1970. By body count the regiment claimed 1,160 enemy dead and took nearly 50 prisoners. More than 800 Marines were wounded in the Que Son Valley and 120 were killed.

The CAP program initiated by III MAF in 1965 continued to be a viable pacification effort in denying the enemy access to local villagers. Typically, a fifteen-man, specially selected Marine platoon operated with a comparably sized Popular Forces platoon based in a specific village. As the Marines worked with the PFs and gained the confidence of the villagers, their effectiveness improved tremendously. As a result, the CAPs started winning fights against local guerrilla units and small VC main-force units. They helped establish local political control over the villages and kept the VC tax collectors from harassing the peasants.

By 1970, the strength of CAP had reached 42 Marine officers and 2,050 enlisted Marines, plus 126 navy corpsmen. Administratively, the CAPs were controlled by four combined-action groups (CAGs), each one responsible for the individual platoons within a specific province.

Most of the CAPs' success was based on their aggressive patrolling. In a typical month more than 1,000 patrols were conducted by the CAPs; nearly three fourths of these were night patrols. In the first six months of 1970, the CAPs claimed nearly 500 enemy killed and more than 80 prisoners. Marine losses were 22 killed and 165 wounded.

One measure of the effectiveness of the CAPs was the number of attacks launched by the enemy on the villages they garrisoned. The better the job the Marines did, the more likely they were to be hit. One such ground attack was directed against Combined-Action Platoon 1-2-3 in Quang Ngai Province in the dark, early morning hours of 8 May. A vastly superior enemy force struck the platoon, wounding LCpl. Miguel Keith in the opening minutes. Disregarding his injuries, the nineteen year old moved to the PFs' firing positions to help calm them and direct their fire. When Keith spotted five enemy soldiers sneaking up on the platoon's CP, he charged them, killing three and wounding the other two. Knocked down by a grenade explosion and again wounded, Keith nonetheless continued fighting. Later, he saw a group of twenty-five enemy soldiers preparing to charge the compound. Though weak from loss of blood, he attacked them, killing at least four and driving off the others. Keith was mortally wounded in his valiant assault, but he had almost single-handedly thwarted the enemy. He became the last Marine to earn a Medal of Honor in South Vietnam.

When redeployment of U.S. forces began in 1969, III MAF concluded that the Combined Action Force (CAF) should be reduced at a proportional rate. Consequently, III MAF decided to deactivate three CAGs in 1970. Only 2d CAG, operating in Quang Nam Province, would remain until the final pullout of American troops.

Reduction of the CAF began in April 1970 with the deactivation of individual platoons in 1st CAG in Quang Tin Province. The deactivation of additional platoons continued at a steady rate until July, when, due to the lack of replacements in the manpower pipeline, the process accelerated. By the end of July, 4th CAG was gone; 1st and 3d CAGs were deactivated by mid-September. The remaining 2d CAG reduced its personnel, too. By the end of September, the unit numbered about 650 Marines and 50 navy corpsmen working in Quang Nam Province with about 900 PFs.

To help take up the slack and continue to maintain a presence at the village level, III MAF authorized the Combined Unit Pacification Program (CUPP). Under the program, ordinary rifle companies were periodically broken down into squads, which were then paired with a PF platoon. The two major differences with the CAP program were that CUPP units were not specially trained for their role, and the companies remained under the operational control of their parent regiments. The CUPP squads could thus be pulled from their pacification assignment at any time and returned to their company.

Although never as effective as CAP units, the CUPP platoons proved to Marine commanders that regular rifle squads, paired with Popular Forces, could perform similar missions. By the end of 1970, though, continued redeployment had made the future of CUPP uncertain.

On 1 May 1970, U.S. Army and ARVN forces made a surprise invasion of Cambodia. Long used as a sanctuary by NVA and VC units operating near Saigon, Cambodia had been secure from overt allied military cross-border operations due to political concerns regarding its ruler, Prince Norodom Sihanouk. Then, in early 1970, political upheaval in Cambodia presented the allies with an opportunity to strike the sanctuaries. Though the invasion was limited in scope and duration, the allied effort did throw the enemy off balance. And the capture of several huge supply caches denied the NVA the logistical support necessary to launch a planned offensive against Saigon.

Marine forces had only a limited, mostly liaison role in the Cambodian incursion. However, III MAF intelligence officers paid close attention to battlefield reports in order to determine what effect the invasion may have on their operations around Da Nang.

Following the withdrawal of U.S. forces from Cambodia, MACV issued orders on 10 June for an aggressive summer campaign in order to exploit the successes of the invasion. The orders directed allied regular forces to attack enemy base camps and main-force units. Among the more aggressive of these efforts would be the 1st Marine Division's Operation Pickens Forest, the division's first named operation of the year. Aimed at the NVA Base Areas 112 and 127 in the mountains of western Quang Nam Province, this campaign would be the responsibility of the 7th Marines. According to intelligence reports, these base areas held headquarters and communication centers, as well as rest and training areas for NVA and VC troops.

As planned by Col. Edmund G. Durning, Jr., and his 7th Marine regimental staff, Operation Pickens Forest would be centered on three fire support bases: Defiant, Darter, and Mace. Fire Support Base Defiant would occupy a hilltop just west of the Song Thu Bon, about fifteen kilometers southwest of An Hoa; Mace would be established about five kilometers northwest of Defiant, and Darter about eight kilometers southwest of Defiant. The latter two fire support bases had been used previously by both U.S. Army and Marine forces and could easily be reopened. As they had on similar operations, rifle companies would occupy the fire support bases, securing them and the surrounding area. Once these positions were established, other rifle companies would helicopter into outlying LZs, then sweep toward the fire support bases, driving any enemy into the blocking Marines.

D day for Operation Pickens Forest began at 0800 on 16 July, when CH-46Ds and CH-53s loaded with men and materiel descended on their fire support bases. Company C, 1/5 (opconned to the 7th Marines), helicoptered into FSB Defiant. Ninety minutes later the 1st Battalion, 7th Marines command group, Companies C and D, and supporting mortars landed at FSB Mace. Not long afterward, the 2d Battalion command group came into FSB Dart. Individual rifle companies were then helicoptered into various LZs in the surrounding areas to begin their sweeps. None of the landings was opposed. By 1600 the entire attack force was in position. Colonel Durning called it "a beautiful example of air-ground teamwork."

For the first two weeks of the operation, the enemy avoided sustained contact. Any fighting was usually against small stay-behind groups of NVA protecting the main force as they abandoned their base camps. This lack of enemy contact resulted in the early reduction of Operation Pickens Forest forces. On 26 July, the 1/7 command group and Company B returned to LZ Baldy. Two days later, Company C, 1/5, returned to its parent regiment. The 2d Battalion, 7th Marines would continue the operation.

The heaviest action of the operation came on 30 July. That day Company E was patrolling both sides of the Thu Bon River. Where the river flowed into a narrow, seven-hundred-meter-deep gorge, two squads of Marines aboard rubber boats looked for enemy-occupied caves in the sheer rock walls. They were like sitting ducks.

As the Marines on the top of the cliffs watched in horror, a force of about fifty enemy soldiers hidden in deep caves opened fire. Within seconds the boats were riddled with bullets. Two Marines were dead and four were wounded. The rest of Company E returned fire as the swift water swept the floundering Marines downriver. Though air support was called in to napalm the enemy, the gorge was too narrow for the planes to be accurate.

That evening, Company C, 1/5, returned to Operation Pickens Forest. The Marines were dropped by CH-46D helicopters in a clearing south and west of the site of Company E's fight, in the hope that they could catch the fleeing enemy. Though they did kill one VC sniper and detain a number of suspects, members of Company C could not find the main body of enemy troops. They returned to 5th Marine control on 1 August.

After another week of patrolling the Thu Bon Valley with minimal results, the focus of 2/7 shifted farther west. Beginning on 9 August, the battalion commander, Lt. Col. Vincent A. Albers, Jr., began shifting his companies twenty-five kilometers west to FSB Hatcher. In conjunction with an ARVN operation in the same area, Albers's rifle companies patrolled but found few signs of the enemy. The strongest contact came on 20 August when a platoon from Company H was ambushed about three kilometers northwest of the fire support base.

First Lieutenant Craig A. Edwards quickly led the rest of his company into the firefight to help the beleaguered platoon. As soon as he arrived, he pushed forward to the scene of the ambush. Four men, including the platoon leader, lay wounded just meters away from one enemy machine-gun nest. Intent only on saving the casualties, Edwards disregarded the stream of enemy bullets passing within inches of his body to charge headlong at the enemy emplacement. He threw grenades into the position, wrecking the gun and killing the crew. As he returned to the casualties, another machine gun raked the area with streams of hot lead.

As he lay there Edwards saw an enemy grenade plop down near the wounded. He kicked it away, then rolled between it and the casualties as it exploded. A large hunk of shrapnel tore a deep furrow in his leg. Ignoring the pain, the young officer used a machete to cut a path through the underbrush to a nearby riverbank. Then, accompanied by a corpsman, Edwards low-crawled back to the casualties. With enemy bullets plowing up the ground all around him, the gutsy lieutenant and corpsman pulled one casualty back to the safety of the defiladed riverbank. They then returned for another man.

By this time another Company H platoon had flanked the enemy position. The riflemen poured a heavy volume of M16 and M60 fire at the enemy, finally killing them. Edwards then directed the rescue of the other two men. Once they were safely aboard the medevac helicopter, Edwards finally consented to his own evacuation. The lieutenant's devotion to his comrades earned him a Navy Cross.

Reinforced by Companies F and G, Company H pursued the enemy. The Marines never were able to reestablish contact with them. They did find three enemy dead, however. Company H suffered one dead and nine wounded in the five-hour fight.

Four days later Albers's CP and his four companies returned to LZ Baldy, and Operation Pickens Forest came to an end. Ninety-nine enemy soldiers were killed during the operation; four Marines died and fifty-one were wounded. Though the operation achieved no spectacular results, the Marines' efforts did disrupt enemy activities in the area and destroy several supply caches.

As the year progressed, the 7th Marines continued its operations in the Que Son Valley while its sister regiments, the 1st and 5th, maintained their high level of small-unit operations in defense of Da Nang. The 1st Marines defended the Rocket Belt and the 5th Marines operated around An Hoa.

One thorn in the side of the 1st Marines disappeared in the summer of 1970. Because the Da Nang Anti-Infiltration System had never worked as envisioned and was proving impossible to maintain, 1st Marine Division headquarters requested permission from III MAF to abandon the system. On 3 May, III MAF approved the request. Between late July and 15 August the system was dismantled.

Now, to block infiltration of the Rocket Belt, the 1st Marines instituted a program of constant squad-sized patrols, running both day and night. Even so, contact with the enemy was limited to brief exchanges of small arms fire and grenades with small bands of NVA or VC.

To determine if the enemy was massing for an attack on Da Nang, the regiment launched Operation Dubois Square, on 9 September, in the mountains northwest of Da Nang. After ten days of methodically searching the steep, jungle-covered slopes and boulder-strewn ravines, the regiment's only significant campaign of the summer ended without the Marines having made any contact with the enemy.

The 5th Marines spent most of July and August moving its headquarters and support units from An Hoa to Camp Reasoner on Division Ridge outside Da Nang as part of the continuing Vietnamization program. The regiment's 2d Battalion would continue operations around An Hoa until ARVN forces took over the AO in the fall. The 3d Battalion, 5th Marines concentrated its efforts in the northern Arizona Territory and on Charlie Ridge; 1/5 served as the division's reserve.

A typical operation for the field battalions during this period consisted of several companies conducting cordon and search efforts against specific hamlets suspected of harboring enemy soldiers. If contact was made, it usually consisted of a brief flurry of gunfire as small groups of VC were flushed from hiding places in and around the village. In all of August, the 5th Marines killed twenty-nine enemy soldiers while losing six dead and sixty wounded.

Though scheduled to redeploy in the early fall of 1970, the 7th Marines kept the pressure on the enemy within its TAOR. As was true throughout the Marines' TAOR, enemy contact was infrequent. However, in late August intelligence reports indicated that the Viet Cong Front 4 Headquarters had taken up residence in the eastern

Que Son Mountains. In response, regimental commander Col. Robert H. Piehl planned to begin Operation Imperial Lake in this area with an intense aerial and artillery bombardment. Four rifle companies would then be helicoptered into twelve landing zones, establishing a tight cordon around the area suspected of harboring the enemy.

The bombardment began at midnight on 31 August. For six hours, ten batteries of 3/11 Marines pounded fifty-three target sites with more than fourteen thousand shells in what was one of the largest artillery barrages of the entire Vietnam War. When the artillery fire ceased, two solid hours of air strikes followed. More than sixty-three tons of aerial ordnance fell on suspected enemy camps in the Que Sons. The effectiveness of the massive bombardment was questionable. Colonel Piehl later said that "one or two enemy bodies. . . ." were found in the target areas.

Nonetheless, at 0900 that day, CH-46 and CH-53 helicopters laden with well-equipped 2d Battalion CP Marines and two platoons of 4.2-inch mortar men of Battery W, 3/11, began touching down at LZ Vulture on Hill 845, one of the highest peaks in the central Que Son Mountains. By noon, all four rifle companies of 2/7 had landed at their LZs ringing LZ Vulture. Over the next four days, the grunts scoured the rugged terrain without finding any enemy.

Finally, on 5 September, Company E encountered a platoon of NVA in a jungle-covered ravine southwest of LZ Vulture. Unable to move deeper into the ravine due to the heavy volume of fire coming from enemy soldiers concealed in caves and behind boulders, Company E was joined by the other three companies that night. Over the next four days, the Marines fought the encircled NVA. The steep terrain, numerous boulders, thick foliage, and many caves favored the enemy's elusive tactics. Though the riflemen tried several times to advance along the bottom of the ravine or down its sides, they were turned back each time by strong small arms and automatic weapons fire.

By 9 September, the Marines had suffered three killed and a dozen wounded. Realizing that his infantry could not dislodge the NVA, Lieutenant Colonel Albers pulled back his rifle companies and called for Marine jets. Nine sorties dropped forty tons of high explosives on the enemy. The next day, the Marines reentered the ravine. This time only sporadic sniper fire greeted them. The companies spent the next week searching for any surviving NVA, killing more than a dozen stragglers.

While 2/7 was fighting near LZ Vulture, 3/7 and units of the U.S. Army's Americal Division conducted Operation Nebraska Rapids to reopen Route 534 between LZ Baldy and Hiep Duc. The infantry units patrolled along the road while Marine engineers searched for mines and repaired the roadbed. The clearing operation lasted for five days, then an ARVN truck convoy made an uneventful trip along the road on 9 September.

On 13 September, 3/7 helicoptered into the Que Son Mountains to join Operation Imperial Lake. The Marines worked south of the 2d Battalion, conducting daytime patrols and night ambushes. Though they had little luck in finding the enemy, Lieutenant Colonel Albers's 2d Battalion did somewhat better. On 16 September, lead by a VC defector, his Company F uncovered a large underground complex consisting of more than the usual caves. Extending more than seventy feet into the ground, this complex included a large kitchen and a hospital complete with an operating room. What made the find even more unusual was the fact that the complex was on the lower slopes of Hill 845, right below LZ Vulture and Albers's CP.

The 7th Marines began departing the Imperial Lake operational area on 18 September in preparation for its redeployment under Operation Keystone Robin Alpha. Accordingly, the 5th Marines shifted its positions to the south to take over from the 7th Marines' AO. At the same time, the 1st Marines sent some of its forces southwest to fill in behind the departing 5th Marines' units. The threat of an enemy attack during this vulnerable period was reduced by taking positive countermeasures. To keep the enemy off balance, Operation Catawba Falls was designed to pound suspected enemy assembly areas with artillery fire. Rifle companies would further unbalance any enemy units by feigning heliborne assaults into their suspected assembly areas.

Operation Catawba Falls began at 0300 on 18 September. Over the next four days, the artillerymen of 2/11 poured more than

11,500 rounds of high explosives into enemy territory. Behind these protective measures, the various units conducted their relocation moves. By 30 September, the realignment was complete. The 5th Marines' 3d Battalion set up at FSB Ross, with its companies deployed in the Que Son Valley; the 2d Battalion operated out of LZ Baldy in the eastern portion of the regiment's new TAOR; the 1st Battalion was assigned duty as the division reserve at Da Nang.

The 7th Marines' redeployment to Camp Pendleton began on 23 September. The official departure ceremony was held at division headquarters on 1 October. By 15 October 1970, III MAF strength stood at 24,527.

Orders issued by MACV, on 21 September, instructed all U.S. forces to concentrate their efforts on small-unit activity designed to protect pacified areas. The 1st Marines focused its patrols on the Rocket Belt around Da Nang and conducted occasional company-sized search and destroy operations on Charlie Ridge. The 5th Marines continued Operation Imperial Lake while protecting, as best it could, the numerous hamlets around LZ Baldy and in the Que Son Valley.

Enemy activity had been infrequent throughout 1970, but it declined even more as the year neared its end. The number of enemy-initiated contacts, ranging from ground probes of night defensive positions to occasional sniper fire, dropped in half from September to November. A large portion of that reduction resulted from unusually heavy monsoon rains and the resultant flooding in Quang Nam Province. Four major typhoons hit the area in October alone, bringing seventeen inches of rain in just one eight-day period. Flash floods inundated the entire area from just south of Da Nang all the way to LZ Baldy and inland to the foothills of the Que Son Mountains. The rapidly rising waters forced the emergency evacuation of several CAP teams and Marine patrols. More than two hundred people, mostly helpless civilians, drowned in the floodwaters.

In early November, as the floodwaters began to recede, Marine infantry units moved back into the bush to hunt for the enemy. The floods had destroyed many of the enemy's usual hiding places, forcing them into the open. Marine patrols, aloft in helicopters, pounced on them as fast as they could. Because numerous VC supply caches had been lost in the floods, enemy supplies were piling up in the Que Son Mountains. Marine patrols working this region as part of the ongoing Operation Imperial Lake uncovered a large number of these supply locations, further hurting the enemy.

The 5th Marines maintained at least one company in the Que Son Mountains as part of the ongoing Operation Imperial Lake. Even as tropical storms pounded the region, the Marines worked the mountains. On 26 October, a patrol from Company H, 2/5, uncovered a deserted base camp. A three-day search of the camp uncovered a substantial quantity of foodstuffs and ammo. In early November, a squad from Company B, 1/5, made a major discovery. A large quantity of documents it found in an abandoned base camp proved to be the master files for the Viet Cong organization for all of Quang Nam Province. The papers included the names of all underground leaders and agents. The information was turned over to the ARVN for processing.

Another major discovery came on Christmas Eve when Company L, 3/5, stumbled upon a large NVA command post. That afternoon a squad from Company L spotted a group of nine NVA, eight men and one woman, sitting in front of a cave. The Marines killed four of the enemy in a flurry of rifle fire, but the others escaped. After searching the area, the patrol realized that it had uncovered an important cave network. Elements of two other companies arrived the next day to help explore the six-cave complex. Besides the normal supplies, the Marines also found a variety of communications equipment. Based on their finds, the Marines felt confident that they had at last uncovered the forward CP of the elusive Viet Cong Front 4 Headquarters.

The last few months of 1970 saw the 1st Marines, now commanded by Col. Paul X. "PX" Kelley, continuing its efforts to protect Da Nang. Constant day and night patrols kept the enemy off balance in their continued attempts to hit Da Nang with rockets and mortars. Contact with enemy forces was limited to brief exchanges of a few rounds of rifle fire with small bands of NVA or VC.

On Christmas Eve, Lt. Gen. Donn J. Robertson took command of III MAF. General McCutcheon had been ill with a spreading cancer for several months. His condition finally reached the point where he could no longer remain in command. General Robertson, who had commanded the 1st Marine Division in the same area from June 1967 to June 1968, was rushed to South Vietnam from his post at U.S. Marine Headquarters to replace McCutcheon.

On 1 January 1971, the role of U.S. forces in South Vietnam changed significantly. On that date all allied units ceased to have tactical areas of responsibility. From then on they would have tactical areas of interest (TAOIs); only ARVN commands could have TAORs. In effect, though, the allied units continued operating in their TAOIs just as they had in their TAORs. The main reason for the change was to lend definition to the primacy of South Vietnam's responsibility for conducting the war. The two Marine regiments remaining in-country continued defending and patrolling in Quang Nam Province as if nothing had changed.

Evidence mounted during the final two months of 1970 that the North Vietnamese Army was preparing for a major offensive in Quang Tri Province. Intelligence sources reported a major increase in the movement of men and vehicles down the Ho Chi Minh Trail. Pilots flying bombing missions reported increased antiaircraft fire. Prisoners and defectors revealed plans for an invasion sometime before the summer of 1971. As a result, MACV revived an old contingency plan for an invasion of Laos. General Abrams's proposal to Washington claimed that the invasion would not only threaten the NVA's plans but would also disrupt the enemy's logistical system while the redeployment of U.S. forces continued. Washington approved the operation.

The III MAF had no role in the planning of Operation Lam Son 719, as the Laotian invasion was named. Indeed, it first learned of the operation only a few days before it was scheduled to begin on 8 February 1971. Marine participation in the invasion would be limited to air support, transportation units, and increased patrols in their TAOIs.

The invasion of Laos started as planned. As the first major test of South Vietnam's ability to conduct an offensive operation on its own, the campaign was closely watched by MACV. Numerous deficiencies among the ARVN units were immediately apparent, with some units literally falling apart under the slightest pressure from the NVA.

Despite the problems, the offensive was proclaimed a success because it did temporarily disrupt the flow of supplies into South Vietnam.

Lam Son 719 had no effect on plans for redeploying the remaining U.S. Marine units. According to MACV's plans, the next redeployment phase, Operation Keystone Robin Charlie, would remove 12,400 Marines from South Vietnam, including the 5th Marines. Until the redeployment actually began, the 5th Marines continued to sweep the Que Son Mountains in the ongoing Operation Imperial Lake. The regiment's responsibilities also included protection of LZ Baldy and FSB Ross.

The level of enemy activity continued to decline in the early weeks of 1971. Rarely did the Marines encounter the enemy in groups larger than six men. One time that they did was on 25 January. Four kilometers northeast of FSB Ross, a platoon from Company L, 3/5, heard voices and sounds of movement in the jungle nearby. The platoon leader dispatched a squad to investigate. They spotted a group of ten enemy soldiers walking toward them. Instantly reacting, the squad members poured M16 fire at the VC. In seconds it was over; nine of the enemy lay dead on the dirt trail, the tenth man having escaped. As the squad spread out to police the nearby area, a sudden burst of AK-47 fire drove them to the ground. The squad maneuvered toward the source of the firing but found nothing. When the Marines returned to the site of the original ambush, they discovered that five of the enemy bodies had been dragged away.

That would prove to be the last significant action for the 3d Battalion. By 15 February, the battalion had ended its combat operations. That same day it formally passed control of FSB Ross to the ARVN. Two weeks later the regiment withdrew its 2d Battalion and its headquarters from field operations. By the end of March, the two battalions and the headquarters element were on the way back to Camp Pendleton. The 1st Battalion was in the final stages of its redeployment and would depart in a matter of weeks.

As of April 1971, the 1st Marine Regiment was the only active infantry unit of the III MAF. As a result, all the regiment's line units were spread thin, covering large TAOIs. The 1st Battalion maintained its presence in the Rocket Belt, guarding against infiltrators, and also rotated its rifle companies in and out of the Que Son Mountains as part of Operation Imperial Lake. The efforts of the 2d Battalion were focused on the area south of Da Nang, where it continually searched for the enemy among the numerous hamlets and villages dotting the region. The 3d Battalion not only guarded the Hai Van Pass but also contributed a platoon for the protection of an artillery fire base in the Que Sons.

During the first few weeks of April, enemy contacts were extremely limited. Booby traps presented a far greater danger to the Marine patrols than enemy small arms fire. As the U.S. presence in South Vietnam rapidly decreased, the infantry units placed greater reliance on artillery support. Unless a Marine patrol had a clear advantage, it would not engage a superior enemy force. Instead, artillery fire would be called in on the enemy. No one wanted to be responsible for the last Marine casualties of the war.

On 7 April 1971, orders for its last major operation of the war were issued by III MAF. Information that U.S. prisoners of war were being held at an isolated camp in the mountainous terrain of western Quang Nam Province had been received by MACV. Though III MAF intelligence officers doubted the accuracy of the reports, they recognized that the plight of American POWs had become, and would remain, a hot political item. If there was any chance to rescue POWs from the grasp of their captors, the Marines wanted to be in on it.

Operation Scott Orchard began when two teams from the 1st Recon Battalion air-assaulted into the abandoned FSB Dagger in the Que Sons at 1045 on 7 April. After a brief firefight with a small enemy force, the fire support base was declared secured. At 1100 helicopters started bringing in the howitzers of the 1st Battalion, 11th Marines. The next day five, rifle companies, three from 2/1 and one each from the 1st and 3d Battalions, 1st Marines, all opconned to 2/1, were inserted into separate LZs around FSB Dagger. From 8 to 11 April, the companies thoroughly scoured the rugged country west of FSB Dagger. Though they uncovered several small abandoned enemy camps, they found no evidence of a POW camp. On 11 April, the infantry companies were withdrawn from the AO and returned to their primary TAOI. At midnight that same day, Operation Scott Orchard, the last search and destroy operation for the Marines, ended. The rifle companies had suffered no casualties. The operation claimed just four enemy dead, three of whom were felled by supporting artillery fire.

While Operation Scott Orchard was in full swing, elements of the U.S. Army's Americal Division began moving into the Que Son Mountains, replacing the departing Marine units. On 13 April, the 1st Marine Division formally turned over the area south of the Thu Bon River to the Americal Division. That same day, 1/1 ceased combat operations and began preparations for their redeployment under Operation Keystone Oriole Alpha. The men of 2/1 altered their positions to fill in the resulting gap.

The next day the III Marine Amphibious Force ended its six-year role in the war. General Robertson moved his command to Okinawa. At the same time he activated the 3d Marine Amphibious Brigade (MAB). Its commander was Maj. Gen. Alan J. Armstrong, an aviator who also commanded what remained of the 1st Marine Air Wing. All Marine units remaining in South Vietnam, consisting of about 15,500 officers and men, were assigned to the 3d MAB.

The two active infantry battalions of the 1st Marines continued saturation patrolling of their respective TAOIs. The 2d Battalion operated south of Da Nang; the 3d Battalion kept one company in regimental reserve and the other three in the fields north and northwest of Da Nang. Members of both battalions experienced few contacts with the enemy. Those that did occur were only brief exchanges of fire. It was obvious that neither the NVA nor the VC had any desire to stand and fight or in any way induce the allies to end their redeployment plans.

The last week of U.S. Marine Corps ground combat operations in South Vietnam began on 1 May 1971. That same day, 3/1 stood down and moved to Da Nang to prepare for its embarkation. The Americal Division's 196th Infantry Brigade extended its TAOI north to cover nearly all of Quang Nam Province.

The final week of ground combat operations was a quiet one for the Marines of the 2d Battalion, 1st Marines, the last operational infantry unit the Marine Corps fielded in South Vietnam. The battalion's rifle companies ran more than 100 small-unit patrols that last week. They experienced no enemy contact, encountered no booby traps, and took no casualties.

1970–71   311

At noon on 7 May 1971, Operation Imperial Lake ended. This final Marine operation had lasted eight months and involved elements of all three remaining Marine infantry regiments. In its final months the operation's scope had been expanded to cover nearly all Marine patrol and ambush activities outside their parent units' immediate vicinity. The operation claimed more than 300 enemy dead and more than 200 captured weapons. The operation cost 24 dead and 170 wounded Marines.

Also on 7 May, all units of the 3d MAB ceased combat operations. The 1st Battalion, 11th Marines fired the last Marine artillery round of the war. The regimental headquarters company and the 3d Battalion were on their way to the United States by 13 May. The 2d Battalion, 1st Marines turned over their TAOI to two companies of the 196th Infantry Brigade.

The Marines' long-standing commitment to civic action and pacification programs ended on 11 May. On that day the 2d CAG headquarters turned over its compound near Hoi An to the ARVN. In the preceding weeks all the remaining CAPs had been closed down.

On 19 May 1971, the commander of 2/1, Lt. Col. Roy E. Moss, his command group, and the battalion colors boarded planes bound for Camp Pendleton. The last 186 members of the battalion sailed from Da Nang aboard the USS *Denver* on 1 June.

With all of its combat and support units gone, the 3d MAB turned over its remaining facilities to either the U.S. Army or the ARVN. The 3d Marine Amphibious Brigade was formally deactivated on 27 June 1971. General Armstrong had departed for Hawaii with a dozen members of his staff the previous day. The balance of the brigade staff followed over the next few days.

The six-year U.S. Marine Corps involvement in the long, often frustrating, occasionally victorious war in South Vietnam was nearly at an end. With all Marine ground combat, aviation, and support units redeployed, the only Marines remaining in South Vietnam were the approximately 550 officers and men serving as embassy guards, on the MACV staff, or as advisers to the South Vietnamese Marine Corps.

Chapter Eight
1972–75

With the departure of the last ground combat units, the only U.S. Marines still fighting the NVA or VC were those serving as advisers to the South Vietnamese Marine Corps (VNMC). Since the original Geneva Convention cease-fire agreement went into effect in 1954, the United States had provided advisers to the South Vietnamese military. When the South Vietnamese Marine Corps was formed in late 1954, one U.S. Marine lieutenant colonel was assigned to assist the infant service. As the VNMC grew over the next fifteen years, so did the number of U.S. Marines assigned to the advisory staff.

By mid-1971, the VNMC was a division-sized force, boasting nine battalions organized into three brigades: Marine Brigades 147, 258, and 369. The Marine Advisory Unit assigned to the VNMC consisted of forty-one officers and ten enlisted men. The majority of the officers were in the field, advising the commanders of individual VNMC battalions. In the field, the U.S. Marine advisers lived the same life as their VNMC comrades. They slept in the same bunkers, ate the same food, and experienced the same horrors of combat as the South Vietnamese.

Though this close association did much to foster good relationships between individual advisers and their advisees, many senior VNMC officers felt that, overall, the U.S. Marine advisers were superfluous. By 1971 most of the VNMC officers had been at war for years, whereas many of the U.S. Marine officers assigned to adviser duty had, at best, one previous tour of combat duty. Because of the way the U.S. forces rotated its officers between combat and staff duties, this meant that the typical U.S. Marine officer had just six months or less of actual combat experience. Consequently, some U.S. Marine officers felt more like glorified fire support coordinators than true advisers. The situation had deteriorated to the point where Col. Joshua W. Dorsey III, the then-current senior adviser, was making plans to pull all his Marines from the battalion advisory level. Instead, he planned to consolidate his men at the brigade level, forming a liaison team that could be dispatched as needed to respond to various tactical situations.

Since the mid-1960s, the VNMC, along with the ARVN Airborne, had served as the Joint General Staff General Reserve of the Republic of Vietnam. As such, it could be, and had been, deployed to any area of South Vietnam to meet any contingency. Beginning in April 1971, two VNMC brigades moved north to Quang Tri Province. Initially, they served under the operational control of the 1st ARVN Division. Later, when the 3d ARVN Division was formed on 1 November 1971, the Vietnamese Marines transferred to its control.

Enemy contact was relatively light throughout the summer and fall of 1971. The U.S. Marine advisers serving during this period could do little to improve the combat efficiency of their allies. Instead, most of the advisers' time was spent training their counterparts in small unit tactics, the use of American weapons, and the coordination of air and artillery support.

In November 1971, responsibility for the defensive positions along the DMZ, as well as the rest of Quang Tri Province, was transferred from the veteran 1st ARVN Division to the rookie 3d ARVN Division. Most of the positions that the ARVN occupied were old American defensive positions oriented along the main avenues of approach from the west and the north. For example, the combat bases at Gio Linh, Con Thien, Cam Lo, and Dong Ha had once formed the infamous Leatherneck Square, which had witnessed so much heavy fighting in 1967 and 1968. Now the ARVN positions were simply known by their alphanumeric designations—Alpha 1 through 4 and Charlie 1 through 4.

As 1971 ended, signs of heightened enemy activity in northern Quang Tri Province increased. On the night of 12 December, the NVA attacked a Regional Forces outpost three kilometers east of Charlie 3, just north of Cam Lo. Though the enemy attack failed, its intensity made everyone nervous. During this time period, Marine advisers at Alpha 4 (Con Thien) reported seeing truck headlights moving across the DMZ at night. The enemy activity continued into the new year. Then, beginning in early February, FSB Fuller, between Cam Lo and the Rockpile, received a daily mortar barrage. About the same time, ARVN troops at the Rockpile reported hearing trucks moving around them nearly every night. Intelligence sources for MACV reported enemy troop buildups along the DMZ and the western borders of both Quang Tri and Thua Thien Provinces. Other sources indicated that enemy artillery was being moved to the west of the VNMC positions. Increasingly, groups of enemy soldiers as large as thirty were spotted maneuvering in broad daylight.

In response, in early March 1972, ARVN forces launched a major operation to the southwest of Hue near the U.S. Army's 101st Airborne Division's old FSB Bastogne. The discipline and strength of the enemy forces encountered, later identified as the 324B NVA Division, stunned the American advisers. However, despite the enemy troop buildup there, the prevailing allied opinion was that the main enemy threat would be against the II Corps tactical zone, not I Corps. Analysts for MACV did not believe that the ARVN defensive positions along the DMZ were worthy of major enemy ground attack. The next few weeks would test that conclusion.

Combat Outposts Sarge and Nui Ba Ho, both located south of the Rockpile along Route 9 and occupied by elements of the 4th VNMC Battalion, stood astride the historical invasion routes leading due east to Quang Tri City and southeast to Hue. There had been relative quiet in this area for some time. Then, on the morning of 30 March 1972, a platoon-sized patrol from Nui Ba Ho ran into an equal-sized NVA force about one kilometer northwest of the outpost. A short time later, elements of the 8th VNMC Battalion, patrolling out of FSB Holcomb, about nine kilometers to the southeast, made contact with an NVA force moving from the south. As these separate fights developed, an intense barrage of NVA 120mm and 130mm artillery bombarded VNMC Brigade 147 headquarters at Mai Loc, seven kilometers east of Nui Ba Ho, and the VNMC artillery group located at Camp Carroll. The ferocity of these barrages kept the ARVN artillery from helping their infantry brethren. Not long afterward, NVA artillery shells began falling on the 3d ARVN

Division headquarters at Ai Tu, just a few kilometers north of Quang Tri City on Highway 1. Then, the shells started falling on Nui Ba Ho and Sarge.

Although not immediately apparent to the allies, the NVA had launched a well-organized attack against ARVN positions throughout Quang Tri Province. More than twelve thousand artillery shells pounded key ARVN positions that day while more than twenty-five thousand well-trained and well-armed North Vietnamese Army regulars, amply supported by Soviet- and Chinese-built tanks, moved into position to attack the ARVN bases. The enemy infantry units included the 304th, 308th, and 324B NVA Divisions, as well as three infantry regiments from the B-5 Front, three artillery regiments, two tank regiments, and two Viet Cong sapper battalions.

In contrast, the fledgling 3d ARVN Division had but five regiments of infantry, including six South Vietnamese Marine battalions, nine battalions of artillery, and various armor and ranger units. The NVA outnumbered the ARVN by at least three to one. So violent was the initial enemy attack that many novice ARVN soldiers simply sat stunned while the NVA easily overran them.

Located two thousand meters south of Nui Ba Ho, Outpost Sarge took more than five hundred NVA artillery rounds the first day. While Sarge's defenders hunkered down in their bunkers, NVA infantry attacked Nui Ba Ho. The Marines there held their positions during the vicious fighting and repelled the enemy.

In response to these offensive moves, the three VNMC battalions of Brigade 258 headed north from positions south of Quang Tri City. They set up around Dong Ha and the vital road junction of Highway 9 and Highway 1.

As those South Vietnamese Marines finalized their new positions, the NVA renewed their attack on Nui Ba Ho. At dawn on 31 March (a low overcast, drizzly day), the NVA launched a major infantry assault against the outpost's north perimeter. Though the defenders repulsed three successive ground attacks, they could not hold out against a renewed artillery barrage. Trench lines and bunkers took repeated direct hits from the high explosives, collapsing under the blasts. In the command bunker the U.S. Marine adviser, Capt. Ray L. Smith (who had commanded Company A, 1/1, during the Hue fighting in 1968), frantically called for air support. He was told that the low clouds prevented any.

As darkness fell, the NVA attacked in force from the south. Pressed from two directions, the Vietnamese Marines began to give ground. At 2200 Smith realized that the end was near. He grabbed a radio and his M16 and crept from the command bunker. Outside he was greeted by a pitch-black, overcast night punctuated by the sharp flashes of exploding artillery shells. As he oriented himself, Smith realized that no friendly troops were nearby. But there were plenty of enemy soldiers. Dropping to the rain-sodden ground, he low-crawled past a group of NVA swarming just outside the bunker. "The NVA were as confused as I by then. I ran right by them without being detected," Smith said. On the back side of the hill he found a group of South Vietnamese Marines. When he realized that they were afraid to move through the nearby barbed wire barrier because of booby traps, he took command of the more than two dozen men.

Looking around, Smith found a gap in the first band of wire and began guiding the confused Marines through it. At that moment an NVA soldier popped out of the darkness just five feet behind Smith and began firing into the group. Reacting instantly, Smith whirled and fired, dropping the enemy rifleman. Afraid that his shot would alert other nearby NVA, Smith pushed his way to the front of the milling column, which was held up by the outer band of razor-sharp concertina wire. Realizing that something had to be done or they would all die, Smith unhesitatingly threw himself backward onto the wire. As the sharp blades sliced into his flesh, the terrified Vietnamese scrambled over Smith and the barrier.

Once the Marines had cleared the wire, Smith carefully extracted himself. Nearly nude, and with uncountable rivers of blood streaming down his body, Smith joined the others. As they cautiously made their way toward Mai Loc, he continued to call artillery fire on the abandoned base. The next day Smith and his harried followers arrived at brigade headquarters.

Nui Ba Ho had fallen in less than forty-eighty hours.

To the south, Outpost Sarge continued to be hit with massive artillery and infantry assaults. Despite a torrential monsoonal downpour, the determined enemy sent repeated infantry attacks against the base. They succeeded. By 0200 on 1 April, the NVA had captured nearly all of the outpost. At 0345 the VNMC command group evacuated the base.

For all practical purposes the 4th VNMC Battalion was gone.

To the north, the situation was just as bad, if not worse. The four infantry regiments of the NVA B-5 Front poured across the DMZ. The inexperienced ARVN defenders folded before them. By 1700 on 1 April, the 57th ARVN Regiment had abandoned Alpha 2, Alpha 4, Charlie 1, and Charlie 2. To the west of Dong Ha, the bases at Fuller, Khe Gio, and Holcomb were also lost. Soldiers and civilians thronged southward, intermixed with NVA artillery forward observers and sappers.

Late that afternoon, reports of NVA tanks streaming across the DMZ created further panic. Any of the few soldiers of the 3d ARVN Division who had held their posts before now discarded weapons, uniforms, and equipment and joined the frightened mobs fleeing south. By nightfall on 1 April, every ARVN combat position north of the Cam Lo River had fallen. And the NVA were advancing on Dong Ha.

Easter Sunday, 2 April 1972, dawned with a grim situation for the defenders of northern Quang Tri Province. The 3d ARVN Division had moved its headquarters south to the Citadel in Quang Tri City. At least one of its regiments, the 57th, had completely disintegrated. The VNMC Brigade 147 at Mai Loc continued to receive a near constant barrage of NVA artillery fire. Reports of several dozen Soviet-built PT76 and T54 tanks headed down Highway 1 for Dong Ha added to the desperate situation. It was obvious that the enemy would have to be stopped at Dong Ha or they would have an open road all the way south to Quang Tri City and Hue.

Guarding Dong Ha was the 3d VNMC Battalion, with Capt. John W. Ripley as its adviser. Before dawn on 2 April, the battalion commander, Maj. Le Ba Binh, was given orders by his brigade commander to hold Dong Ha and its bridges "at all costs." The only support he would receive to help accomplish the suicidal mission would be the M48 battle tanks of the 20th ARVN Tank Battalion.

As the rifle companies of the 3d VNMC Battalion deployed toward the side-by-side railroad and vehicle bridges over the Bo Dieu River (a tributary of the Cua Viet bisecting Dong Ha), NVA maneuvering on the north bank called in an artillery barrage. In what Captain Ripley described as an "absolute firestorm," shells blew apart buildings and flung the South Vietnamese Marines and civilians into the air like rag dolls. The South Vietnamese Marines had to pull back and continue their advance to the bridges from a less exposed position.

As they completed the maneuver, enemy soldiers from the 36th NVA Regiment began crossing the partially destroyed railroad bridge. To block their advance Captain Ripley hastily called for gunfire from U.S. Navy ships cruising offshore. Responding instantly to the desperate request, the four destroyers of the gunfire support task force delivered an incredibly accurate barrage of 5-inch shells. For more than an hour the destroyers poured a continuous stream of the deadly rounds into the area. The enemy pulled back. When Ripley noticed enemy tanks maneuvering a few hundred meters north of the river, he directed a naval fire mission on them. All were destroyed.

Throughout the day, more NVA tanks came barreling down Highway 1. Some were hit by South Vietnamese Air Force A-1E Skyraiders, others by naval gunfire, and still others by fire from the mounted guns of the 20th ARVN Tank Battalion. Despite these losses the enemy tankers pressed forward.

Just after noon, a lone NVA tank started across the Dong Ha bridge. A very brave South Vietnamese Marine advanced into the open and drove off the armored vehicle with a single well-placed shot from a light antitank weapon. Though impressed with the man's courage, Ripley knew that other NVA tanks would soon try another crossing. He realized that the bridge would have to be destroyed.

The complications of command responsibility in the Vietnamese military delayed the decision. No one wanted to take responsibility for destroying a vital bridge that the ARVN might well need themselves for any future counterattack. While the questions moved slowly up the ARVN chain of command, Captain Ripley's U.S. Marine commander, Lt. Col. Gerald H. Turley, at brigade headquarters at Ai Tu, took matters in his own hands. He radioed Ripley to destroy the bridge.

As Ripley walked up Highway 1 toward the bridge, U.S. Army major James E. Smock, the adviser to the 20th ARVN Tank Battalion, pulled up next to him on an ARVN tank. "Hey, Marine!" Smock yelled. "Climb aboard and let's go blow a bridge."

Together the two Americans rode the M48 tank to within one hundred meters of the bridge and dismounted behind an abandoned bunker. Open space swept by NVA small arms fire lay between them and the bridge. Disregarding the danger, the two Americans dashed forward to the base of the bridge. There they found a small band of ARVN engineers preparing TNT and C-4 plastic explosives. In front of them a high, chain-link fence topped by razor-sharp concertina wire guarded the bridge's approaches. After visually examining the structure, Ripley realized that the explosive charges, in about twenty wooden ammo crates weighing fifty pounds each, would have to be placed in staggered alignment under the bridge's main girders. Whoever did this would be dangerously exposed to enemy fire as he worked. Ripley unhesitatingly volunteered for the suicide mission.

After swinging his body up and over the chain-link fence, Ripley made his way underneath the bridge. At the same time, Major Smock pushed the boxes of TNT over the fence. Hanging from one of the structure's main I beams, Ripley inched his way hand over hand out over the water to study the bridge's construction. Satisfied that he now knew where to place the charges, he swung his way back to shore.

Ripley manhandled one of the heavy, awkward ammo boxes up into the girders, then pushed the crate down the I beams as he hung below the bridge. He finally worked the box into the desired spot.

Back and forth, Ripley scurried along the I beams, placing box after box into position. His hands ached and his arms burned from the physical strain, but he persisted in his mission. Finally, he had enough charges in place to ensure the bridge's destruction.

Nearly exhausted, Ripley next set about preparing the fuse. To be on the safe side he built both a burnable fuse and an electrical detonator using blasting caps and communications wire. While Smock and several of the ARVN engineers went off to complete plans for destroying the bridge, Ripley crept back out on the bridge to place the blasting caps, then back to shore to connect the electrical wires to the battery of a nearby abandoned jeep. He ducked as he made the final connection. Nothing happened. Either the battery was bad or the electrical circuit had failed. Realizing that the fate of northern Quang Tri Province rested on his actions, Ripley carefully ignited the burnable fuse. He watched until the smoking, sputtering fuse disappeared from view. Then he crept away to cover. After a tension-filled eternity, the bridge finally blew. Towering clouds of smoke reached skyward as pieces of the structure rained down. Ripley reported the bridge's destruction to brigade headquarters at 1630.

Stymied by Ripley's bold action, the NVA attackers swung westward. The Cam Lo Bridge, directly below the abandoned combat base, was their new objective. With no ARVN troops in the vicinity, and no prospect of any getting there, the local U.S. Army advisers called for naval gunfire. All night, the deadly 5-inch shells pounded the area. The high explosives not only kept the enemy at bay but sufficiently damaged the structure to prevent their using it.

While Captain Ripley engaged in his heroics at Dong Ha, an unusual situation developed at Camp Carroll, which had just been reopened by the ARVN the previous year. Manned by the 56th ARVN Regiment, the camp had undergone only relatively mild attacks during the new enemy offensive. Then, to the surprise of everyone, at 1520 on Easter Sunday, the regiment's U.S. Army adviser radioed the 3d ARVN Division operations center that white flags were suddenly popping up everywhere on the base. As best as could be determined, the traitorous regimental commander had unilaterally surrendered his command. While NVA troops poured through the camp's main gate, one last U.S. helicopter landed and carried away the American adviser and a few ARVN unwilling to surrender so easily.

The unexpected loss of Camp Carroll was a major blow to the defense of Quang Tri Province. It immediately exposed the VNMC Brigade 147 at Mai Loc to ground attack from the north and denied it desperately needed artillery support.

The 147th's commander recommended to 3d ARVN Division headquarters that Mai Loc be evacuated. The division commander, Brig. Gen. Vu Van Giai, agreed. At 1815 on 2 April, the surviving members of the brigade headed for Dong Ha, twenty kilometers east. The last of the South Vietnamese Marines would not complete the journey until noon the next day. For all involved it was a dark, wet, and fear-ridden journey.

The 3d VNMC Battalion continued its defense of Dong Ha. Together with the 20th ARVN Tank Battalion, they battled back repeated enemy attempts over the next few days to capture the ruined, but still important, town. In a near continuous cacophony of explosions, NVA artillery and mortar fire slammed into the town. Throughout the week after Easter, Captain Ripley remained at the forefront of the action, calling in artillery, rallying the battered South Vietnamese Marines, and closely advising Major Binh.

By 6 April, bands of NVA had infiltrated across the Bo Dieu River into the outskirts of Dong Ha. The ARVN commander reinforced the town with several groups of rangers, another armored unit, and a reconstituted 57th ARVN Regiment. Together, the ARVN units repulsed the invaders and retained their hold on the vital town. With less than two hundred of its original seven hundred members on their feet, the 3d VNMC Battalion was pulled off the line, on 7 April, for a well-deserved rest.

Thwarted in their effort to take Quang Tri City from the north, the NVA renewed their attacks from the west. In their way sat FSB Pedro, ten kilometers west of Quang Tri City. Defended by the 6th VNMC Battalion, FSB Pedro was hit at first light, on 9 April, by two battalions of NVA infantry supported by sixteen tanks. Thirty minutes after the attack began, the lead tanks easily rolled over the base's outer defensive perimeter. Many of the South Vietnamese Marines crouching in their fighting holes died when the Soviet-made T54 tanks collapsed the holes' earthen walls with their heavy metal tracks. The majority of the surviving defenders bolted for Ai Tu, ten kilometers north.

At VNMC Brigade 258 headquarters in Ai Tu, a reaction force was hastily assembled. Two companies of the 1st VNMC Battalion—accompanied by eight M48 tanks, a dozen M113 armored personnel carriers (APCs), and adviser Capt. Lawrence H. Livingston, USMC—made up the force. By 0830 the reaction force was moving west down the dirt road leading to FSB Pedro.

A short time later, the column arrived at FSB Pedro. Immediately, a ferocious, close-quarters tank battle developed—a rarity for the

Vietnam War. It was quickly evident the NVA tanks were no match for the better armed M48s; five enemy tanks were destroyed in as many minutes. Within two hours, thirteen of the NVA's sixteen T54 tanks had been destroyed. One escaped and two were captured intact. By early afternoon, FSB Pedro was back in South Vietnamese hands. The NVA tried several times over the next two days to recapture the base, but they were easily driven off each time. Their victory at FSB Pedro was one of the few bright spots for the ARVN in early April.

Despite the heroic efforts of many South Vietnamese units and the personal gallantry of their U.S. advisers, the NVA kept pressing their offensive. Their next major push came on 27 April. At 0630 that day, the 304th NVA Division attacked Ai Tu from the southwest. The 1st VNMC Battalion battled the NVA on the outskirts of the town, stopping two tank-supported infantry attacks, although they were brutally pounded by more than five hundred 82mm mortar rounds and 130mm artillery shells. The South Vietnamese Marines and the ARVN M48 tanks destroyed no less than fifteen enemy T54s.

Although the South Vietnamese Marines blunted the NVA advance on Ai Tu, this enemy attack indirectly contributed to the collapse of Dong Ha. In order to shore up the defenses at Ai Tu, the Vietnamese commanders ordered the 20th Tank Battalion to leave its positions around Dong Ha and move south. When the already jittery troops of the heavily battered 57th ARVN Regiment saw the tanks withdrawing, they bolted. Within a short time the regiment had disintegrated into a panicked pack, streaming south toward Ai Tu. By the afternoon of 27 April, the NVA had occupied Dong Ha without firing a shot. They barely paused as they headed south on Highway 1 toward Ai Tu and Quang Tri City.

At 0200 on 29 April, the NVA launched a tank and infantry assault on the bridge across the Thach Han River that guarded the northern approaches to Quang Tri City. From Ai Tu, ARVN rangers were sent south to help elements of the 7th VNMC Battalion hold the bridge, but they entered the town and kept on going. About the same time, defensive positions around Ai Tu began to crumble. The defending ARVN infantry finally broke and fled south across the Thach Han River. At noon on 30 April, General Giai gave the official order to abandon Ai Tu.

According to a hastily formulated new plan, the South Vietnamese Marines of Brigade 147 would now be responsible for the defense of Quang Tri City. The brigade's three battalions began moving south from Ai Tu the afternoon of 30 April. By nightfall the 1st VNMC Battalion was dug in on the western side of the city, the 4th held the eastern and southern approaches, and the 8th guarded the north.

The new plan for holding Quang Tri City lasted less than twenty-four hours. Early on the morning of 1 May, General Giai decided that further efforts to defend the provincial capital would be fruitless. Rather, he decided to withdraw to a defensive line centered on My Chanh, fifteen kilometers southeast on Highway 1. At 1215 that day, the division's chief of staff strolled into the American advisory team's bunker and, to the utter surprise of all those present, sent a message to all subordinate commands ordering them to fight their way south to My Chanh.

When Lt. Gen. Hoang Xuan Lam, the ARVN corps commander, received this news, he immediately rescinded the order. Lam ordered all units to "stand and die!" Unfortunately, it was too late. Within thirty minutes of receiving the original order, most of General Giai's subordinates had fled. Within hours, the entire Quang Tri City area was in complete chaos. No orderly withdrawal plan was issued. What began as an organized retreat soon turned into a panicked rout. The ARVN soldiers disintegrated into a frightened mob that packed Highway 1 in a southward surge of humanity.

In Quang Tri City about forty Americans remained trapped in the advisory compound. General Giai had originally abandoned the group as he fled with key members of his staff. Unable to break through the tightening ring of NVA, however, Giai returned to the advisory compound. At 1630, U.S. Air Force HH-53 helicopters arrived to evacuate the Americans. General Giai jumped aboard the first aircraft. The American advisers clambered aboard the other machines and made it to safety. And none too soon. As the last HH-53 climbed out of the advisory compound's LZ, a lone NVA soldier dashed forward. He unleashed with his AK-47, firing a full clip of ammo at the departing aircraft. Fortunately, he missed.

Much to the dismay of their U.S. Marine Corps advisers, even the South Vietnamese Marines were not immune to the spreading panic. From its positions around Quang Tri City, VNMC Brigade 147 withdrew in an orderly manner early on the morning of 2 May 1972. All was well as they proceeded south—until enemy armor, supported by infantry and recoilless rifle fire, hit the column from the north, west, and south. The supporting ARVN tank drivers panicked and broke from the column. Soon, effective command and control evaporated and hysteria set in. The once undaunted South Vietnamese Marines threw away their weapons and fled cross-country.

By 2 May, all of Quang Tri Province, including Quang Tri City, had fallen to the NVA. Farther south, Hue was seriously threatened by the NVA who had captured FSB Bastogne, just eighteen kilometers to the southwest. With few exceptions, the 3d ARVN Division had disintegrated into a panicked mob.

Restricted by a war-weary Congress from introducing ground combat troops into South Vietnam, the U.S. military was also limited in response options to air support and equipment replacement; however, both were provided as fast as possible. As the battered ARVN forces consolidated along the My Chanh River, General Lam was replaced by Lt. Gen. Ngo Quang Truong. Truong immediately set about rebuilding his shattered forces. In the subsequent realignment of forces, the VNMC division was given its own TAOR, the area between the Gulf of Tonkin and Highway 1 north of My Chanh.

Once the new defensive line was stabilized, General Truong began operations to move back north. On 12 May, units of VNMC Brigade 369 were lifted by U.S. Marine CH-46 and CH-53 helicopters north of the My Chanh River. Prepped by a barrage of both U.S. air and naval gunfire, the LZs were cold as the South Vietnamese Marines off-loaded. Once on the ground the Marines attacked south. In the meantime, the 9th VNMC Battalion had crossed the My Chanh River and attacked north. The pincers caught the 66th NVA Regiment by complete surprise. By nightfall the VNMC had driven the NVA out of the area.

Stunned by this attack, the NVA responded by launching two attacks against the My Chanh line: one on 21 May and another the next day. Both resulted in heavy fighting and heavy casualties on both sides, but the South Vietnamese Marines held. However, the fighting was not without its terrifying moments. On 22 May, one force of twenty-five NVA tanks penetrated the friendly line, driving all the way back to the brigade headquarters. There, for the first time in combat, a U.S. Army enlisted adviser used the new TOW (tube-launched, optically tracked, wire-guided) antitank missile launcher to destroy an enemy tank that had closed to four hundred meters. Buoyed by this display of gallantry, the headquarters Marines destroyed a total of nine more tanks and armored personnel carriers, forcing the NVA to flee. The My Chanh line had held.

Determined to keep the NVA off balance, General Truong launched yet another attack. On 24 May, U.S. Navy amphibious assault ships landed the 7th VNMC Battalion at Wunder Beach, about fifteen kilometers southeast of Quang Tri City. Once the beachhead was secure, U.S. Marine CH-46 and CH-53 helicopters carried elements of the 4th and 6th VNMC Battalions into an LZ just a few kilometers east of Quang Tri City. Soon after landing, however, both battalions were counterattacked by two NVA regiments. After heavy fighting, the Marines pulled out and returned to the My Chanh line.

After these limited spoiling attacks, General Truong decided to launch a major offensive operation to recapture Quang Tri City. Once again, the Vietnamese Marines were in the forefront. On 8 June, four VNMC battalions started across the river. They advanced behind a curtain of supporting air, artillery, and naval gunfire coordinated by the U.S. Marine advisers. Enemy resistance was strong, particularly in the coastal areas, but the Vietnamese Marines fought harder. Within forty-eight hours they were well established in Quang Tri Province and eager to continue northward.

The final push to retake Quang Tri City began on 28 June. Four VNMC battalions—the 3d, 5th, 7th, and 8th—attacked northwest from the east side of Highway 555; ARVN airborne forces moved along their left flank. When the attackers ran into stubborn resistance, General Truong again used U.S. Marine helicopters to carry South Vietnamese Marines into battle. The 1st and 4th VNMC were heliassaulted into LZs behind enemy lines. Pressed from two flanks, the NVA pulled back.

By early July, the ARVN forces had closed on Quang Tri City. Before the South Vietnamese Marines attacked the city, General Truong wanted to block any NVA reinforcement or resupply of the city from the north. To accomplish that he decided to move one VNMC battalion to the northeast of the city. At 1200 on 11 July, following six hours of preparatory fire, 34 U.S. Marine helicopters carried 840 South Vietnamese Marines of the 1st VNMC Battalion into LZs Blue Jay and Crow, just two kilometers north of Quang Tri City.

The six-hour artillery and naval gunfire barrage seemed to have had little effect on the NVA defenders. Their fire was strong and accurate. Twenty-eight of the friendly helicopters took hits over the LZs. So confusing was the situation that one pilot nearly landed his aircraft on top of an NVA T54 tank. Only the quick response of a nearby hovering Bell Cobra gunship, which blasted the tank with a TOW antitank missile, prevented the troop-laden helicopter from being blown away. Another helicopter landed smack on top of an NVA battalion command post. In all, three U.S. Marine helicopters were shot down, with two U.S. Marines killed and seven wounded; more than forty Vietnamese Marines died in the crashes.

On the ground, the South Vietnamese Marines ran into even heavier fire. A veritable hail of small arms and automatic weapons fire zinged across the LZ, ripping into the Marines. Despite this intense fire, the South Vietnamese Marines crept forward, boldly attacking the NVA in two trench lines flanking the LZ. Overcoming tremendous odds, the brave men overran the NVA line, killing more than one hundred of the enemy while suffering more than fifty dead of their own.

During the fighting, U.S. Marine 1st Lt. Stephen G. Biddulph, the naval gunfire spotter team leader, was hit in the legs by enemy small arms fire. Captain Livingston, still the 1st VNMC Battalion adviser, ignored the stream of enemy lead snapping past him to rush to Biddulph's aid. "He came sliding in beside me like a man stealing second base," remembered Biddulph. Oblivious to the danger, Livingston hoisted Biddulph onto his shoulders and dashed across the bullet-swept ground to a position of relative safety. Livingston then took over Biddulph's radio and directed naval gunfire against on-rushing NVA reinforcements.

Despite the expansion of their perimeter after clearing the two trenches, the South Vietnamese Marines were still taking heavy incoming fire. One troublesome enemy position was in a tree line just fifty meters away. Rallying the South Vietnamese Marines lying around him, Captain Livingston led them in a bold attack on the position. Though knocked to the ground by an exploding grenade, Livingston regained his feet to lead the small force to the edge of the NVA fortifications. The enemy soldiers rushed forward and fought the Marines hand to hand. The fighting was brutal, but the Marines prevailed.

Fighting around the two LZs raged for three more days. Not until 14 July did the South Vietnamese Marines succeed in cutting the NVA's main supply route, Highway 560, into the city. Only then could medevac helicopters come in to carry out the wounded. Lieutenant Biddulph had spent the three days lying in the bottom of a shallow drainage ditch, tended only by Captain Livingston. The helicopter that carried him out was crowded with wounded. "A litter patient lay squarely across my wounded legs," Biddulph recalled. "I held another patient around the body to prevent him from falling out. And we still had to fly over the heads of the enemy to get out." Fortunately, the helicopters made it safely.

Even with their supply line severed, the NVA clung tenaciously to Quang Tri City. The rugged ARVN Airborne Division fought hard for several weeks but could not dislodge the NVA. By 27 July, it was apparent that the ARVN could not retake the city. They were pulled out, and the VNMC division was given the mission.

For the next four weeks the brutal fighting for Quang Tri City continued without letup. At least one full enemy division, the 325th, and elements of the 308th and 320B NVA Divisions stubbornly clung to the nearly ruined city. Several times the enemy even counterattacked out of their fortified positions, but each attack was successfully thrown back. Slowly, the South Vietnamese Marines squeezed the remaining NVA into the Citadel, the ancient, thick-walled imperial city inside Quang Tri City.

As September began it became apparent that the enemy was at

last weakening. General Truong planned a major attack using four battalions of South Vietnamese Marines to throw the NVA out of the Citadel.

On 9 September, the final drive to retake Quang Tri City began with an intense barrage of artillery fire and air strikes on the Citadel. At the same time, U.S. Marine helicopters and U.S. Navy landing craft faked an amphibious attack north of the mouth of the Cua Viet River. This successfully diverted NVA infantry and artillery while the VNMC units closed on the Citadel.

In Quang Tri City, the South Vietnamese Marines made surprisingly rapid progress. By the end of the first day, they had closed on the Citadel's three-meter-thick, ten-meter-high walls, most of which had been reduced to rubble from the constant bombardment. The NVA, however, had constructed numerous, mutually supporting strongpoints among the ruins, slowing the Marines' advance down the wall.

Following day-long, close-quarters fighting on 10 September, the 6th VNMC Battalion finally gained a foothold on the southwest corner of the wall. Early the next day, it pushed a full company into the Citadel. Two more South Vietnamese battalions penetrated the Citadel's north wall on the thirteenth.

At 1245 on 16 September, the flag of the Republic of South Vietnam once again fluttered over Quang Tri City. After 138 days of occupying the provincial capital, the enemy had at last been evicted. The fighting cost the South Vietnamese Marines more than 3,600 casualties.

The battle for Quang Tri Province was a major test of the U.S. Marine Corps' advisory effort. Pushed to the ultimate limit of their ability by the intense fighting, the men responded in a manner consistent with the traditions of all the Marines who had gone to war before them. Providing timely and accurate guidance to their South Vietnamese counterparts, the members of the Marine Advisory Unit repeatedly proved their worth. When the situation required individual initiative and heroism, the Marine advisers responded without hesitation. Three of them, Captains Smith, Ripley, and Livingston, would receive the Navy Cross for their personal gallantry.

* * *

With Quang Tri City once again in their hands, the South Vietnamese set their sights on driving the North Vietnamese invaders completely out of their country. With peace talks under way in Paris, South Vietnam's president Nguyen Van Thieu was concerned that a cease-fire might be put in place before the ARVN had regained their lost territory.

On 7 October, the 8th VNMC Battalion jumped off in the vanguard of the attack north. Heavy monsoon rains slowed its progress but also hampered the enemy. Two weeks later, the 9th VNMC Battalion joined the offensive. The objective for the forces was the Cua Viet River. Control of this vital waterway meant control of Quang Tri Province.

Heavy fighting erupted as the two battalions pushed farther north. The South Vietnamese Marines again placed much reliance on American aerial support and U.S. naval gunfire to destroy the enemy's defenses. The U.S. Marine advisers again played a key role in coordinating the supporting fire. By the end of October, the South Vietnamese Marines had closed to within five kilometers of the Cua Viet River.

After regrouping his forces and committing the 4th VNMC Battalion to the attack, General Truong resumed the offensive on 11 November. Almost immediately, intense NVA artillery and mortar fire crashed among the South Vietnamese. Local ground attacks hit the Marines. Under this heavy pressure their forward momentum slowed, then stopped. Continued torrential monsoon rains restricted air support, making destruction of enemy defensive positions nearly impossible. The adverse weather halted activities by both sides, and the war stalled. Resupply was very difficult due to washed out roads and poor flying weather. Though the enemies constantly patrolled to their respective fronts, there was little actual fighting. It was as if the foes realized that they were sharing a miserable existence and had no interest in making it worse.

As a result, the front lines remained relatively static throughout December 1972. The VNMC battalions could get no closer than four kilometers from the Cua Viet River. The new year began with both sides making probes and counterprobes. As a negotiated cease-fire via the Paris peace talks appeared more likely, General Truong made plans for a concentrated attack to reach the Cua Viet River. At 0655 on 26 January, a combined infantry–armor attack, led by the deputy commandant of the South Vietnamese Marine Corps, headed for the river.

Advancing in two columns moving parallel to the coastline, the attackers came under fire from wire-guided antitank missiles. In the next eighteen hours the columns lost twenty-six M48 tanks and M113 APCs to the enemy missile teams. During this period two allied aircraft flying close air support missions were downed by surface-to-air missiles.

At 0145 on 28 January, a mixed force of 3d, 4th, and 5th VNMC Battalion Marines supported by just three tanks made a last, determined dash to reach the river. At 0700 three hundred South Vietnamese Marines finally broke through the enemy lines. They proudly hoisted the red and yellow South Vietnamese flag on the river's south bank.

At 0745 on 28 January 1973, the USS *Turner Joy,* the same vessel involved in the Gulf of Tonkin incident eight and a half years earlier, fired the final U.S. Navy gunfire support mission of the war.

Fifteen minutes later, the long-anticipated cease-fire went into effect. All U.S. Marine Corps advisers were formally relieved of their duties. That same afternoon they returned to VNMC division headquarters for a final formation. Early the next morning, the advisers boarded aircraft bound for Saigon. From there they would depart for the United States. The U.S. Marine Corps' role in the war in South Vietnam was over.

Almost.

The signing of the Peace Accords in Paris on 27 January 1973 signaled the formal end of hostilities in South Vietnam. Immediately following the cease-fire there was a noticeable decline in combat activity throughout South Vietnam. Although this fostered an air of optimism throughout the world, in reality the North Vietnamese had merely shifted their emphasis from combat to logistics. The north's goal still remained the conquest of the south. The Peace Accords simply allowed the North Vietnamese ample opportunity to refit and rebuild their frontline units, refine lines of communication, and replenish supply caches in the south.

By May 1974, it was obvious to American intelligence analysts that the NVA had used the preceding fifteen months to make substantial improvements to the logistics of their transportation system. The series of foot and bicycle paths that had made up the infamous Ho Chi Minh Trail had been massively expanded and improved. In many instances dirt trails had been upgraded to paved, all-weather roads. The journey from North Vietnam to South Vietnam, which had once taken an individual soldier nearly three months to complete, could now be made in just three weeks.

As a result of these improvements, in less than two years the NVA nearly doubled the artillery pieces and quadrupled the number of tanks it had in South Vietnam. By January 1975 they had more than 400 artillery pieces in the south versus about 225 at the time of the cease-fire. In the same period they went from 150 Soviet-built T54 and Chinese Type 59 tanks to almost 600. They also increased the number of antiaircraft regiments from 13 to 23 and even brought in 4 battalions of surface-to-air missiles.

During this same period U.S. military aid to South Vietnam had been cut by Congress from $2.2 billion to $700 million. Coupled with rampant worldwide inflation, this meant that the ARVN experienced a drastic drop in its purchasing power. Consequently, every aspect of the South Vietnamese military organization suffered significant reductions. These changes had not been lost on North Vietnam.

In late 1973, the NVA had launched a division-sized offensive in Quang Duc Province, in the Central Highlands. By the end of February 1974, they had conquered nearly all of the ARVN's outposts in the province. In mid-May 1974, elements of the 3d NVA Division attacked the Phu Cat air base in coastal Binh Dinh Province. In September, NVA artillery in the nearby mountains began shelling the air base at Phu Bai. In December, the NVA not only initiated offensive action in the Mekong River Delta area south of Saigon but also moved the entire 968th Division into the Central Highlands, the first time since the accords that a full division had entered the south as a complete unit.

The U.S. Marine Corps had only a minimal presence in South Vietnam during this tense period. Per the terms of the Paris Peace Accords, the Military Assistance Command, Vietnam ceased to exist on 29 March 1973. Replacing it was the newly created Defense Attaché Office (DAO). The DAO was staffed by former members of MACV, who essentially performed the same functions in the same offices they'd occupied as part of MACV.

According to the Peace Accords, however, the DAO was allowed only fifty military and twelve hundred civilian personnel. Of the fifty military slots, three were allocated to the U.S. Marines. One of these positions was essentially the same as the former senior adviser to the South Vietnamese Marine Corps; the other two were purely administrative positions.

The largest contingent of U.S. Marines remaining in South Vietnam after the cease-fire was made up of the 5 officers and 140 enlisted men of Company E of the Marine Security Guard Battalion. This specially selected, all-volunteer force provided guards for the American embassy in Saigon and the consulates at Da Nang, Nha Trang, and Bien Hoa, as well as personal security for Ambassador Graham Martin. In the early summer of 1974, this contingent was further reduced when Company E was deactivated and the 90 remaining Marines were reassigned to Company C, headquartered at Hong Kong. Captain (and soon-to-be major) James H. Kean took command of the Marine Detachment, Saigon, and Company C on 16 July.

The small number of U.S. Marines actually stationed in South Vietnam did not mean that the country was ignored by III MAF, still headquartered on Okinawa. As the ARVN gave ground under the renewed NVA offensive, Marine planners prepared a number of contingency plans to deal with a wide variety of situations. One of these covered the evacuation of all Americans, as well as key South Vietnamese citizens, from the country in the event of its loss. Though no one really expected this plan to be implemented, the hours of work and training would eventually pay major dividends.

By late 1974, the North Vietnamese clearly held the upper hand in ground combat operations. Desirous of capitalizing on their advantageous position, North Vietnam's leadership decided to accelerate its plans for the conquest of the south. The first phase of the new effort started in Phuoc Long Province, about 120 kilometers north of Saigon. The NVA planned to use two infantry divisions, a tank battalion, an artillery regiment, and a variety of supporting units to capture the province's populated areas by hitting their centers first, then, in the resulting chaos, destroy the city from within. The enemy commander called this the "blooming lotus" tactic.

The enemy attack on Phuoc Long Province began on 16 December 1974. The blooming lotus worked. By 6 January 1975, the entire province was in enemy hands. The ease with which this victory was achieved, coupled with the lack of a military response from the United States, convinced North Vietnamese's politburo to move even faster.

The NVA next launched a series of coordinated attacks in the Central Highlands on 1 March 1975, attacks that signaled the beginning of the end of South Vietnam. Within three days, they had cut Highway 19, the main east-west road that connected Pleiku with the coast. By 9 March, they had surrounded Ban Me Thuot, Darlac Province's capital. Using two full infantry divisions, the 10th and 316th, the NVA hit the city the next day. Their attack was a complete success. Rather than put up much of a defense, the soldiers of the 23d ARVN Division deserted and fled. By 18 March, Ban Me Thuot was in enemy hands, and the 23d ARVN Division was no more.

Before Ban Me Thuot actually fell, President Thieu made the first of several calamitous decisions that ultimately spelled doom for his country. On 14 March, he ordered the commander of Military Region II (formerly II Corps tactical zone) to abandon the Central Highlands. In Thieu's mind, giving up undefendable territory to the NVA would allow the struggling ARVN to do a better job of defending selected, more favorable territory.

The South Vietnamese Army's II Corps retreat from the Central Highlands began on 16 March. Within hours, the NVA had determined the ARVN's intent. North Vietnamese Army chief of staff Gen. Van Tien Dung received the news with astonishment. "If a whole army corps was fleeing at full tilt, then why? On whose orders?" Dung ordered all his available forces to close on the retreating ARVN. They had put their own head in the noose and he would tighten it. Every available NVA artillery tube was brought to bear on the long column. With enemy artillery shells crashing into the throngs of escaping civilians and soldiers, the retreat quickly turned into a rout. At several points, NVA infantry ripped into the column, fragmenting and destroying any last vestige of command control. The NVA chased the surviving South Vietnamese all the way to the coast. In the process they killed and captured thousands of ARVNs and their arms and equipment. For example, of the seven thousand ARVN Rangers that began the retreat, only nine hundred ultimately reached safety. The II Corps lost fully 75 percent of the twenty-thousand-plus soldiers it had on its rolls on 16 March.

This momentous disaster occurred in less than ten days. In that short span of time the NVA captured six provinces, destroyed two ARVN divisions as well as tens of thousands of Regional and Popular Forces, and cut the country in two. South Vietnam's death knell had begun to sound. The country had less than five weeks to live.

At the same time that President Thieu ordered the evacuation of the Central Highlands, he ordered General Truong, the Military Region I commander, to yield the elite ARVN Airborne Division. Concerned for the security of Saigon, and troubled by the lack of an available reserve force, Thieu wanted the elite paratroopers in the capital. Truong vehemently opposed the move, even flying to Saigon to make his case, but he was ultimately overruled. On 17 March, the airborne division began pulling out of its positions around Da Nang.

Taking advantage of this situation, and keenly aware of the increasing panic building among both soldiers and civilians, on 19 March, the NVA attacked and quickly recaptured Quang Tri City. General Truong tried to establish a new defensive line based on Hue, but he abandoned that effort on 24 March. He then tried to conduct an orderly withdrawal to Da Nang, but once again panic set in. Any semblance of order collapsed as everyone, military and civilian, rushed to save themselves.

The massive surge of terror-filled refugees overwhelmed Da Nang. Law and order quickly collapsed. The defense of the city evaporated as more and more soldiers deserted. On 30 March, the NVA simply walked into the city and captured it without firing a shot. They found hundreds of planes, helicopters, tanks, and other vehicles, as well as tons of materiel, abandoned.

Among the casualties in the loss of most of Military Region 1 was the majority of the South Vietnamese Marine Corps. Assigned a rear-guard role during the various withdrawals, the South Vietnamese Marines were not immune to the panic that gripped their brethren. Many of them simply donned civilian clothes and disappeared amidst the throngs of fleeing residents. Others were killed or captured as the NVA clashed with the Marines. In all, more than half the South Vietnamese Marine Corps was lost in this short period.

With Da Nang swarming with tens of thousands of refugees, the United States reacted by ordering the U.S. Marines to help evacuate them from the city and return them to areas still controlled by the Government of South Vietnam (GVN). Accordingly, on 25 March, the III MAF commander, Maj. Gen. Carl W. Hoffman, ordered the 1st Battalion, 4th Marines to support evacuation operations at Da Nang.

Moving rapidly, the newly designated BLT 1/4 arrived off the northern coast of South Vietnam on several U.S. Navy ships by 3 April. The next day, the first huge influx of refugees boarded the SS *Durham,* anchored off Cam Ranh Bay. Various vessels of the Military Sealift Command (MSC) also began taking on refugees at this time. To provide security aboard the jam-packed MSC ships, individual platoons from the rifle companies of BLT 1/4 were ordered aboard each vessel. This assignment required considerable professionalism, because the Marines were required to not only deal with frightened refugees who had left all their possessions behind as they fled, but also with many ARVN deserters who operated as little more than armed thugs.

Once order was established, the navy and MSC ships sailed for ports designated by Saigon as the destination for the refugees. During the voyage the U.S. Marines maintained order and helped control the distribution of food and water. Attached U.S. Navy corpsmen provided a wide variety of medical assistance to the many sick and injured refugees. A major problem with thousands of people crowded aboard the ships was the sanitary conditions. The Marines organized the more cooperative refugees into cleanup squads to rid the ships of waste material. In some instances, high-pressure water hoses were required to wash the decks of filth and waste.

By 10 April, the evacuation of the refugees was completed. The majority of them were deposited on Phu Quoc Island, off the west coast of South Vietnam in the Bay of Thailand. This isolated island was selected because the GVN did not want the refugees unloaded near any major population centers where their horror stories might contribute to a general panic. The South Vietnamese government had good cause to be worried.

As April 1975 began, the NVA were in complete control of both Military Regions (MRs) I and II. Actual combat was light for the first few days of the month as the enemy divisions consolidated their positions and began preparing for their final drive on Saigon. On 3 April, NVA divisions in MR I and MR II headed south. Those in MR IV moved north and east toward the capital.

Tay Ninh Province, northwest of Saigon, saw the first renewal of fighting. A massive combined arms attack, beginning on 7 April, quickly eliminated the ARVN from the western half of the province. The NVA then began attacks against ARVN positions in the eastern region of the province.

Fighting then erupted at Xuan Loc, the capital of Long Khanh Province, northeast of Saigon. On 9 April, the 341st NVA Division attacked the strategic city, which guarded Route 1 on its way to South Vietnam's capital. The defending ARVN troops of the 18th Division fought bravely, holding their positions, repulsing several fierce NVA attacks, and even launching several counterattacks. But the enemy was determined to take Xuan Loc and be in Saigon by the end of April.

General Dung elected to modify his original plan and bypass Xuan Loc. Instead of punishing frontal assaults, he decided to outflank the city and nip away at its perimeter. Leaving elements of three divisions behind to accomplish this task, he steered the rest of his forces toward Bien Hoa and Saigon. Dung's tactics worked.

On 17 April, the NVA overran the 48th ARVN Regiment holding the western edge of Xuan Loc. With the earlier loss of the 52d ARVN Regiment to the northwest of the city, it appeared that in a matter of hours Xuan Loc would be lost. The remaining soldiers of the 18th ARVN Division and 1st Airborne Brigade faced annihilation. To avoid that loss, the South Vietnamese Joint General Staff ordered Xuan Loc evacuated. On the evening of 20 April, the remaining ARVN forces successfully withdrew. Overriding the military consequences of this decision, however, were its fateful political ramifications.

The next day, President Thieu resigned and fled to Taiwan. Vice President Tran Van Huong temporarily replaced him. Six days later, the National Assembly elected Gen. Duong Van Minh to be South Vietnam's new president. As Minh took the oath of office on the evening of 28 April, the ceremony was shattered by the crashing explosions of bombs dropping on Tan Son Nhut air base from captured South Vietnamese A-37 planes. The country now had less than forty-eight hours left. It was once again time for the U.S. Marines to take action.

Operation Frequent Wind

During South Vietnam's series of disastrous defeats in late March and early April, the III MAF began assembling a force capable of evacuating Americans and key South Vietnamese from the capital. On 26 March, General Hoffman reactivated the 9th Marine Amphibious Brigade. Brigadier General Richard E. Carey, assistant commander of the 1st Marine Air Wing, was placed in command. The brigade's major units were BLT 2/4, Marine Heavy Helicopter Squadron 462, and Logistic Support Unit 2/4. In all, there were some six thousand Marines and navy corpsmen plus more than eighty different types of helicopters in the 9th MAB.

On 9 April, the brigade staff left Okinawa for the waters off South Vietnam. General Carey and the others arrived off Vung Tau on the command vessel *Blue Ridge* three days later. They immediately began the complicated planning for the evacuation. The operation was code-named "Frequent Wind."

After setting up a liaison with officials of the U.S. embassy and reviewing the plans with them, General Carey decided that the primary evacuation site would be the DAO office complex (formerly MACV headquarters) at Tan Son Nhut air base. Those to be evacuated would assemble there upon receipt of a prearranged signal. Marine CH-53 helicopters would then pick them up, move them to one of more than a dozen ships waiting off Vung Tau, and return for another load. This process would continue until all evacuees were handled.

By the last week of April, the 9th MAB had completed their preparations. All General Carey needed was the order to put the plan into effect.

Early on the morning of 29 April, the NVA fired a salvo of rockets at Tan Son Nhut air base. The barrage marked the beginning of their last push to capture Saigon. With eighteen NVA infantry divisions bearing down on the city, the end was not far away. Besides damaging the base's runways, the rockets also caused the last two U.S. Marine combat deaths in South Vietnam. Corporal Charles McMahon, Jr., of Woburn, Massachusetts, and LCpl. Darwin W. Judge, of Marshalltown, Iowa, were members of the Embassy Security Guard, assigned to provide protection at the DAO complex. At 0400, while manning a checkpoint just outside the complex's main gate, both died when a rocket slammed head-on into their position.

Several hours later, U.S. Ambassador Graham Martin toured the area. After viewing the damage from the rockets, the ambassador placed a phone call to Secretary of State Henry Kissinger: he was ready to close the embassy. At 1051 on Tuesday, 29 April 1975, General Carey received word to commence Operation Frequent Wind.

As soon as the commander of Regimental Landing Team 4, Col. Alfred M. Gray, Jr. (a future commandant of the Marine Corps), received notification of the activation of Operation Frequent Wind, he wasted no time in putting the plan into motion. Aboard the various ships of the task force, individual Marines sprang into action. Crewmen on the eight aircraft carriers readied the helicopters that would take the infantrymen into Saigon and bring out the evacuees. The preparatory tasks had a ring of familiarity: both of the helicopter squadrons (Heavy Helicopter Squadrons 462 and 463) as well as BLT 2/4 had conducted the evacuation of Phnom Penh, Cambodia, two weeks earlier in Operation Eagle Pull.

With L hour set for 1500, the first wave of twelve CH-53s from HMH 462 departed the USS *Okinawa* at 1430. Aboard the helicopters were a command group and members of Companies F and H. The first wave touched down inside the DAO compound at 1506. Greeted by the cheers and shouts of the Americans and South Vietnamese awaiting evacuation, the Marines jumped off the helicopters and rushed to their assigned positions around the compound.

Within minutes, guides had loaded the first group of evacuees aboard the helicopters. With rotors churning the air, the dozen CH-53s left the compound and headed seaward. Minutes later the second wave of helicopters landed. More Marines ran to hold the perimeter. More evacuees were loaded. So far, Operation Frequent Wind was working as planned.

Throughout the evacuation process, enemy artillery shells and rockets hit on and around Tan Son Nhut. Though some rounds came close, fortunately none struck the compound itself.

General Carey and Colonel Gray had arrived at the DAO compound by helicopter at 1350. They quickly established a command post in the compound. As they coordinated the arrival and departure of the successive waves of helicopters, General Carey received a shocking call from the American embassy—more than two thousand people needed to be picked up at the downtown embassy building.

In the planning for the operation, the main embassy compound had been rejected as an evacuation point. With just a one-ship LZ and a small rooftop landing pad, the compound was judged too small to handle a mass evacuation. But now General Carey had no choice. He had to get those people to safety.

General Carey immediately ordered three platoons of Marines aboard helicopters and sent them to the American embassy. They arrived there about 2100. Their first task was to help the Marine embassy guard detachment control the crushing throng of frantic South Vietnamese civilians clamoring at the compound's main gate.

Once the situation at the embassy was stabilized, General Carey began diverting inbound helicopters there. Over the next few hours, CH-46 and CH-53 helicopters flew in and out of both the DAO compound and the embassy, carrying the evacuees to the safety of the offshore ships.

At 2205 the last helicopter load of evacuees lifted off from the DAO compound. The Marines of BLT 2/4 then began pulling back from their perimeter positions to await their own evacuation. Leaving Colonel Gray in charge, General Carey departed the compound at 2250 to return to the *Blue Ridge* to coordinate the final evacuation efforts from the embassy. At 0030 on 30 April, thermite grenades, previously placed by the Marines, exploded in the DAO compound buildings. As the fires spread, the last two helicopters carrying the remaining Marine ground security forces lifted off. The nine-hour DAO operation resulted in the evacuation of 395 American citizens and 4,475 Vietnamese and third-world nationals.

In the meantime, the evacuation process at the embassy continued. One helicopter touched down at either the LZ or the rooftop pad every ten minutes. Each time one did, the near-panicked South Vietnamese rushed to board the craft that would carry them to freedom.

The frenzied evacuation continued into the early morning hours of 30 April. As the number of evacuees steadily decreased, General Carey ordered a helicopter to extract Ambassador Graham Martin. At 0458 on 30 April 1975, Capt. Gerald L. Berry lifted his CH-46 from the embassy helipad. Aboard his helicopter was Ambassador Martin. With his departure the American embassy was officially closed.

When Ambassador Martin departed, there were still several dozen Marines from the security guard detachment and BLT 2/4 remaining in the embassy. By 0600 only the officer in charge, Major Kean, and ten enlisted men remained. Kean barricaded the building's main doors and herded the Marines to the top floor. Dodging small arms fire from frustrated South Vietnamese unable to be evacuated, Kean and his men waited on the rooftop. When South Vietnamese forced their way into the building, the Marines used tear gas to hold them at bay. Finally, at 0750, a CH-46 from HMM 146, a medium helicopter squadron, appeared in the sky. By 0752 the eleven Marines were safely aboard the helicopter and on their way to the *Okinawa*.

In spite of its complexity, Operation Frequent Wind went surprisingly well. In addition to the nearly 5,000 people evacuated from the DAO compound, 978 U.S. citizens and 1,120 third-world nationals were extracted from the embassy. Regrettably, in one of the few mistakes made, the bodies of McMahon and Judge were left behind. Not until a year later did the North Vietnamese release their remains.

More than 680 sorties were flown during Operation Frequent Wind. Amazingly, only two helicopters were lost. In one crash, both the pilot and copilot were killed; in the other, the pilot and copilot survived.

Later on 30 April, 1975 North Vietnamese Army troops entered Saigon. Within hours, President Minh surrendered his country. The war for South Vietnam was over.

The departure of Major Kean and his 10 Marines signaled the end of more than 20 years of U.S. Marine Corps involvement in South Vietnam. At the peak of the war in 1968, more than 86,000 Marines were ashore in South Vietnam—more than 25 percent of the Marine Corps' total strength. In all, more than 500,000 Marines served in-country during the war. Of these, 13,070 were killed in action and 88,630 were wounded, a casualty total greater than the Marine Corps suffered in World War II.

During the six years of major U.S. Marine Corps participation in South Vietnam, Marines fought a variety of wars under a wide range of conditions. From wave-crashing amphibious landings on sandy beaches to muscle-fatiguing humps through thick, triple-canopied jungle covering steep mountainsides, the Marines pursued the enemy wherever he might be. Though shackled by political considerations that hampered its offensive operations, and operating under a command that had no clear strategy for winning the war, the U.S. Marine Corps performed admirably. Whatever task the Marines were given—from securing Chu Lai to defending Khe Sanh to recapturing Hue to evacuating thousands of helpless refugees from Saigon—those who fought in South Vietnam continued the proud tradition of their brethren who have fought America's wars from the Revolution to Korea. Despite the many hardships they faced, they demonstrated the one characteristic that binds Marines of all generations—*Semper Fidelis,* Always Faithful.

Bibliography

Bowman, John S., ed. *The Vietnam War Almanac.* New York: World Almanac Publications, 1985.

Casey, Michael, et al. *The Vietnam Experience: The Army at War.* Boston, Massachusetts: Boston Publishing Co., 1987.

————. *The Vietnam Experience: Flags Into Battle.* Boston, Massachusetts: Boston Publishing Co., 1987.

Cosmas, Graham A., and Lt. Col. Terrence P. Murray, USMC. *U.S. Marines in Vietnam: Vietnamization and Redeployment, 1970–1971.* Washington, D.C.: Government Printing Office, 1986.

Dougan, Clark, and David Fulghum. *The Vietnam Experience: The Fall of the South.* Boston, Massachusetts: Boston Publishing Co., 1985.

Dougan, Clark, and Stephen Weiss. *The Vietnam Experience: Nineteen Sixty-Eight.* Boston, Massachusetts: Boston Publishing Co., 1983.

Doyle, Edward, and Samuel Lipsman. *The Vietnam Experience: America Takes Over.* Boston, Massachusetts: Boston Publishing Co., 1982.

Dunham, George R., Maj. USMC, and Col. David A. Quinlan, USMC. *U.S. Marines in Vietnam: The Bitter End, 1973–1975.* Washington, D.C.: Government Printing Office, 1990.

Esper, George, and the Associated Press. *The Eyewitness History of the Vietnam War, 1961–1975.* New York: Ballantine Books, 1983.

Fulghum, David, and Terrence Maitland. *The Vietnam Experience: South Vietnam on Trial.* Boston, Massachusetts: Boston Publishing Co., 1984.

Hammel, Eric. *Fire in the Streets.* Chicago, Illinois: Contemporary Books, 1991.

Hemingway, Al. *Our War Was Different.* Annapolis, Maryland: Naval Institute Press, 1994.

Lipsman, Samuel, and Edward Doyle. *The Vietnam Experience: Fighting For Time.* Boston, Massachusetts: Boston Publishing Co., 1983.

Lipsman, Samuel, and Stephen Weiss. *The Vietnam Experience: The False Peace.* Boston, Massachusetts: Boston Publishing Co., 1985.

Maitland, Terrence, and Peter McInerney. *The Vietnam Experience: A Contagion of War.* Boston, Massachusetts: Boston Publishing Co., 1983.

Maitland, Terrence, and Stephen Weiss. *The Vietnam Experience: Raising the Stakes.* Boston, Massachusetts: Boston Publishing Co., 1982.

Melson, Charles D., Maj. USMC, and Lt. Col. Curtis G. Arnold, USMC. *U.S. Marines in Vietnam: The War That Would Not End, 1971–1973.* Washington, D.C.: Government Printing Office, 1991.

Murphy, Edward F. *Vietnam Medal of Honor Heroes.* New York: Ballantine Books, 1987.

Nolan, Keith William. *Battle For Hue, Tet 1968.* Novato, California: Presidio Press, 1983.

————. *Death Valley.* Novato, California: Presidio Press, 1987.

————. *The Magnificent Bastards.* Novato, California: Presidio Press, 1994.

————. *Operation Buffalo.* Novato, California: Presidio Press, 1991.

Pisor, Robert. *The End of the Line.* New York: Ballantine Books, 1982.

Prados, John, and Ray W. Stubbe. *Valley of Decision.* Boston, Massachusetts: Houghton Mifflin Co., 1991.

Schuon, Karl. *U.S. Marine Corps Biographical Dictionary.* New York: Franklin Watts, Inc., 1963.

Shulimson, Jack. *U.S. Marines in Vietnam: An Expanding War, 1966.* Washington, D.C.: Government Printing Office, 1982.

Shulimson, Jack, and Maj. Charles M. Johnson, USMC. *U.S. Marines in Vietnam: The Landing and the Buildup, 1965.* Washington, D.C.: Government Printing Office, 1978.

Smith, Charles R. *U.S. Marines in Vietnam: High Mobility and Standdown, 1969.* Washington, D.C.: Government Printing Office, 1988.

Stanton, Shelby L. *The Rise and Fall of an American Army.* Novato, California: Presidio Press, 1985.

————. *Vietnam Order of Battle.* Washington, D.C.: U.S. News Books, 1981.

Telfer, Gary L., Maj. USMC, Lt. Col. Lane Rogers, USMC, and V. Keith Fleming, Jr. *U.S. Marines in Vietnam: Fighting the North Vietnamese, 1967.* Washington, D.C.: Government Printing Office, 1984.

Vetter, Lawrence C. *Never Without Heroes.* New York: Ivy Books, 1996.

Index